子連れ狼

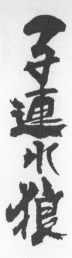

LONE WOLF AND CUB

子連れ狼

story
KAZUO KOIKE

art
GOSEKI KOJIMA

DARK HORSE COMICS

LON
v. 21

translation
DANA LEWIS

lettering & retouch
DIGITAL CHAMELEON

cover illustration
MATT WAGNER

publisher
MIKE RICHARDSON

editor
TIM ERVIN-GORE

assistant editor
JEREMY BARLOW

consulting editor
TOREN SMITH for **STUDIO PROTEUS**

book design
DARIN FABRICK

art director
MARK COX

Published by Dark Horse Comics, Inc., in association
with MegaHouse and Koike Shoin Publishing Company.

Dark Horse Comics, Inc.
10956 SE Main Street, Milwaukie, OR 97222
www.darkhorse.com

First edition: May 2002
ISBN: 1-56971-593-9

1 3 5 7 9 10 8 6 4 2

Printed in Canada

To find a comics shop in your area, call the
Comic Shop Locator Service toll-free at 1-888-266-4226.

$9.95
12/1/15
DC

i14123368

FRAGRANCE
OF DEATH

子連れ狼

By **KAZUO KOIKE**
& GOSEKI KOJIMA

VOLUME
21

A NOTE TO READERS

Lone Wolf and Cub is famous for its carefully researched re-creation of Edo-Period Japan. To preserve the flavor of the work, we have chosen to retain many Edo-Period terms that have no direct equivalents in English. Japanese is written in a mix of Chinese ideograms and a syllabic writing system, resulting in numerous synonyms. In the glossary, you may encounter words with multiple meanings. These are words written with Chinese ideograms that are pronounced the same but carry different meanings. A Japanese reader seeing the different ideograms would know instantly which meaning it is, but these synonyms can cause confusion when Japanese is spelled out in our alphabet. *O-yurushi o* (please forgive us)!

LONE WOLF AND CUB

TABLE OF CONTENTS

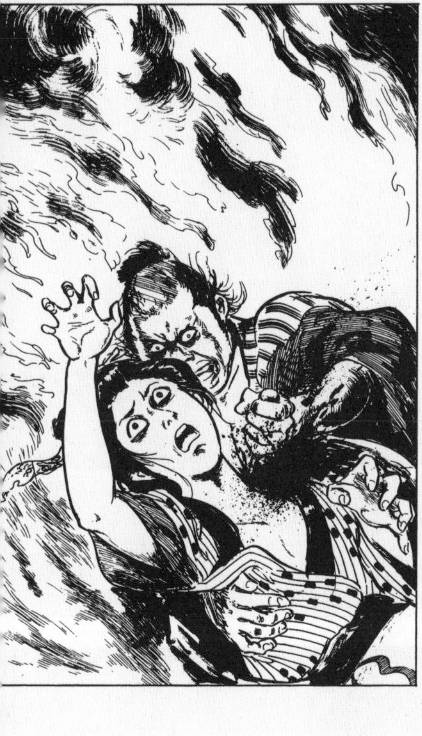

the hundred and third

Poison Currents

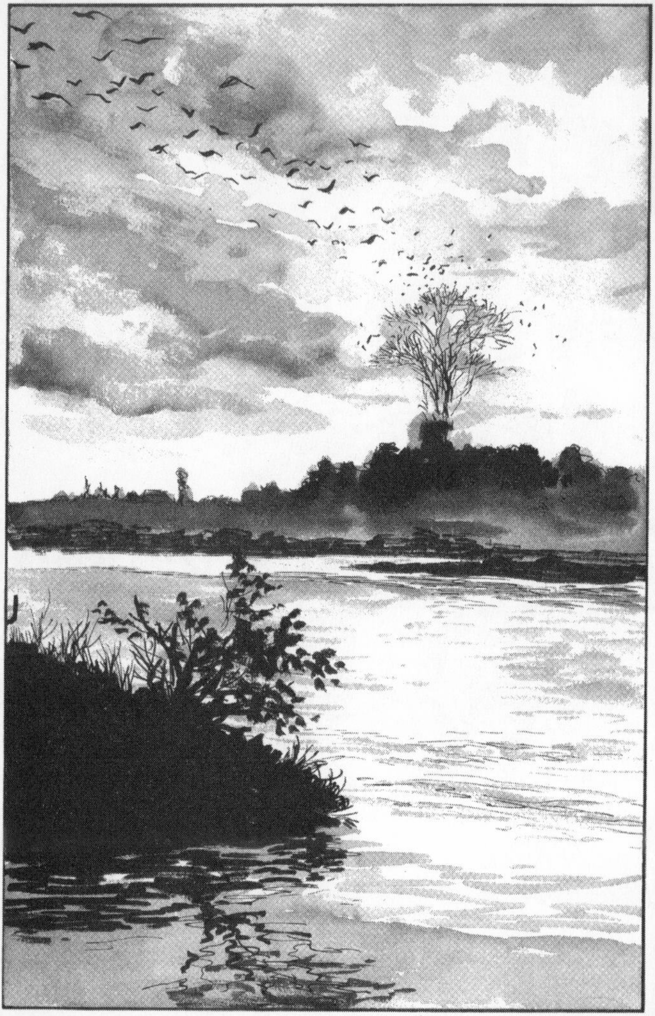

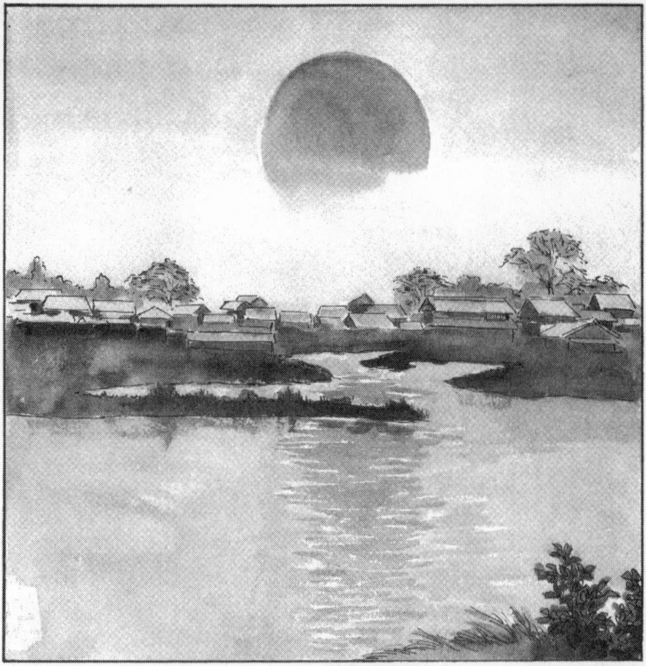
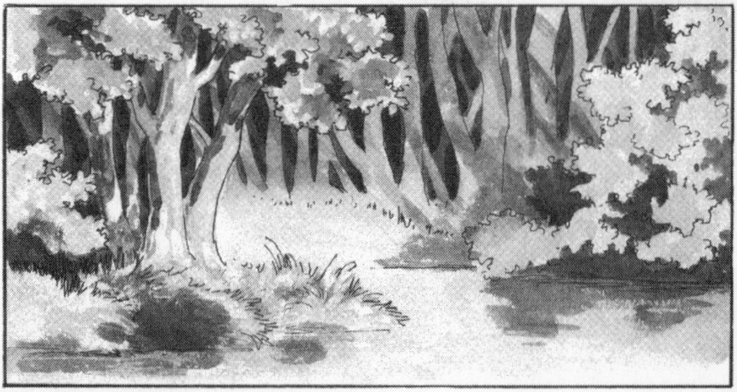

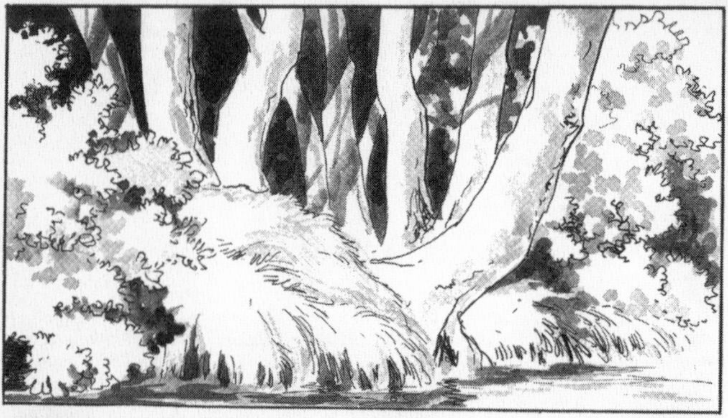

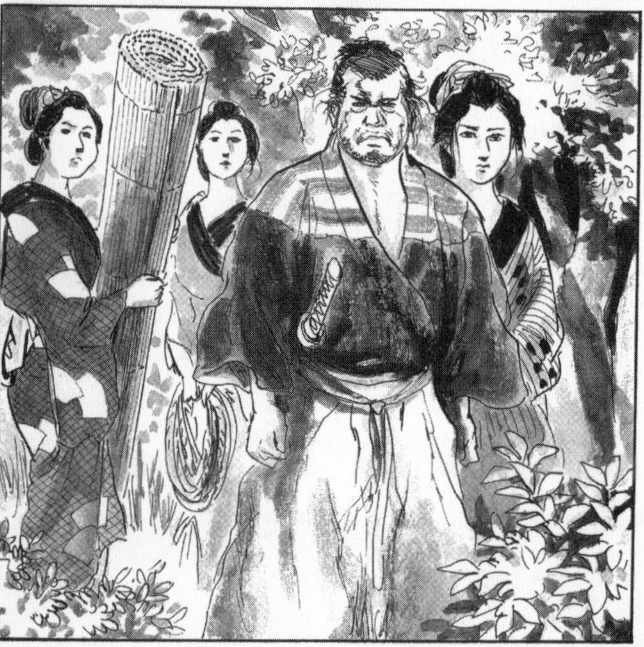

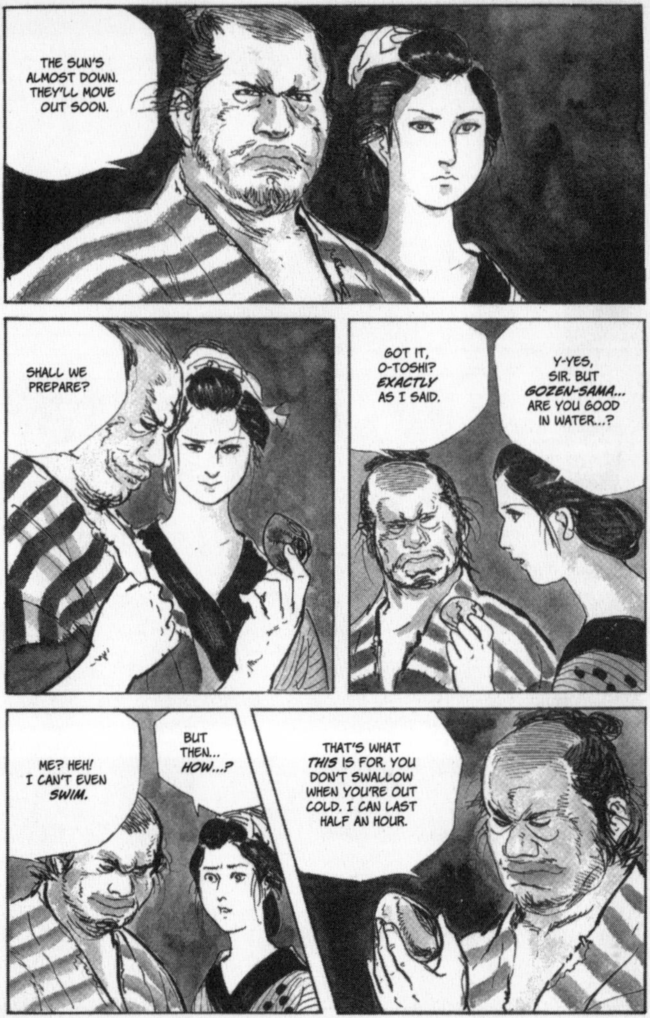
THE SUN'S ALMOST DOWN. THEY'LL MOVE OUT SOON.
SHALL WE PREPARE?
GOT IT, O-TOSHI? *EXACTLY* AS I SAID.
Y-YES, SIR. BUT *GOZEN-SAMA*... ARE YOU GOOD IN WATER...?
ME? HEH! I CAN'T EVEN *SWIM.*
BUT THEN... *HOW...?*
THAT'S WHAT *THIS* IS FOR. YOU DON'T SWALLOW WHEN YOU'RE OUT COLD. I CAN LAST HALF AN HOUR.

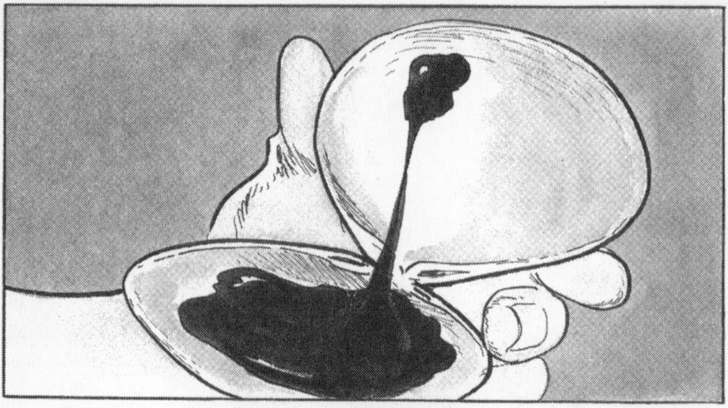
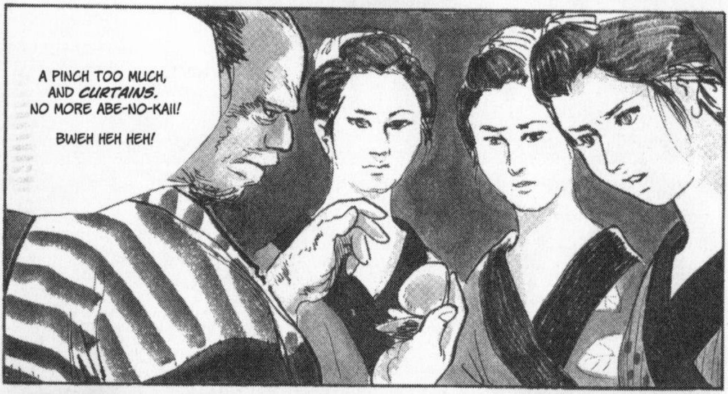
A PINCH TOO MUCH, AND *CURTAINS.* NO MORE ABE-NO-KAII!
BWEH HEH HEH!
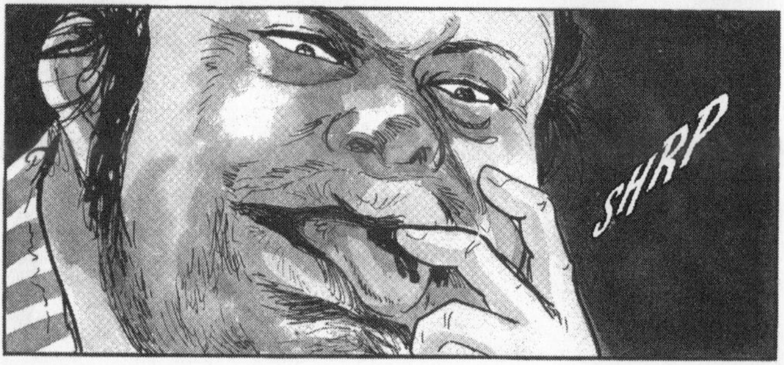
SHIRP

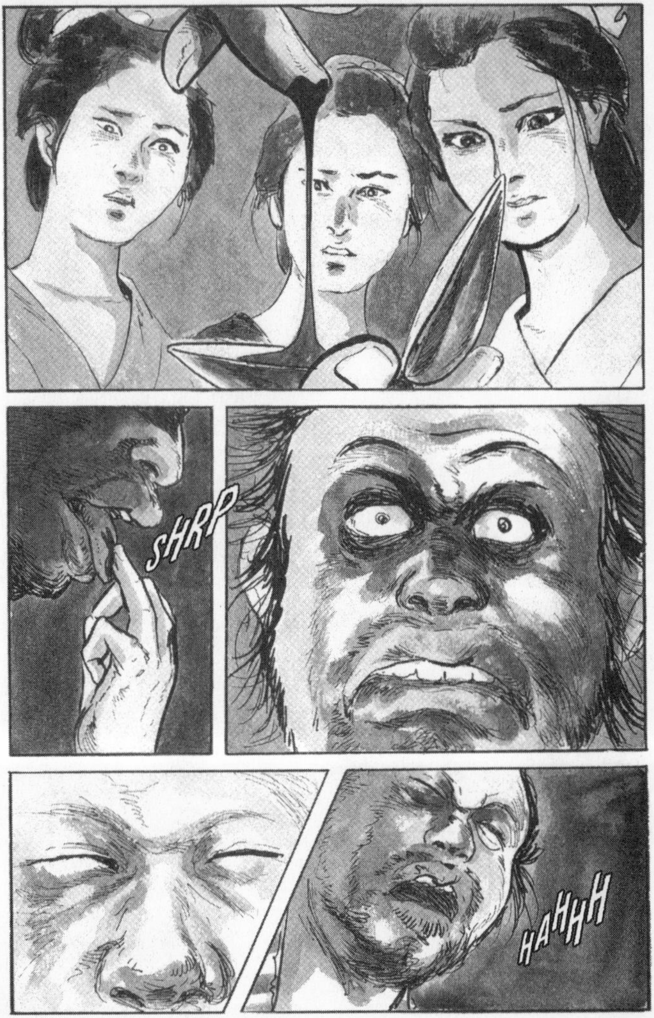
SHRP
HAHHH

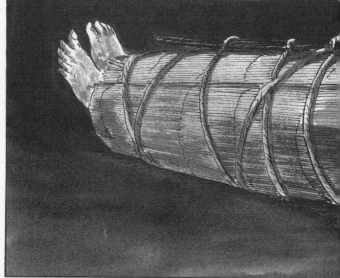

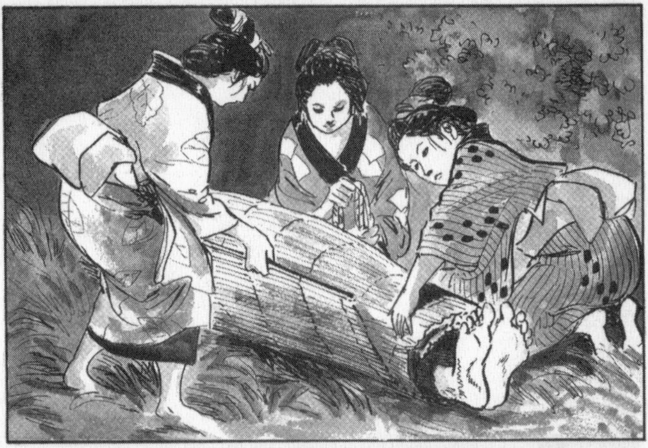

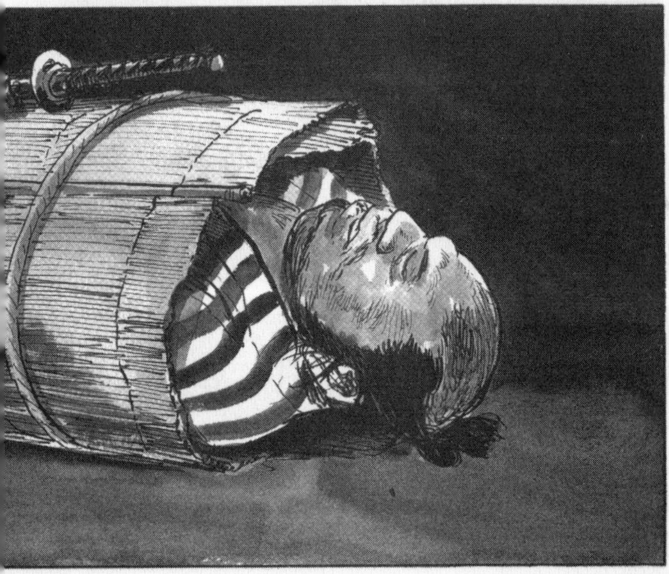

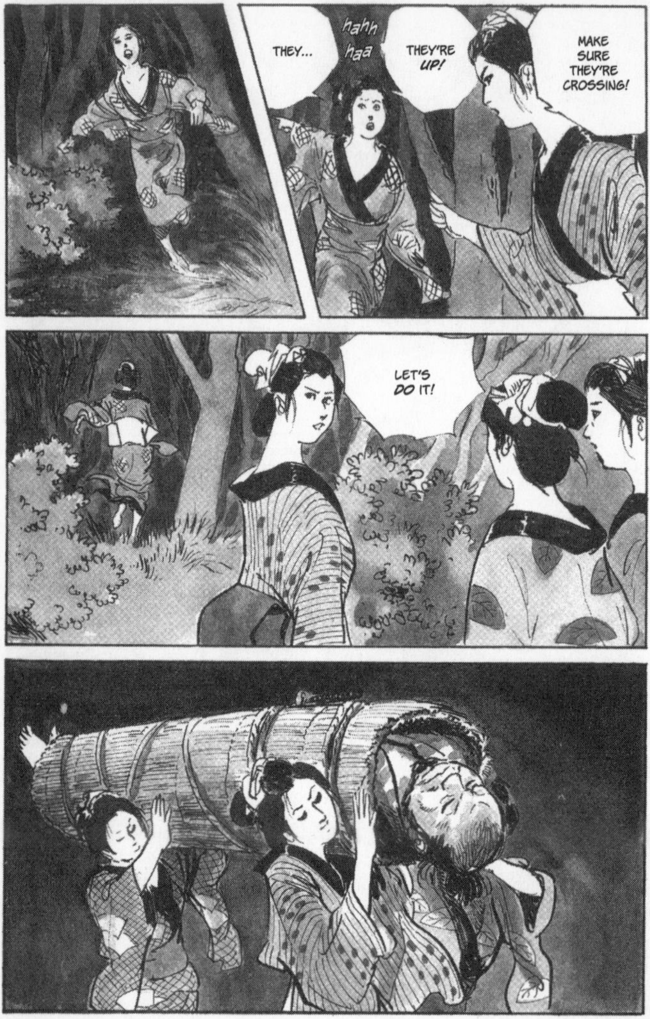
THEY...
hahh haa
THEY'RE *UP!*
MAKE SURE THEY'RE CROSSING!
LET'S *DO* IT!

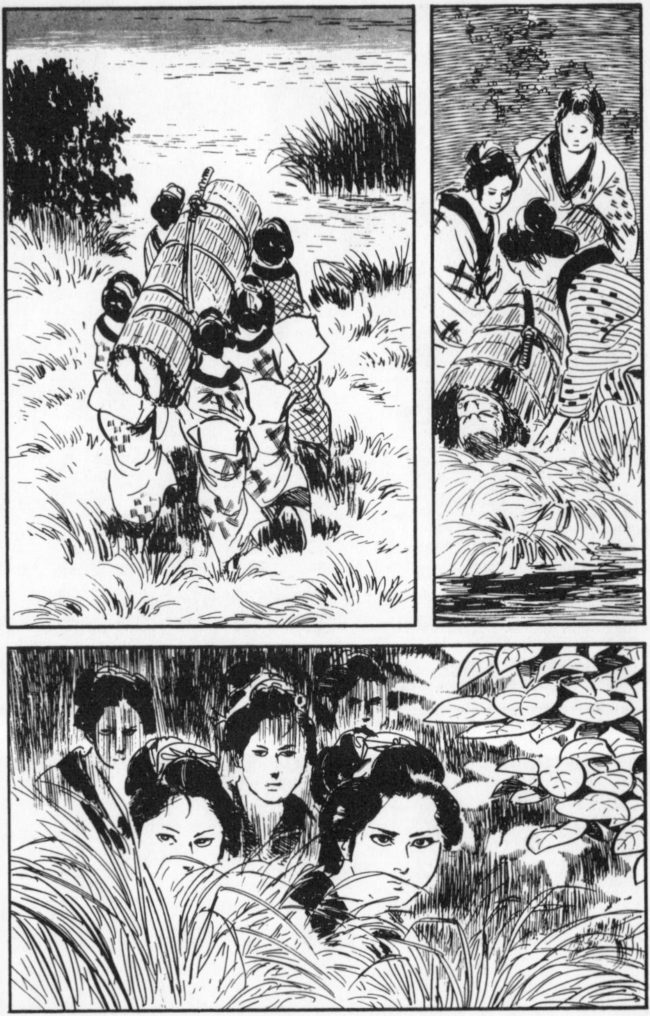

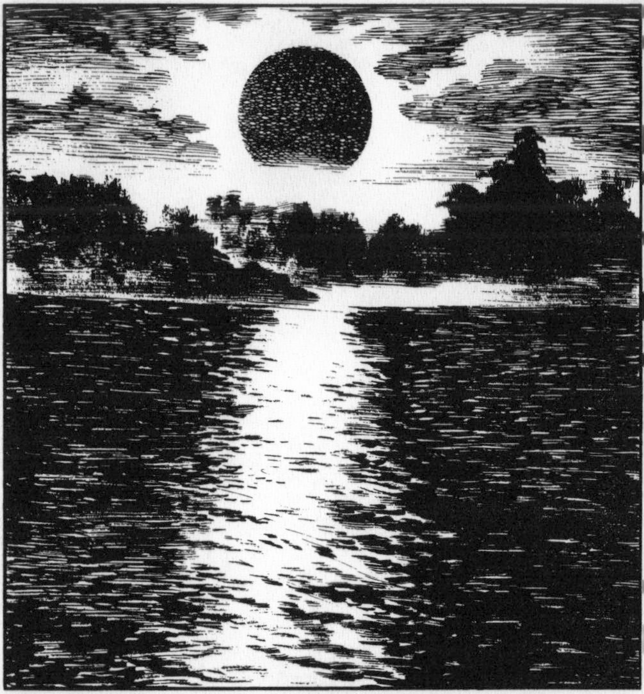

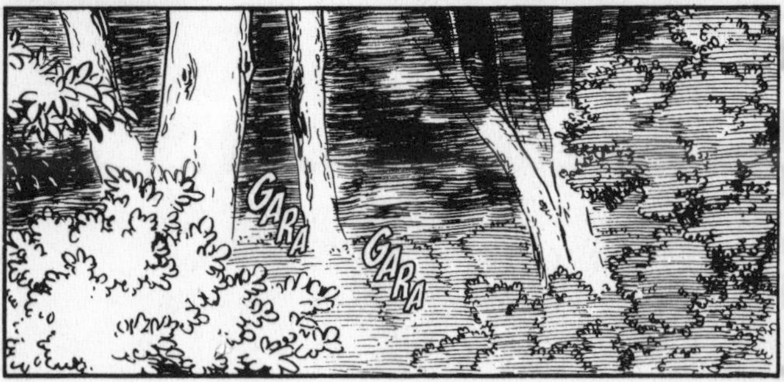
GARA
GARA

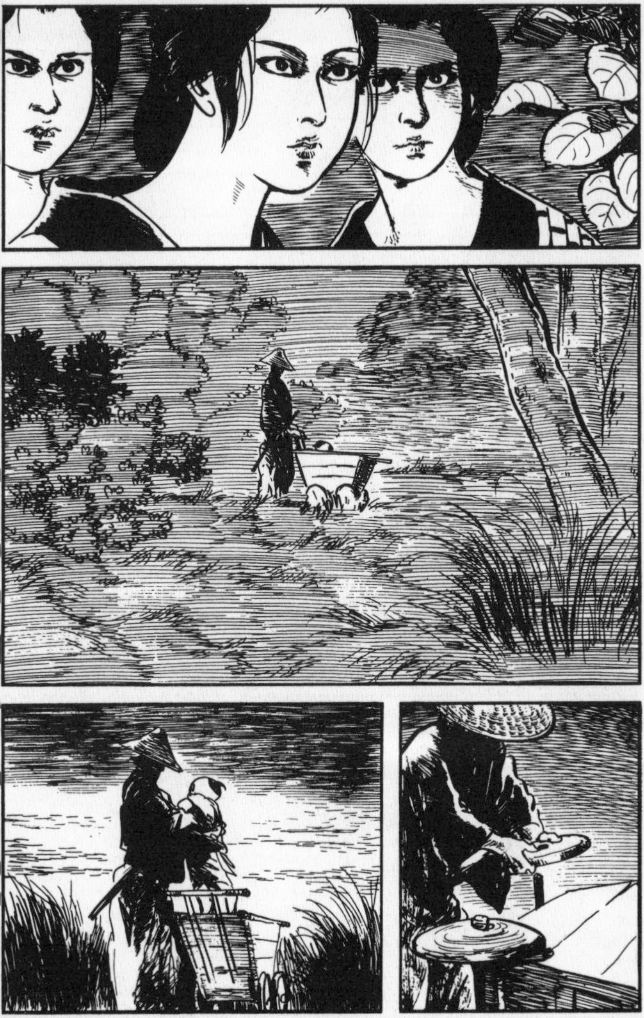

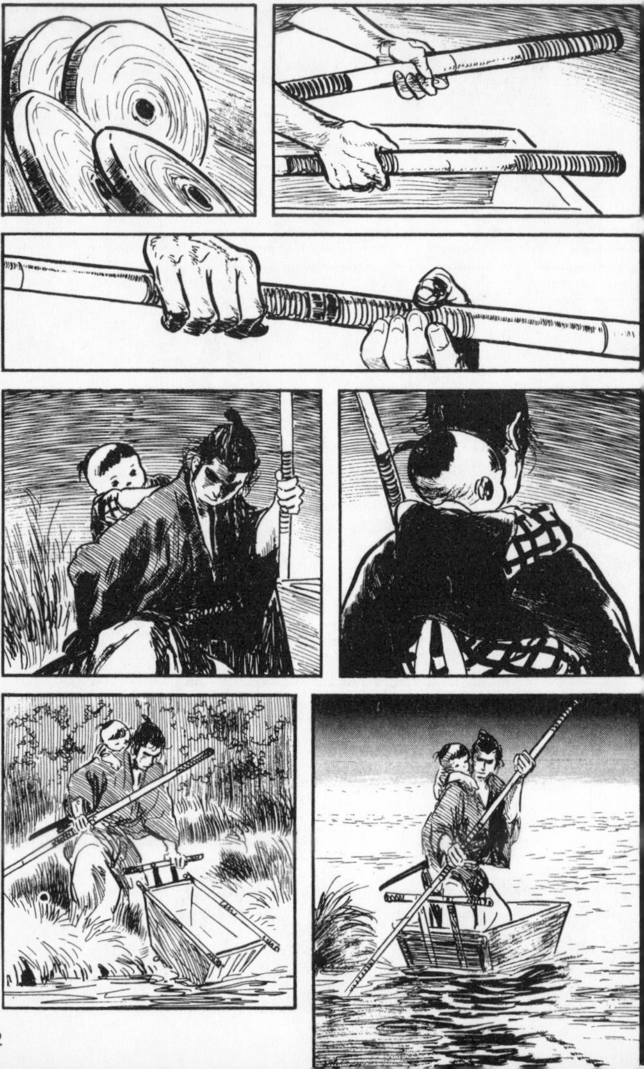

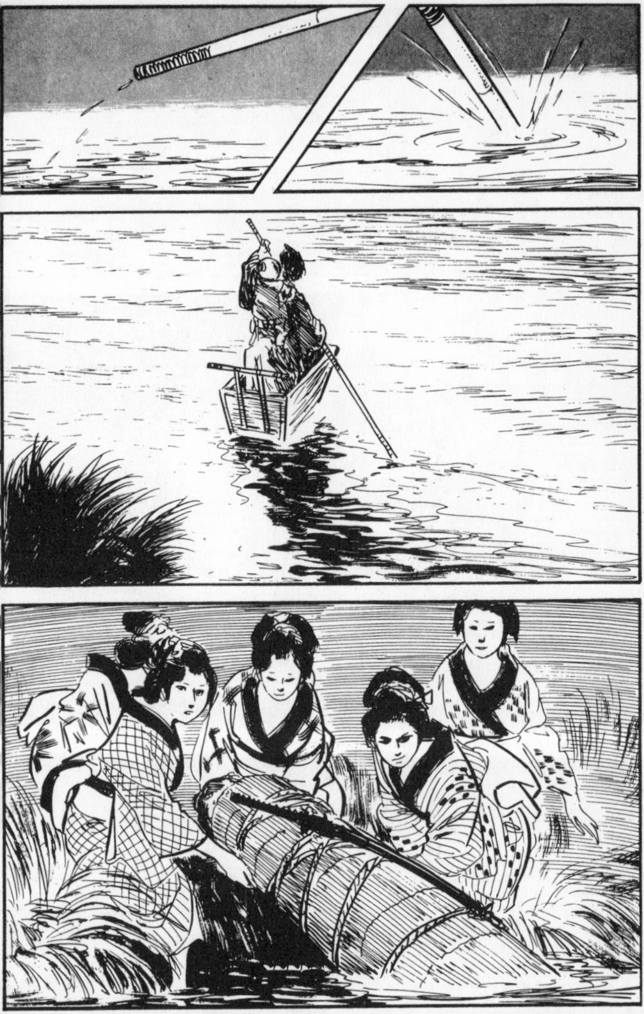

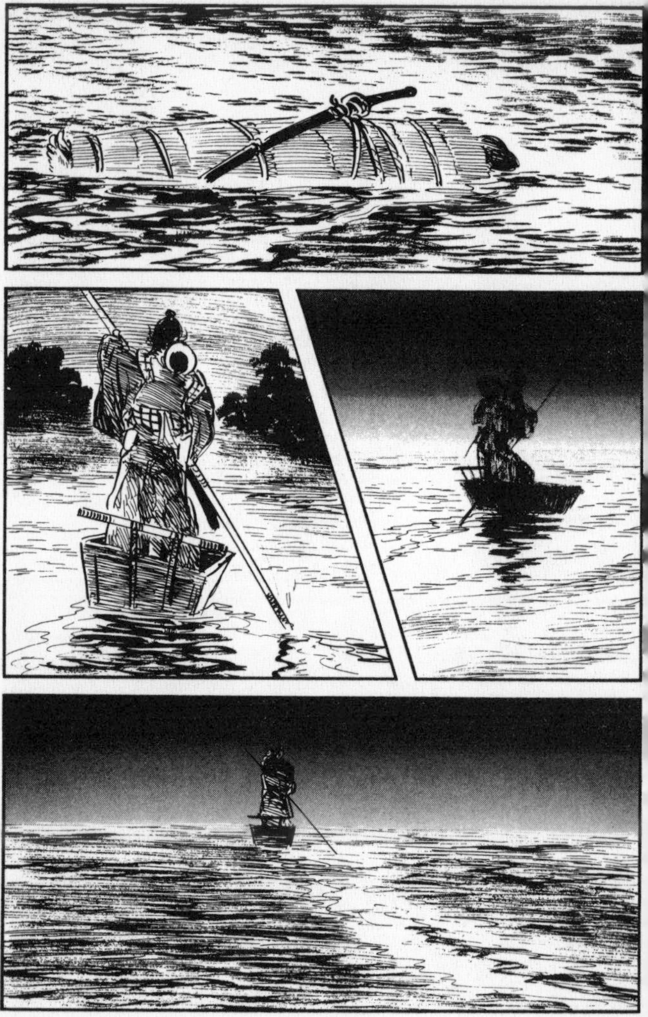

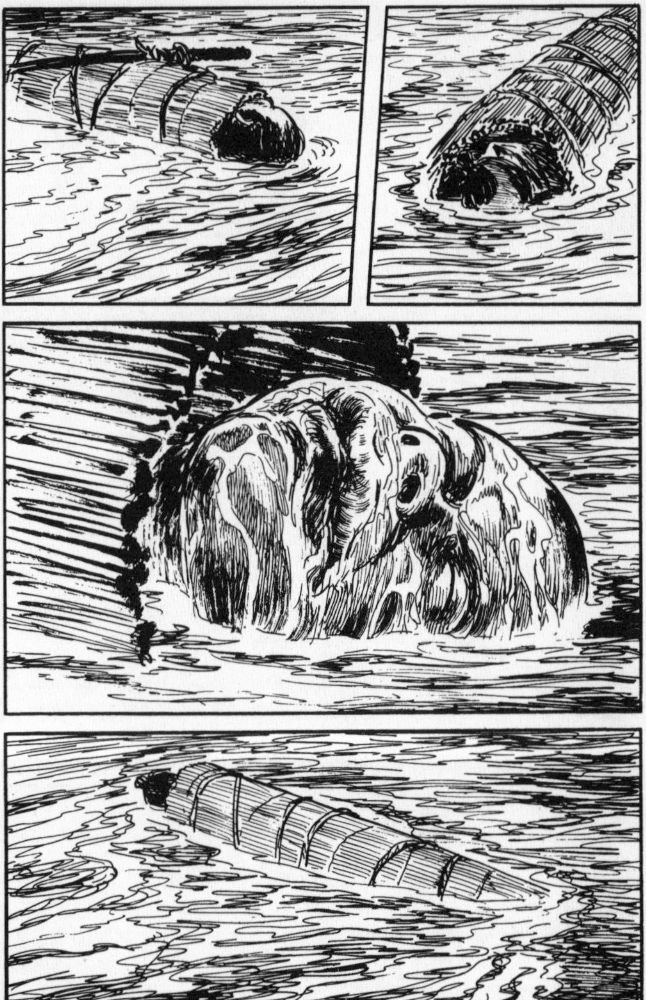

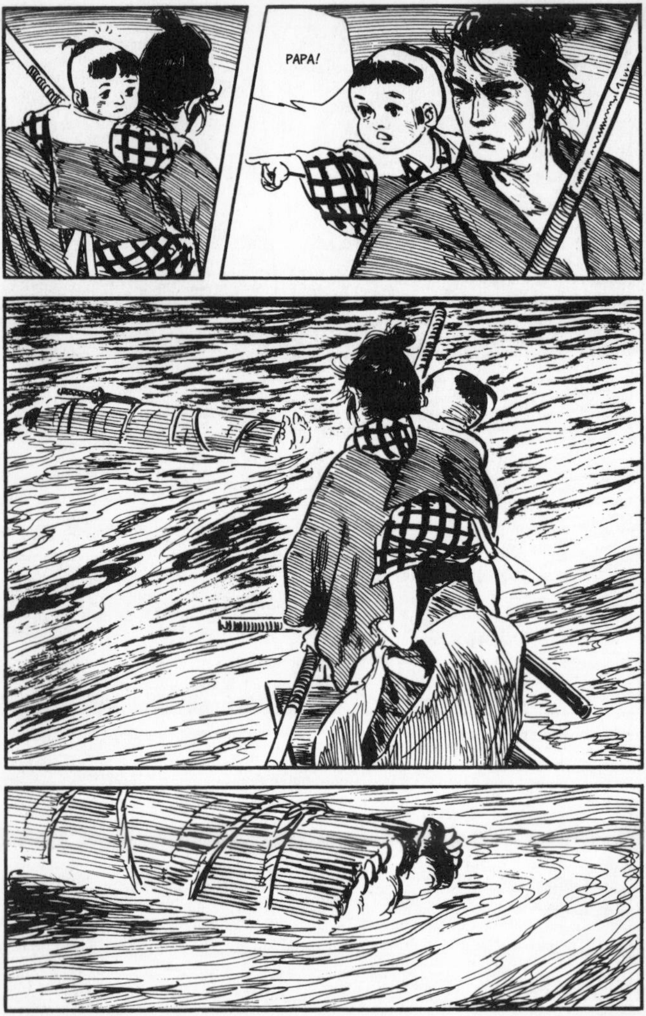
PAPA!

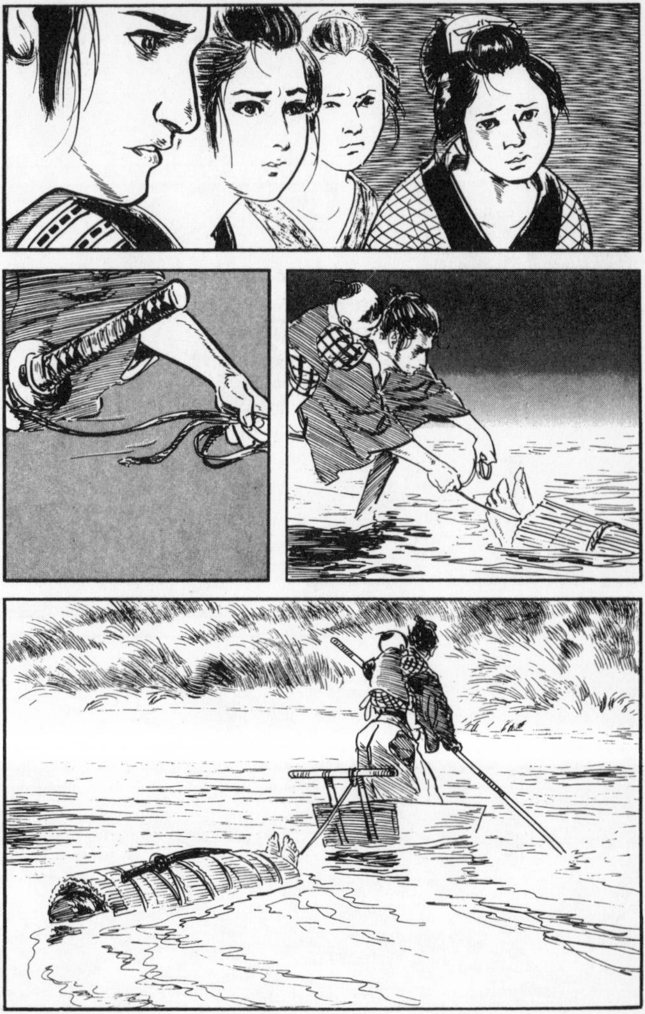

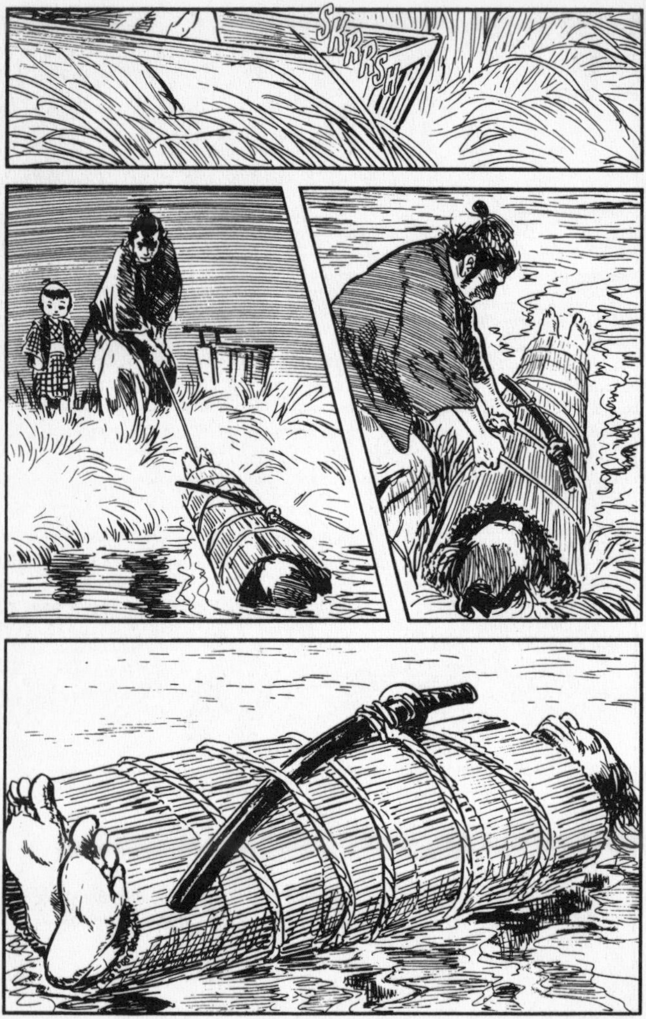
SKRRSH

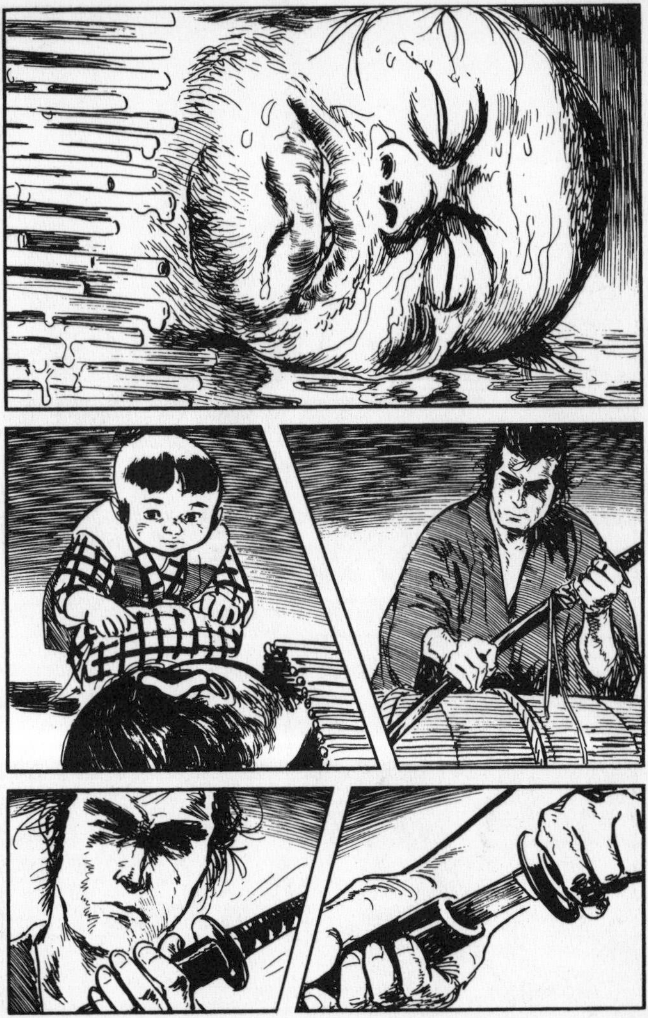

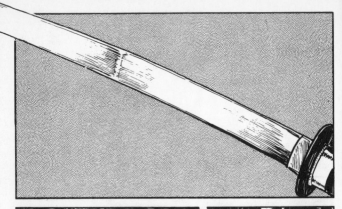

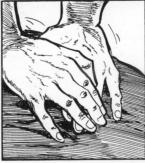

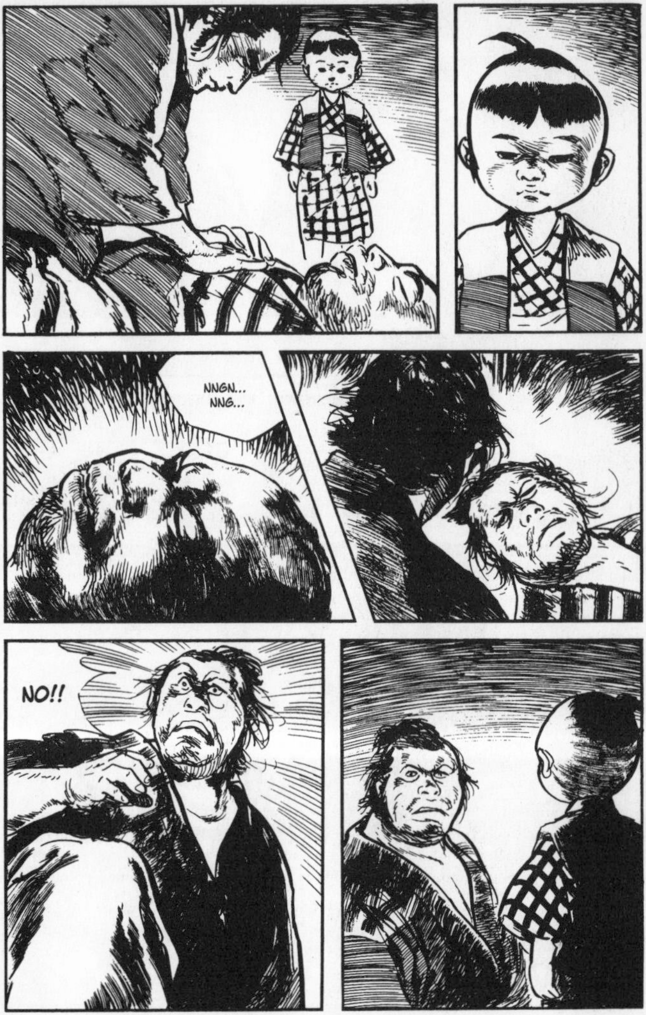
NNGN...
NNG...
NO!!

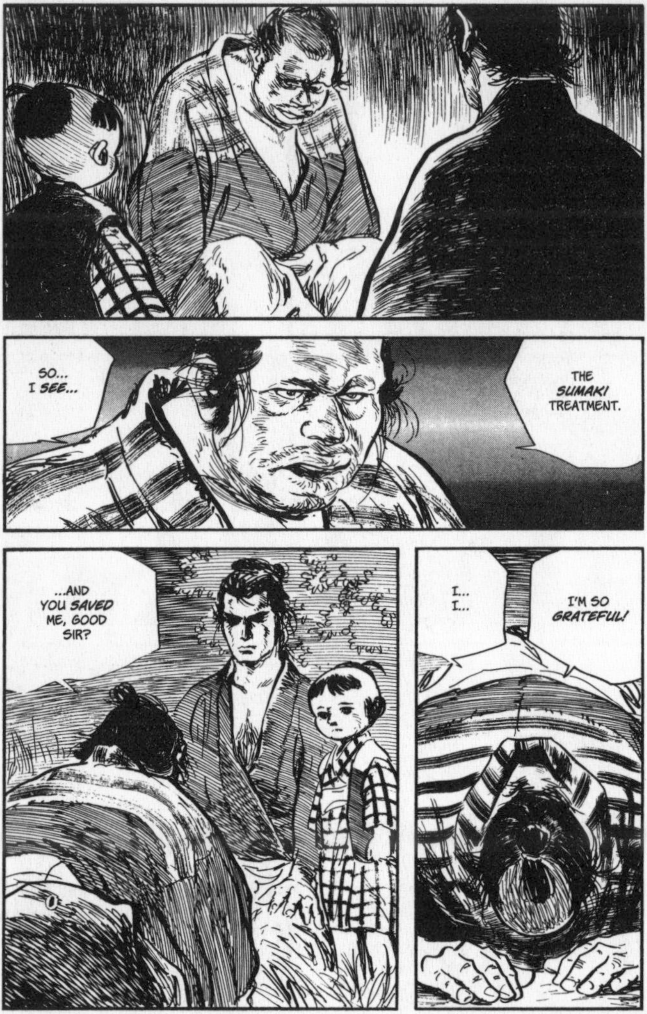
SO... I SEE...
THE *SUMAKI* TREATMENT.
...AND YOU *SAVED* ME, GOOD SIR?
I... I...
I'M SO *GRATEFUL!*

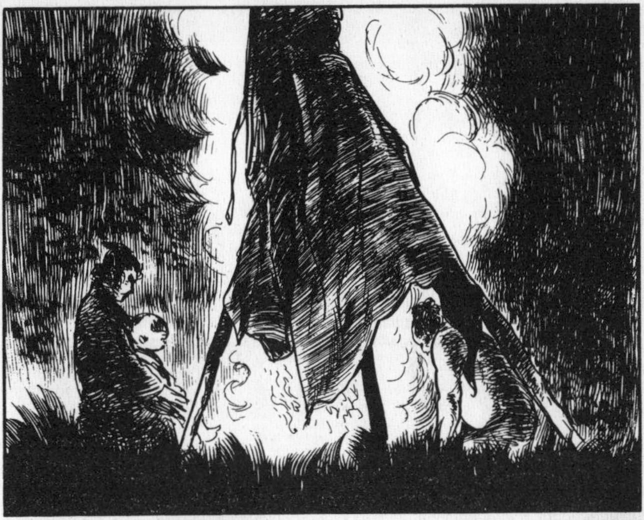

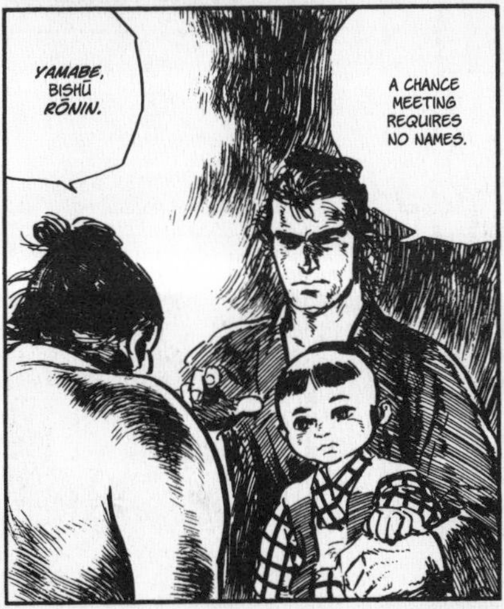
YAMABE, BISHŪ RŌNIN.
A CHANCE MEETING REQUIRES NO NAMES.

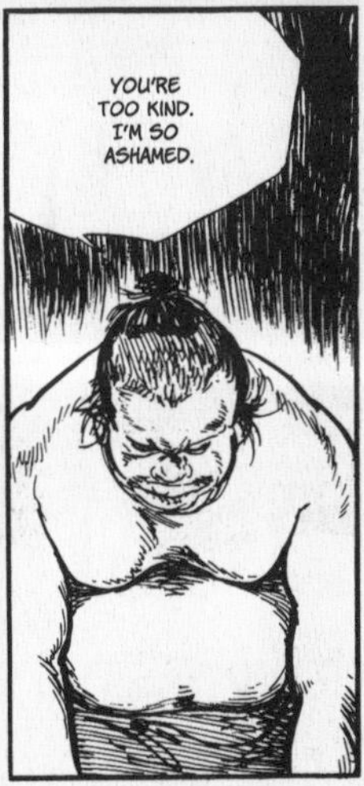
YOU'RE TOO KIND. I'M SO ASHAMED.

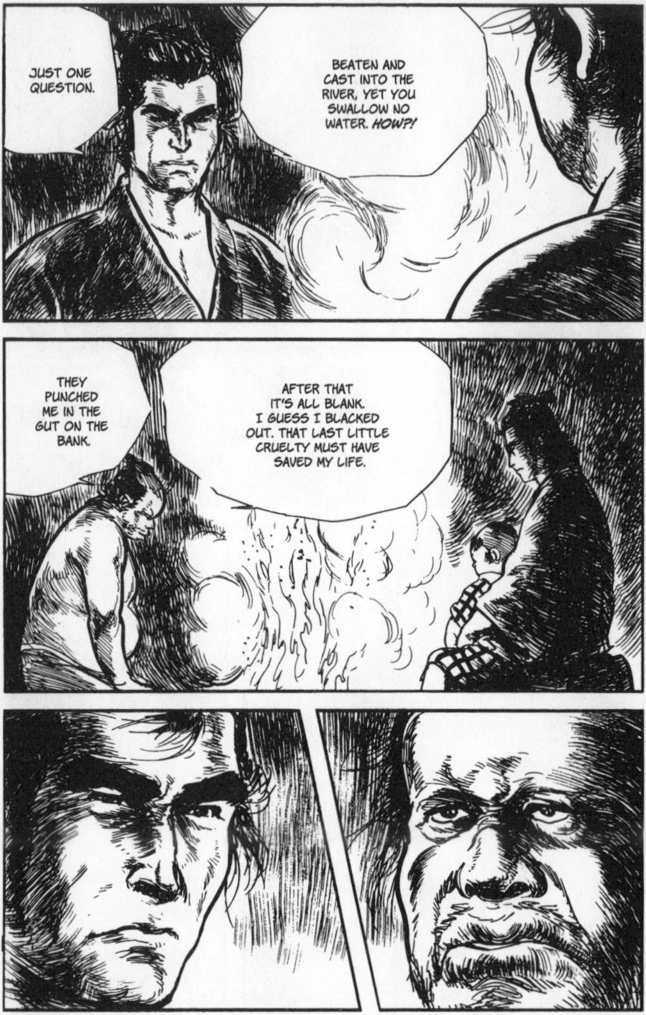
JUST ONE QUESTION.
BEATEN AND CAST INTO THE RIVER, YET YOU SWALLOW NO WATER. *HOW?!*
THEY PUNCHED ME IN THE GUT ON THE BANK.
AFTER THAT IT'S ALL BLANK. I GUESS I BLACKED OUT. THAT LAST LITTLE CRUELTY MUST HAVE SAVED MY LIFE.

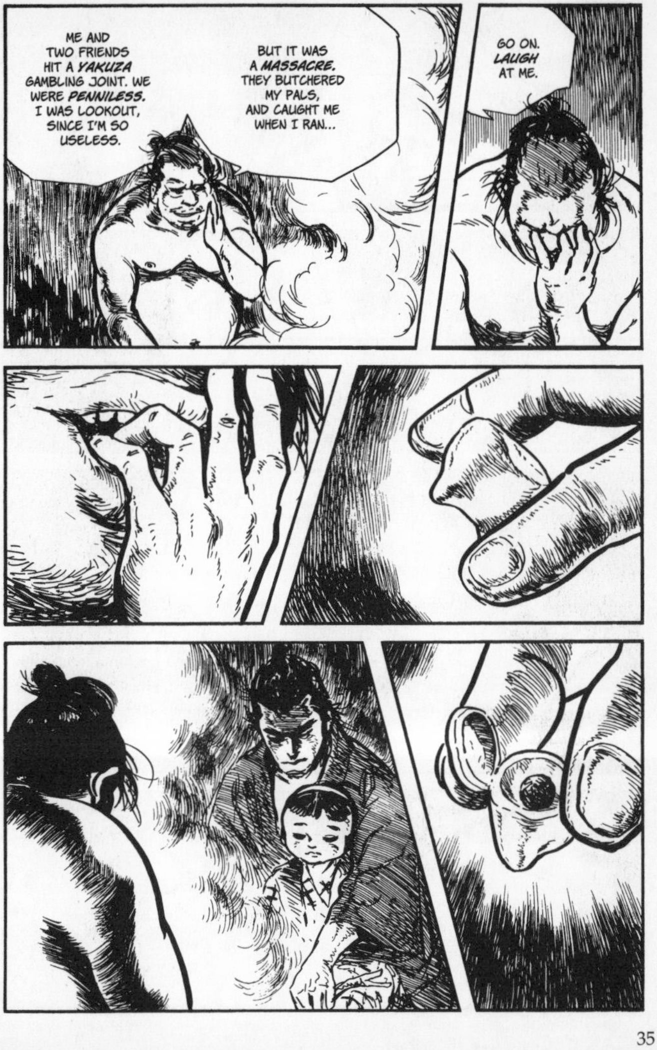
ME AND TWO FRIENDS HIT A *YAKUZA* GAMBLING JOINT. WE WERE *PENNILESS.* I WAS LOOKOUT, SINCE I'M SO USELESS.
BUT IT WAS A *MASSACRE.* THEY BUTCHERED MY PALS, AND CAUGHT ME WHEN I RAN...
GO ON. *LAUGH* AT ME.

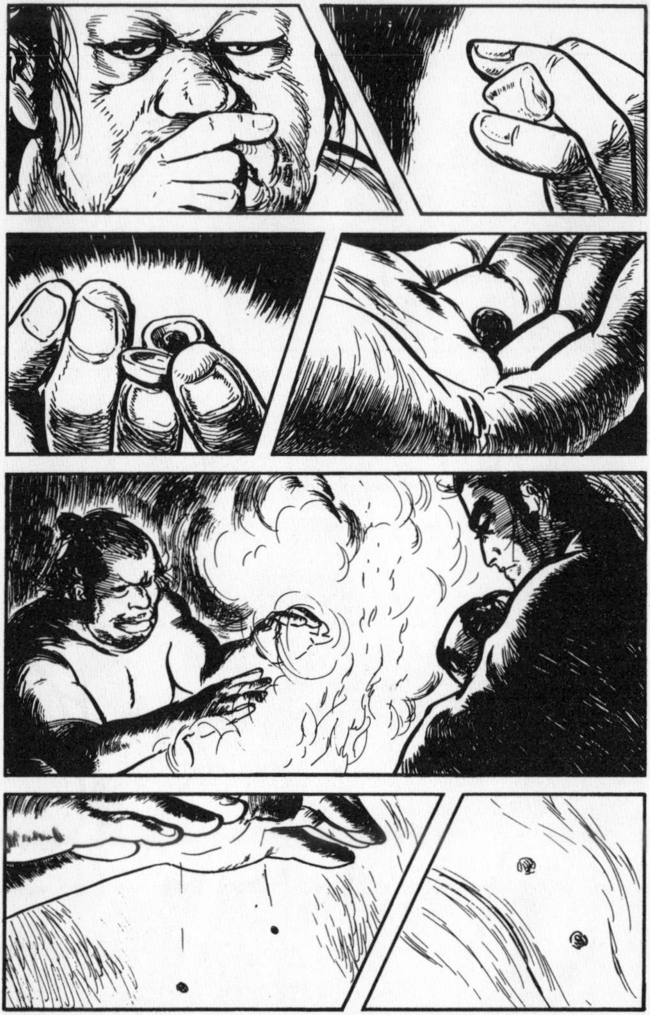

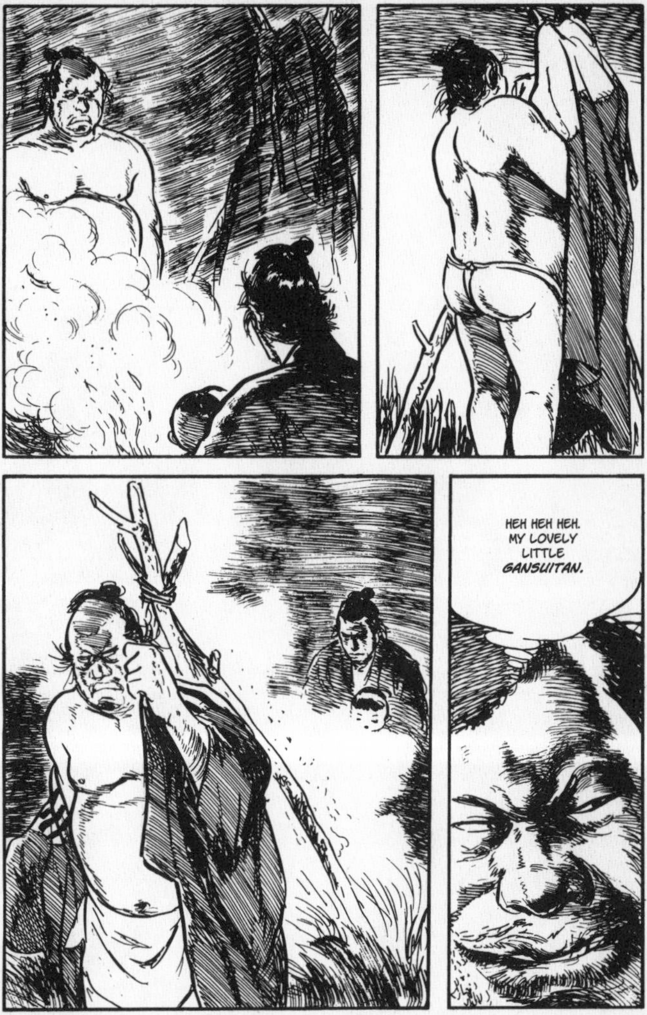
HEH HEH HEH. MY LOVELY LITTLE *GANSUITAN.*

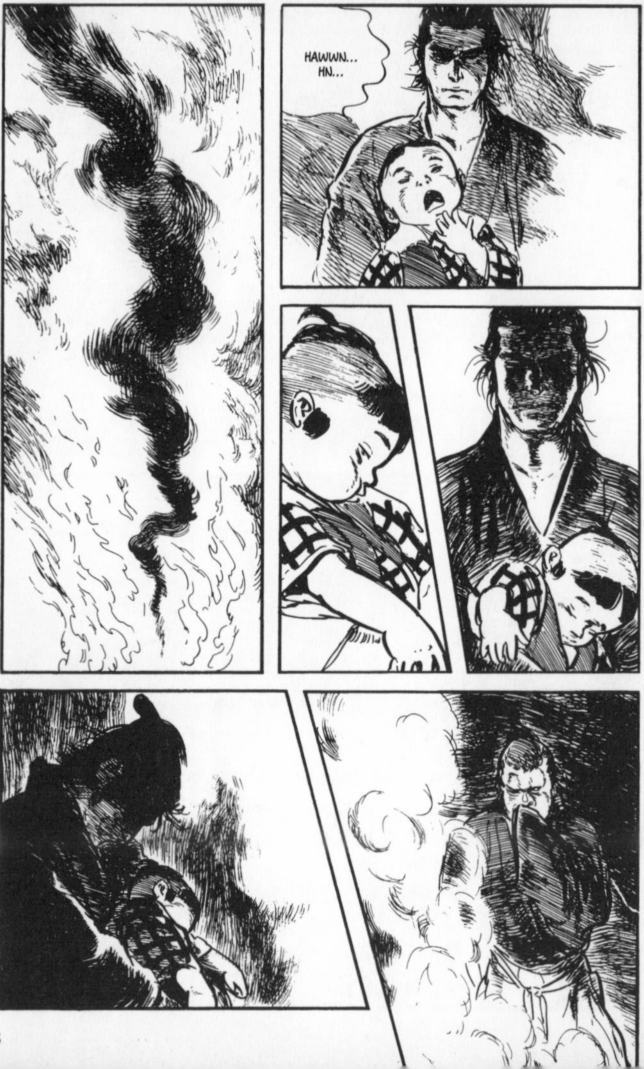
HAWWN... HN...

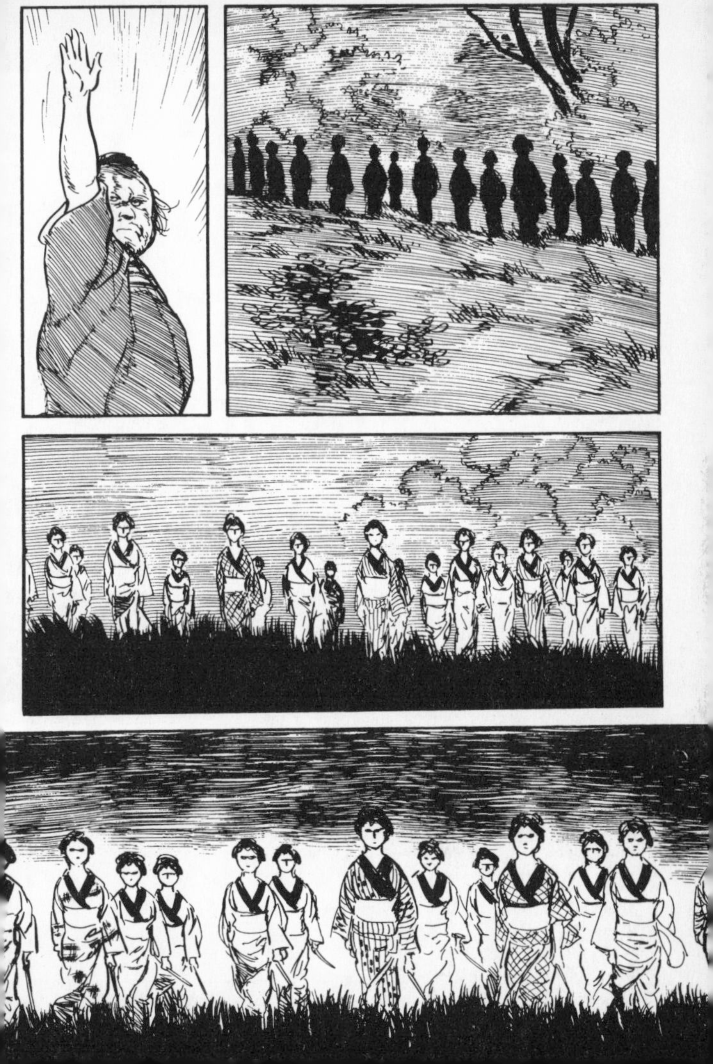

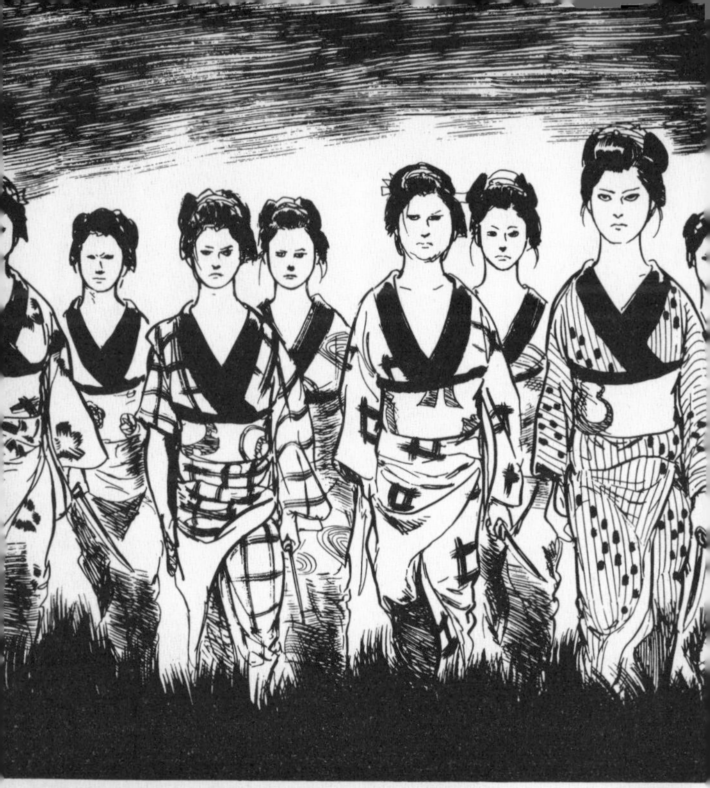
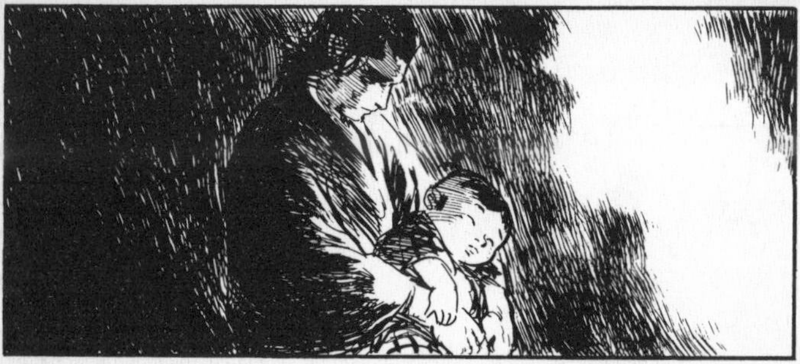

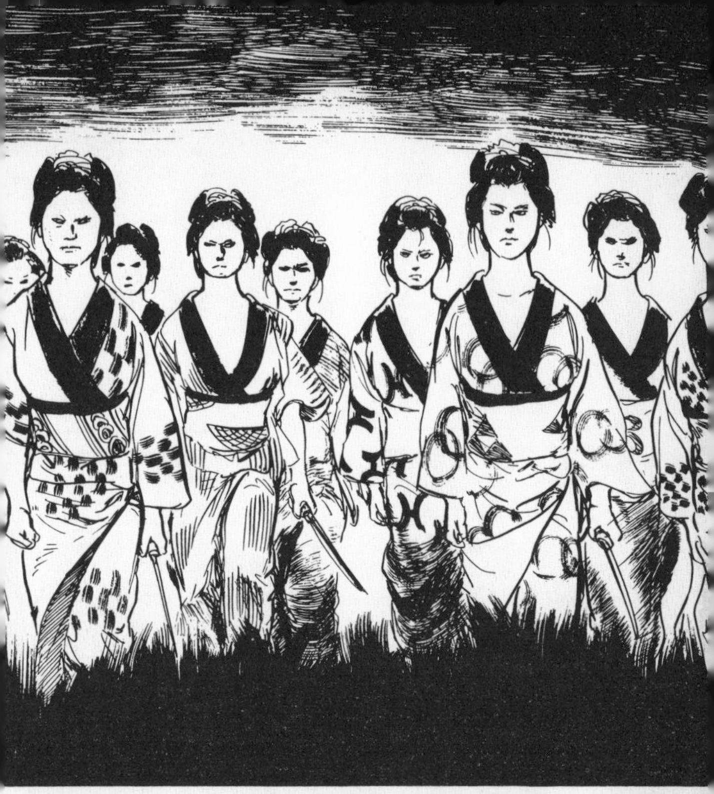

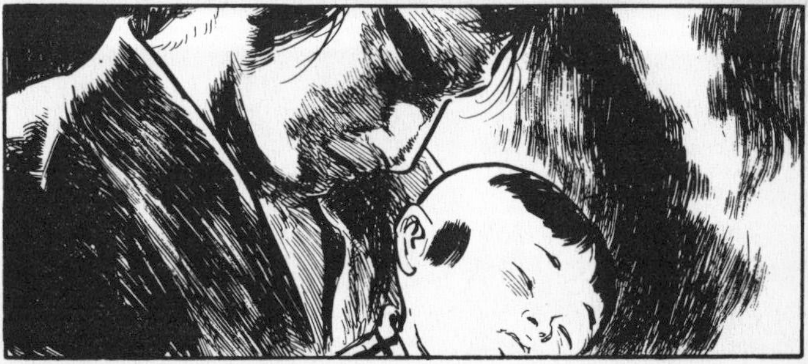

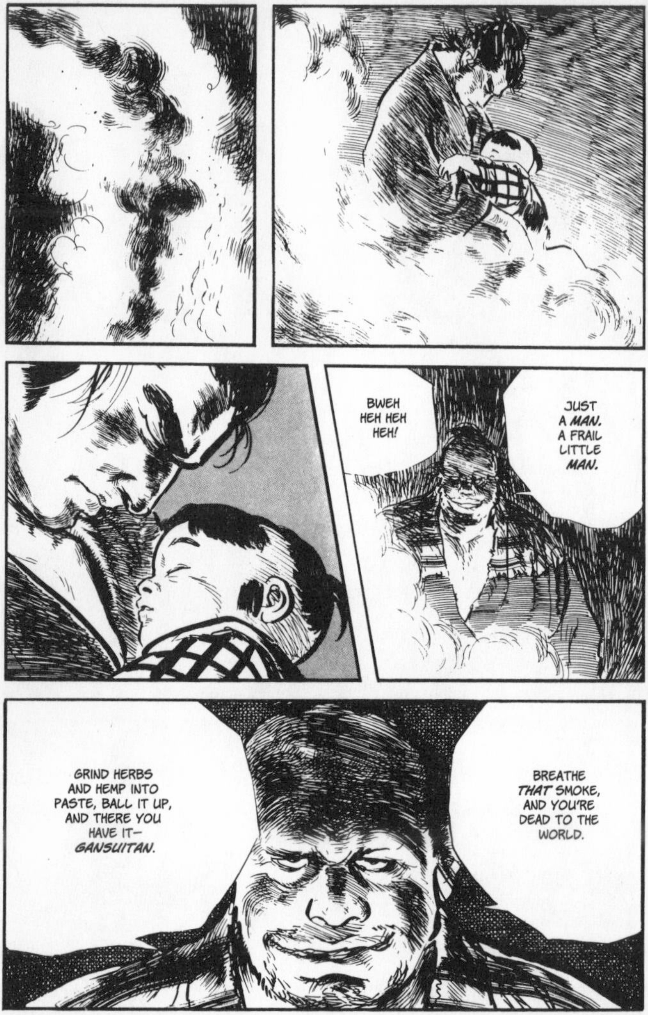

BWEH HEH HEH HEH!
JUST A *MAN.* A FRAIL LITTLE *MAN.*
GRIND HERBS AND HEMP INTO PASTE, BALL IT UP, AND THERE YOU HAVE IT— *GANSUITAN.*
BREATHE *THAT* SMOKE, AND YOU'RE DEAD TO THE WORLD.

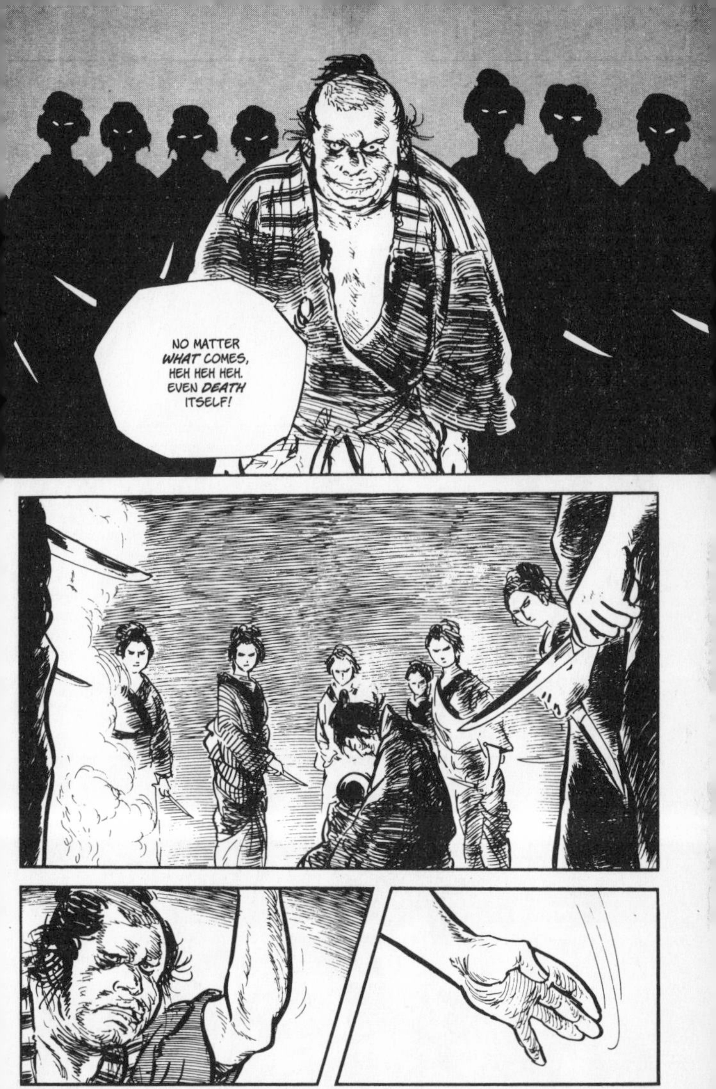
NO MATTER *WHAT* COMES, HEH HEH HEH. EVEN *DEATH* ITSELF!

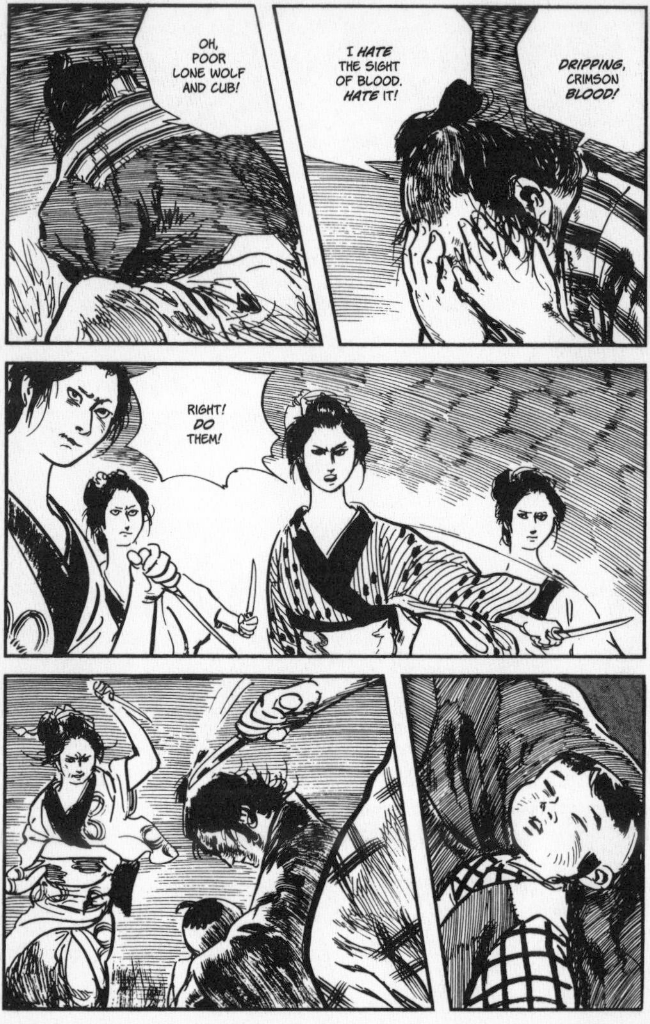
DRIPPING, CRIMSON BLOOD!
I HATE THE SIGHT OF BLOOD. HATE IT!
OH, POOR LONE WOLF AND CUB!
RIGHT! DO THEM!

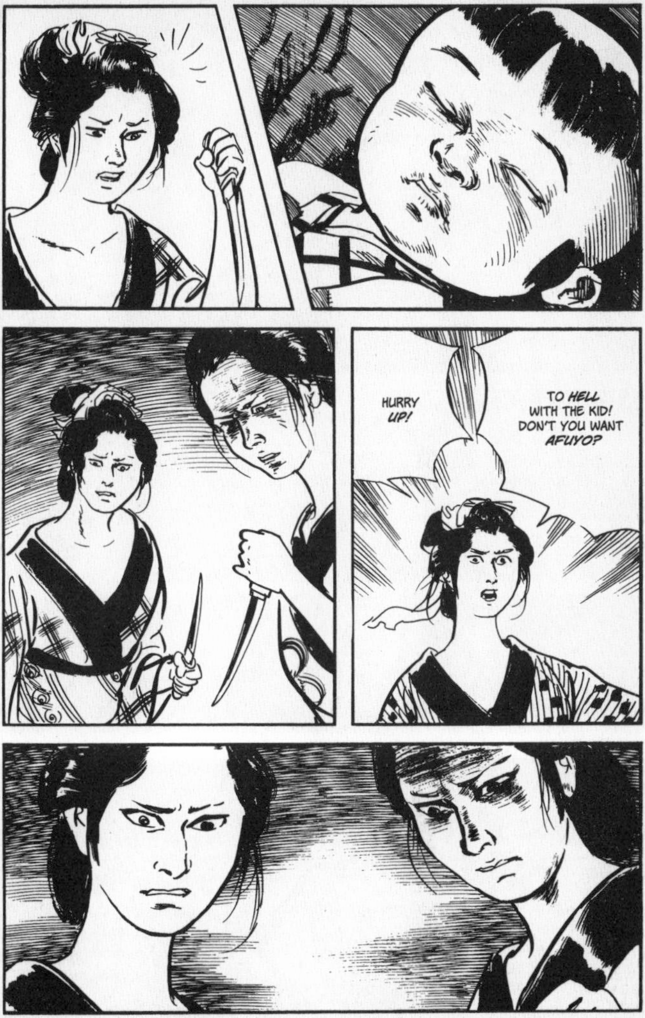
TO HELL WITH THE KID! DON'T YOU WANT AFUYO?
HURRY UP!

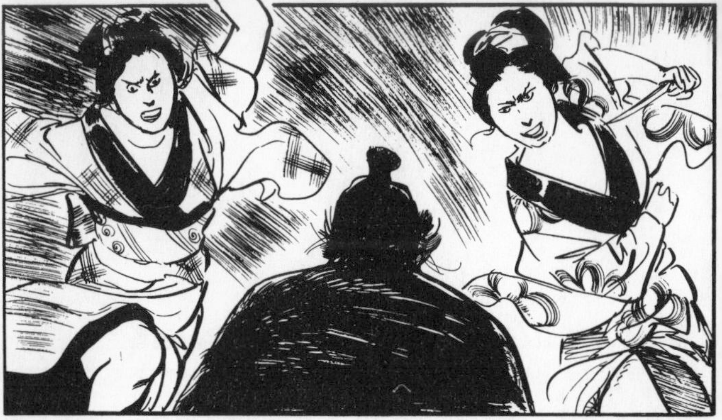

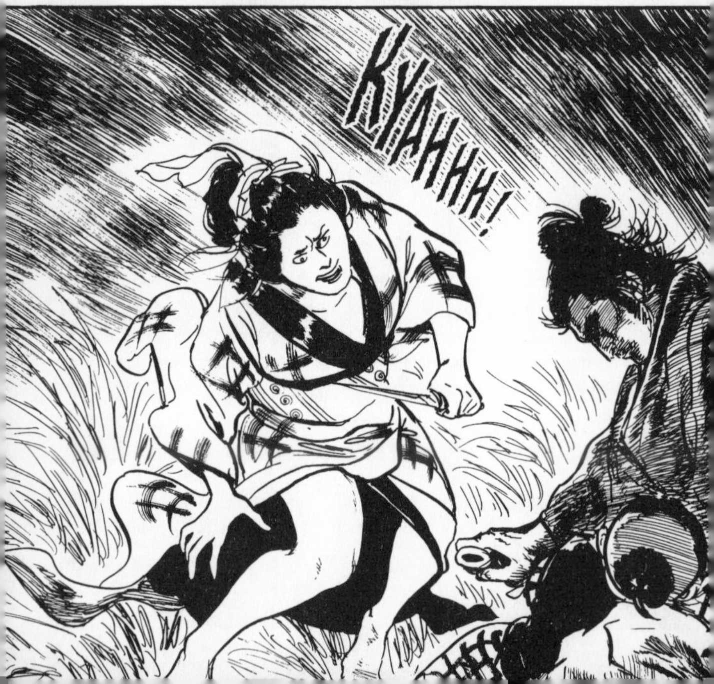
KYUHHHH!

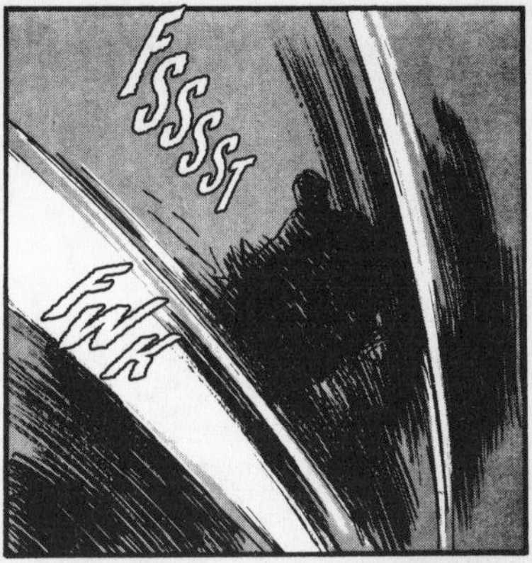
FSSSST
FWK
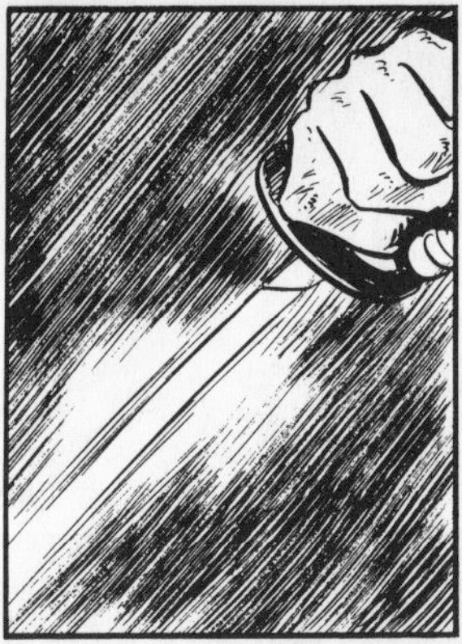
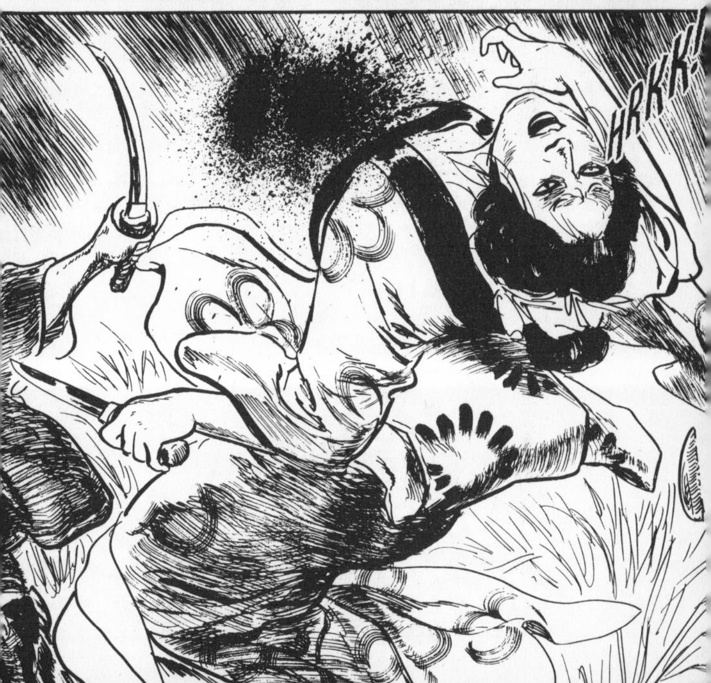
HRKK!

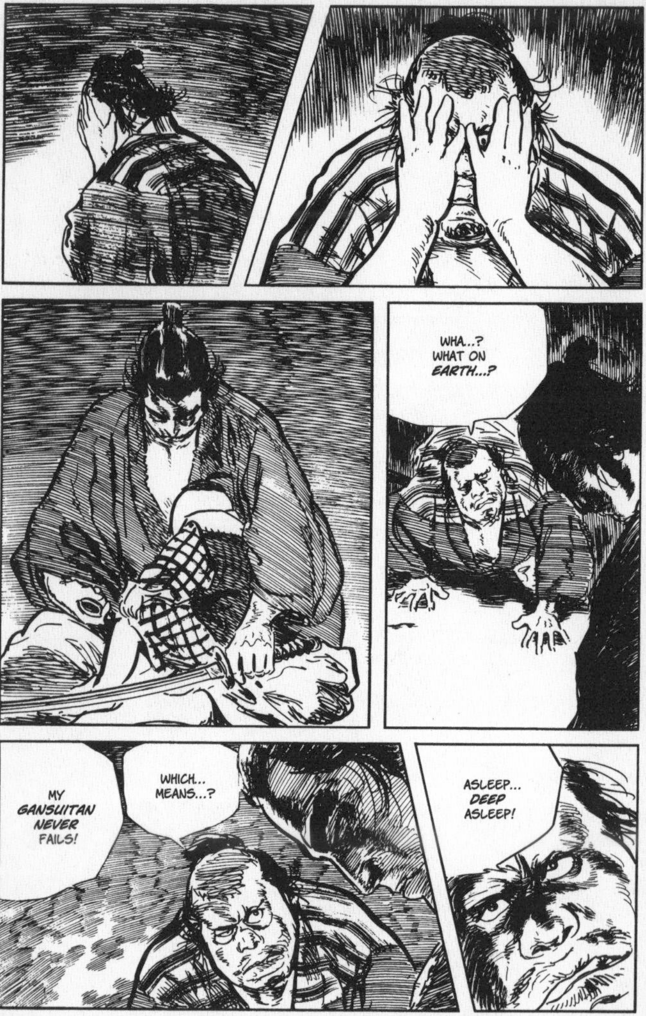
WHA...? WHAT ON *EARTH*...?
MY *GANSUITAN* *NEVER* FAILS!
WHICH... MEANS...?
ASLEEP... *DEEP* ASLEEP!

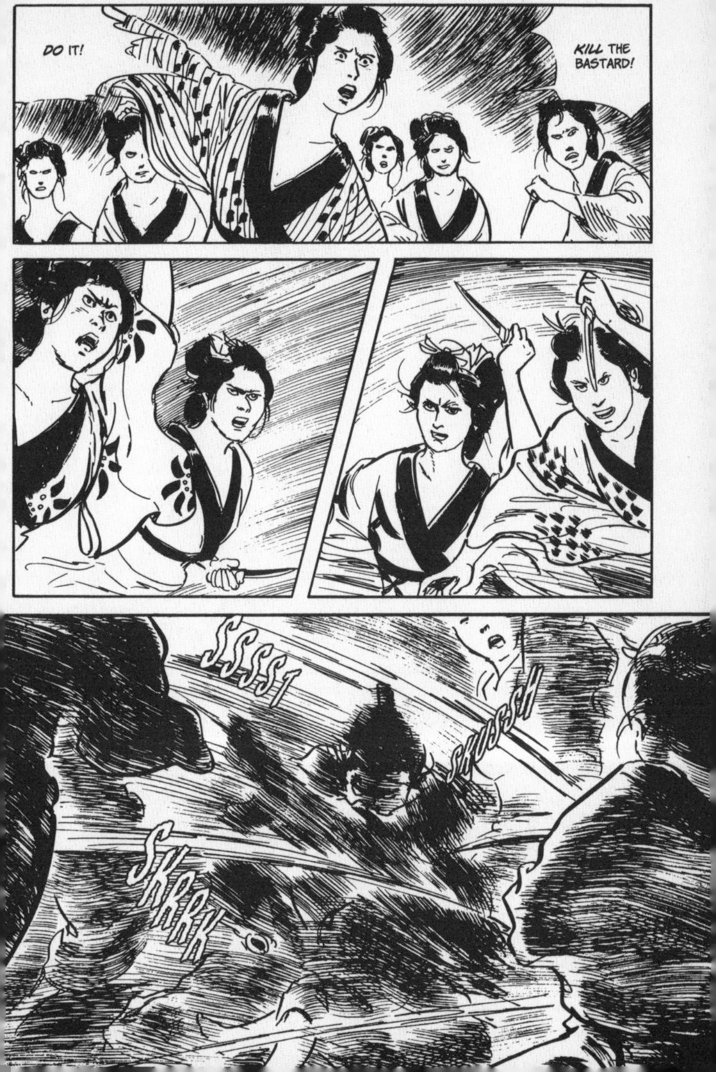
KILL THE BASTARD!
DO IT!
SSSST
SHUSSH
SKRRK

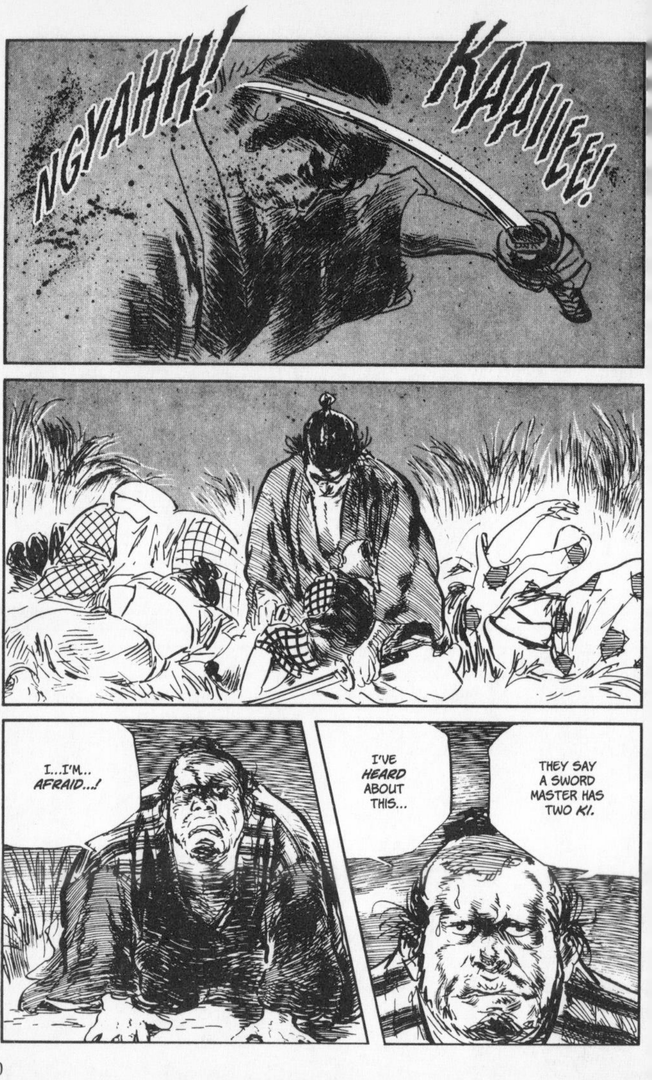
NGYAHH!
KAAIIEE!
I...I'M.. *AFRAID*...!
I'VE *HEARD* ABOUT THIS...
THEY SAY A SWORD MASTER HAS TWO *KI*.

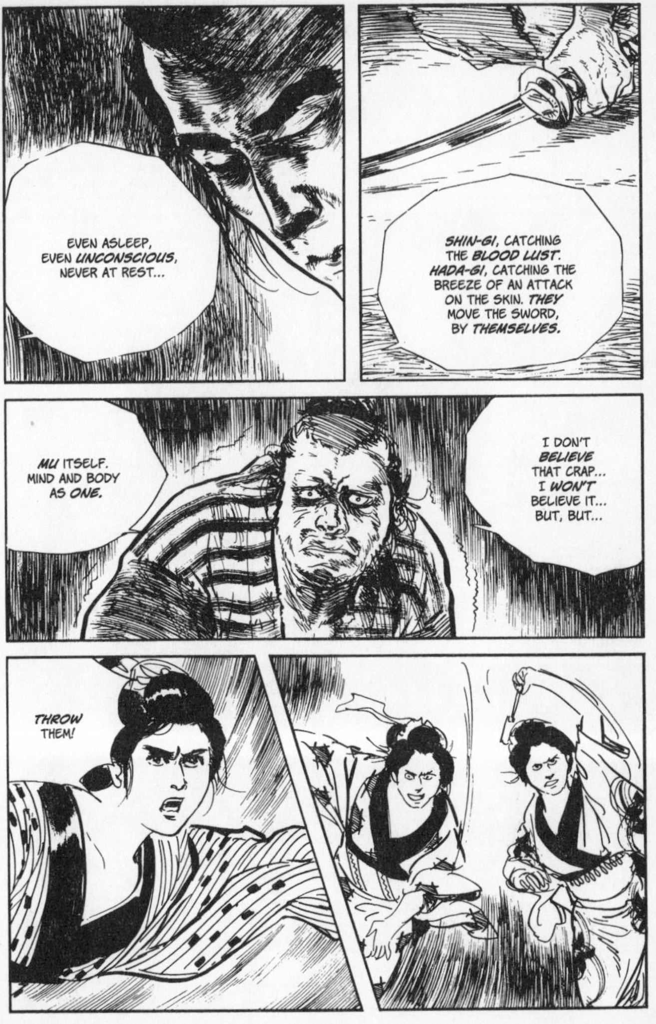
EVEN ASLEEP, EVEN UNCONSCIOUS, NEVER AT REST...
SHIN-GI, CATCHING THE BLOOD LUST. HADA-GI, CATCHING THE BREEZE OF AN ATTACK ON THE SKIN. THEY MOVE THE SWORD, BY THEMSELVES.
MU ITSELF. MIND AND BODY AS ONE.
I DON'T BELIEVE THAT CRAP... I WON'T BELIEVE IT... BUT, BUT...
THROW THEM!

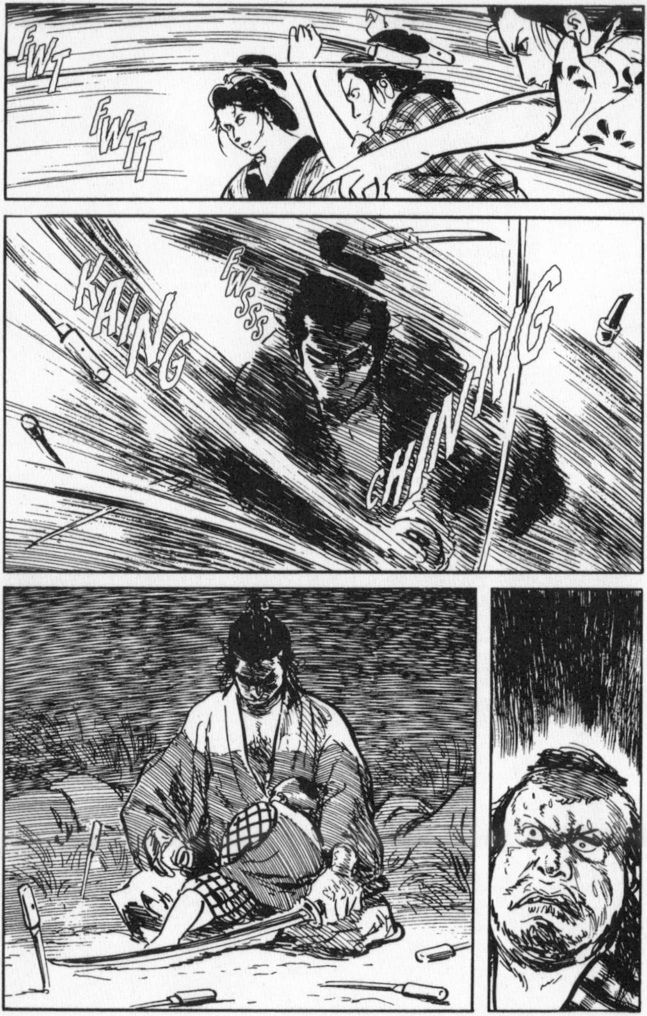
FWT
FWTT
CHINING
FWSSS
KAING

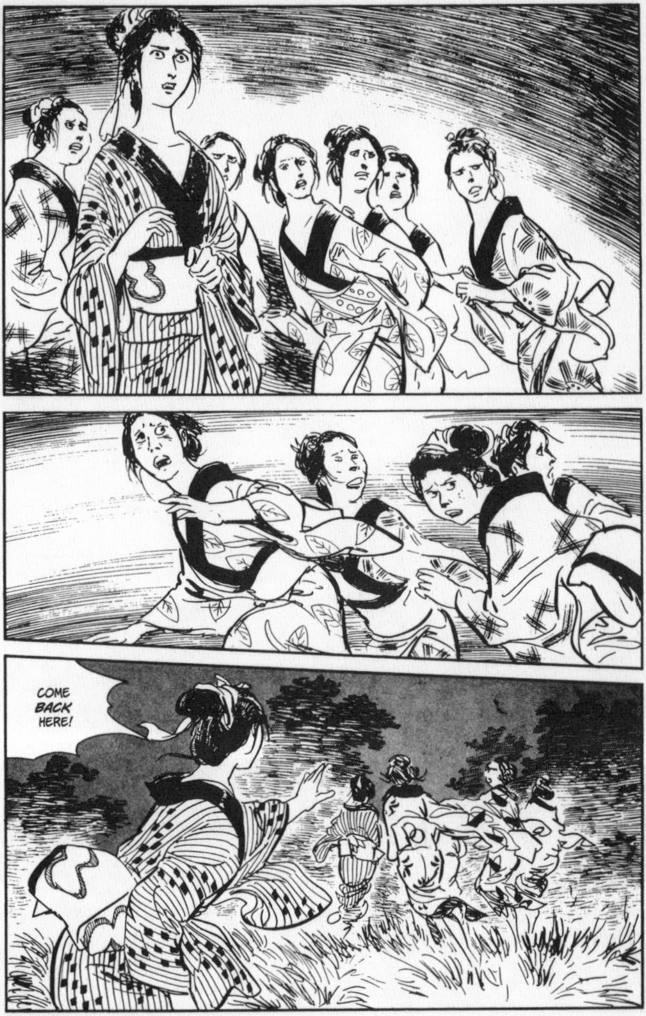
COME BACK HERE!

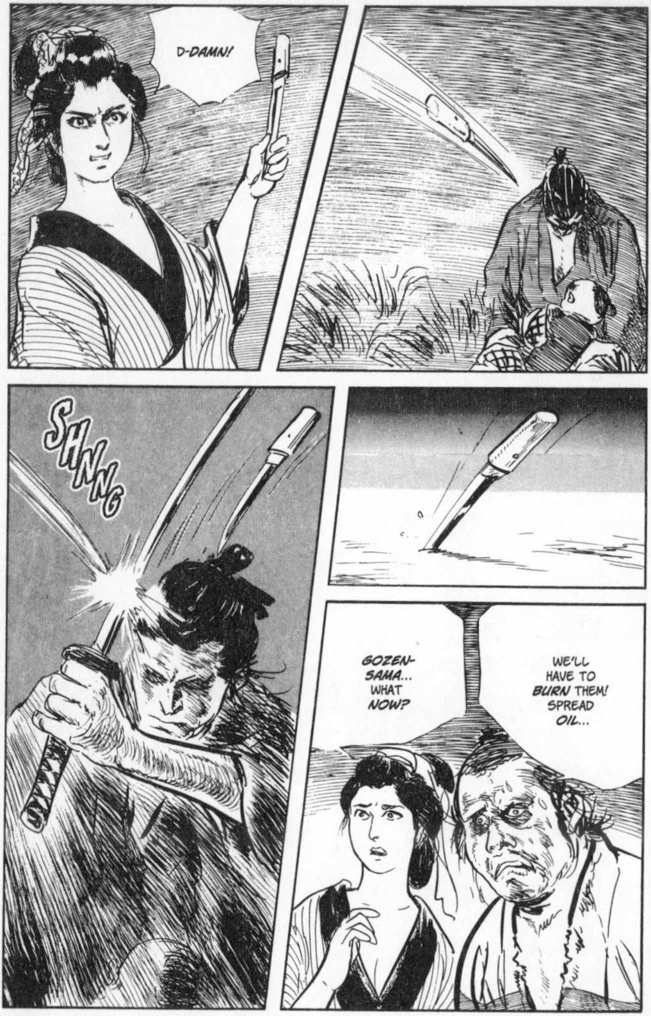
D-DAMN!
SHNNG
GOZEN-SAMA... WHAT NOW?
WE'LL HAVE TO BURN THEM! SPREAD OIL...

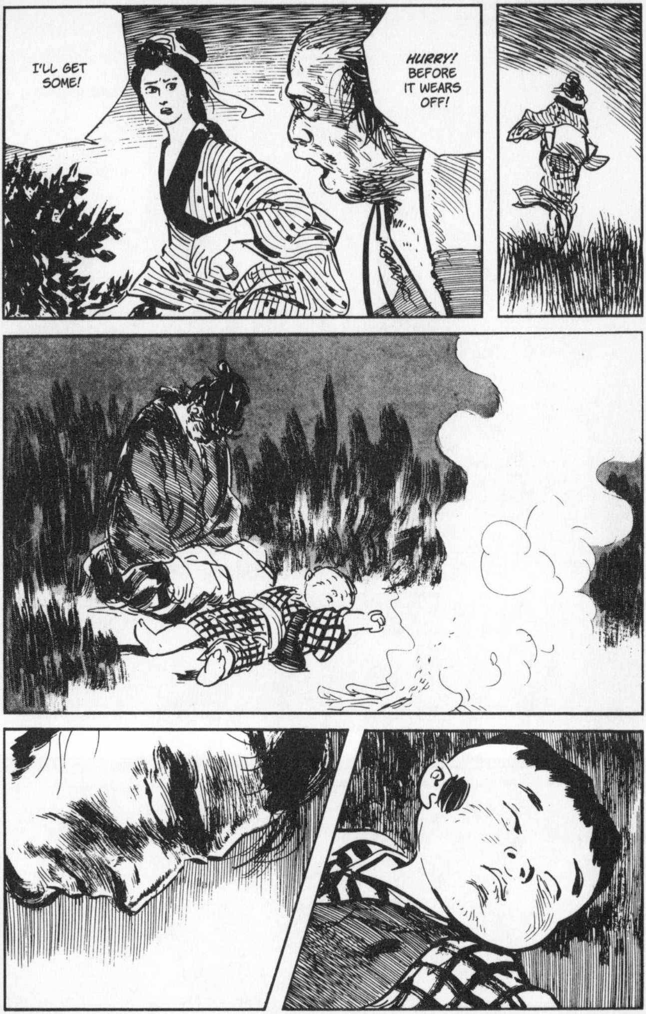
I'LL GET SOME!
HURRY! BEFORE IT WEARS OFF!

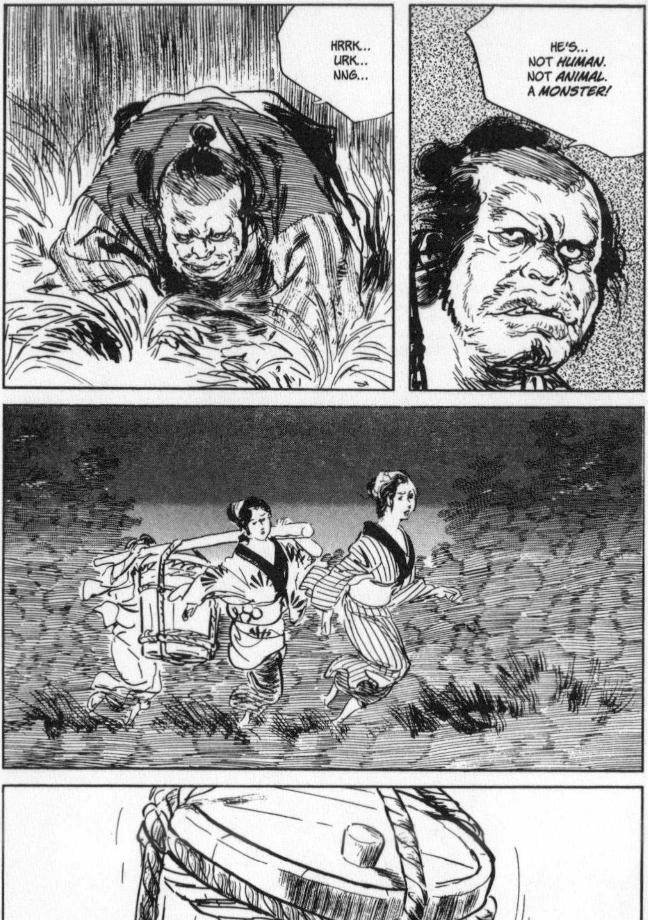
HE'S... NOT *HUMAN*. NOT *ANIMAL*. A *MONSTER!*
HRRK... URK... NNG...

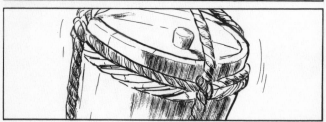

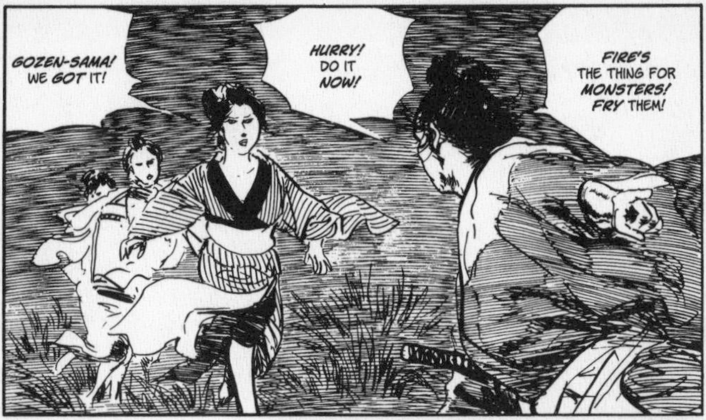
FIRE'S THE THING FOR MONSTERS! FRY THEM!
HURRY! DO IT NOW!
GOZEN-SAMA! WE GOT IT!

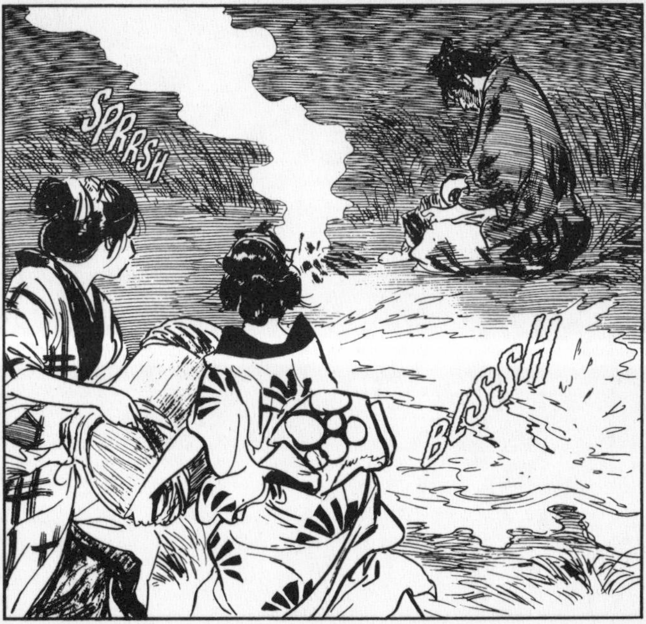
BLSSH
SPRRSH

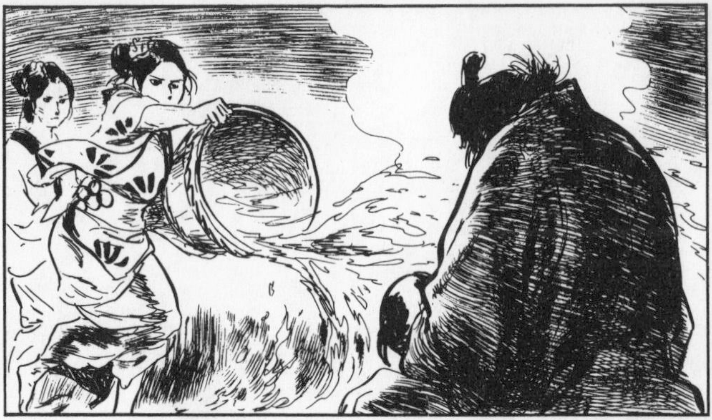

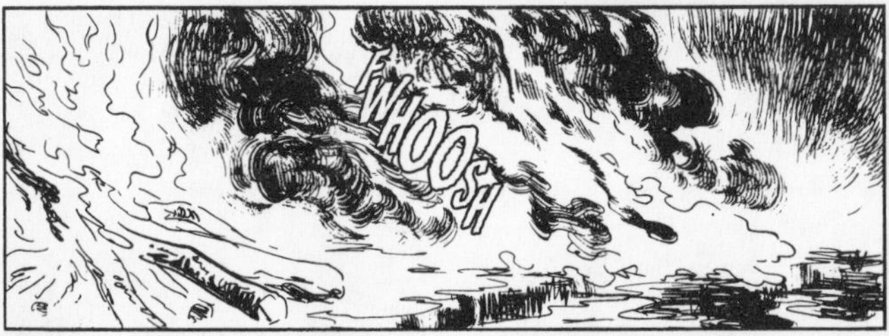
FWHOOSH

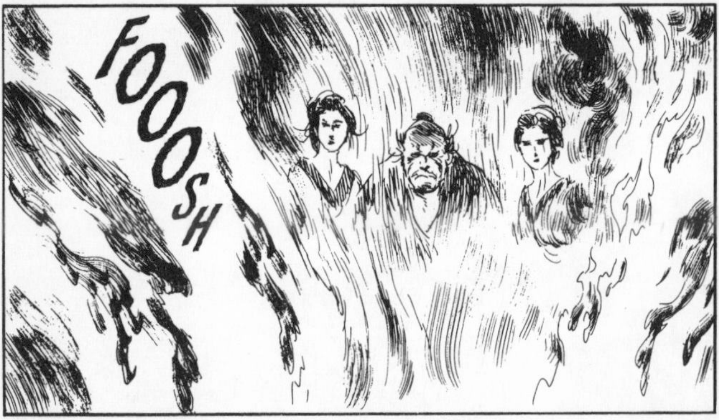
FOOOSH

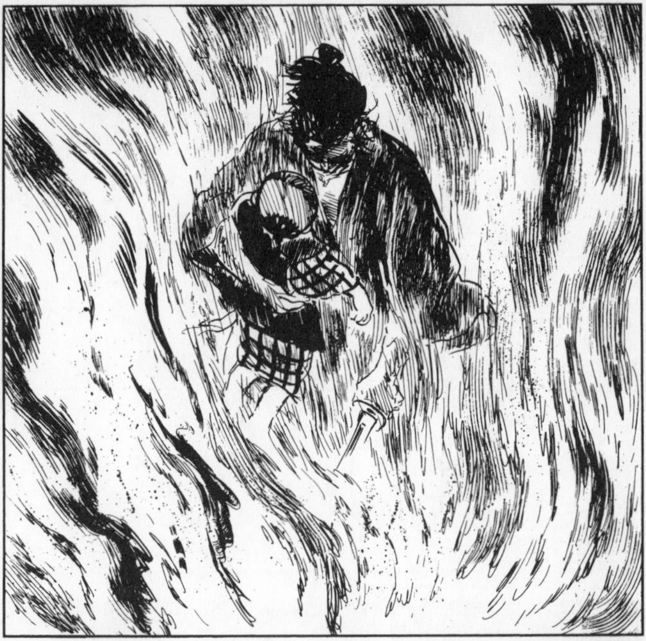
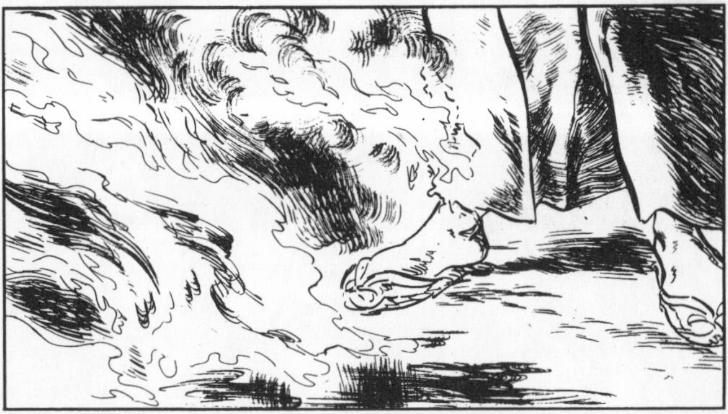

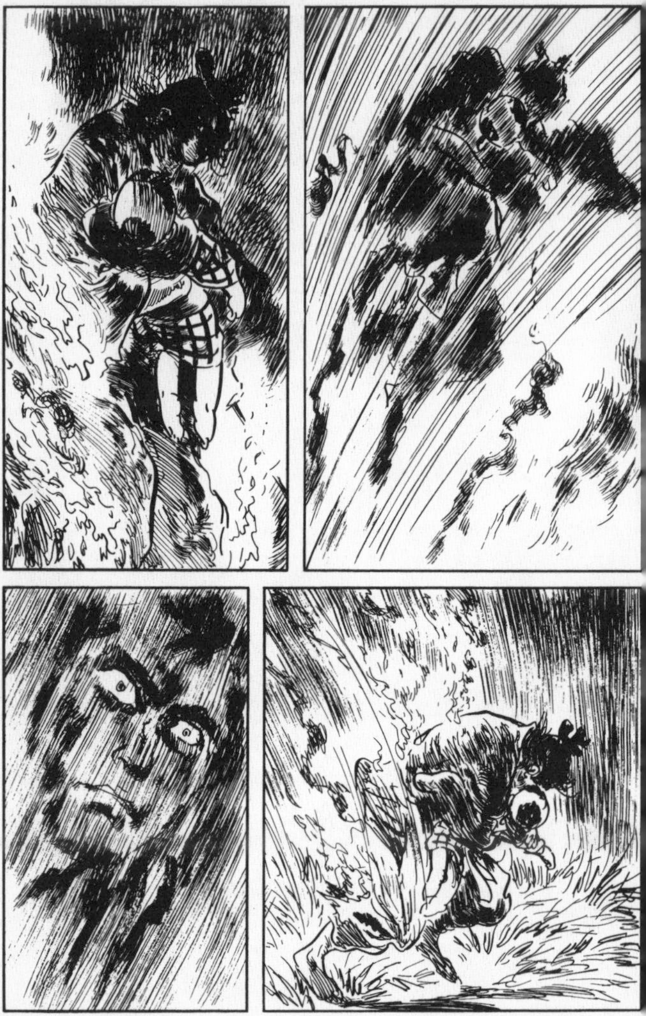

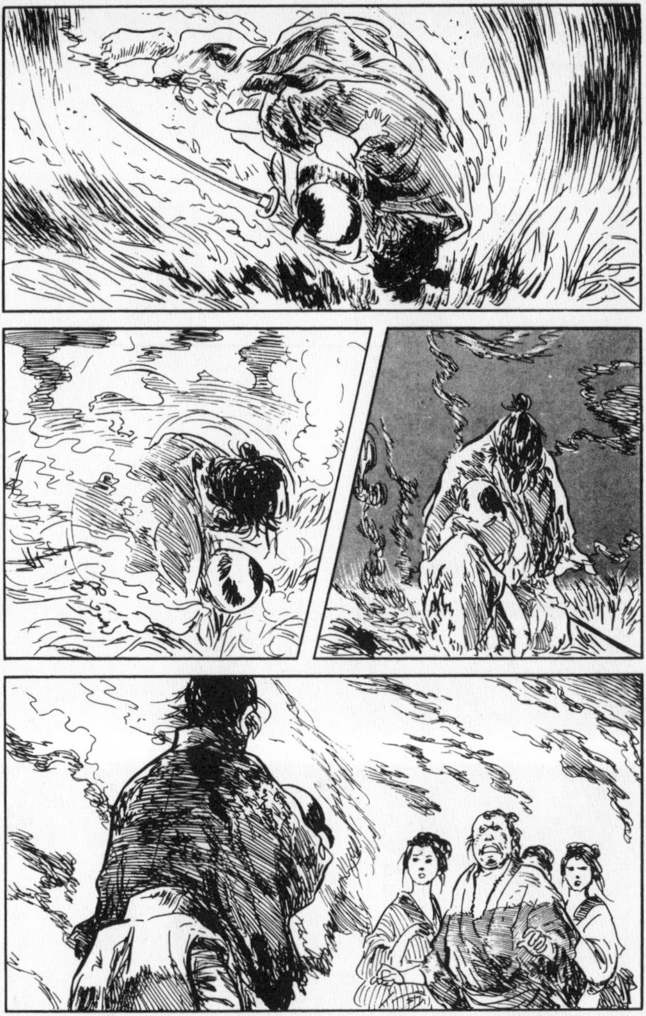

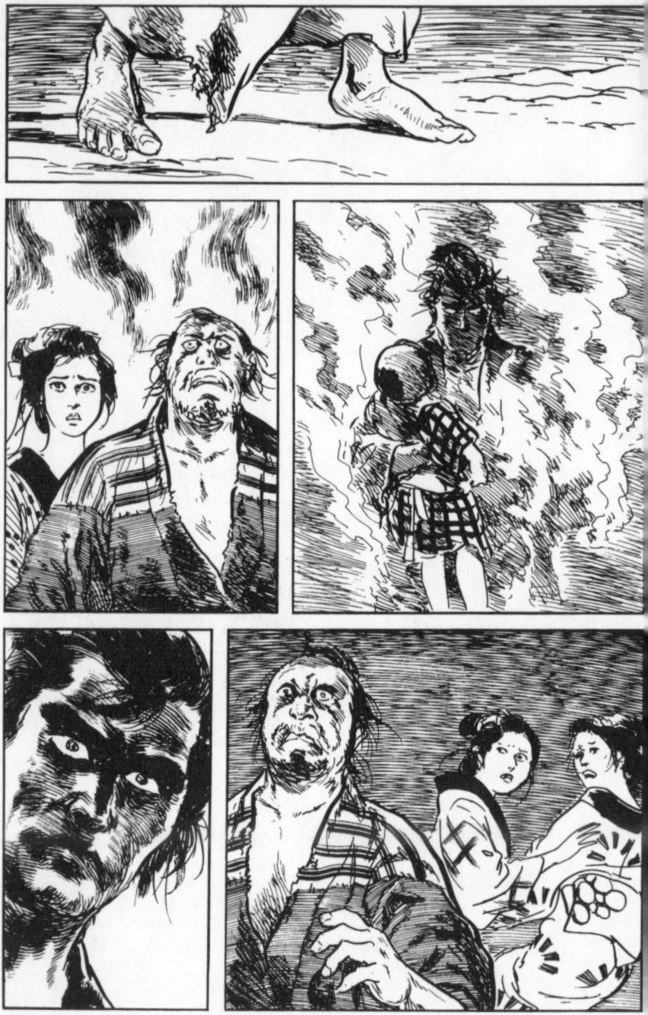

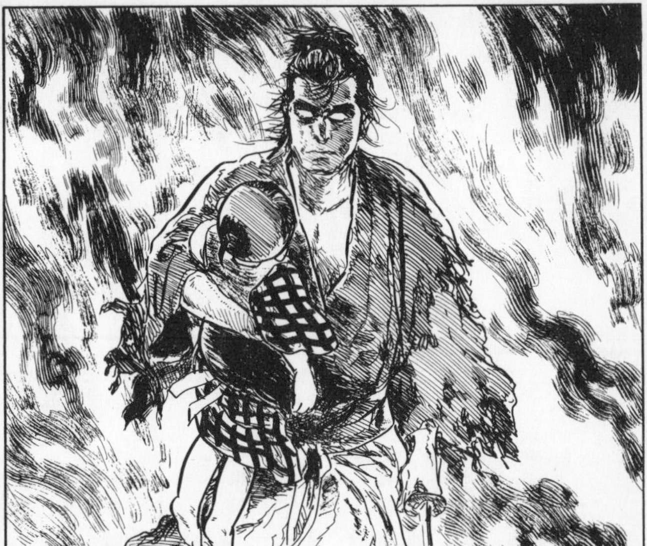

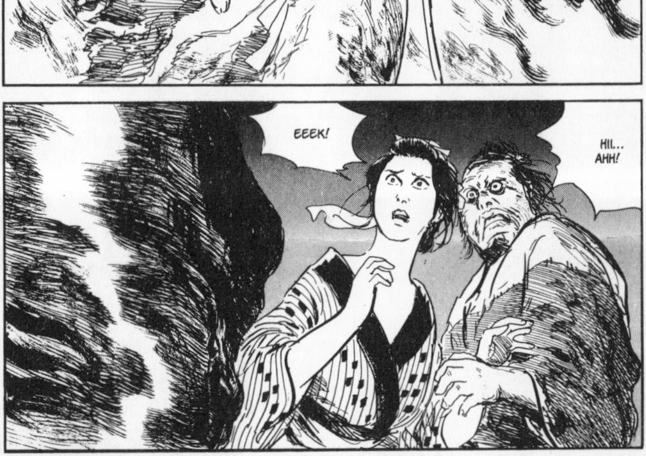
HII...
AHH!
EEEK!

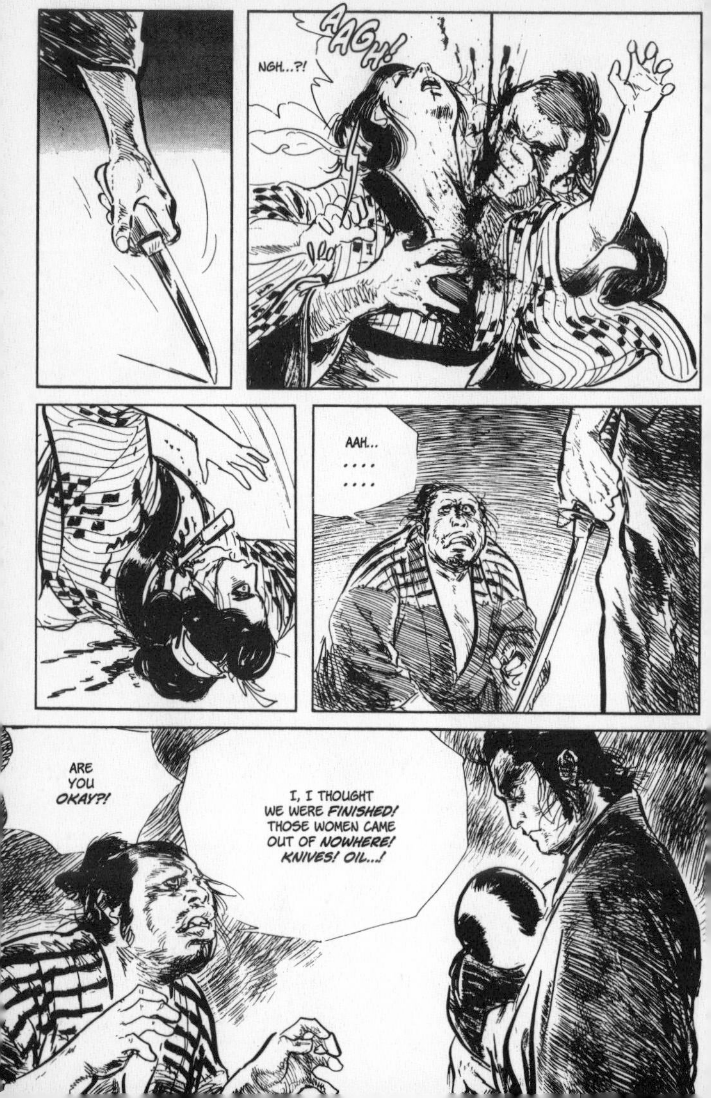
AAGH!
NGH...?!
AAH...
....
....
ARE YOU OKAY?!
I, I THOUGHT WE WERE FINISHED! THOSE WOMEN CAME OUT OF NOWHERE! KNIVES! OIL...!

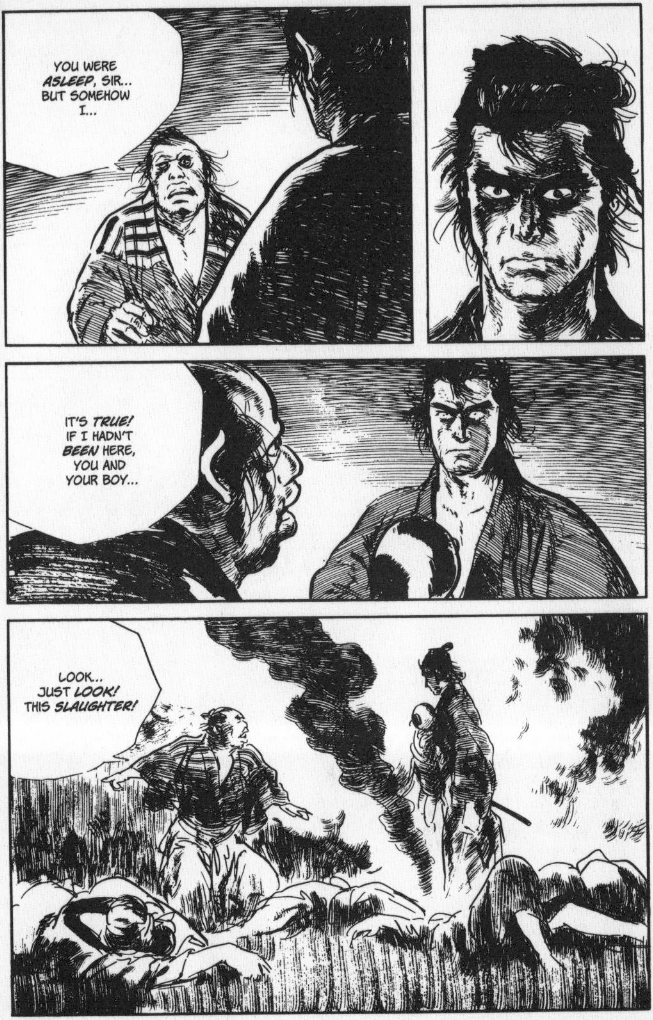
YOU WERE ASLEEP, SIR... BUT SOMEHOW I...
IT'S TRUE! IF I HADN'T BEEN HERE, YOU AND YOUR BOY...
LOOK... JUST LOOK! THIS SLAUGHTER!

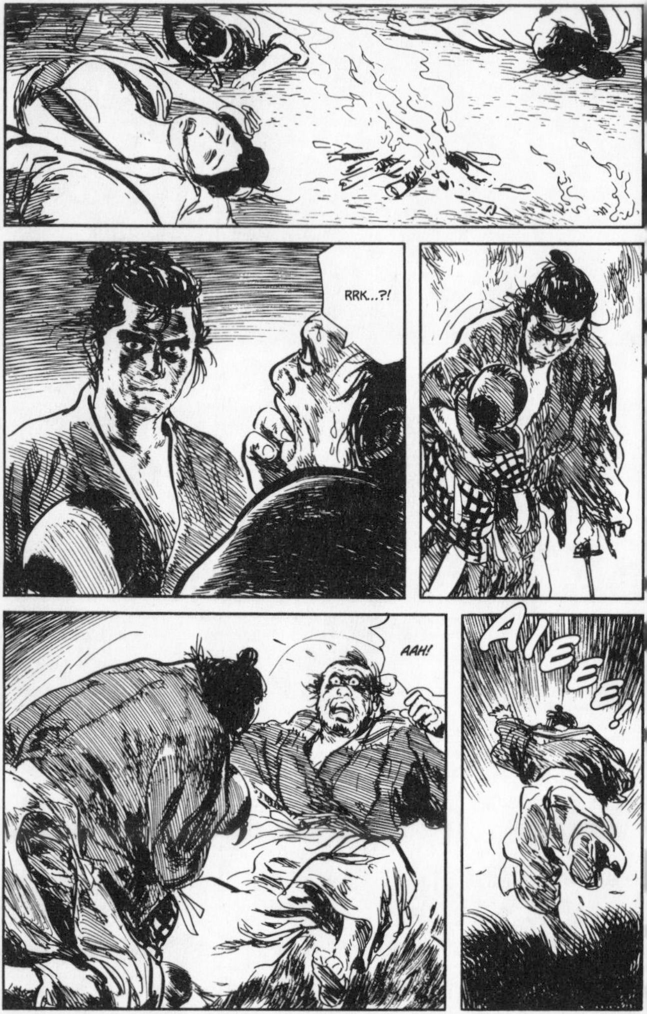
RRK...?!
AIEEE!
AAH!

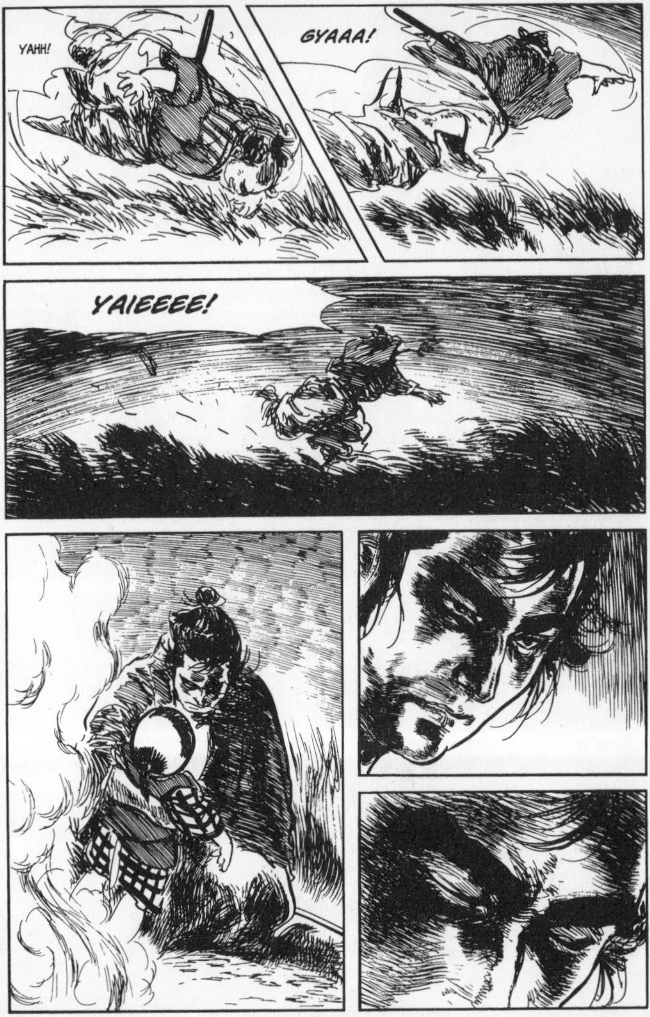
GYAAA!
YAHH!
YAIEEEE!

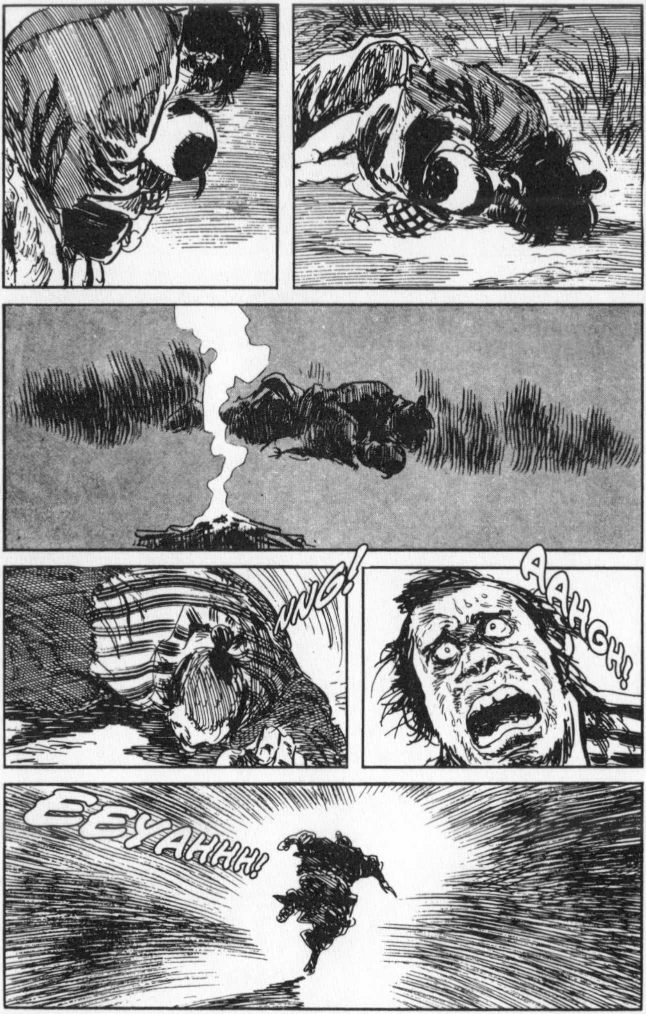
AAHGH!
NNG!
EEYAHHH!

the hundred
and fourth

Flood

of

Fire

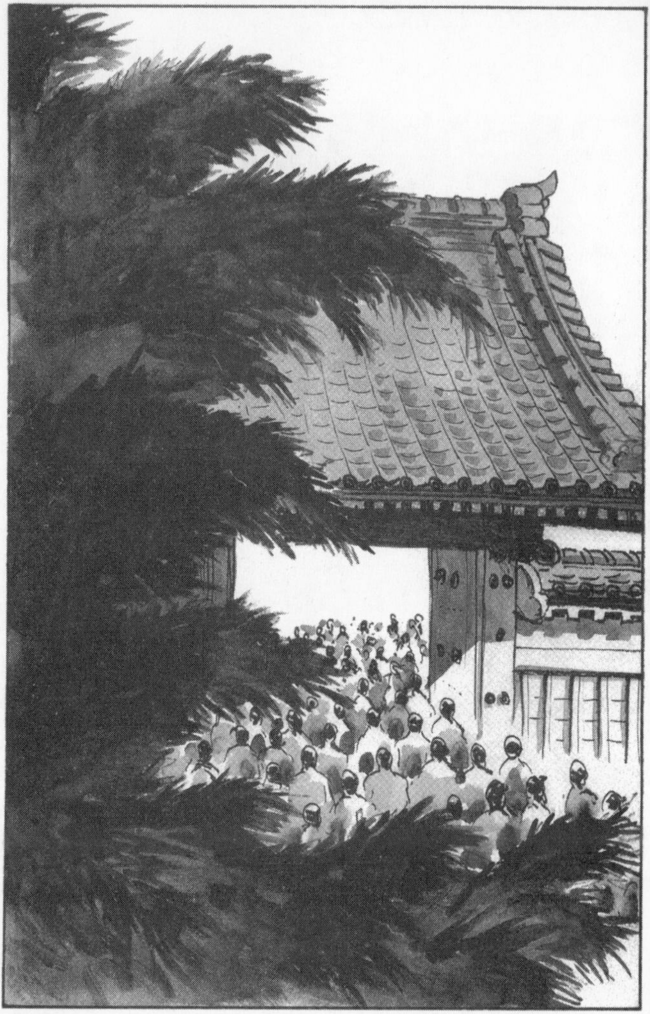

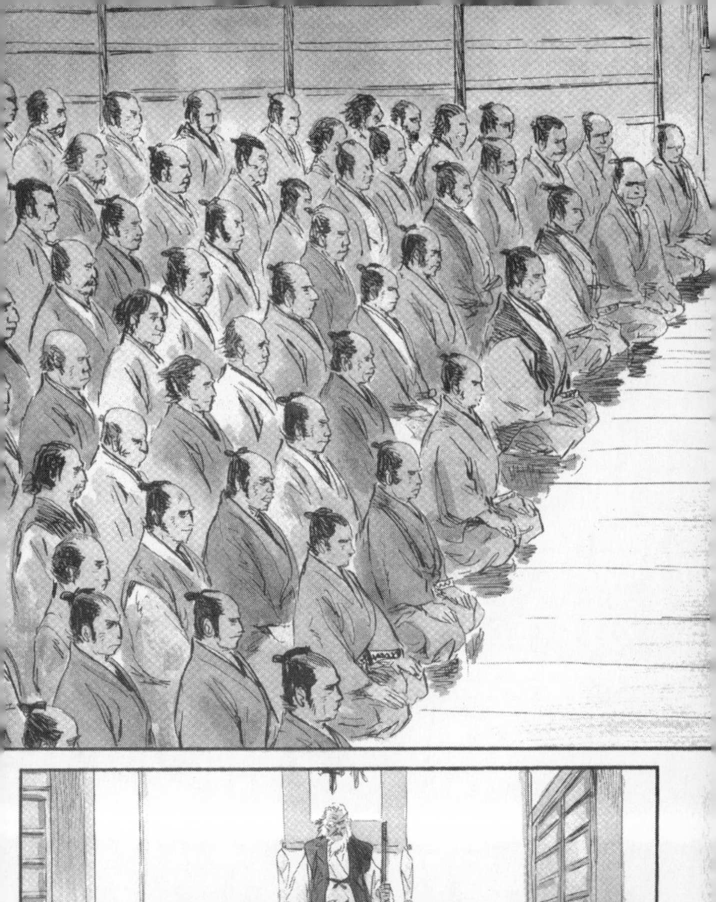
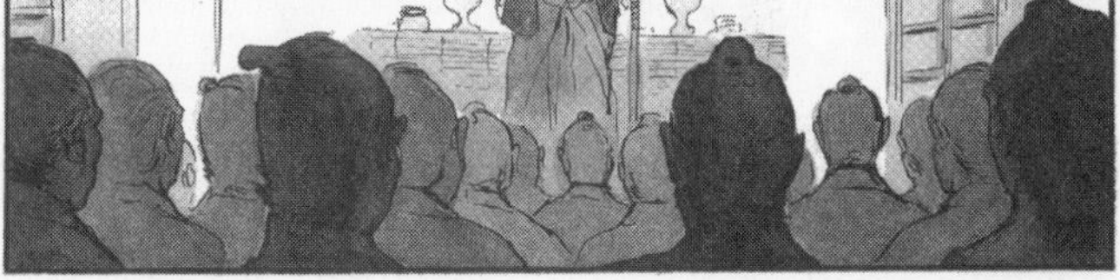

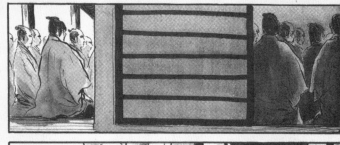

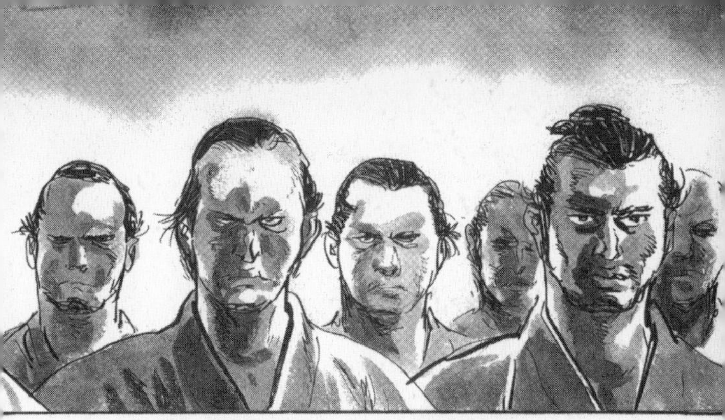
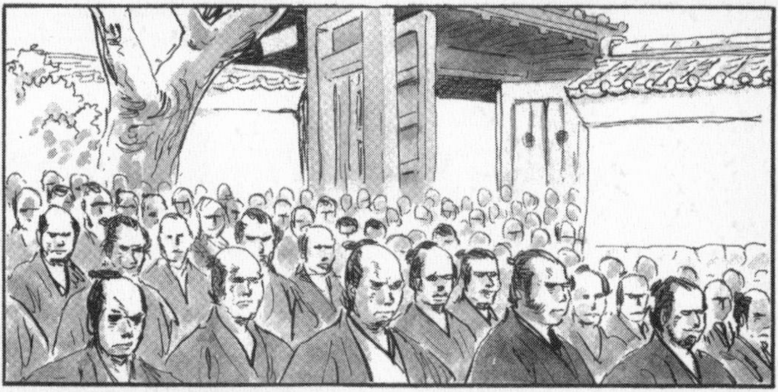
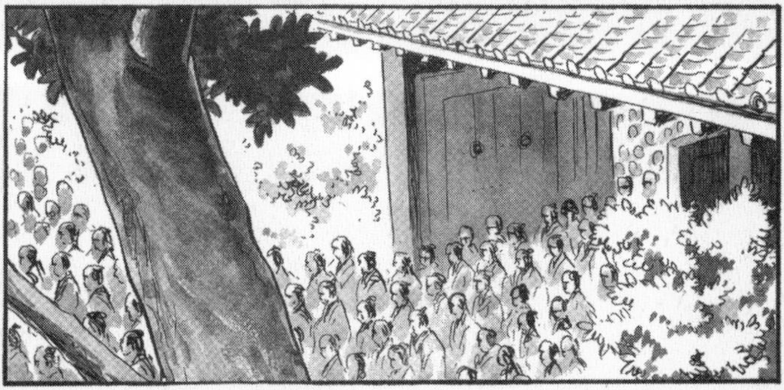

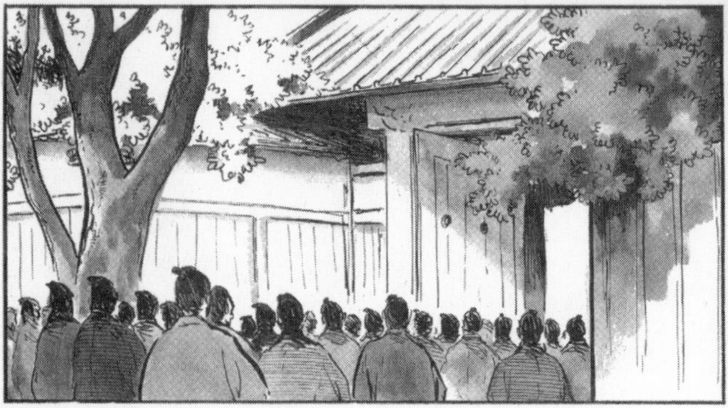
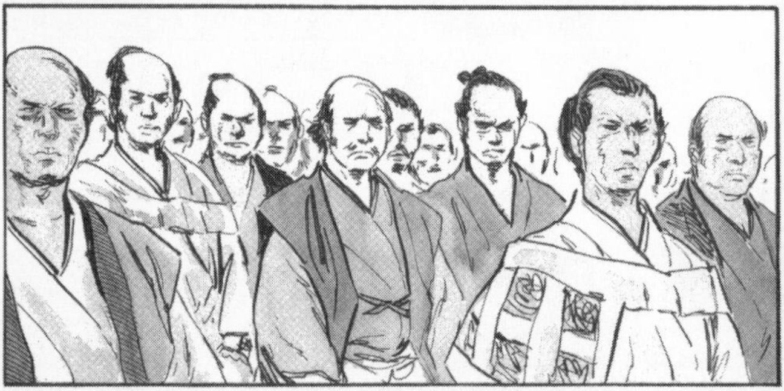
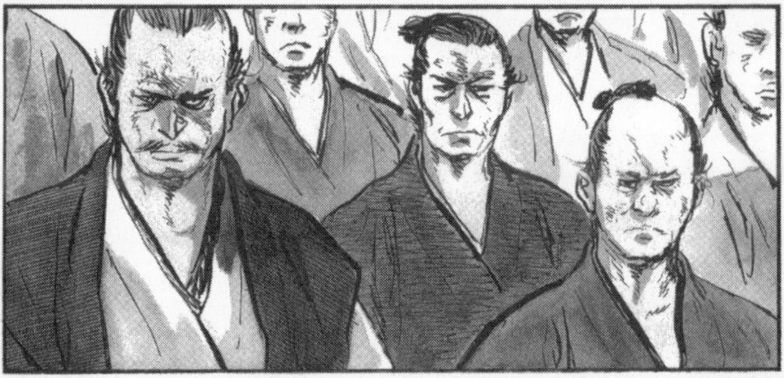

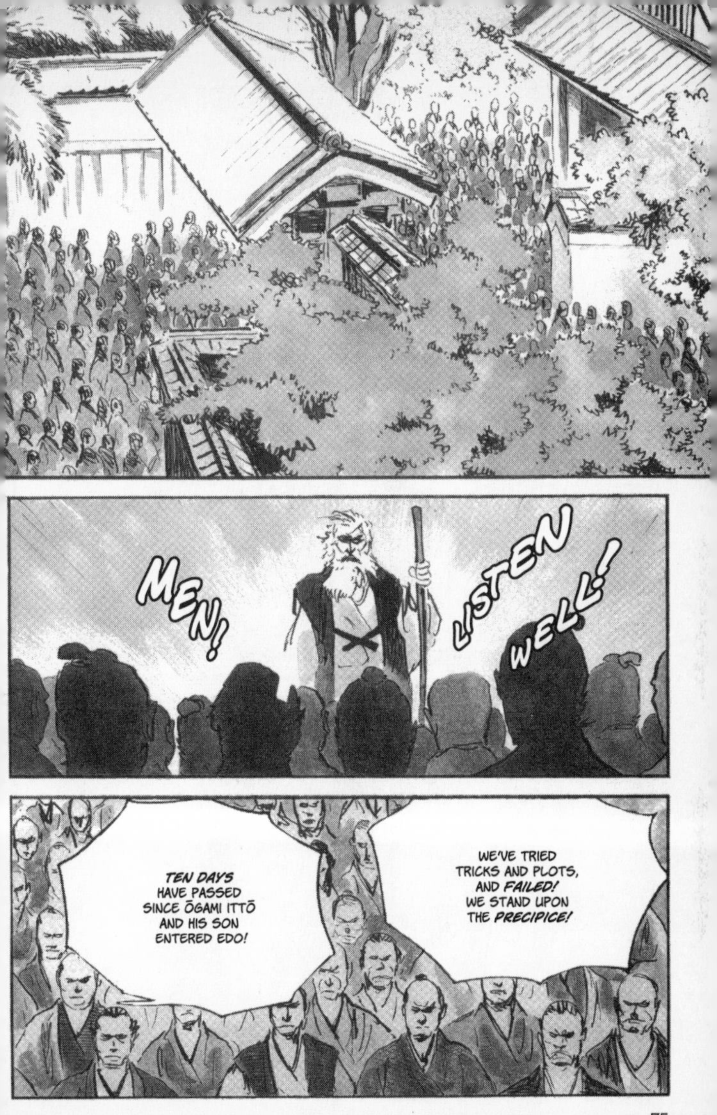
MEN!
LISTEN WELL!
WE'VE TRIED TRICKS AND PLOTS, AND FAILED! WE STAND UPON THE PRECIPICE!
TEN DAYS HAVE PASSED SINCE ŌGAMI ITTŌ AND HIS SON ENTERED EDO!

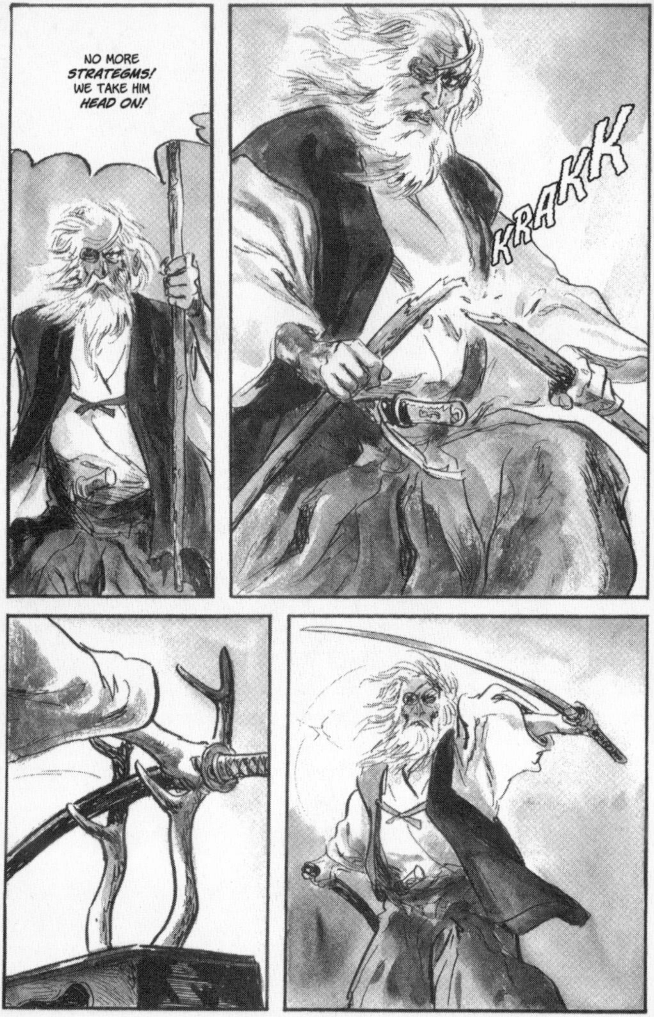
NO MORE STRATEGMS! WE TAKE HIM HEAD ON!
KRAKK

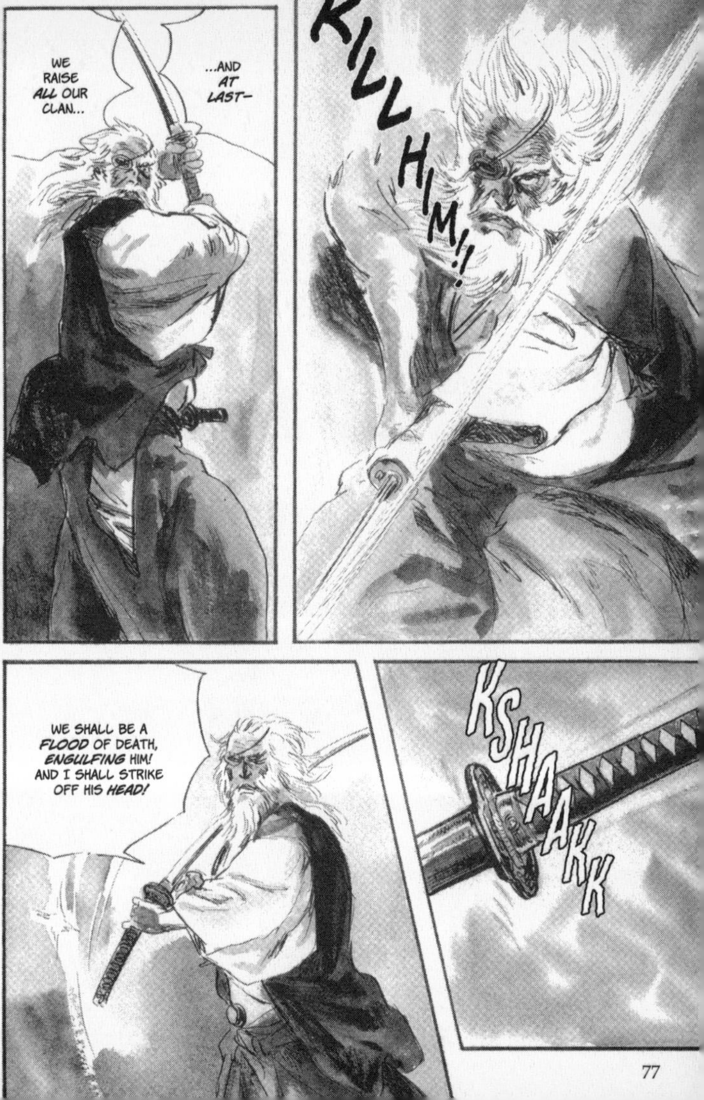
WE RAISE ALL OUR CLAN...
...AND AT LAST—
KILL HIM!!
WE SHALL BE A FLOOD OF DEATH, ENGULFING HIM! AND I SHALL STRIKE OFF HIS HEAD!
KSHAAKK

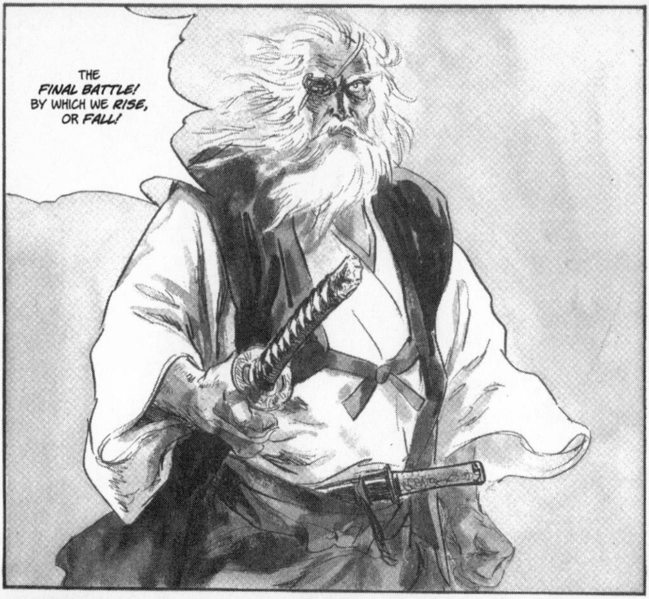
THE *FINAL BATTLE!* BY WHICH WE *RISE*, OR *FALL!*

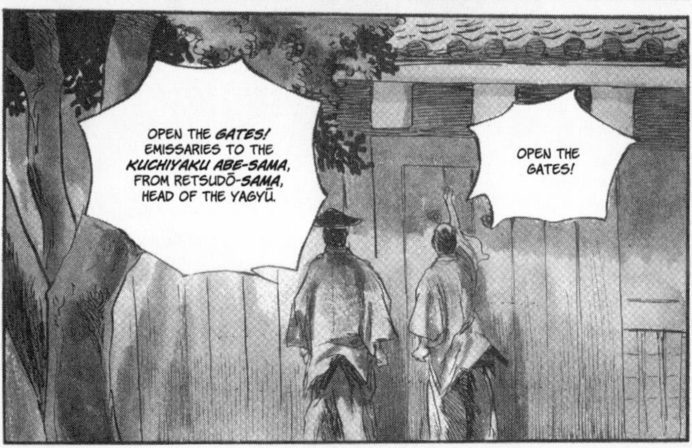
OPEN THE GATES!
OPEN THE *GATES!* EMISSARIES TO THE *KUCHIYAKU ABE-SAMA*, FROM RETSUDŌ-*SAMA*, HEAD OF THE YAGYŪ.

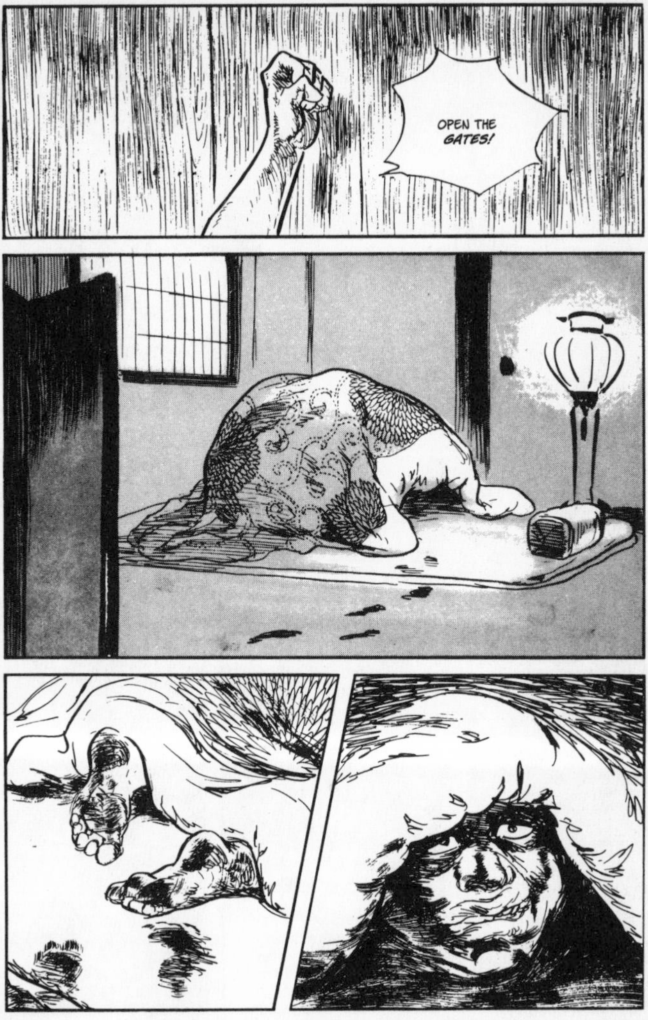
OPEN THE GATES!

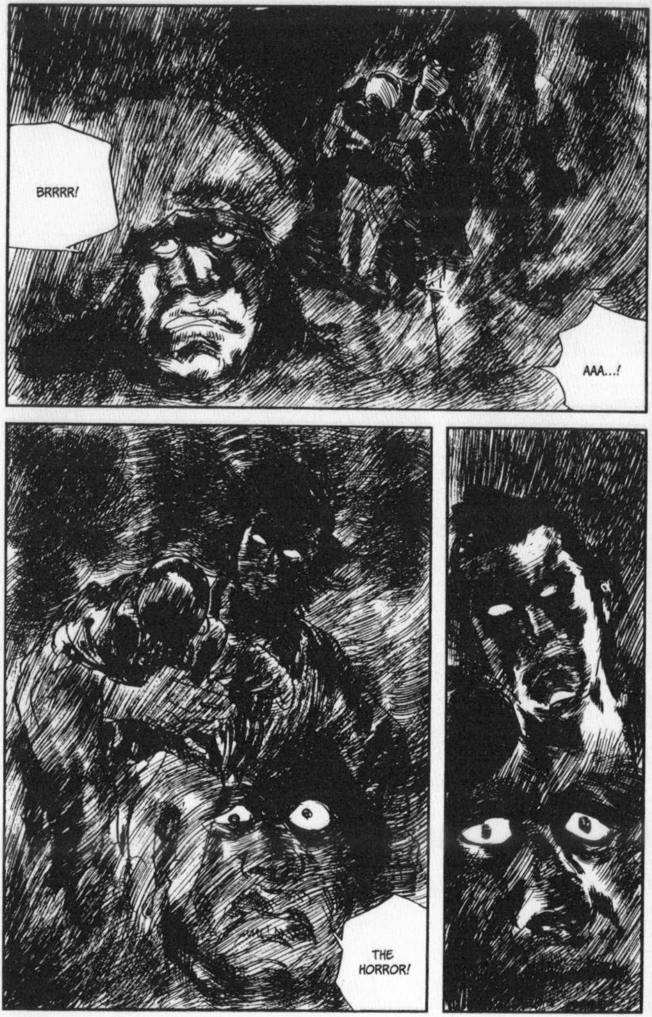
BRRRR!
AAA...!
THE HORROR!

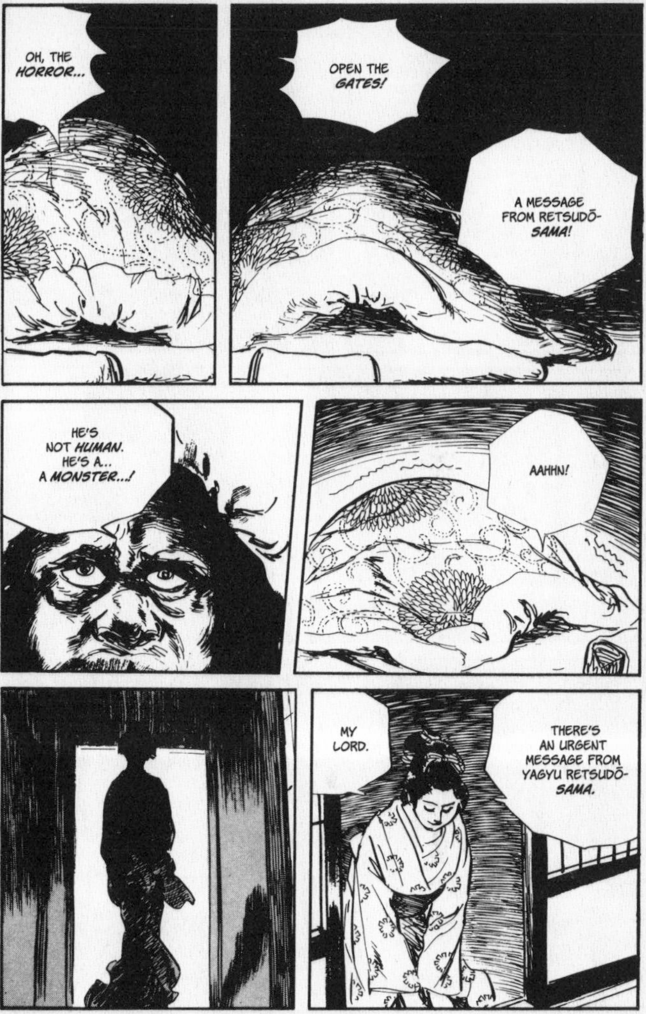
OPEN THE GATES!
A MESSAGE FROM RETSUDŌ-SAMA!
OH, THE HORROR...
AAHHN!
HE'S NOT HUMAN. HE'S A... A MONSTER...!
MY LORD.
THERE'S AN URGENT MESSAGE FROM YAGYU RETSUDŌ-SAMA.

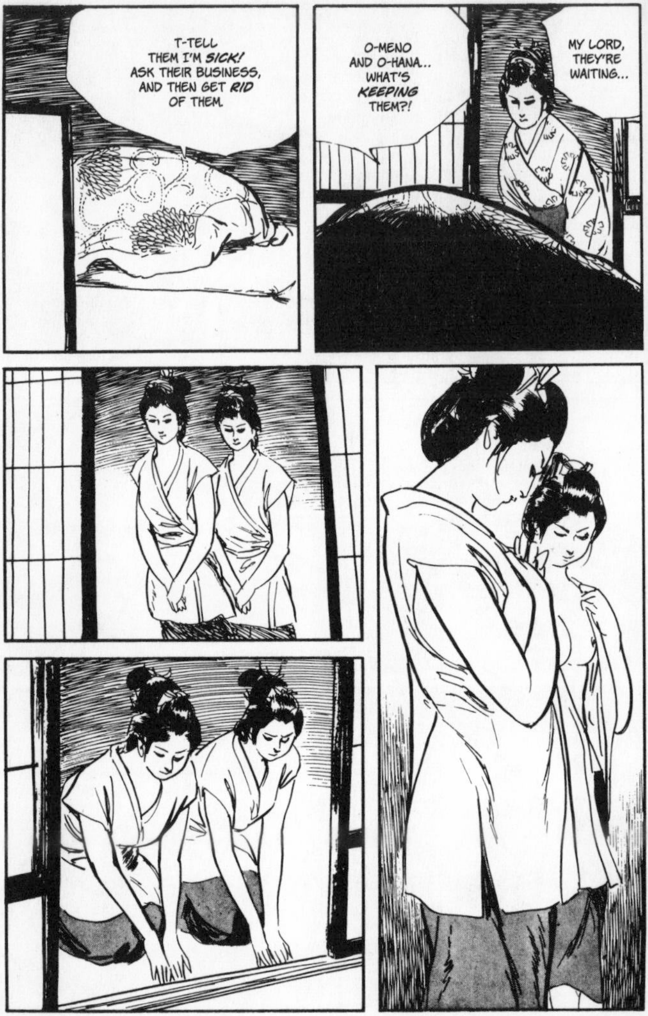
MY LORD, THEY'RE WAITING...
O-MENO AND O-HANA.. WHAT'S KEEPING THEM?!
T-TELL THEM I'M SICK! ASK THEIR BUSINESS, AND THEN GET RID OF THEM.

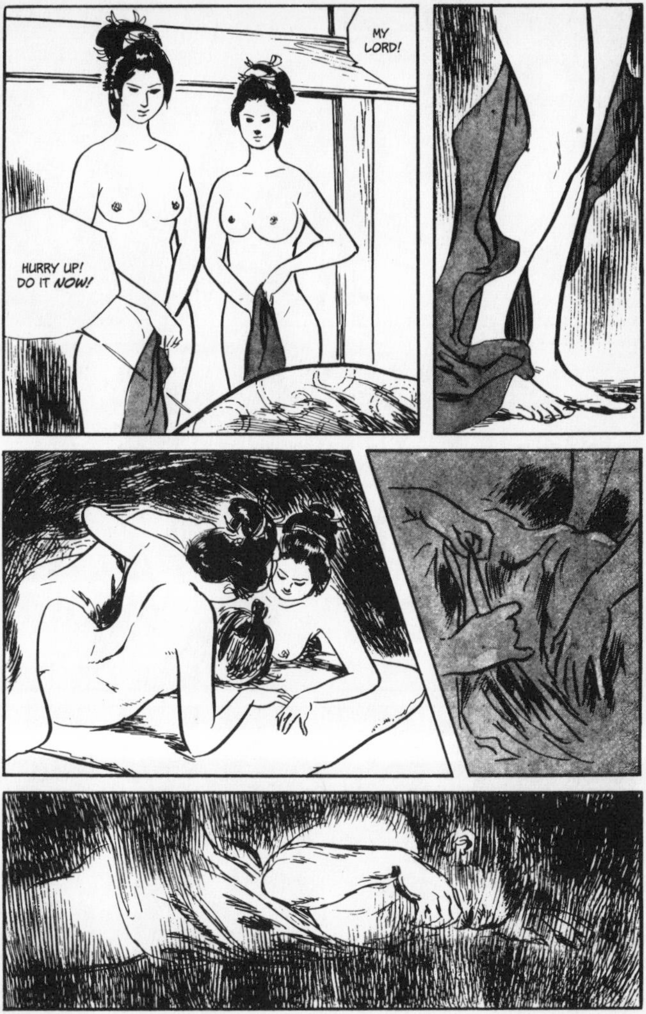
MY LORD!
HURRY UP! DO IT NOW!

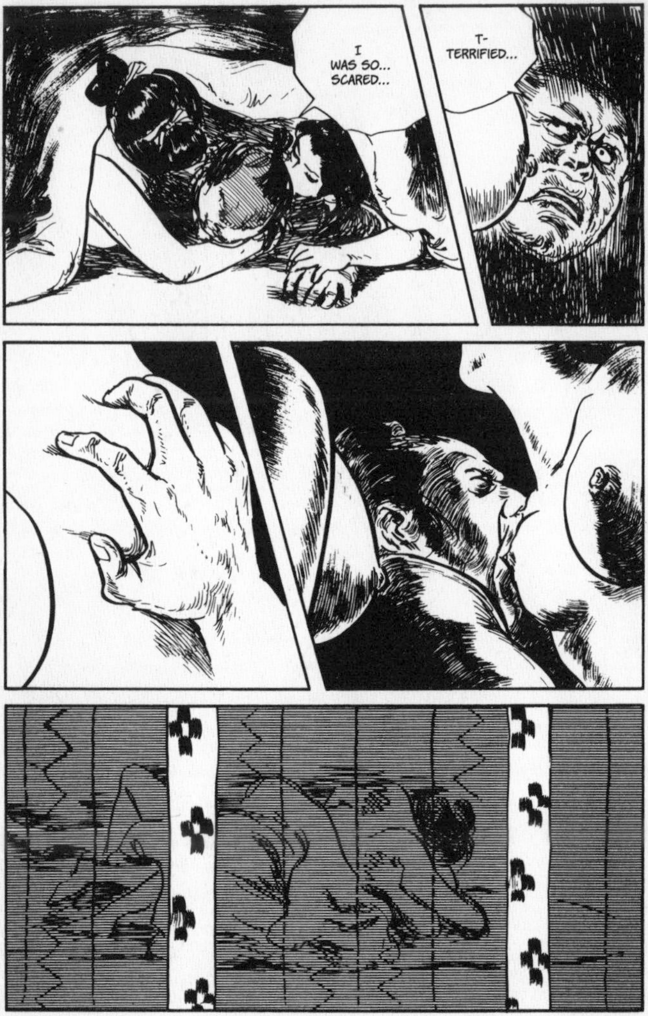
T-
TERRIFIED...
I
WAS SO...
SCARED...

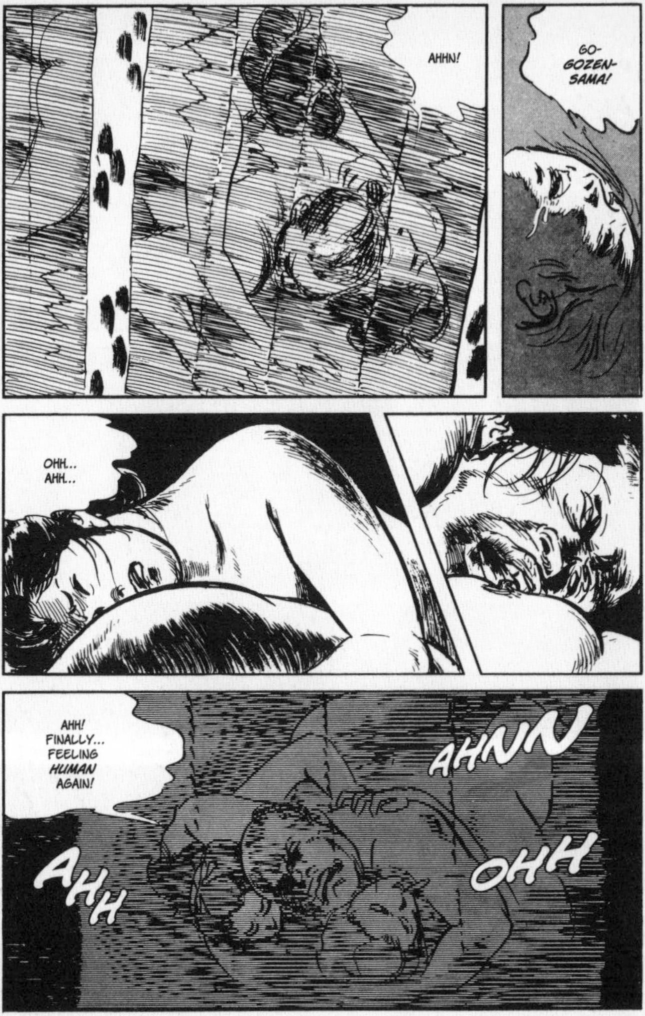
GO-GOZEN-SAMA!
AHHN!
OHH... AHH...
AHHN
AHH! FINALLY... FEELING HUMAN AGAIN!
OHH
AHH

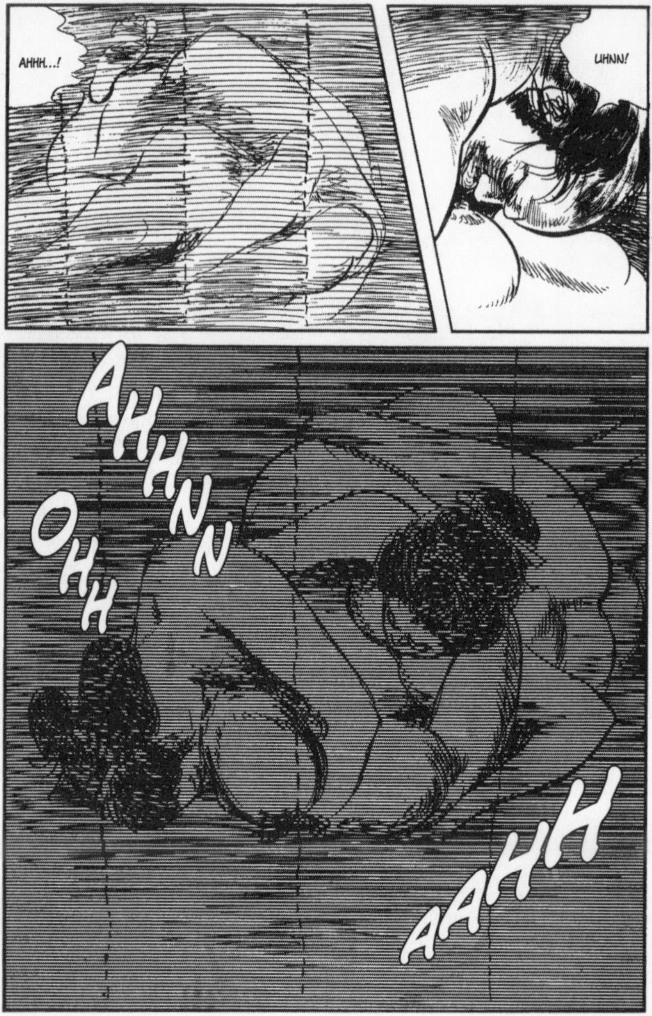
UHNN!
AHHH...!
AHHNNN
OHH
AAHH

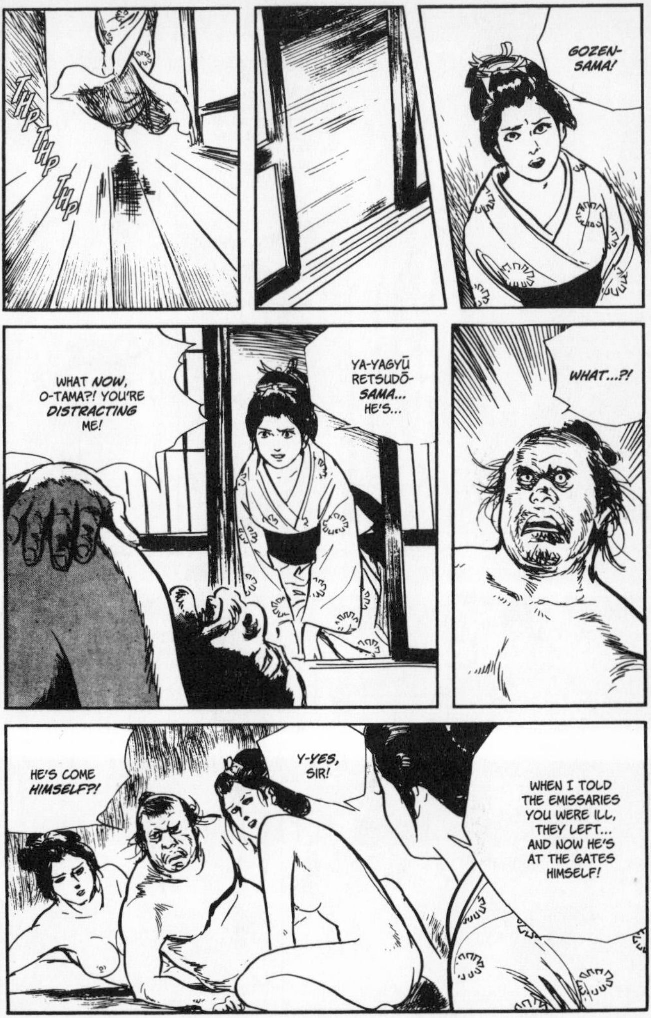
THP THP THP
GOZEN-SAMA!
WHAT NOW, O-TAMA?! YOU'RE DISTRACTING ME!
YA-YAGYŪ RETSUDŌ-SAMA... HE'S...
WHAT...?!
HE'S COME HIMSELF?!
Y-YES, SIR!
WHEN I TOLD THE EMISSARIES YOU WERE ILL, THEY LEFT... AND NOW HE'S AT THE GATES HIMSELF!

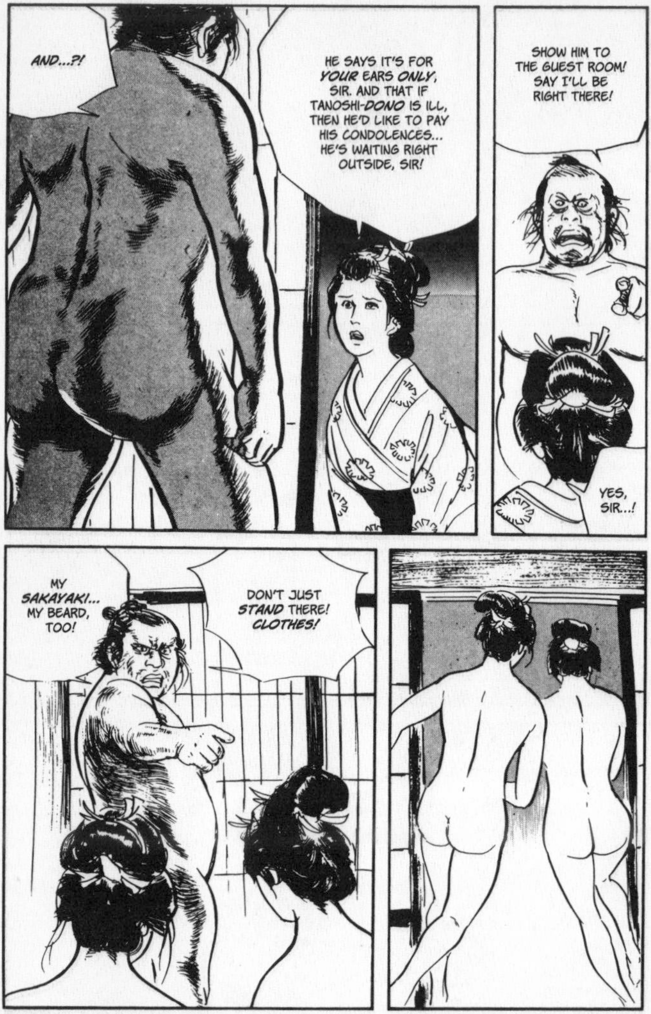
AND...?!
HE SAYS IT'S FOR *YOUR* EARS *ONLY*, SIR. AND THAT IF TANOSHI-*DONO* IS ILL, THEN HE'D LIKE TO PAY HIS CONDOLENCES... HE'S WAITING RIGHT OUTSIDE, SIR!
SHOW HIM TO THE GUEST ROOM! SAY I'LL BE RIGHT THERE!
YES, SIR...!
MY *SAKAYAKI*... MY BEARD, TOO!
DON'T JUST *STAND* THERE! *CLOTHES!*

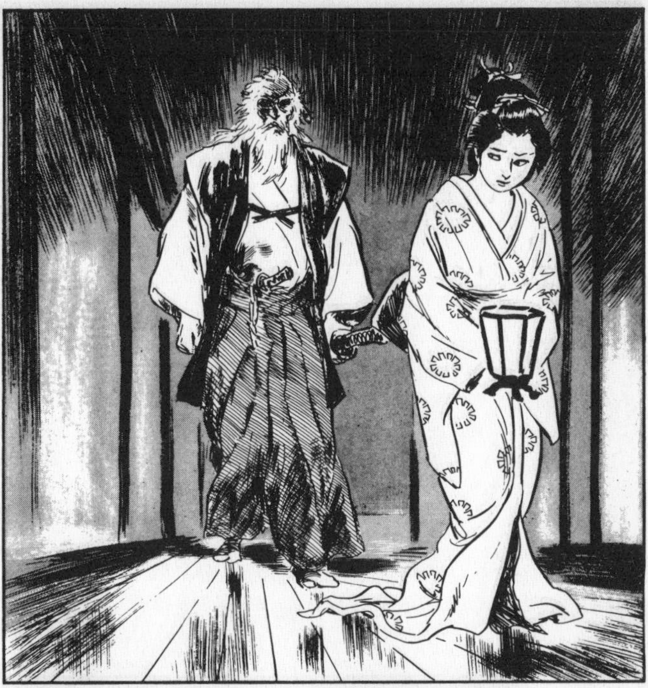
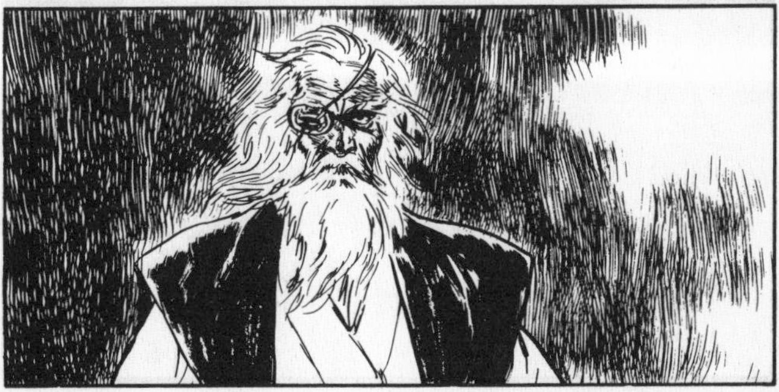

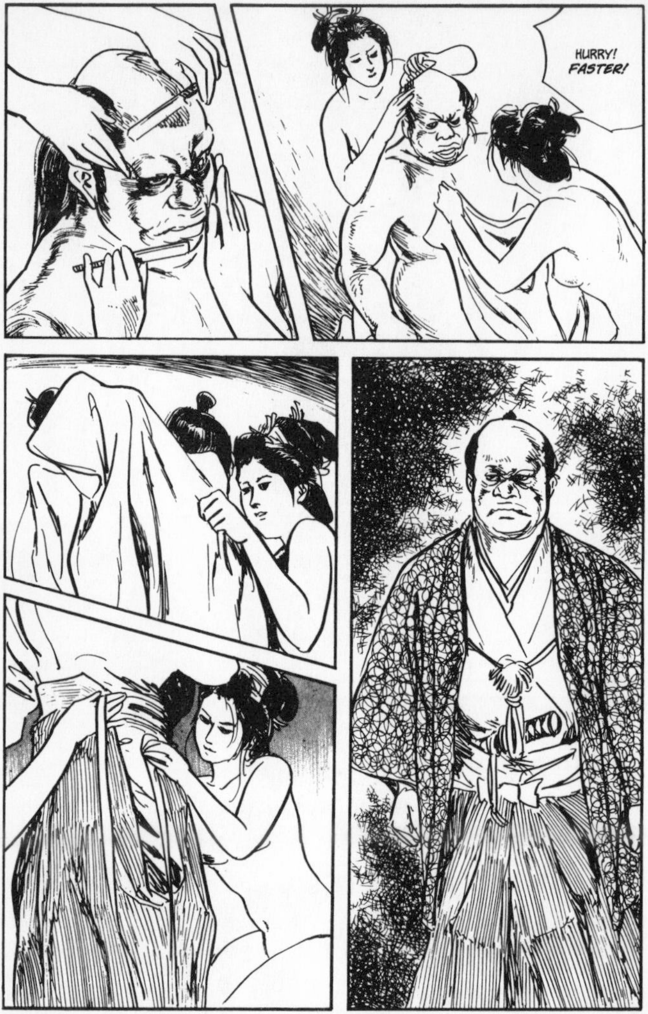
HURRY!
FASTER!

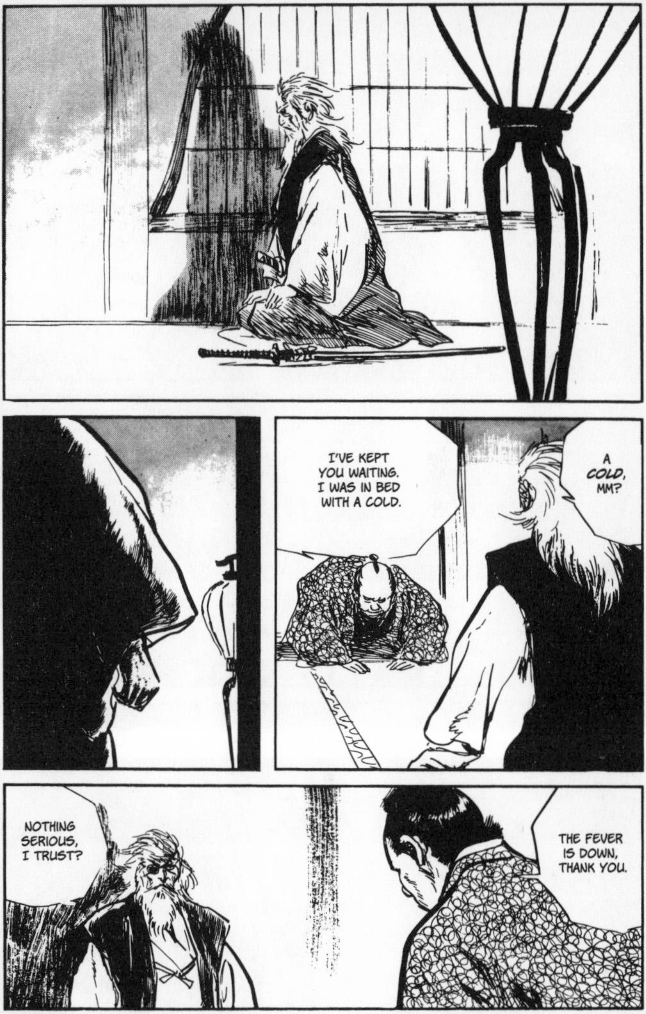
I'VE KEPT YOU WAITING. I WAS IN BED WITH A COLD.
A COLD, MM?
NOTHING SERIOUS, I TRUST?
THE FEVER IS DOWN, THANK YOU.

WHAT BUSINESS BRINGS MY LORD HERE...?
THE *YAGYŪ* WILL KILL LONE WOLF. YOUR SERVICES ARE NO LONGER NEEDED.
BUT *WHY?!*
IF THERE'S FIGHTING IN EDO, THERE'LL BE A *SCANDAL!* INNOCENT PEOPLE COULD DIE!
WASN'T THAT WHY WE DECIDED THAT I WOULD KILL HIM FOR YOU?
WHY THIS SUDDEN CHANGE...?
AND *LONE WOLF?*

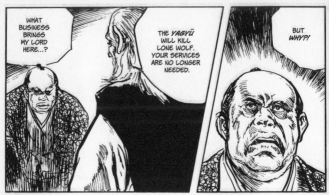

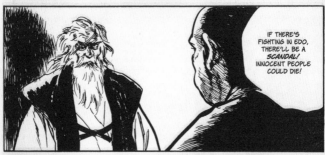

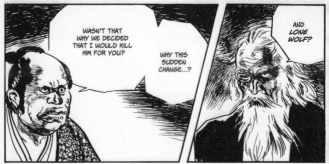

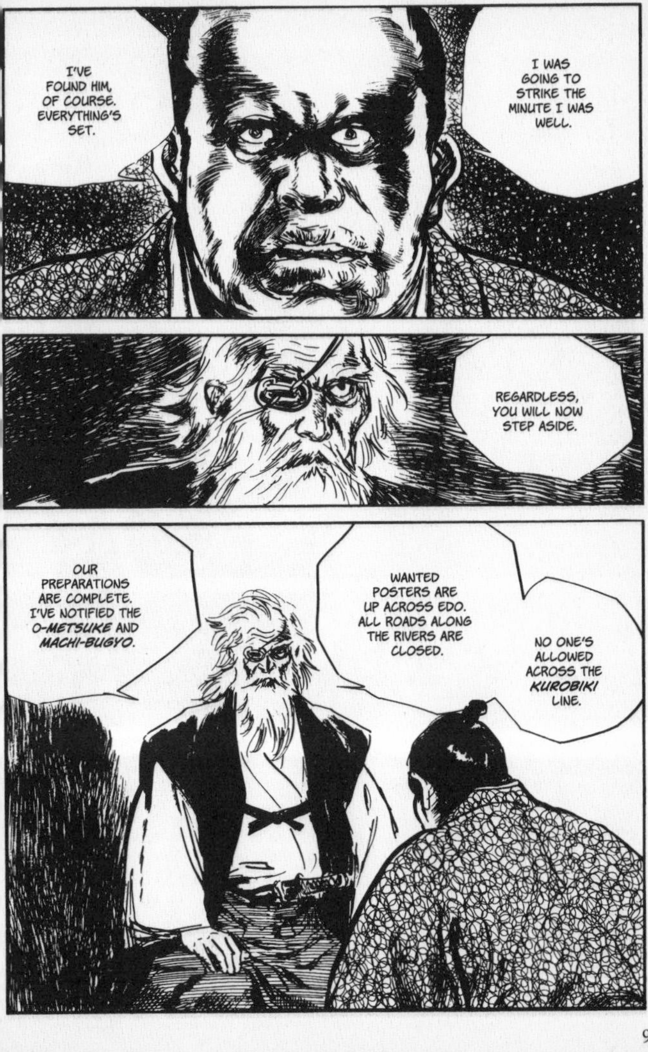
I'VE FOUND HIM, OF COURSE. EVERYTHING'S SET.
I WAS GOING TO STRIKE THE MINUTE I WAS WELL.
REGARDLESS, YOU WILL NOW STEP ASIDE.
OUR PREPARATIONS ARE COMPLETE. I'VE NOTIFIED THE *O-METSUKE* AND *MACHI-BUGYO*.
WANTED POSTERS ARE UP ACROSS EDO. ALL ROADS ALONG THE RIVERS ARE CLOSED.
NO ONE'S ALLOWED ACROSS THE *KUROBIKI* LINE.

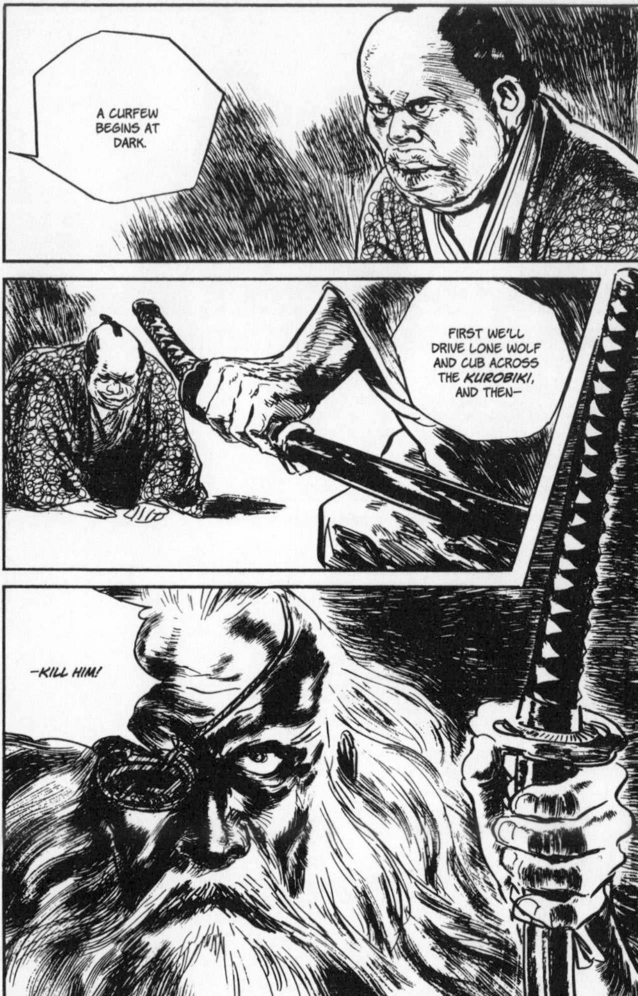
A CURFEW BEGINS AT DARK.
FIRST WE'LL DRIVE LONE WOLF AND CUB ACROSS THE *KUROBIKI*, AND THEN–
–KILL HIM!

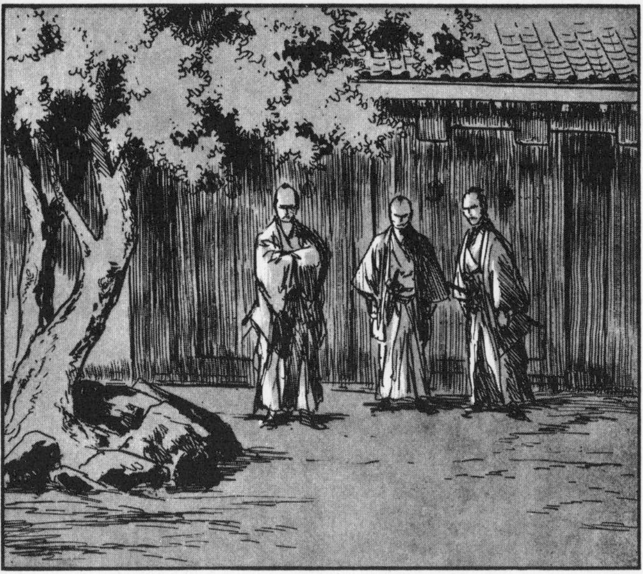
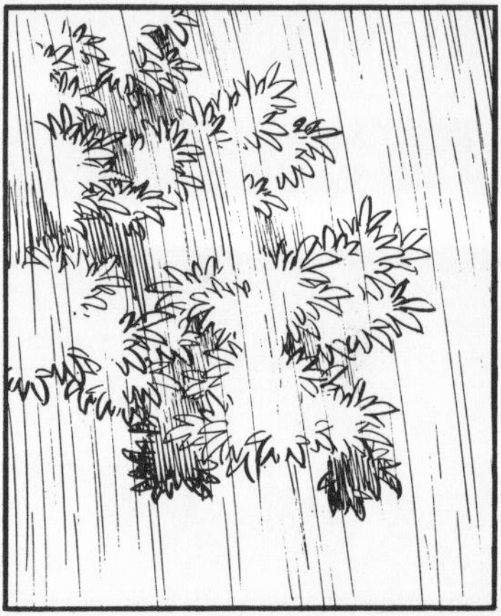
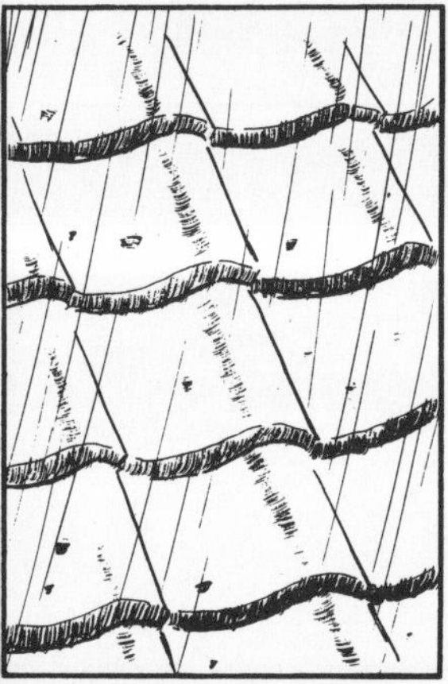

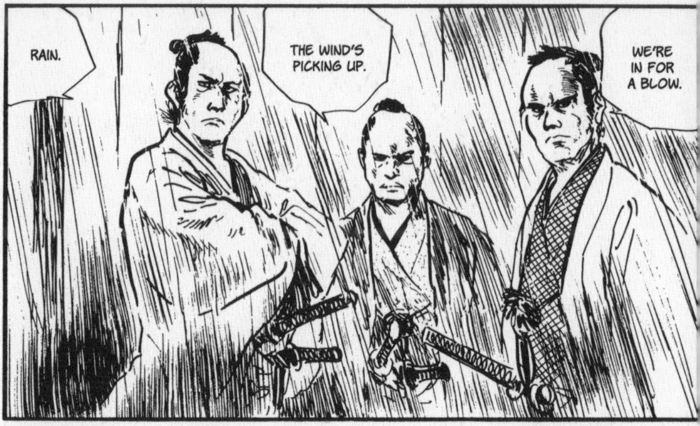
RAIN.
THE WIND'S PICKING UP.
WE'RE IN FOR A BLOW.

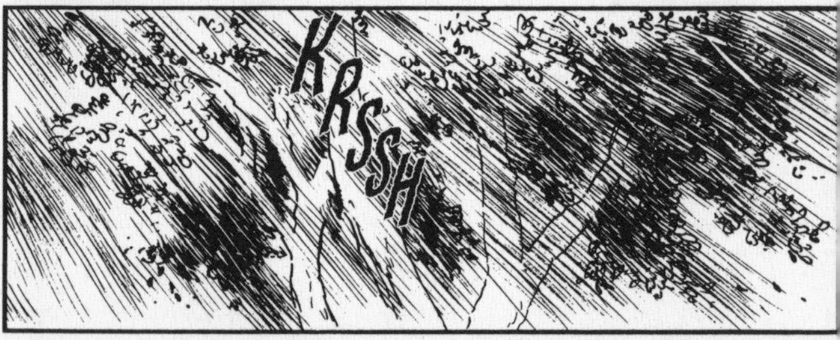
KRSSH

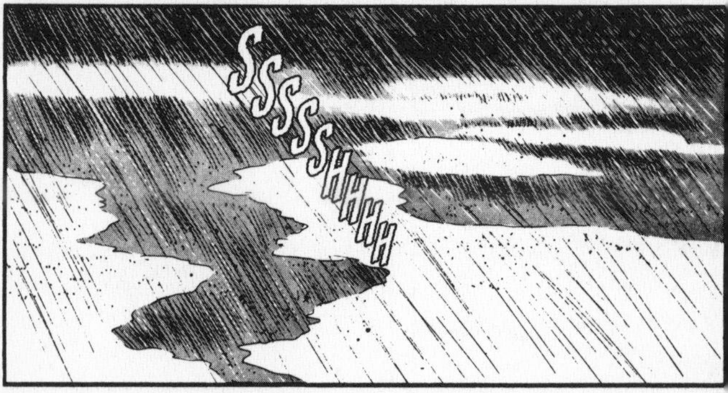
SSSSSHHHHH

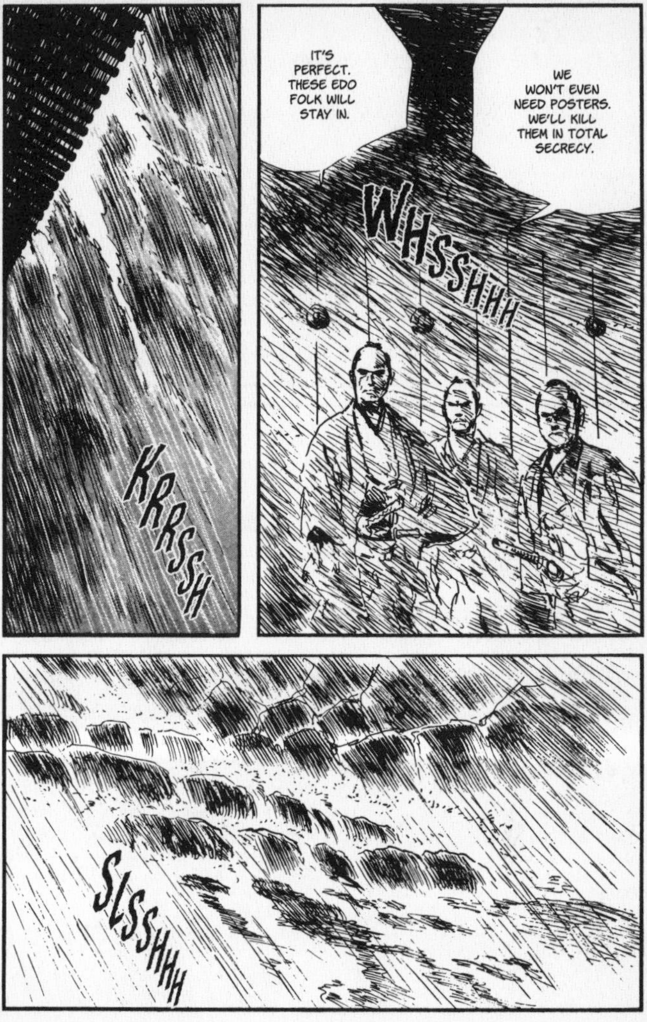
IT'S PERFECT. THESE EDO FOLK WILL STAY IN.
WE WON'T EVEN NEED POSTERS. WE'LL KILL THEM IN TOTAL SECRECY.
WHSSHHH
KRRSSH
SLSSHHH

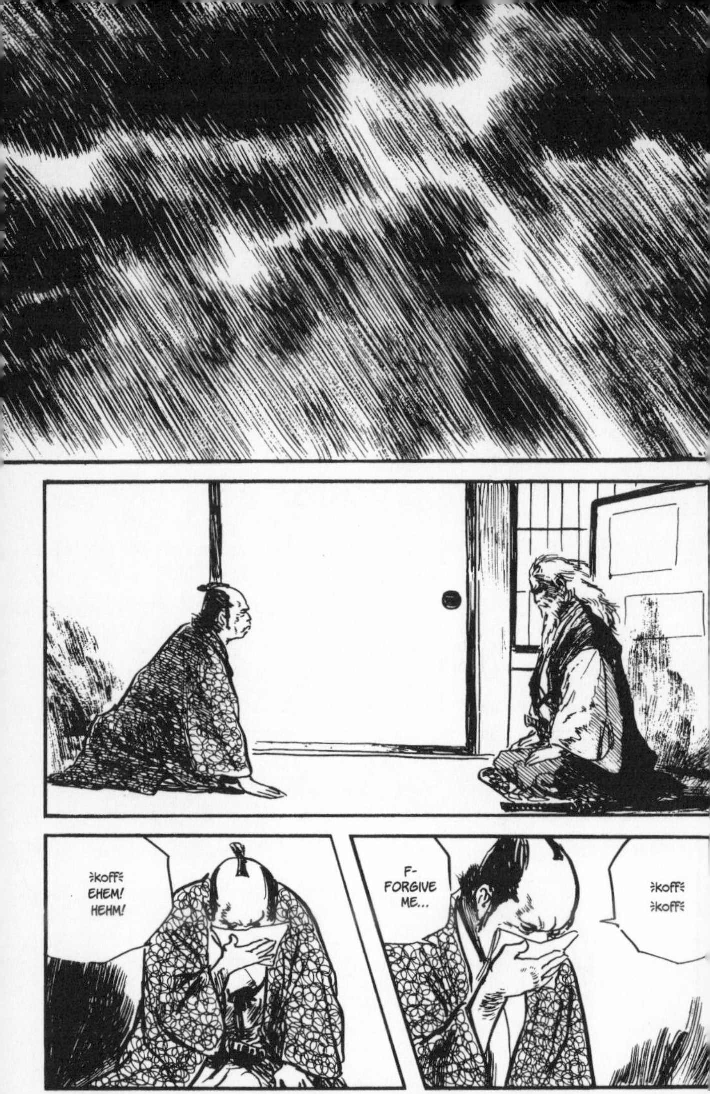
koff *koff*
F- FORGIVE ME...
koff EHEM! HEHM!

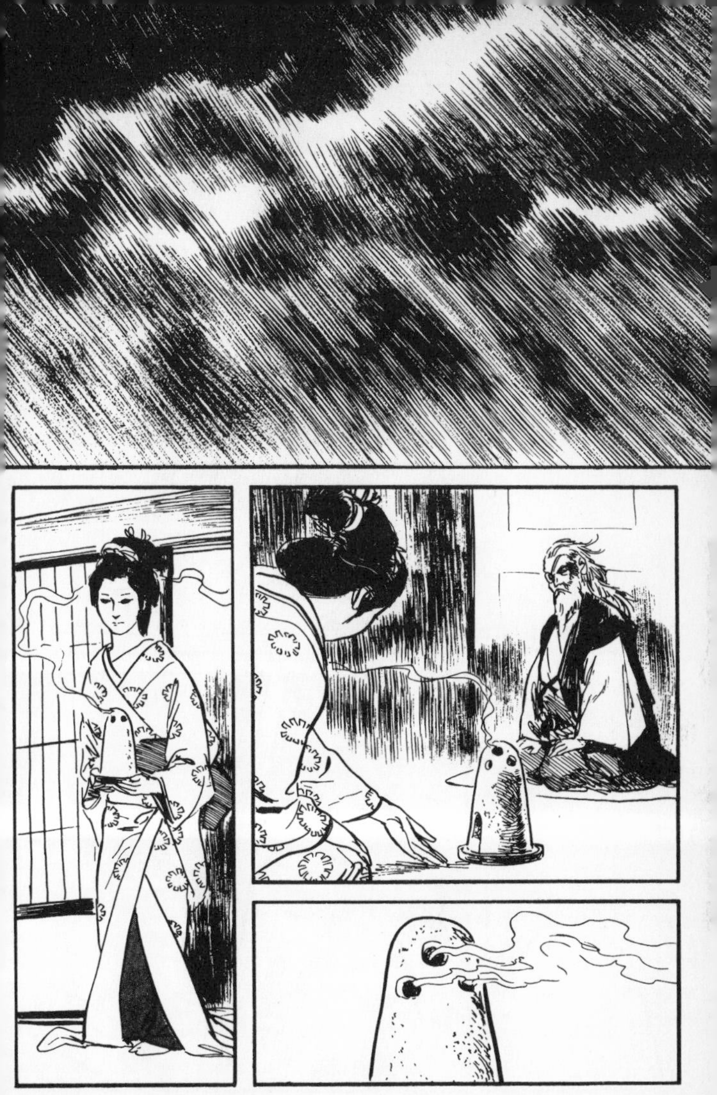

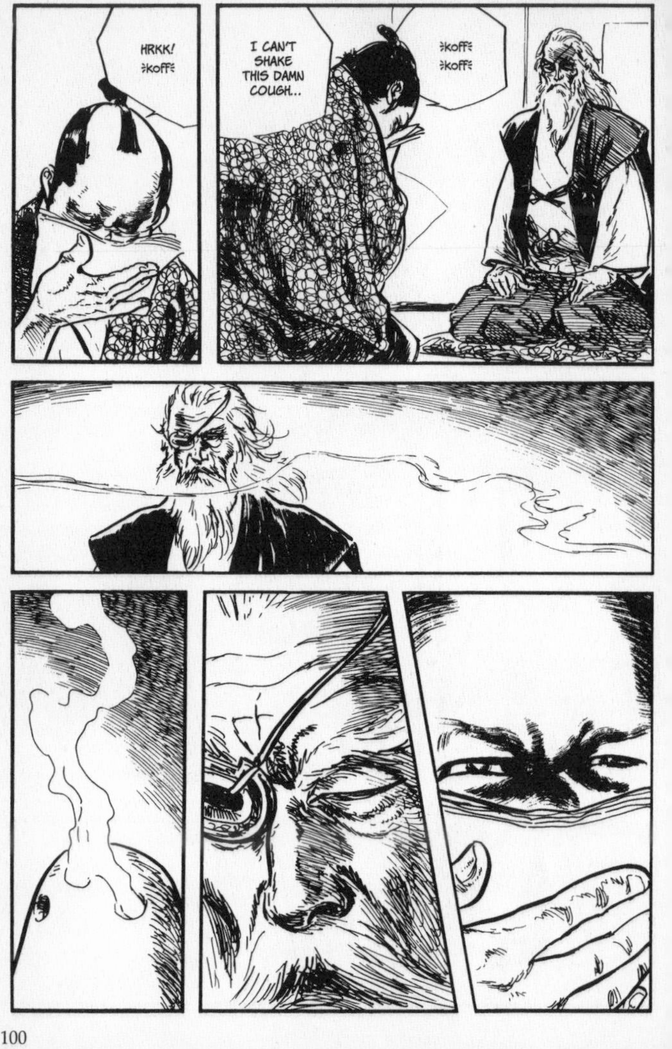
koff koff
I CAN'T SHAKE THIS DAMN COUGH...
HRKK! koff

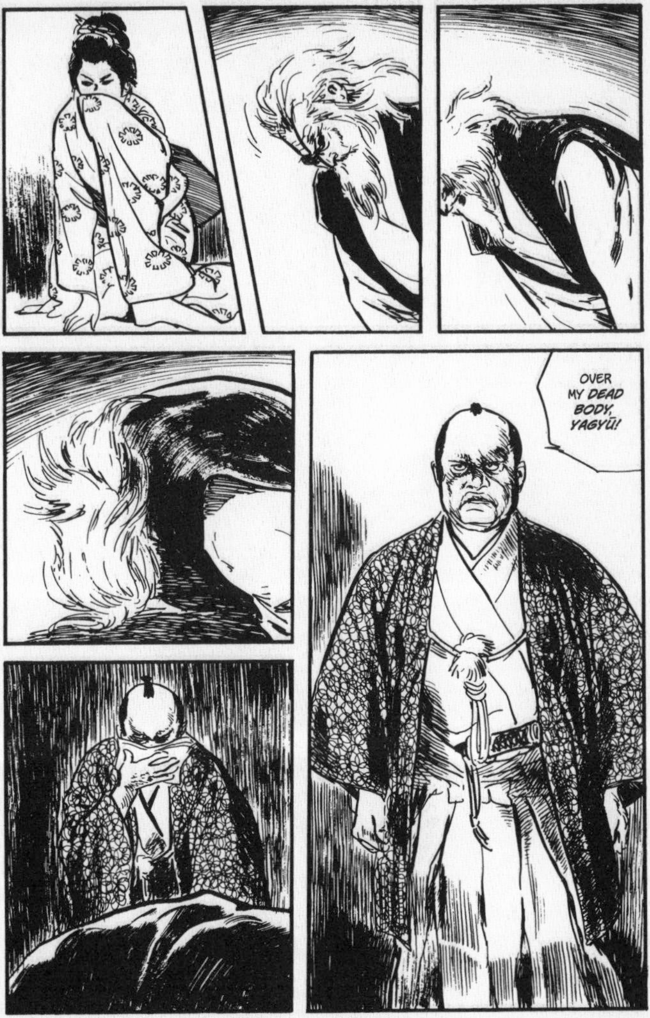
OVER MY DEAD BODY, YAGYŪ!

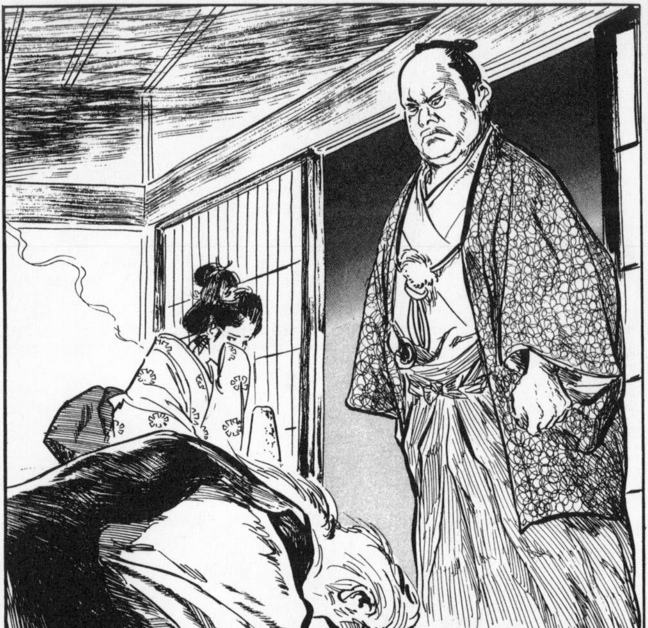

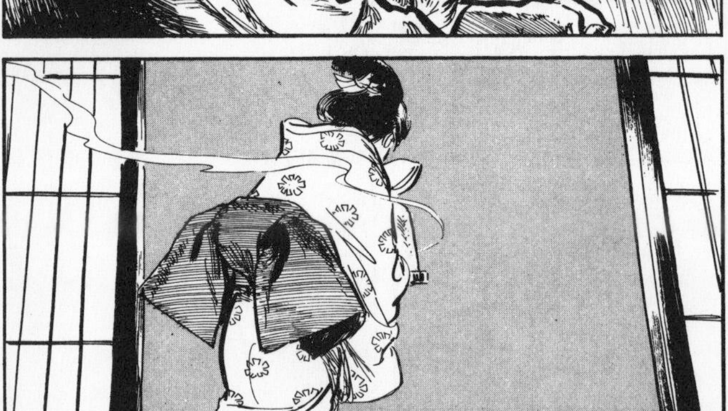

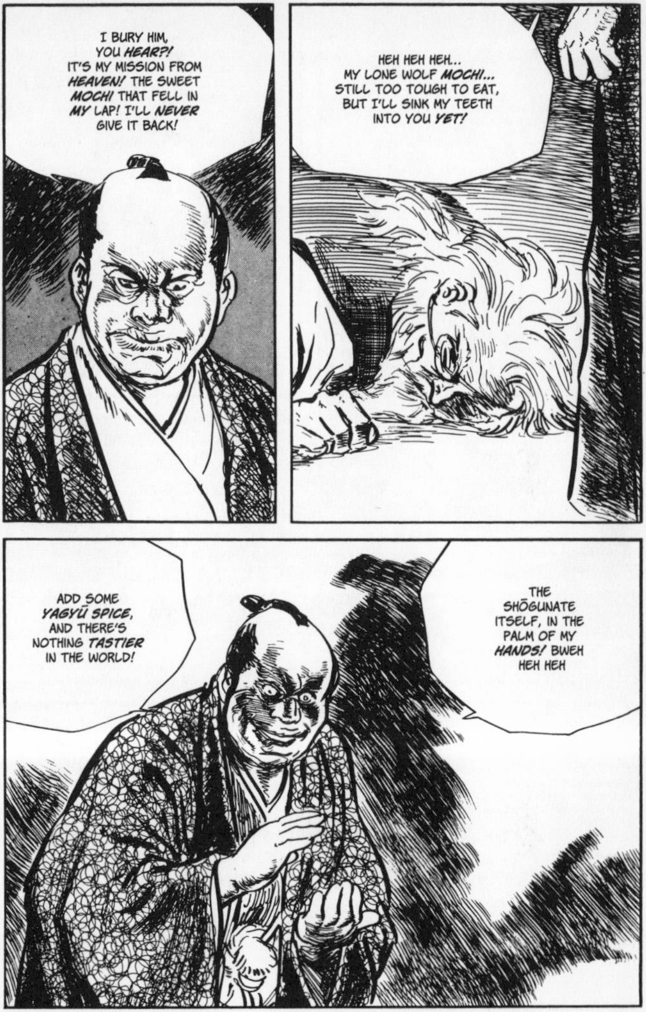
I BURY HIM, YOU HEAR?! IT'S MY MISSION FROM HEAVEN! THE SWEET MOCHI THAT FELL IN MY LAP! I'LL NEVER GIVE IT BACK!
HEH HEH HEH... MY LONE WOLF MOCHI... STILL TOO TOUGH TO EAT, BUT I'LL SINK MY TEETH INTO YOU YET!
ADD SOME YAGYŪ SPICE, AND THERE'S NOTHING TASTIER IN THE WORLD!
THE SHŌGUNATE ITSELF, IN THE PALM OF MY HANDS! BWEH HEH HEH

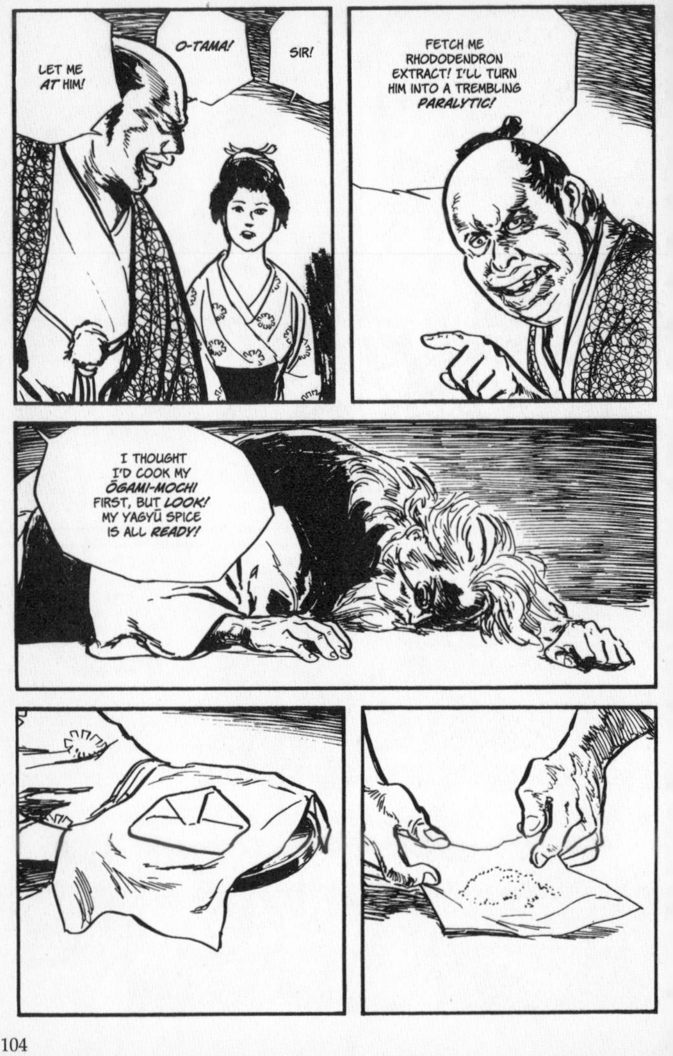
LET ME AT HIM!
O-TAMA!
SIR!
FETCH ME RHODODENDRON EXTRACT! I'LL TURN HIM INTO A TREMBLING PARALYTIC!
I THOUGHT I'D COOK MY ŌGAMI-MOCHI FIRST, BUT LOOK! MY YAGYŪ SPICE IS ALL READY!

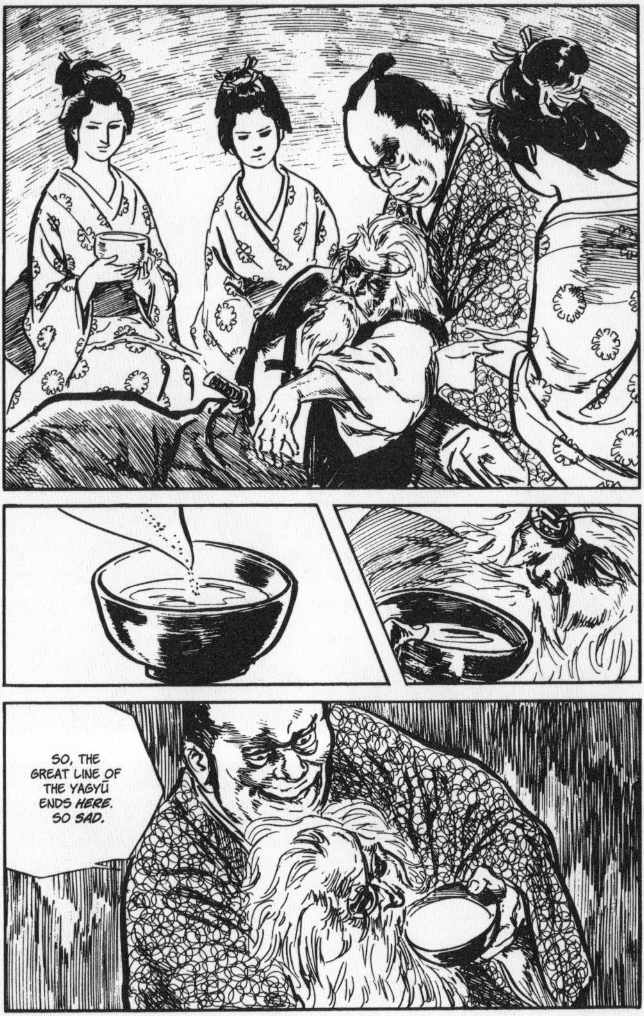
SO, THE GREAT LINE OF THE YAGYŪ ENDS *HERE*. SO *SAD*.

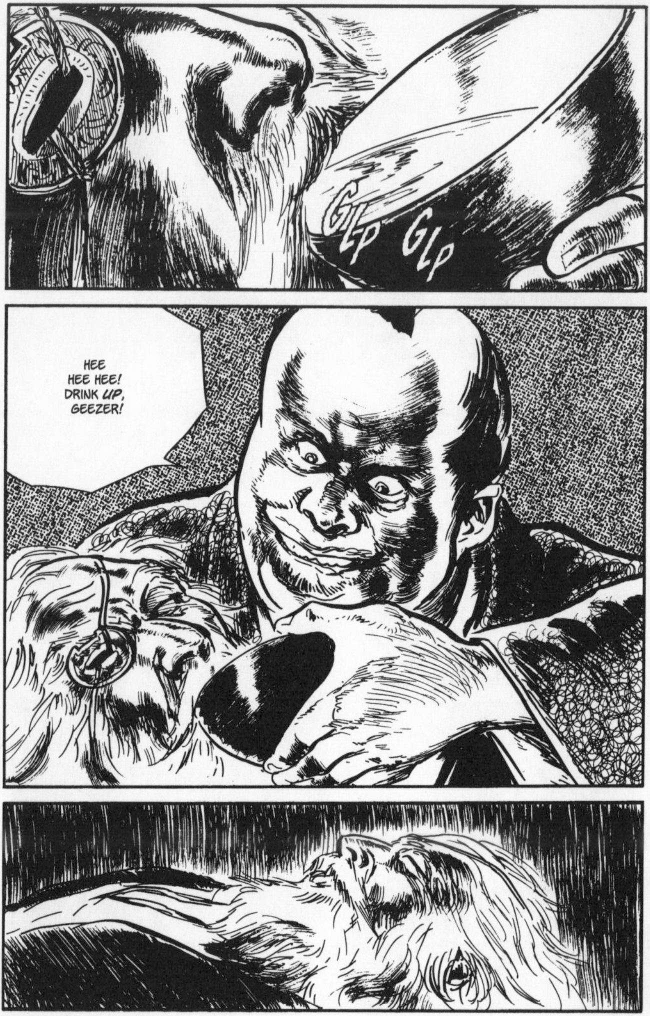
GLP GLP
HEE HEE HEE! DRINK UP, GEEZER!

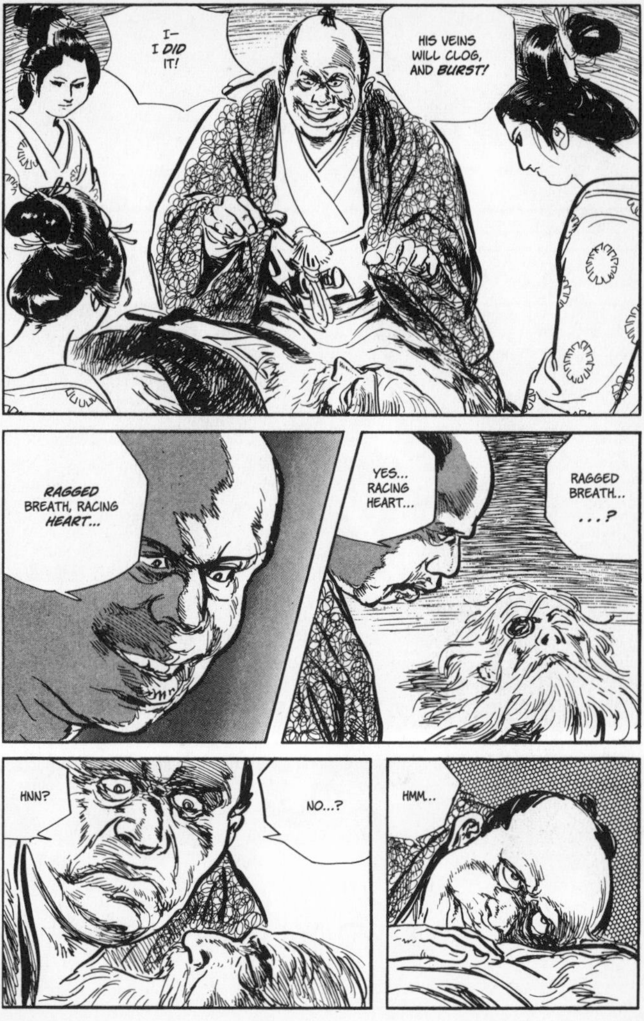
I— I *DID* IT!
HIS VEINS WILL CLOG, AND *BURST!*
RAGGED BREATH, RACING *HEART*...
YES... RACING HEART...
RAGGED BREATH...
...?
HNN?
NO...?
HMM..

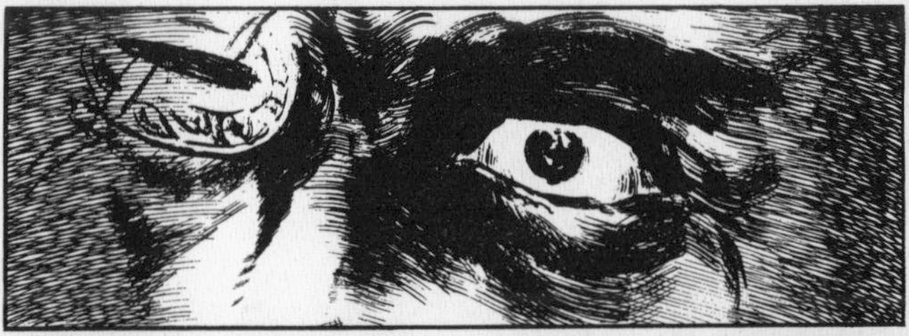
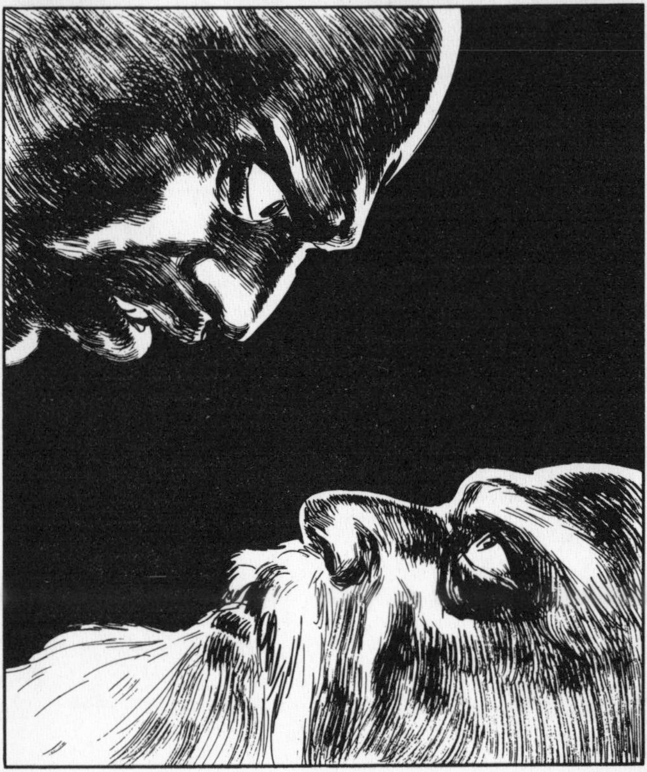

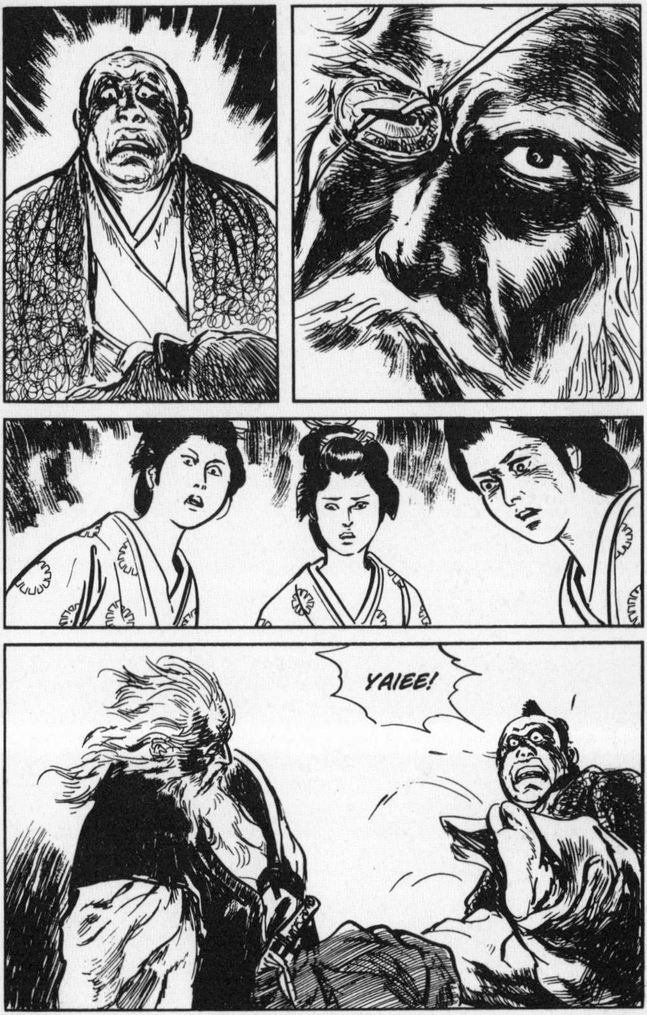
YAIEE!

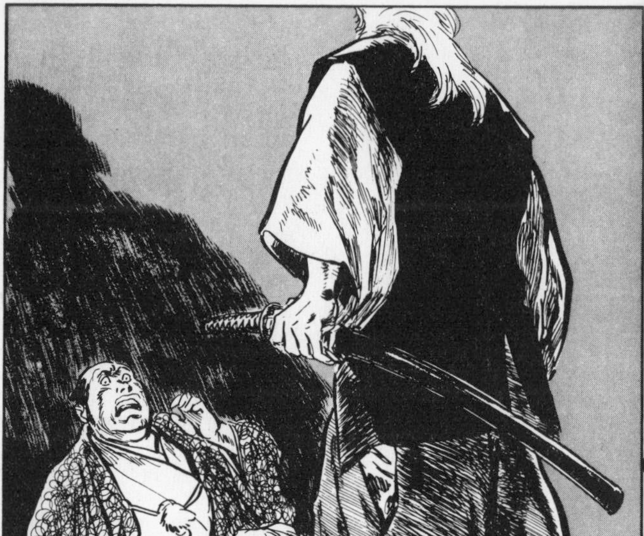

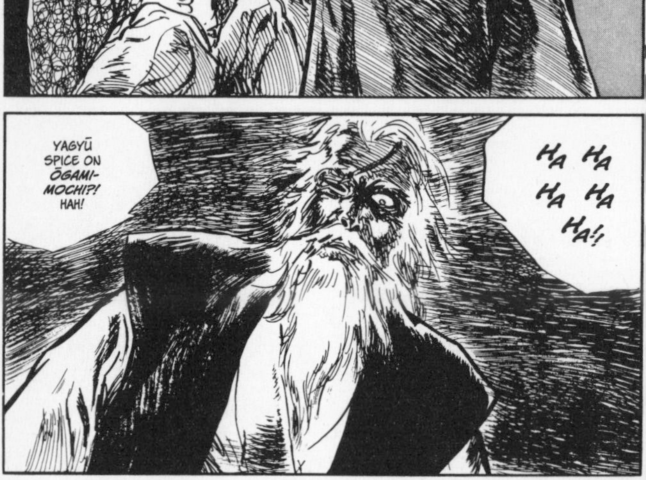
HA HA HA HA HA!!
YAGYŪ SPICE ON ŌGAMI-MOCHI?! HAH!

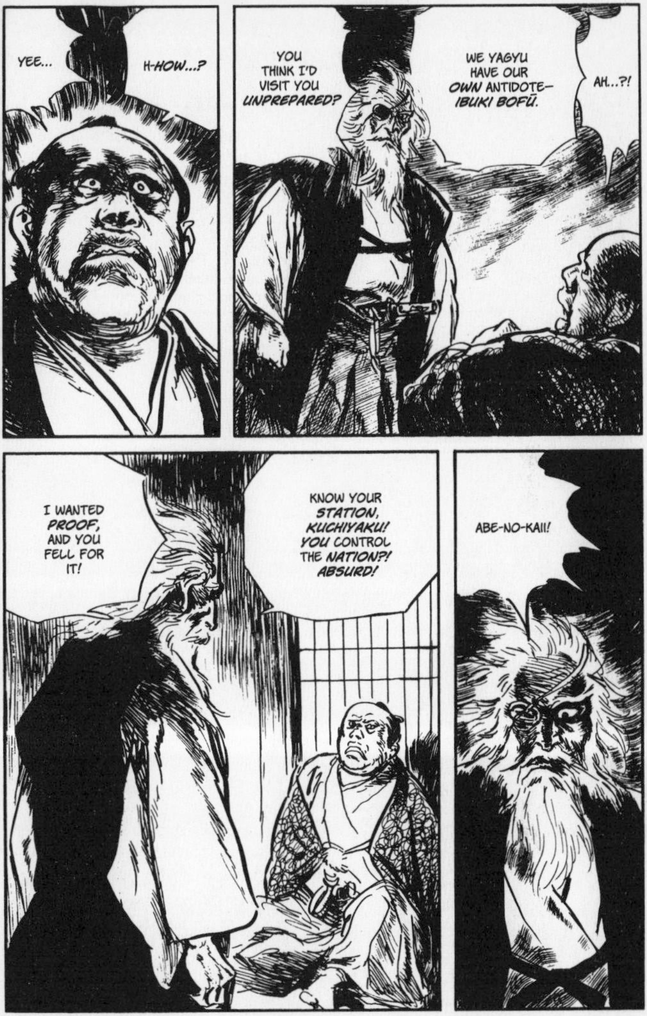
YEE...
H-HOW...?
YOU THINK I'D VISIT YOU UNPREPARED?
WE YAGYU HAVE OUR OWN ANTIDOTE-IBUKI BOFŪ.
AH...?!
I WANTED PROOF, AND YOU FELL FOR IT!
KNOW YOUR STATION, KUCHIYAKU! YOU CONTROL THE NATION?! ABSURD!
ABE-NO-KAII!

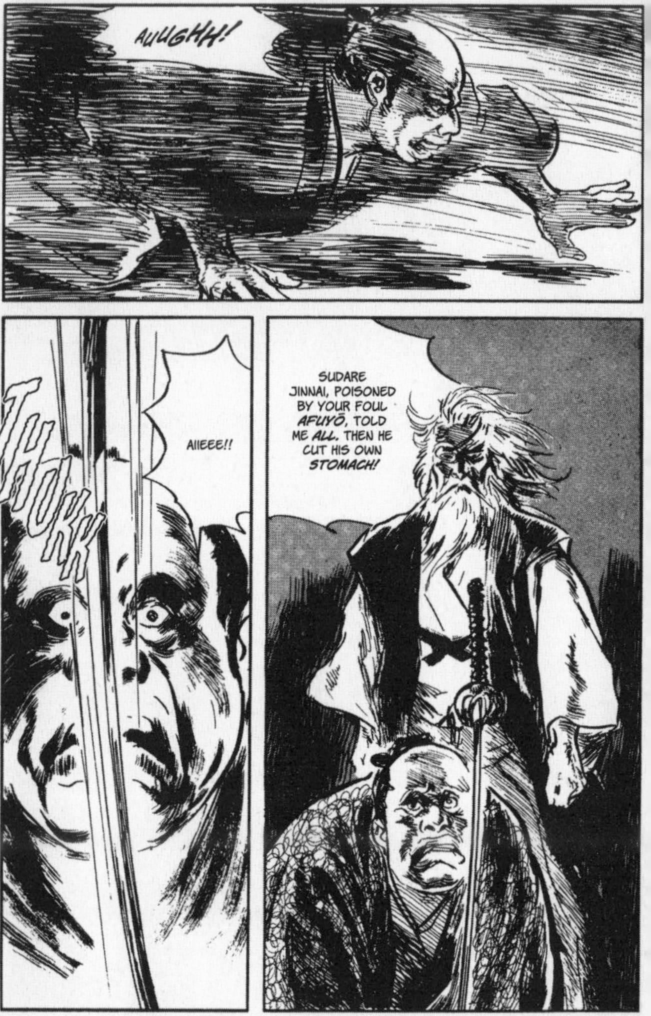
AUUGHH!
SUDARE JINNAI, POISONED BY YOUR FOUL *AFUYŌ*, TOLD ME *ALL*. THEN HE CUT HIS OWN *STOMACH!*
AIIEEE!!
THUKK

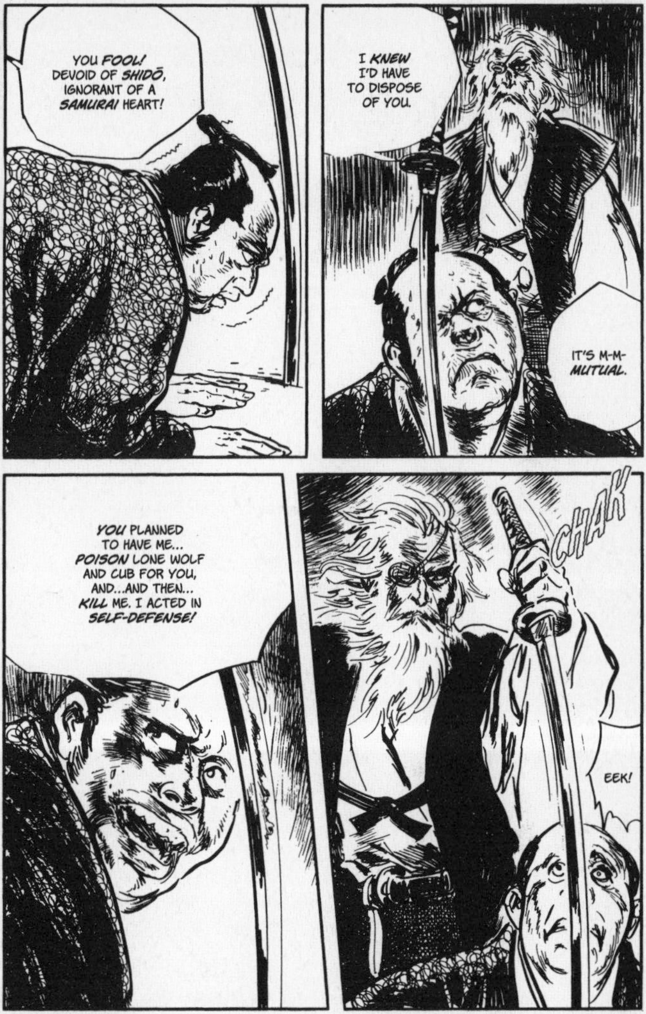
YOU FOOL! DEVOID OF SHIDŌ, IGNORANT OF A SAMURAI HEART!
I KNEW I'D HAVE TO DISPOSE OF YOU.
IT'S M-M-MUTUAL.
YOU PLANNED TO HAVE ME... POISON LONE WOLF AND CUB FOR YOU, AND...AND THEN... KILL ME. I ACTED IN SELF-DEFENSE!
CHAK
EEK!

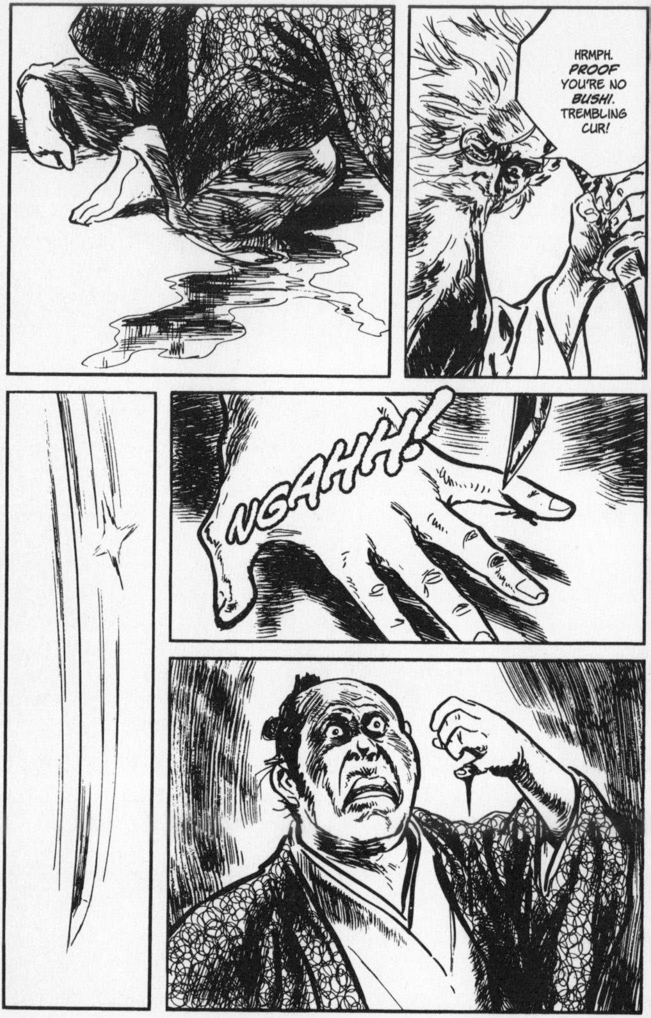
HRMPH. *PROOF* YOU'RE NO *BUSHI*. TREMBLING CUR!
NGAHH!

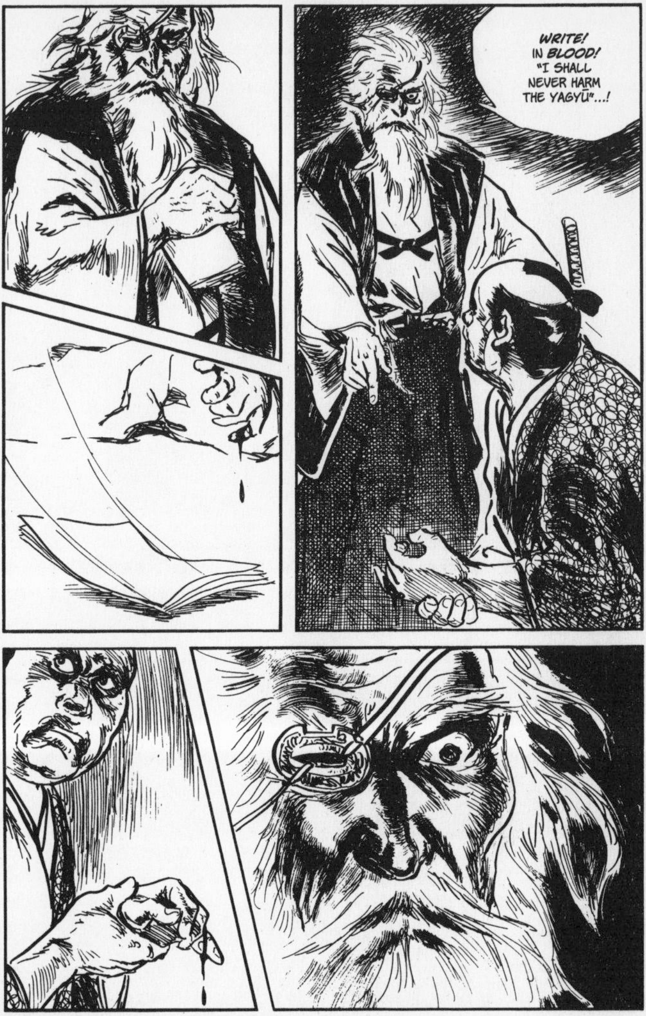
WRITE! IN BLOOD! "I SHALL NEVER HARM THE YAGYŪ"...!

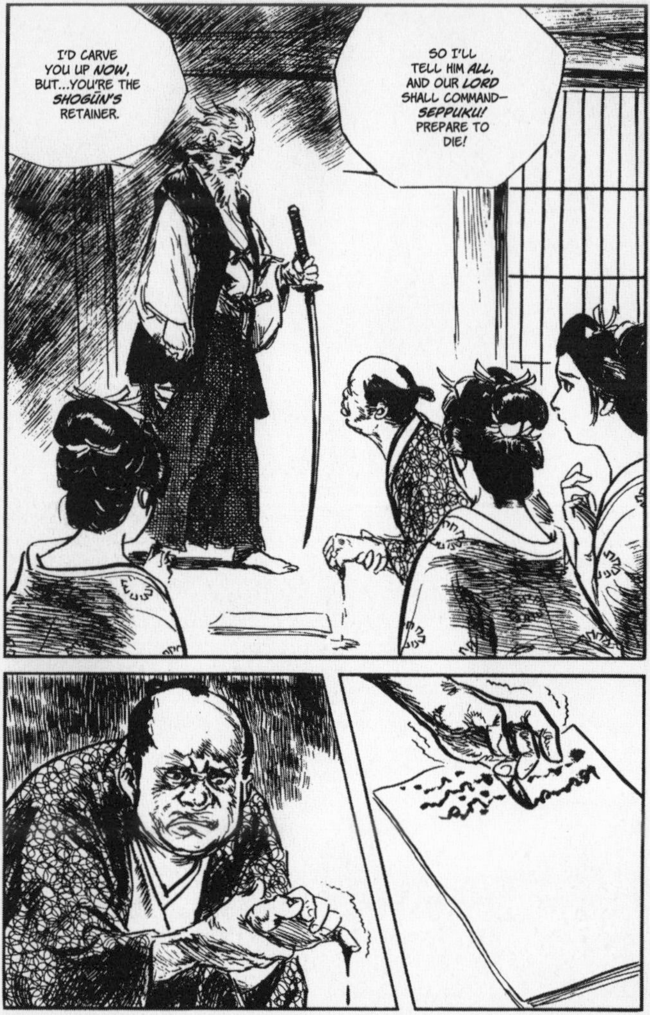
I'D CARVE YOU UP *NOW*, BUT...YOU'RE THE *SHOGŪN'S* RETAINER.
SO I'LL TELL HIM *ALL*, AND OUR *LORD* SHALL COMMAND— *SEPPUKU!* PREPARE TO DIE!

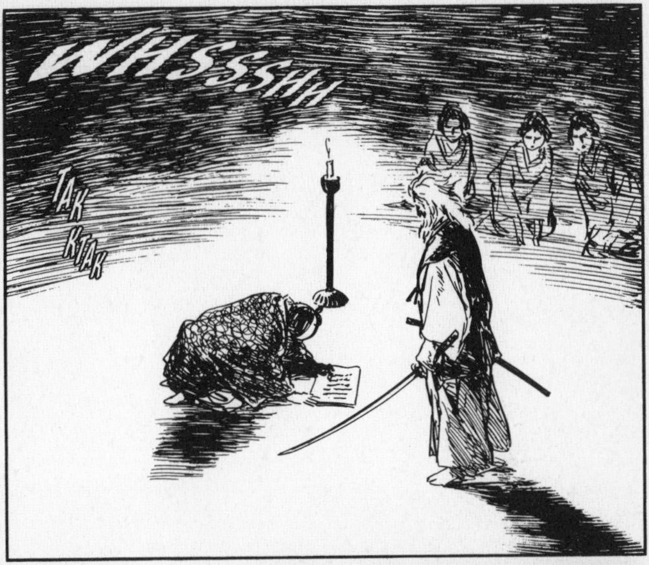
WHSSSHH
TAK KTAK
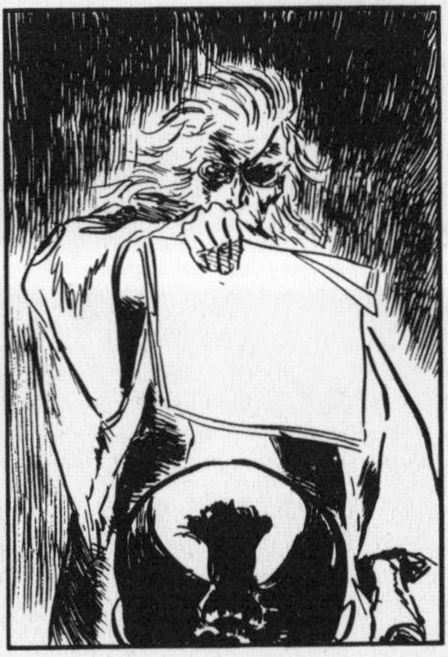
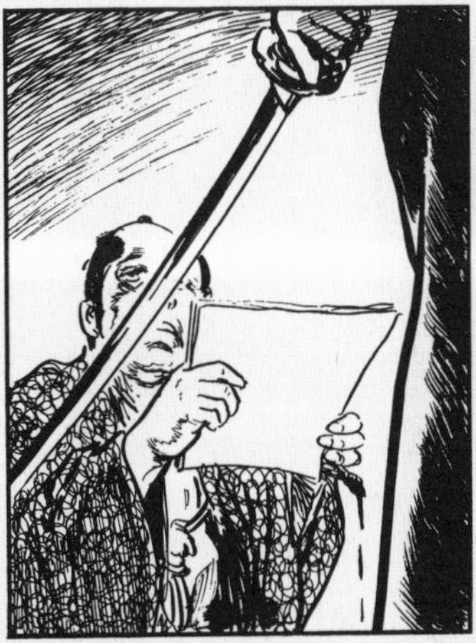

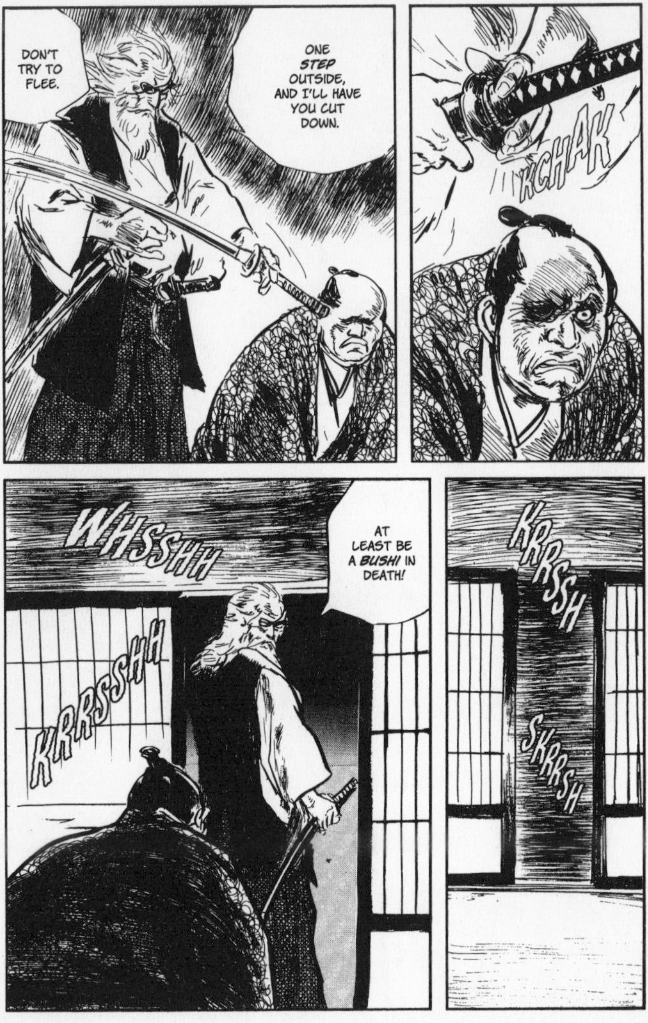
DON'T TRY TO FLEE.
ONE *STEP* OUTSIDE, AND I'LL HAVE YOU CUT DOWN.
KCHAK
WHSSHH
AT LEAST BE A *BUSHI* IN DEATH!
KRRSSHH
KRRSSH
SKRRSH

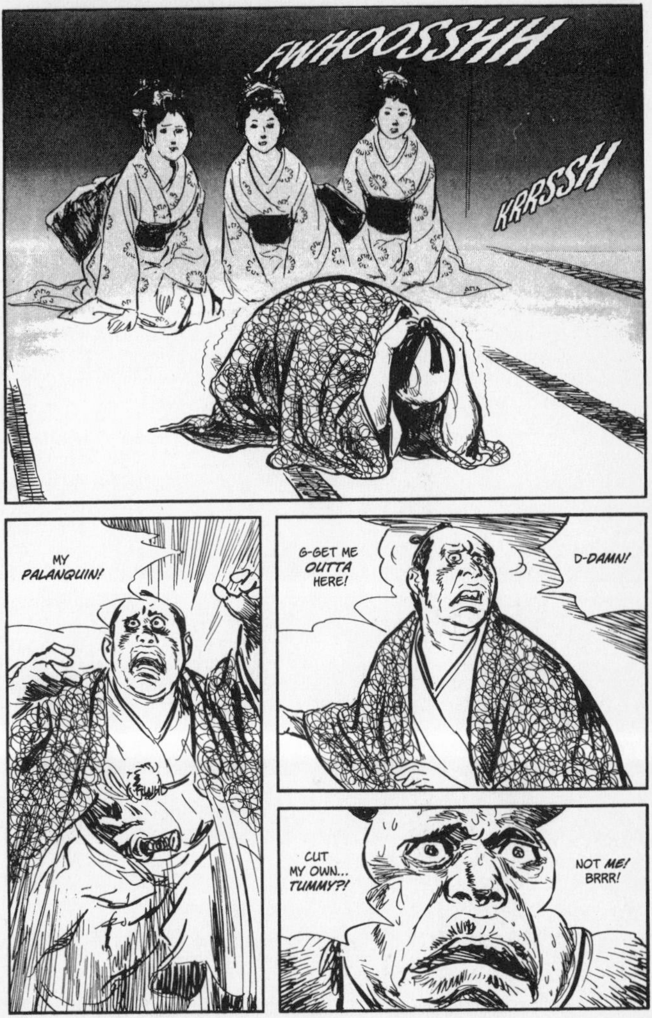
FWHOOSSHH
KRRSSH
D-DAMN!
G-GET ME OUTTA HERE!
NOT ME! BRRR!
CUT MY OWN... TUMMY?!
MY PALANQUIN!

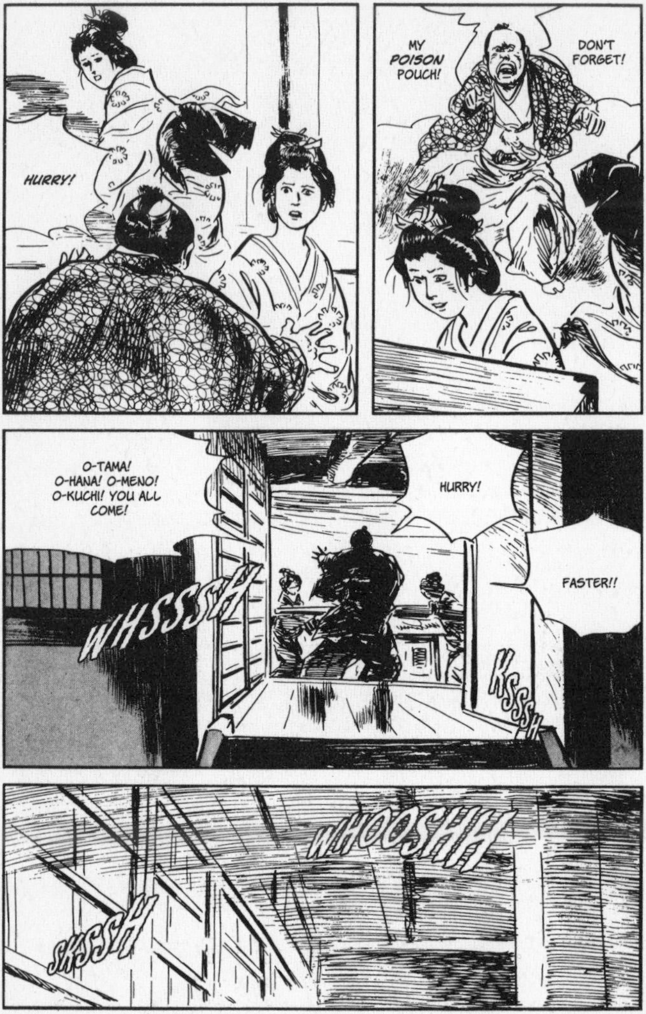
HURRY!
MY POISON POUCH!
DON'T FORGET!
O-TAMA! O-HANA! O-MENO! O-KUCHI! YOU ALL COME!
HURRY!
FASTER!!
WHSSSH
KSSSH
WHOOSHH
SKSSSH

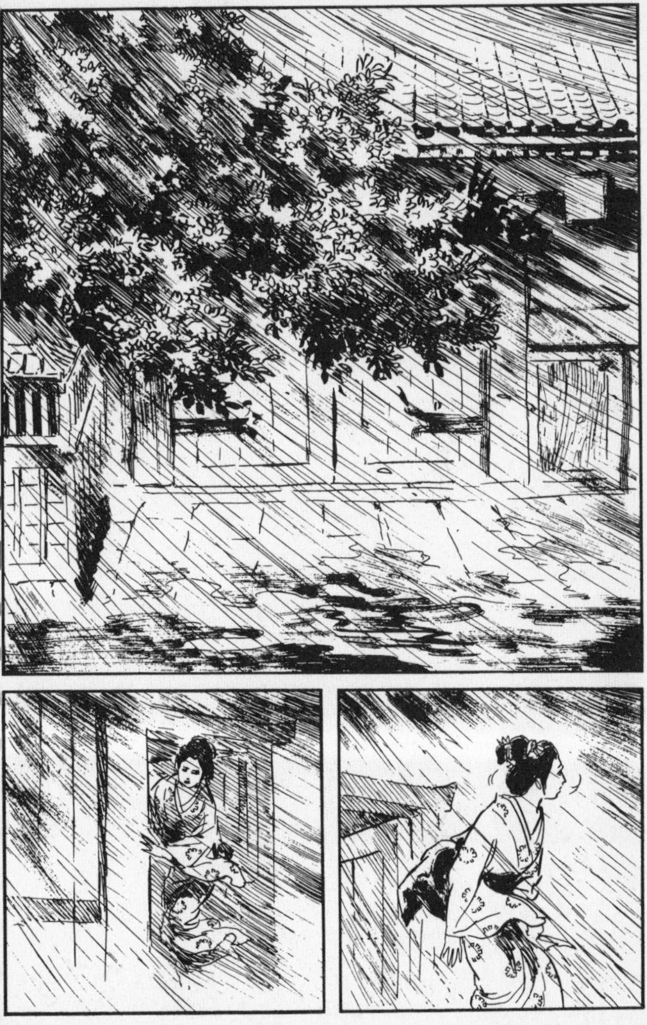

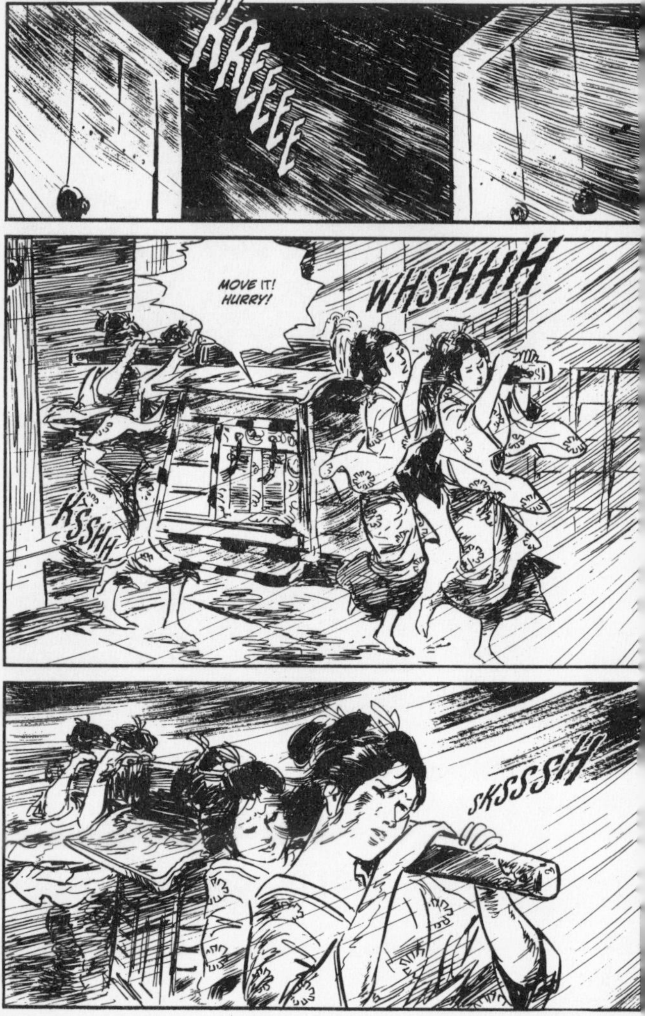
KREEEE
WHSHHH
MOVE IT! HURRY!
KSSHH
SKSSSH

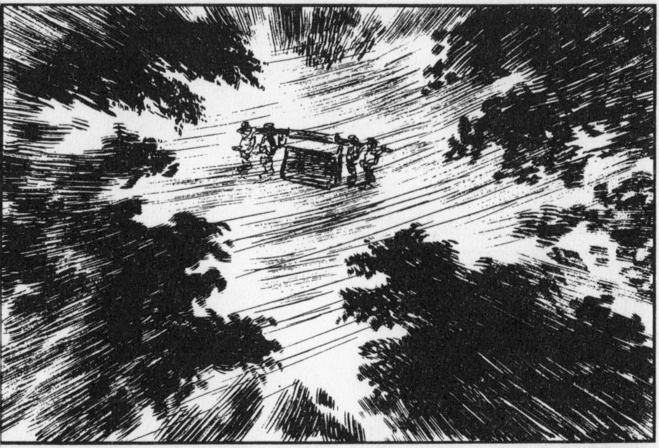
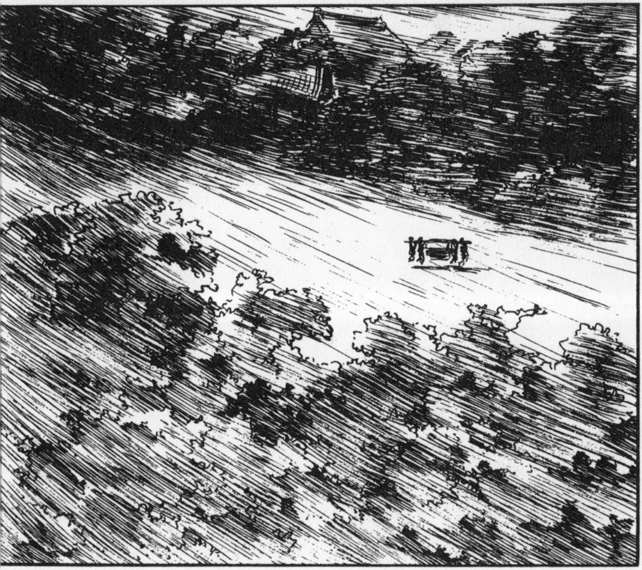

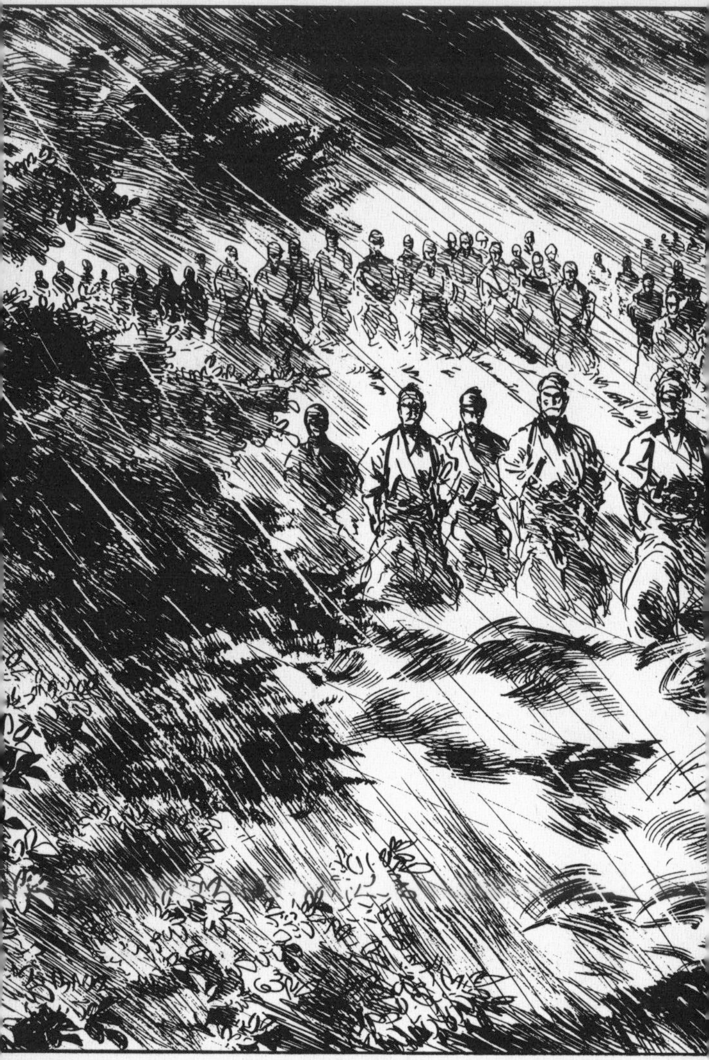

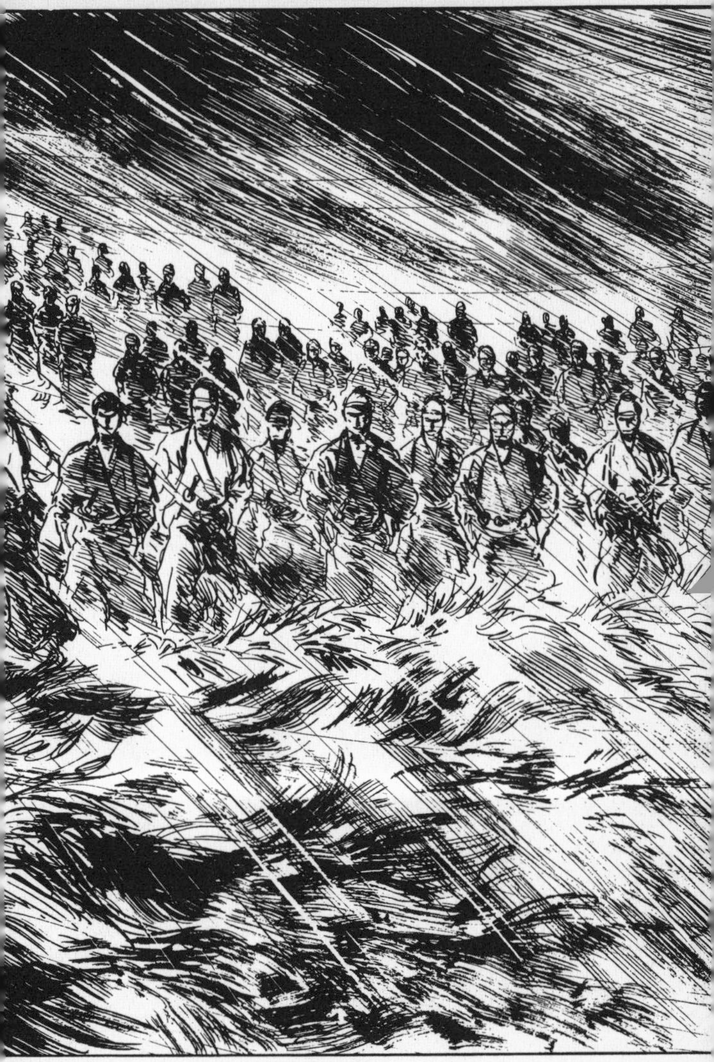

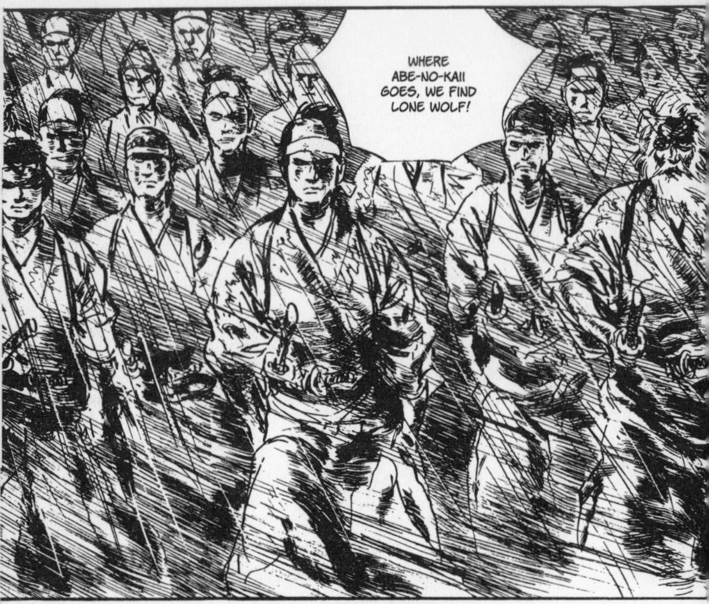
WHERE ABE-NO-KAII GOES, WE FIND LONE WOLF!

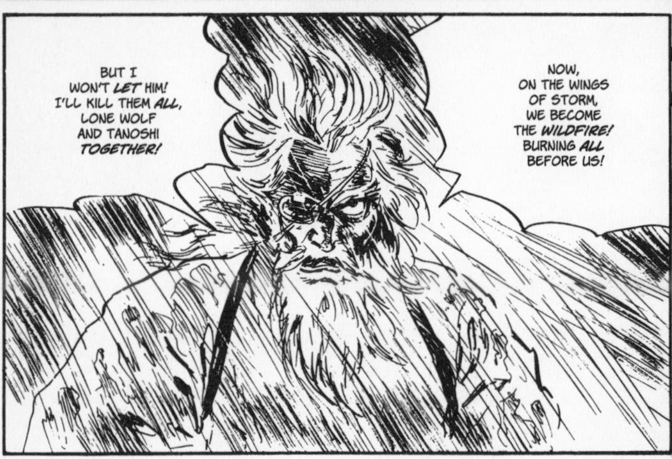
NOW, ON THE WINGS OF STORM, WE BECOME THE *WILDFIRE!* BURNING *ALL* BEFORE US!
BUT I WON'T *LET* HIM! I'LL KILL THEM *ALL*, LONE WOLF AND TANOSHI *TOGETHER!*

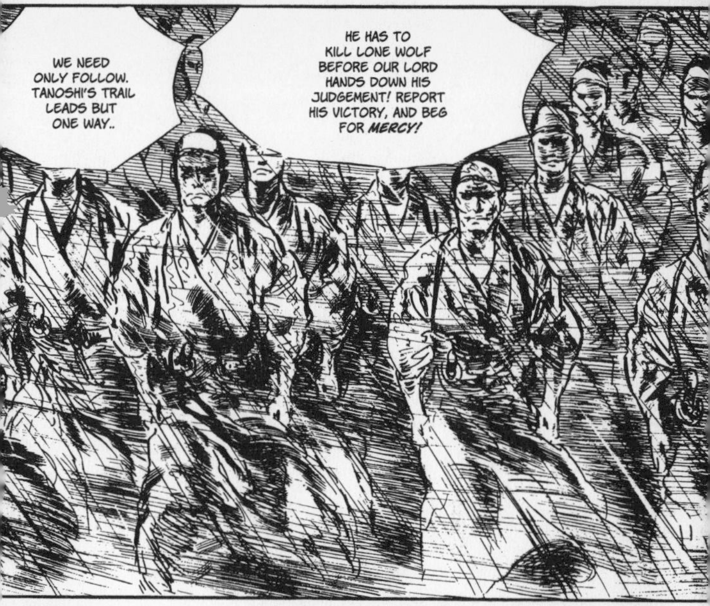
HE HAS TO KILL LONE WOLF BEFORE OUR LORD HANDS DOWN HIS JUDGEMENT! REPORT HIS VICTORY, AND BEG FOR *MERCY!*
WE NEED ONLY FOLLOW. TANOSHI'S TRAIL LEADS BUT ONE WAY..

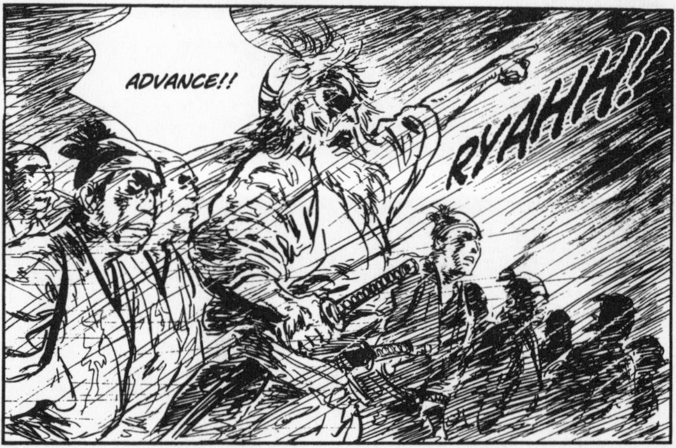
RYAHH!!
ADVANCE!!

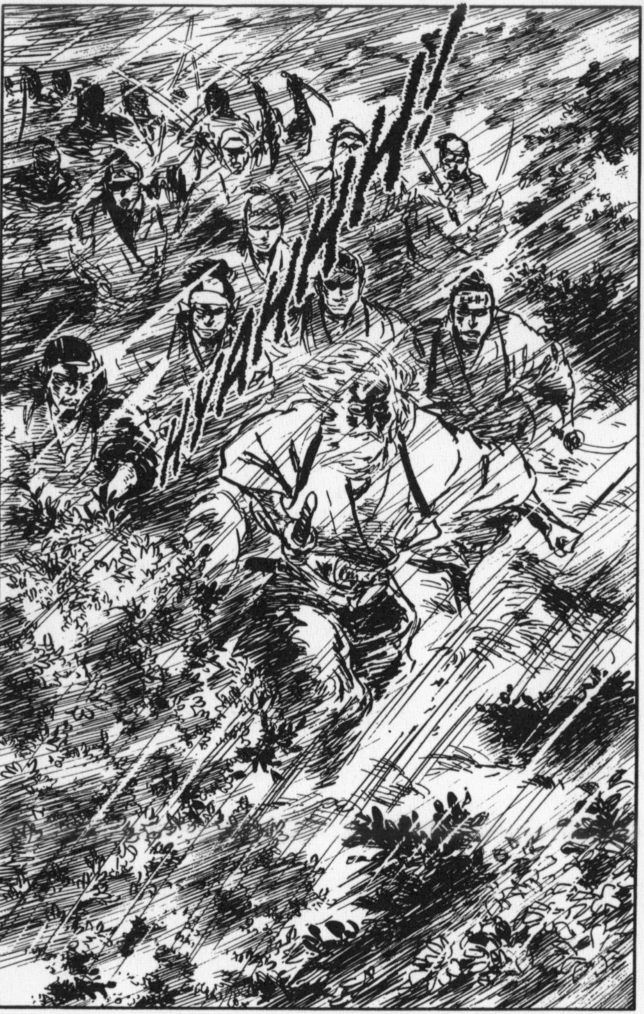

the hundred
and fifth

Fire,
Water,
and
Poison

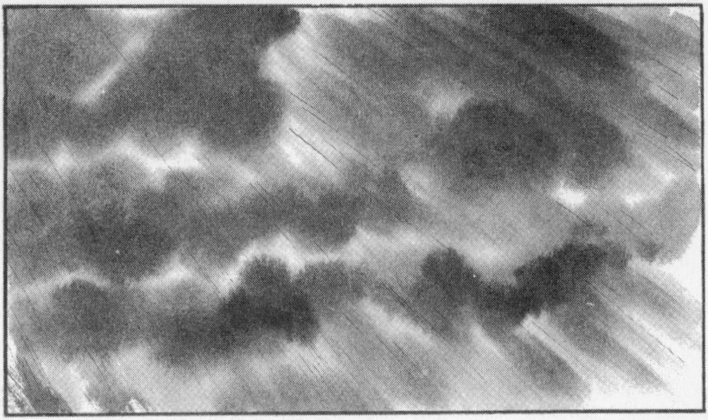

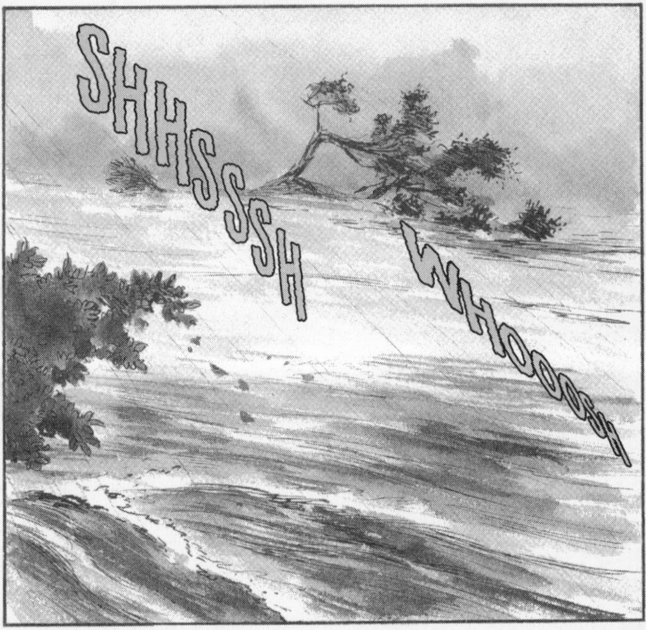
SHHSSSSH
WHOOOSH

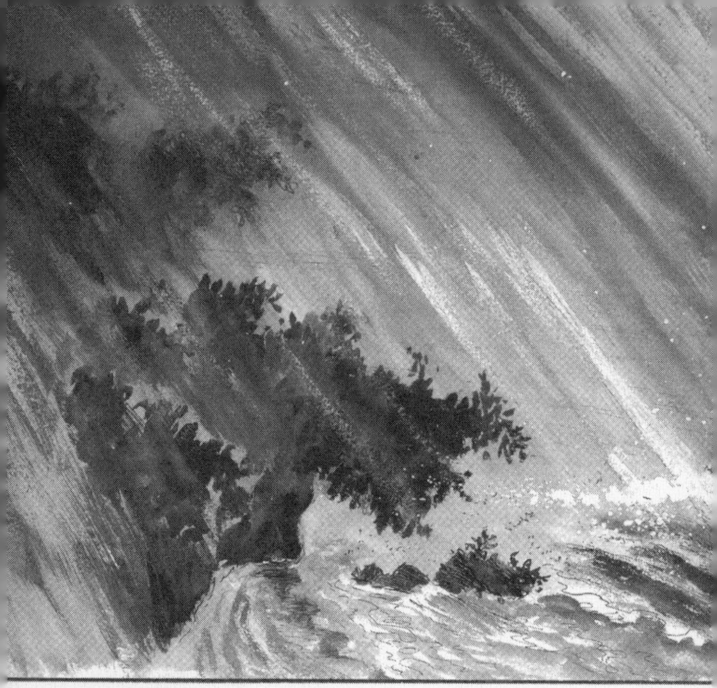
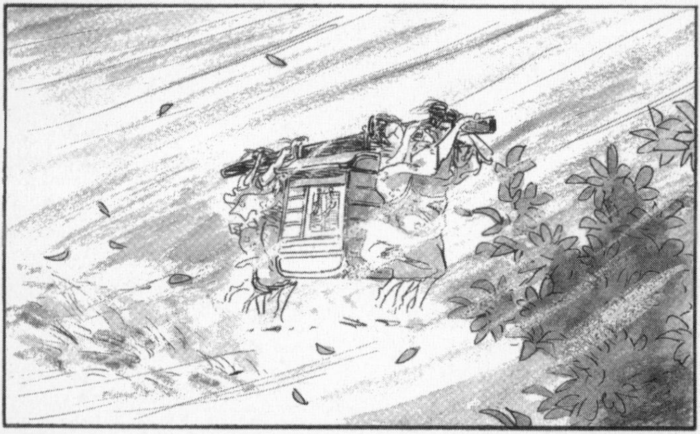

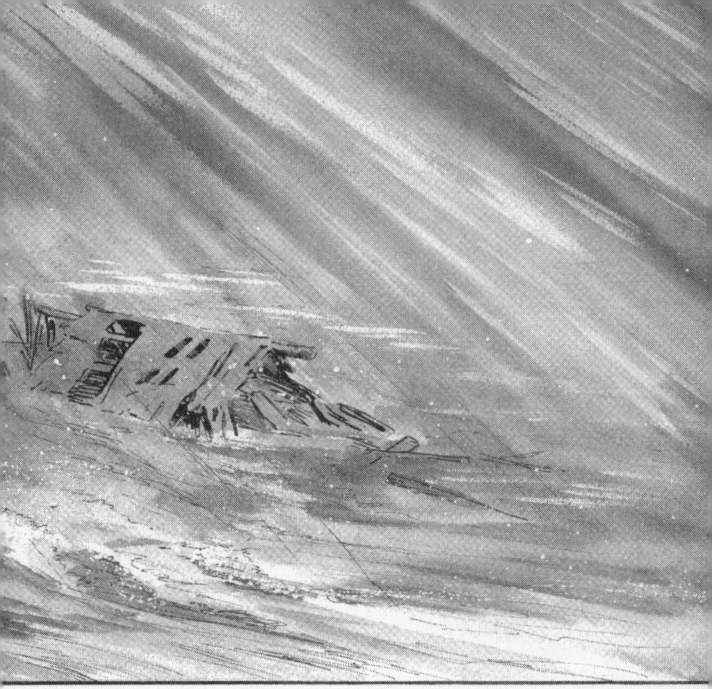

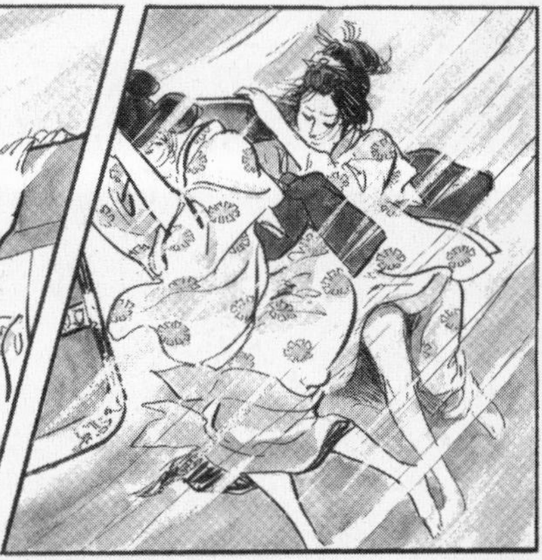

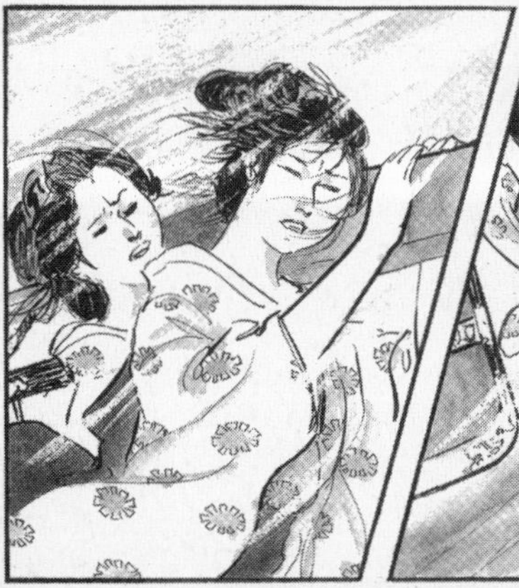

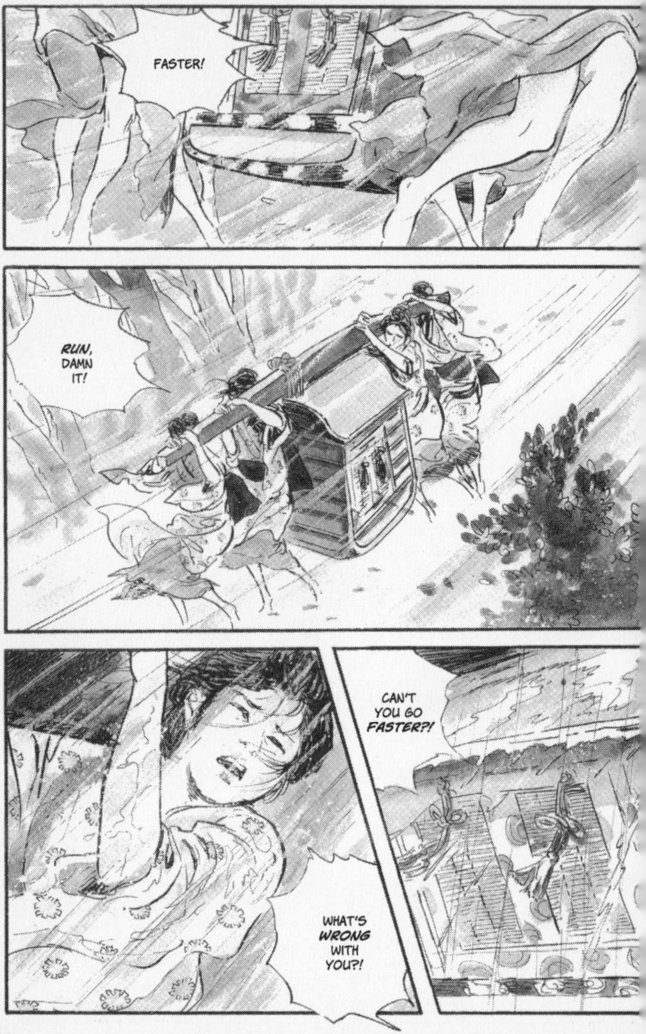
FASTER!
RUN, DAMN IT!
CAN'T YOU GO FASTER?!
WHAT'S WRONG WITH YOU?!

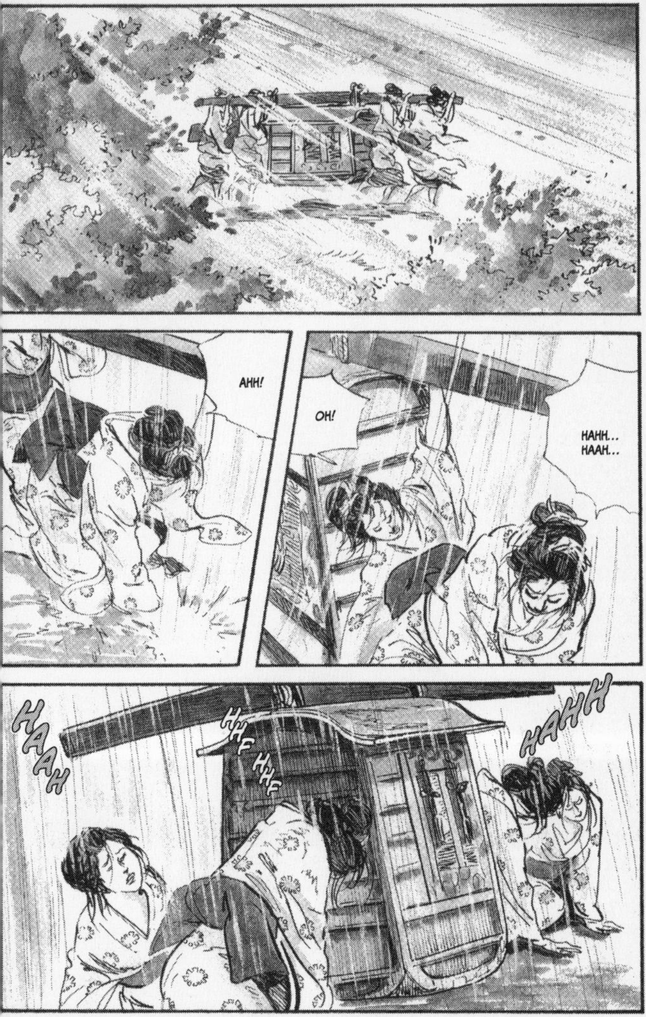
HAHH...
HAAH...
OH!
AHH!
HAHH
HHF HHF
HAAH

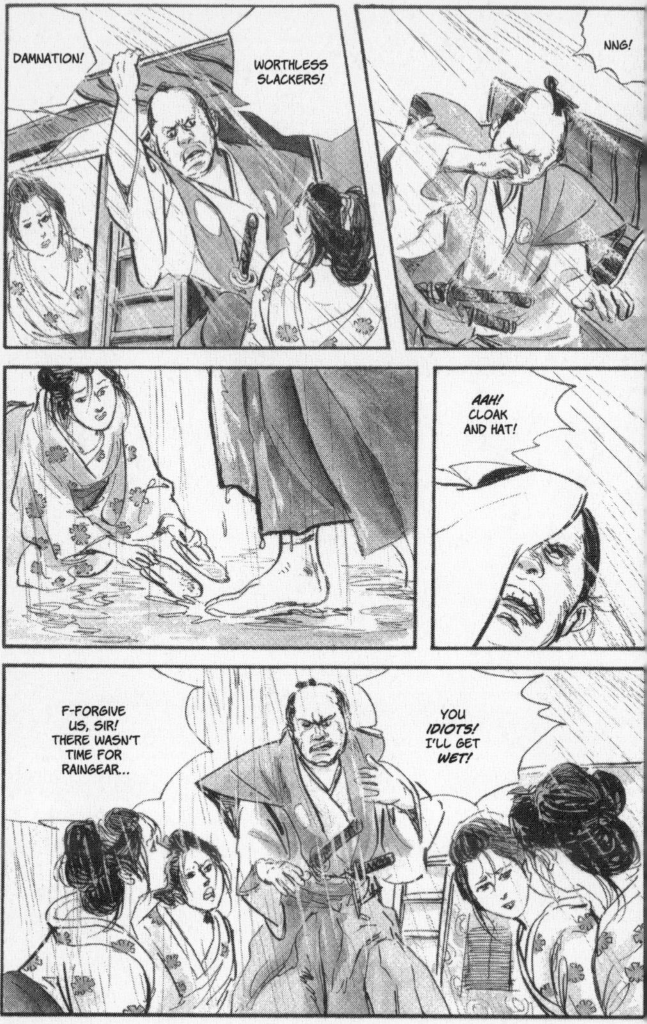
NNG!
WORTHLESS SLACKERS!
DAMNATION!
AAH! CLOAK AND HAT!
YOU *IDIOTS!* I'LL GET *WET!*
F-FORGIVE US, SIR! THERE WASN'T TIME FOR RAINGEAR...

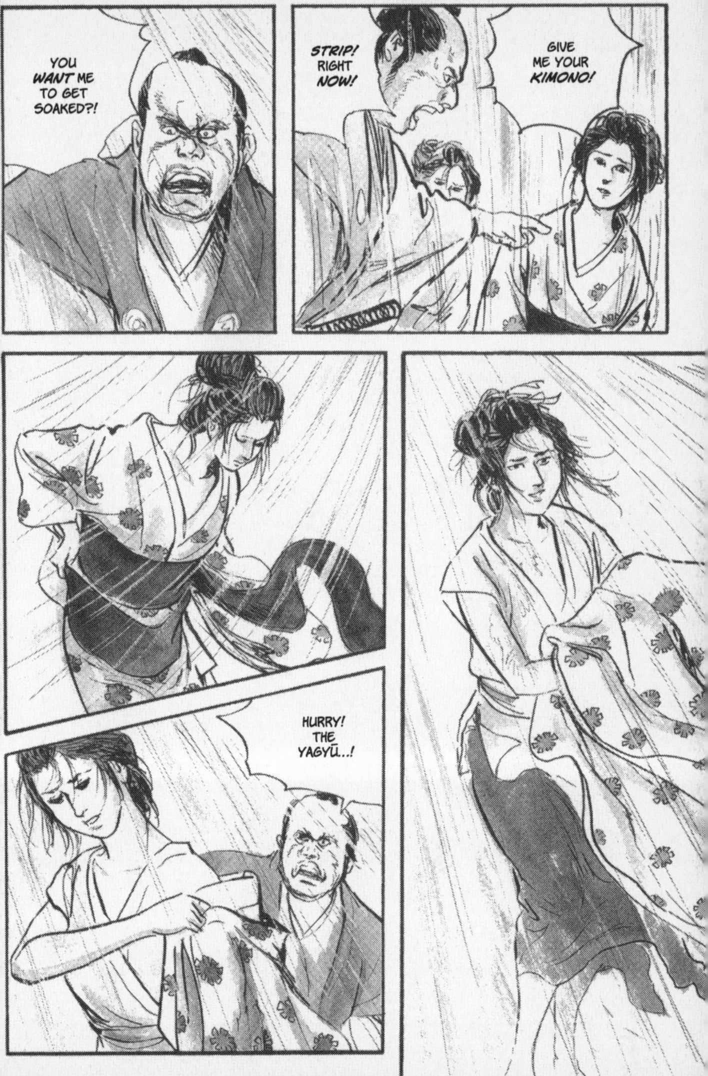
YOU WANT ME TO GET SOAKED?!
STRIP! RIGHT NOW!
GIVE ME YOUR KIMONO!
HURRY! THE YAGYŪ...!

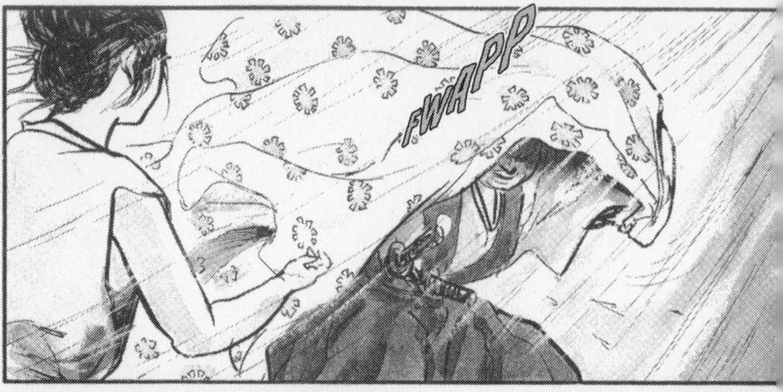
FWAPP
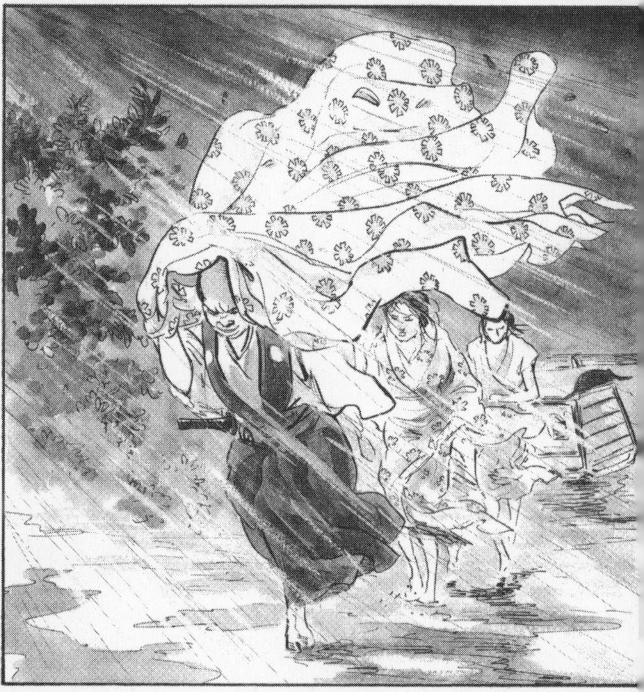

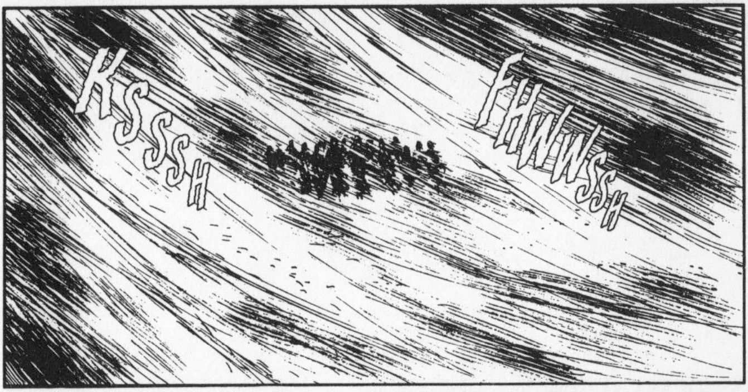
FHWWSSH
KSSSH
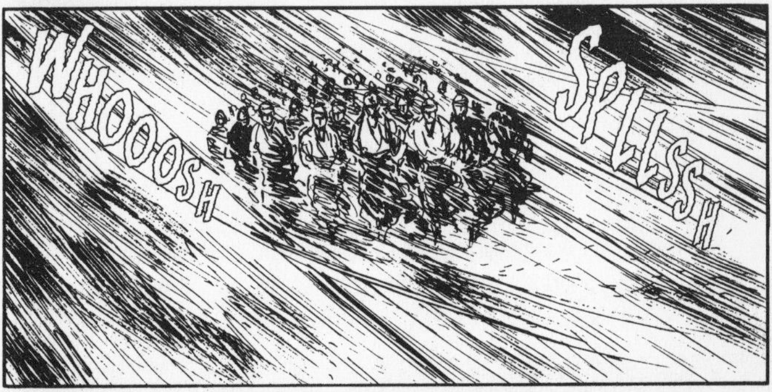
SPLLSSH
WHOOOSH
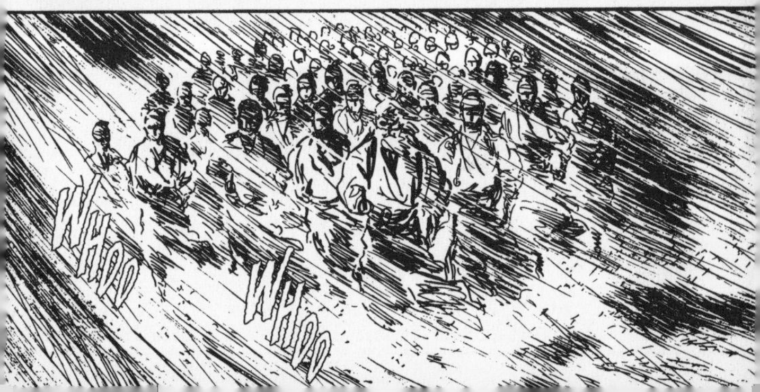
WHOO
WHOO

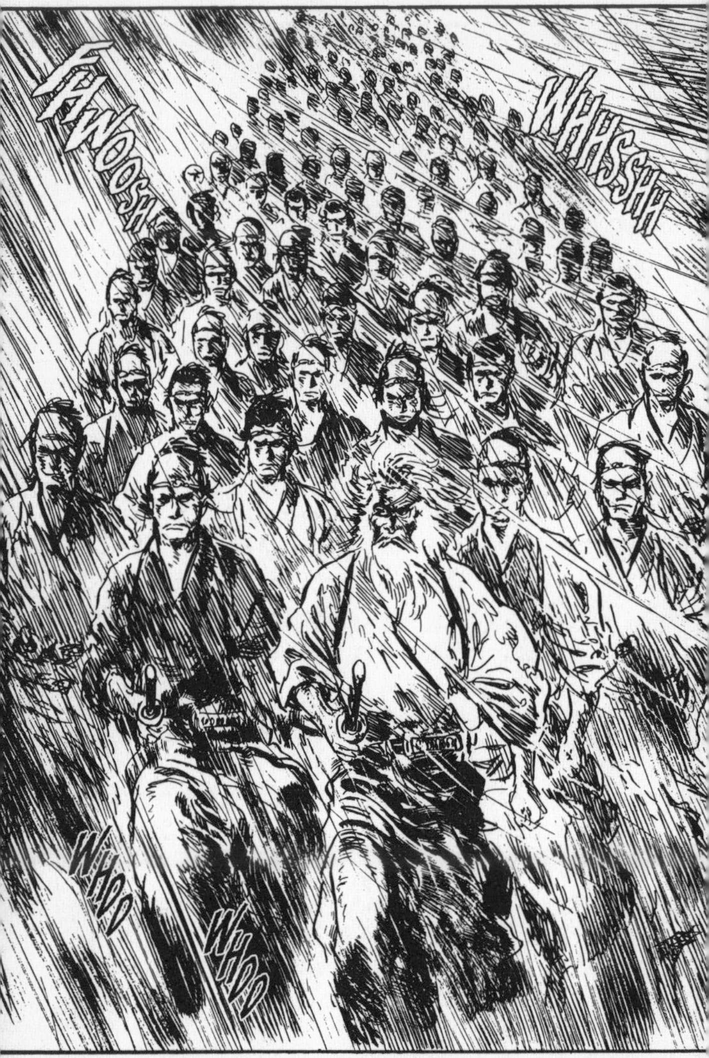
WHSSHH
WHOOSH
WHOO
WHOO

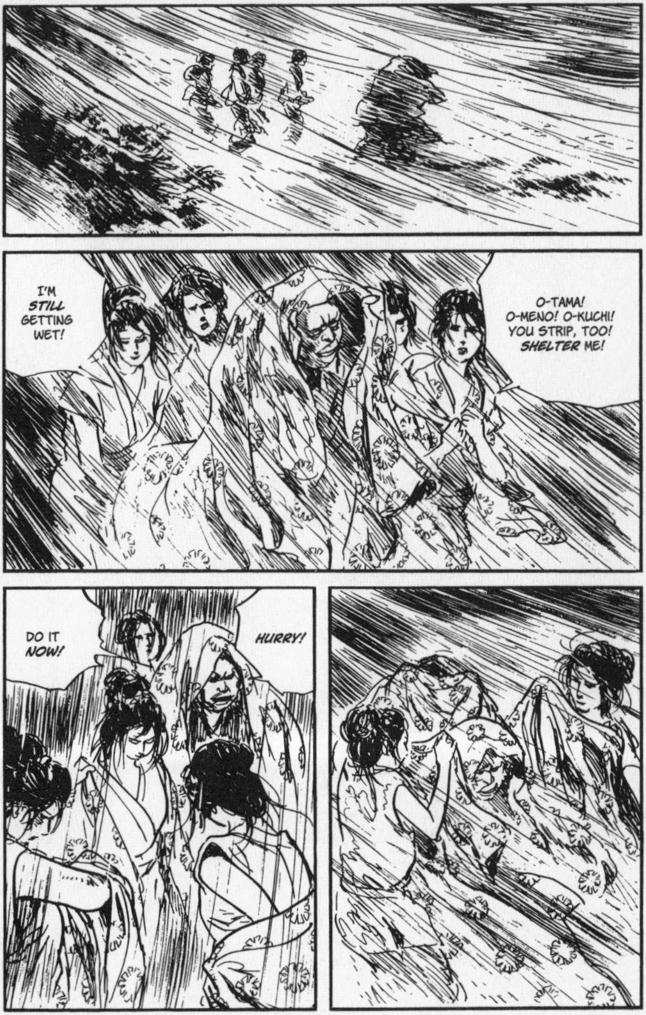
O-TAMA! O-MENO! O-KUCHI! YOU STRIP, TOO! SHELTER ME!
I'M STILL GETTING WET!
HURRY!
DO IT NOW!

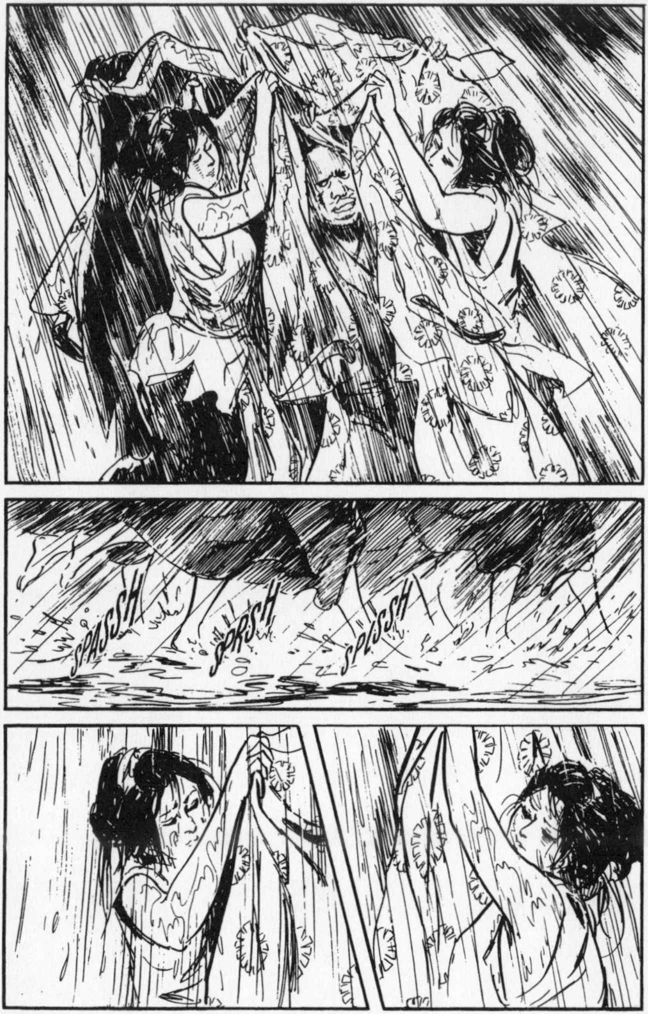
SPLSSH
SPRSH
SPASSH

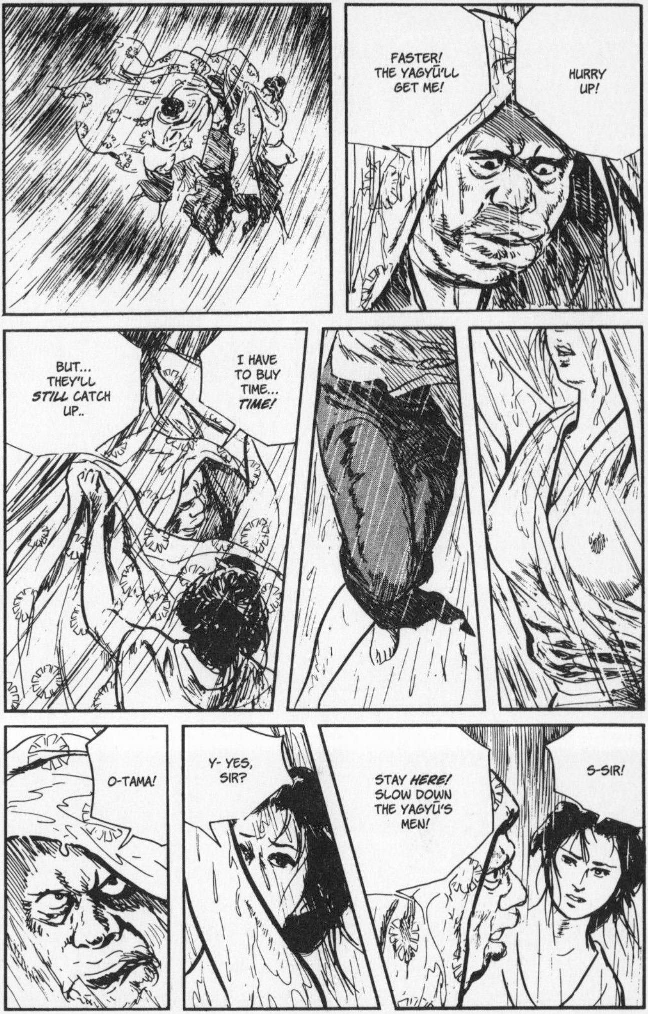
FASTER! THE YAGYŪ'LL GET ME!
HURRY UP!
BUT... THEY'LL STILL CATCH UP..
I HAVE TO BUY TIME... TIME!
O-TAMA!
Y- YES, SIR?
STAY HERE! SLOW DOWN THE YAGYŪ'S MEN!
S-SIR!

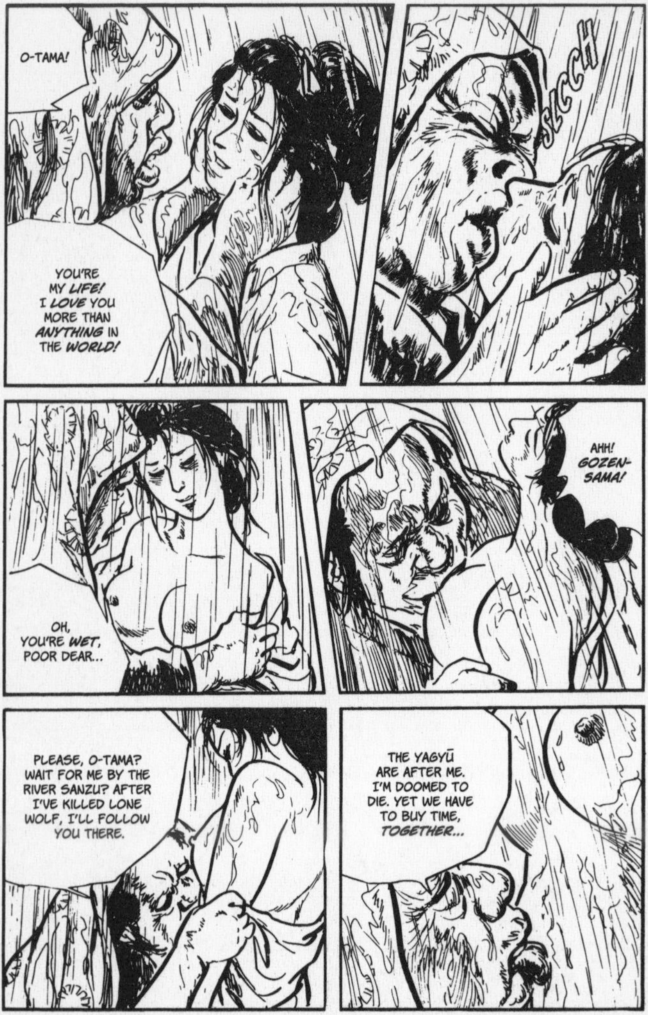
O-TAMA!
YOU'RE MY *LIFE!* I *LOVE* YOU MORE THAN *ANYTHING* IN THE *WORLD!*
SLCCH
OH, YOU'RE *WET*, POOR DEAR...
AHH! *GOZEN-SAMA!*
PLEASE, O-TAMA? WAIT FOR ME BY THE RIVER SANZU? AFTER I'VE KILLED LONE WOLF, I'LL FOLLOW YOU THERE.
THE YAGYŪ ARE AFTER ME. I'M DOOMED TO DIE. YET WE HAVE TO BUY TIME, *TOGETHER...*

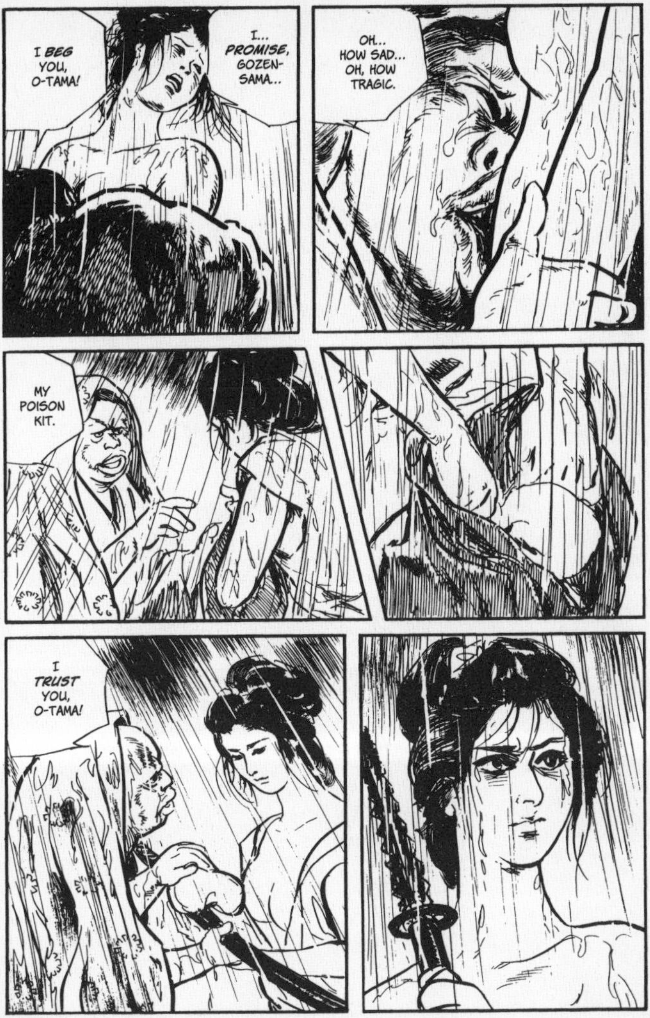
I BEG YOU, O-TAMA!
I... PROMISE, GOZEN-SAMA...
OH... HOW SAD... OH, HOW TRAGIC.
MY POISON KIT.
I TRUST YOU, O-TAMA!

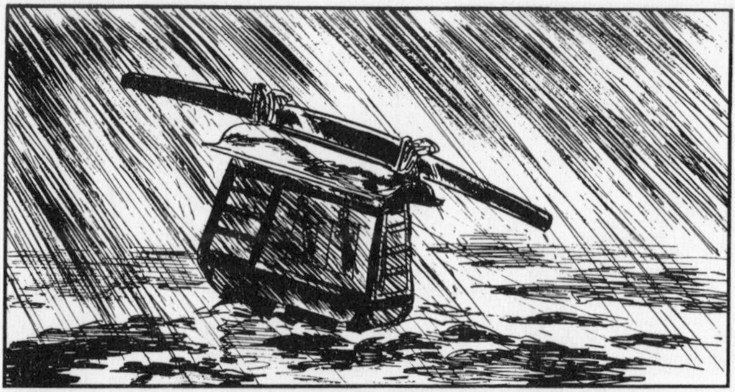
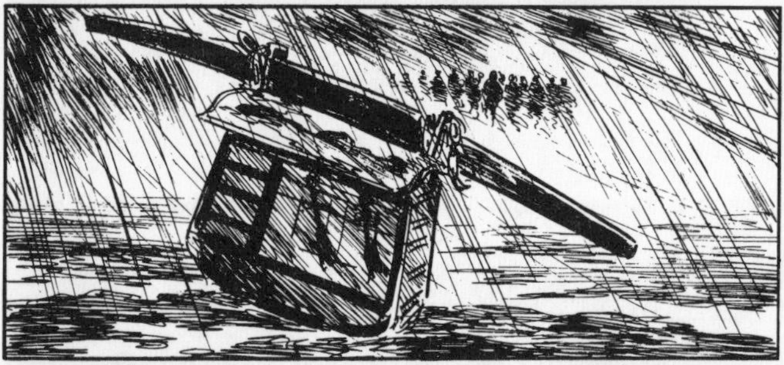
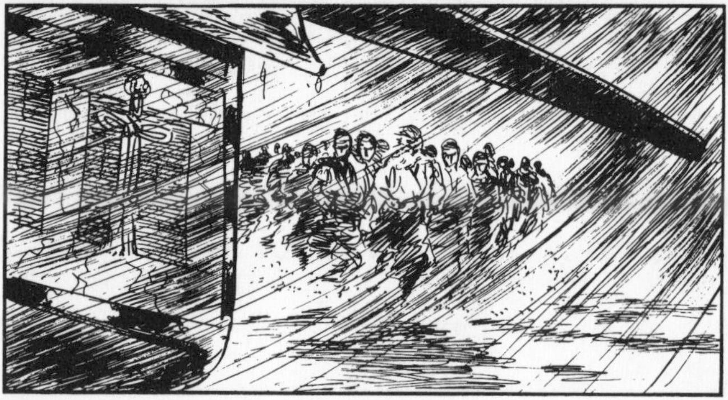

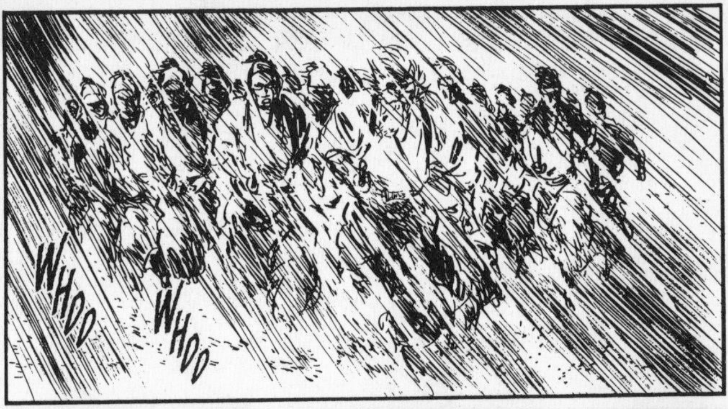
WHOO
WHOO

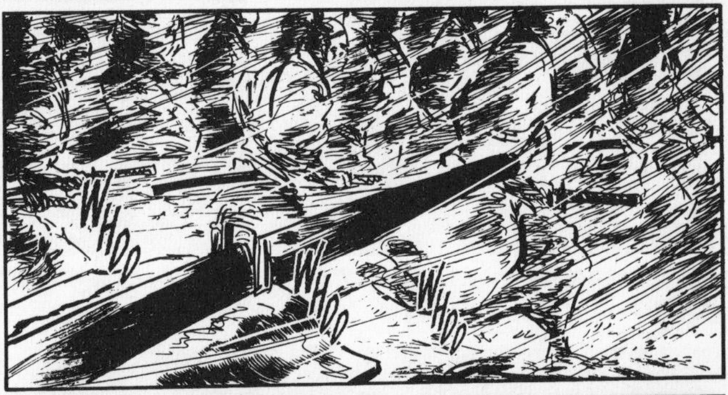
WHOO
WHOO
WHOO

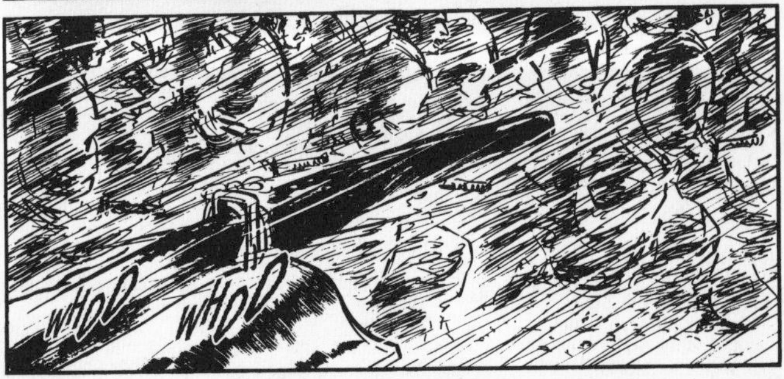
WHOO
WHOO

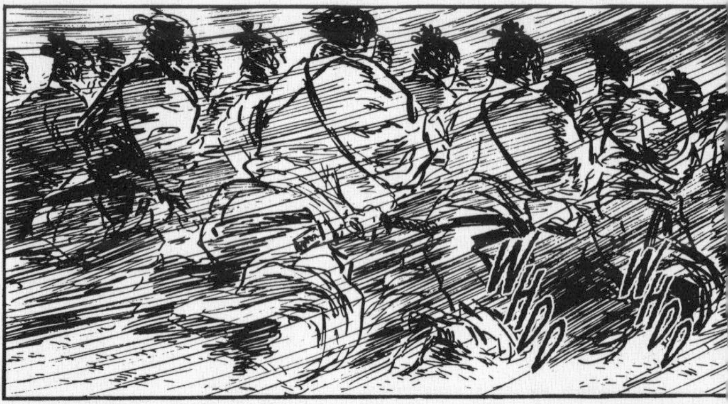
WHOO
WHOO

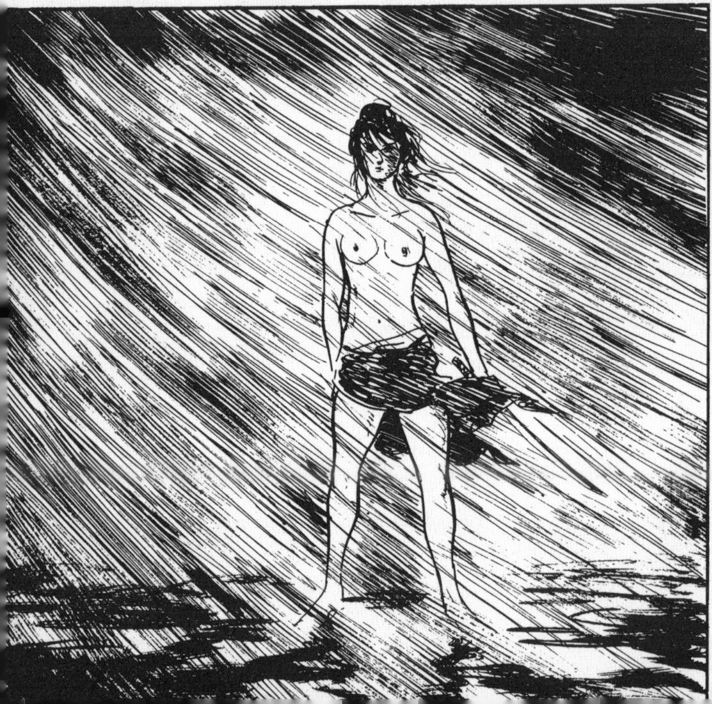

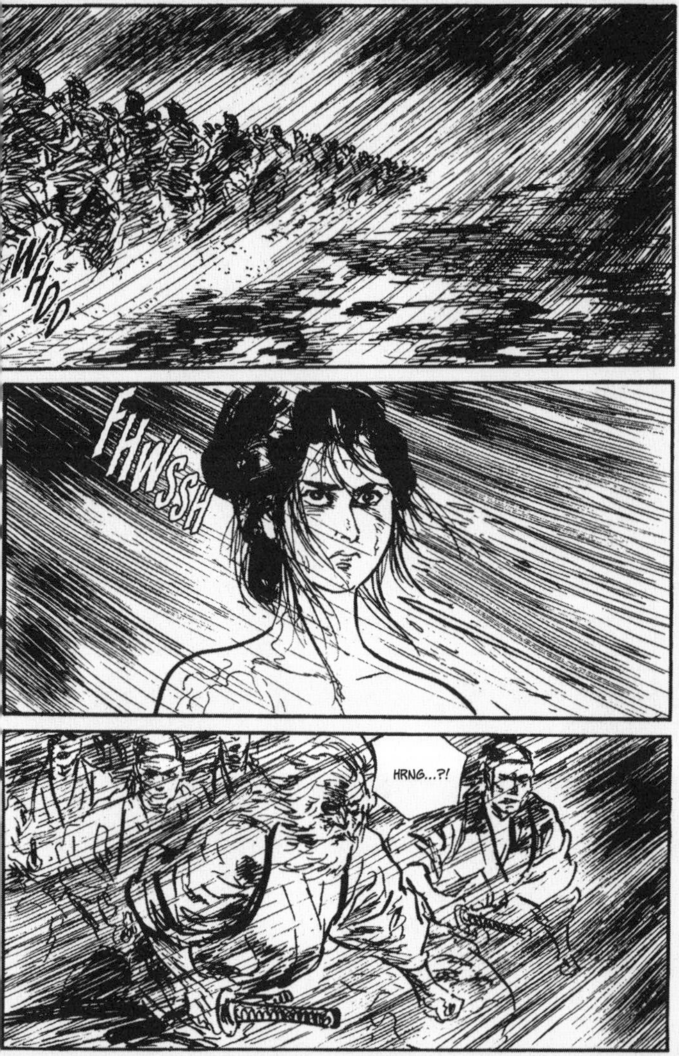
WHOO
FHWSSH
HRNG...?!

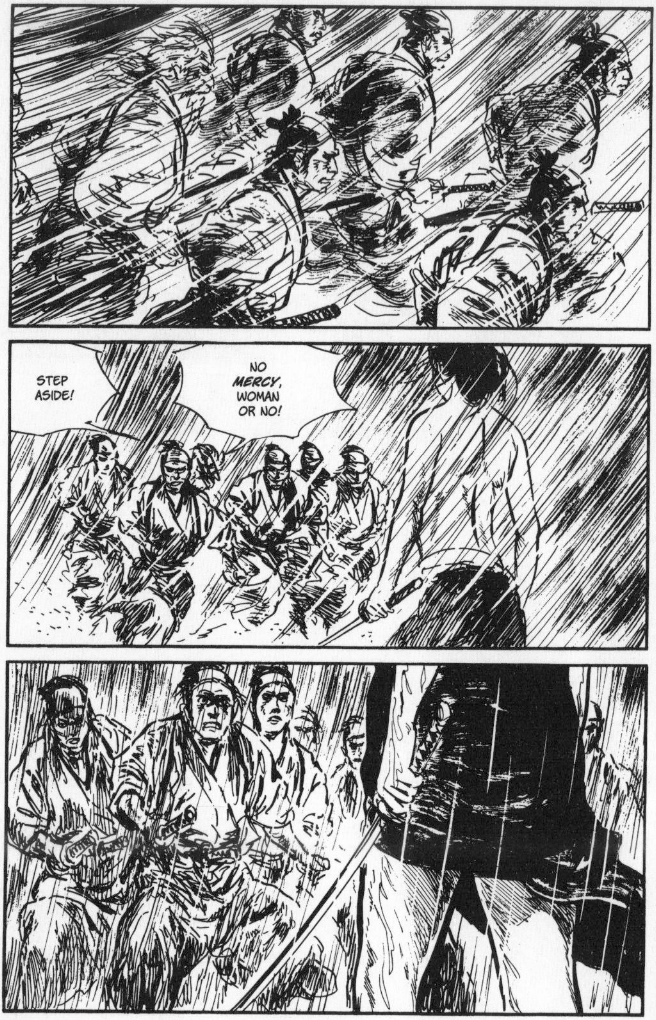
NO MERCY, WOMAN OR NO!
STEP ASIDE!

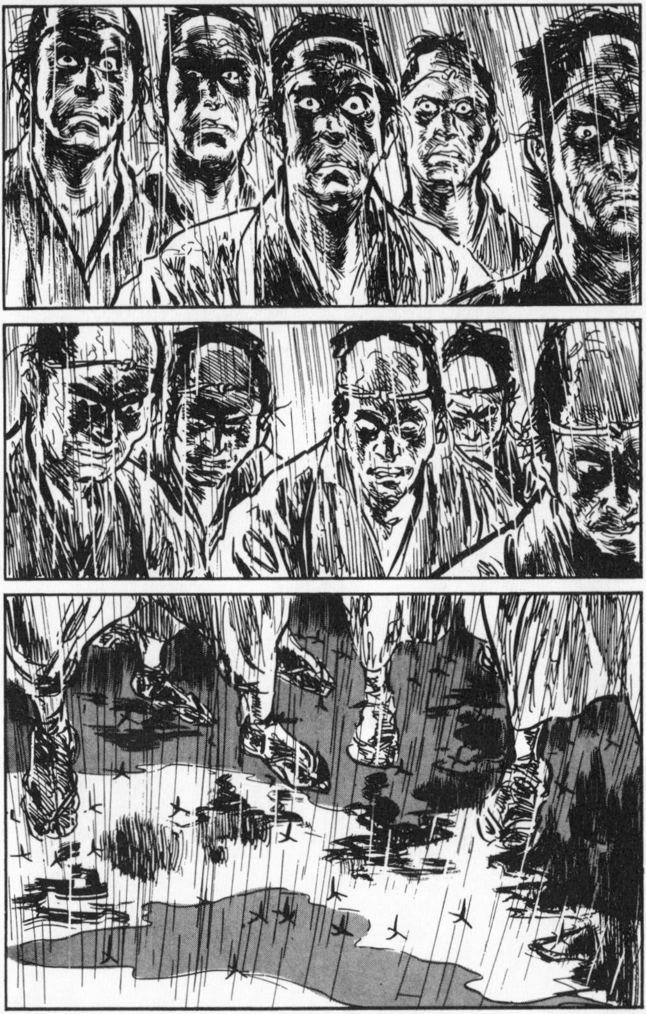

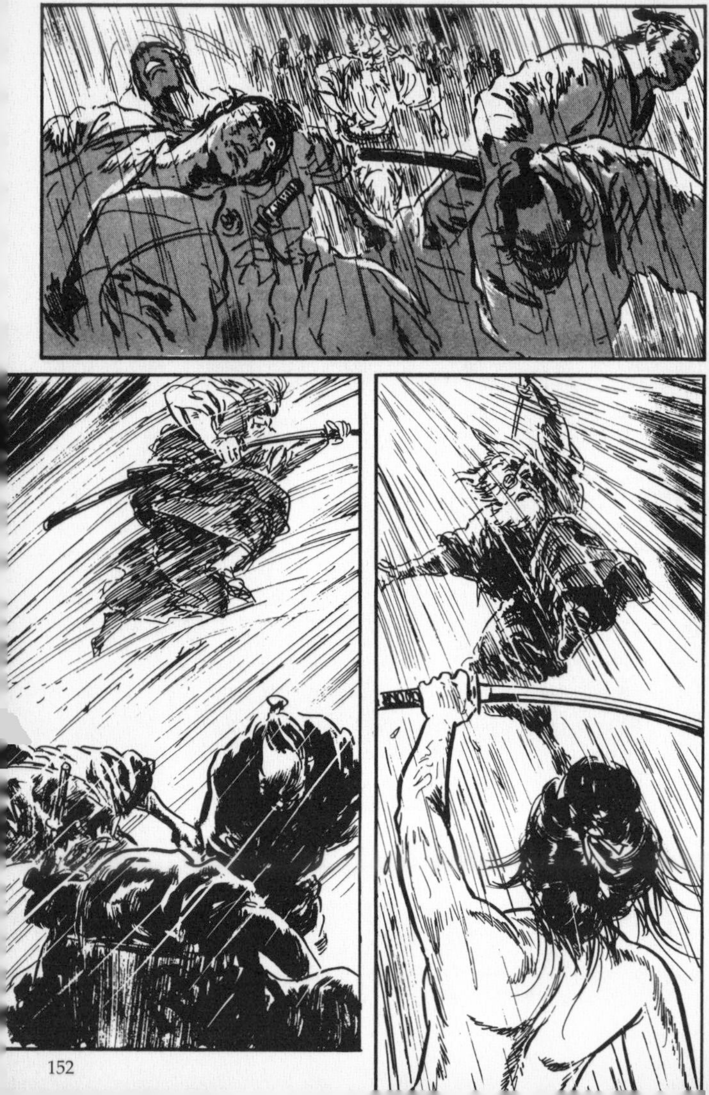

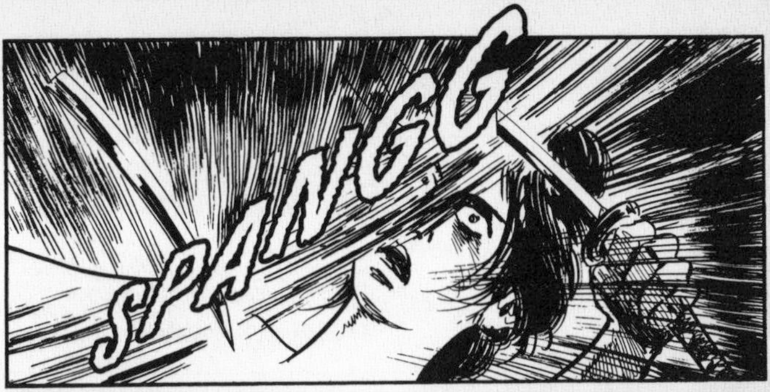
SPANGG
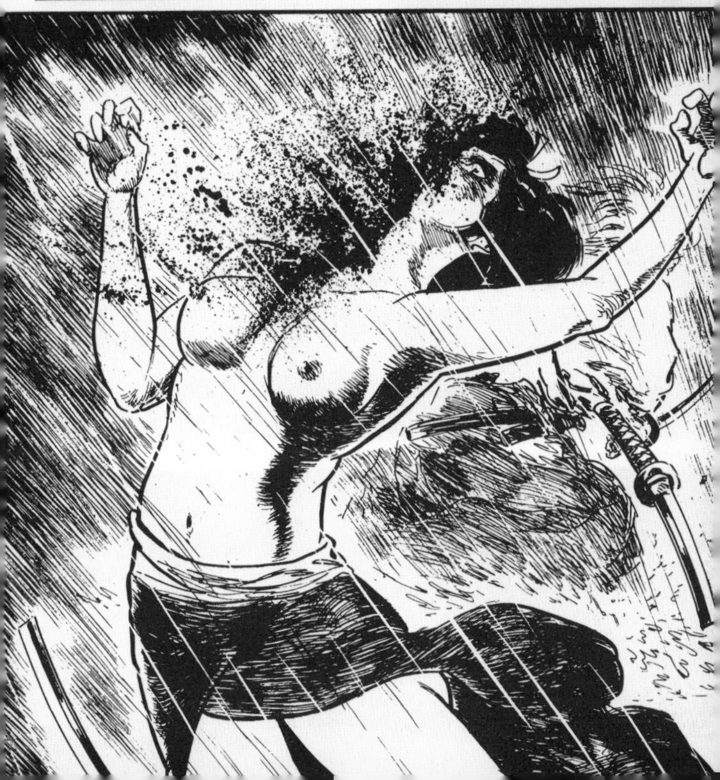

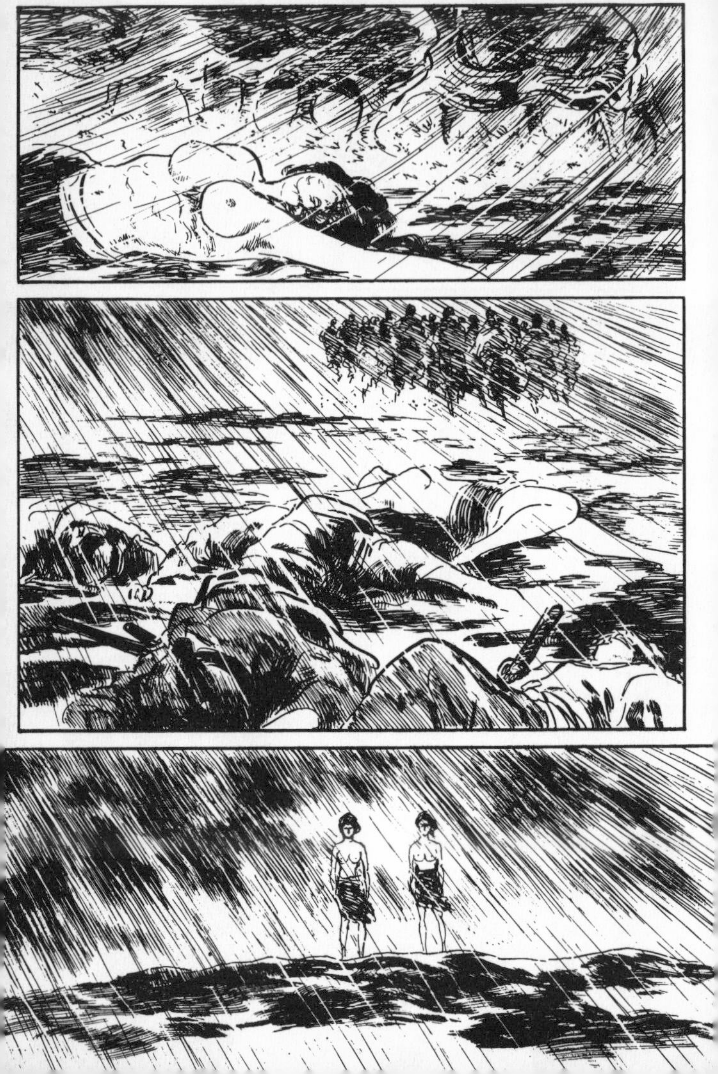

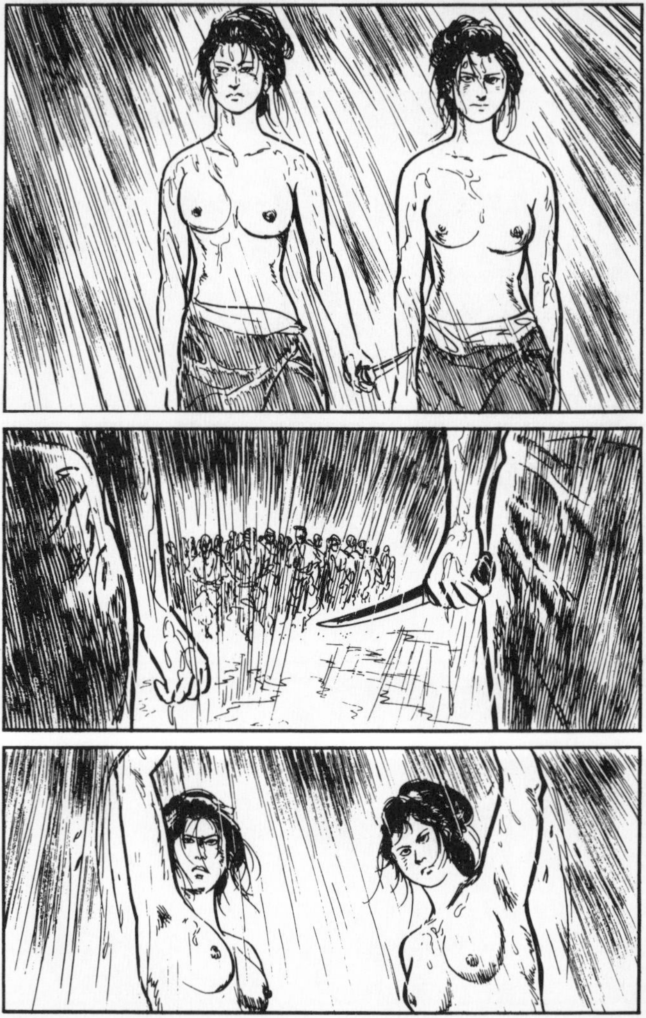

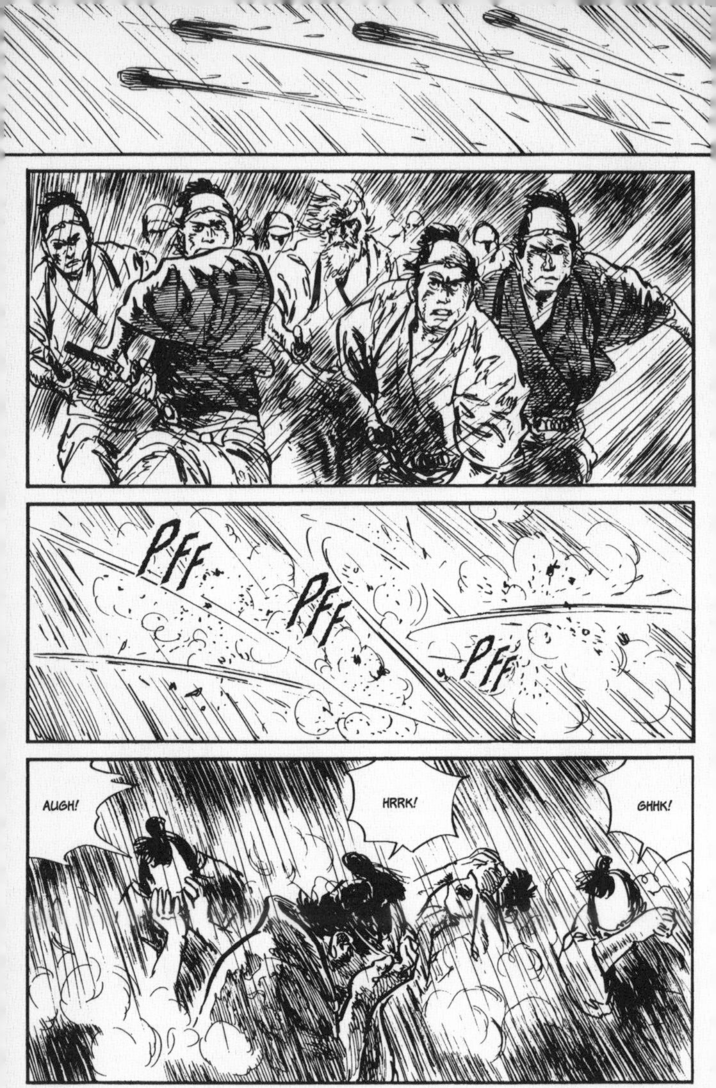
PFF
PFF
PFF
GHHK!
HRRK!
AUGH!

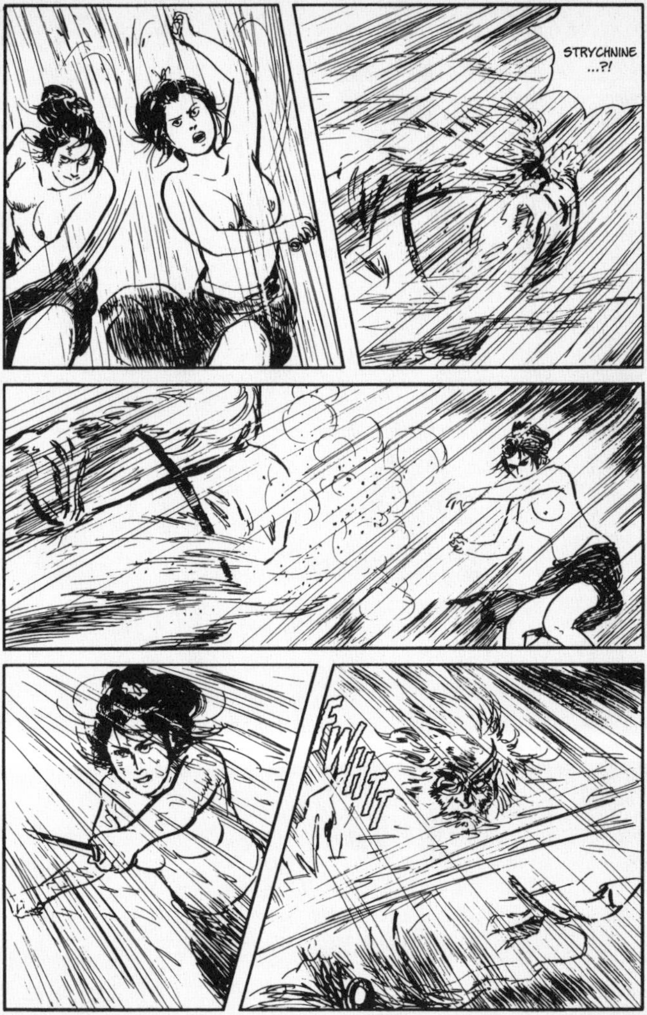
STRYCHNINE ...?!
FWHTT

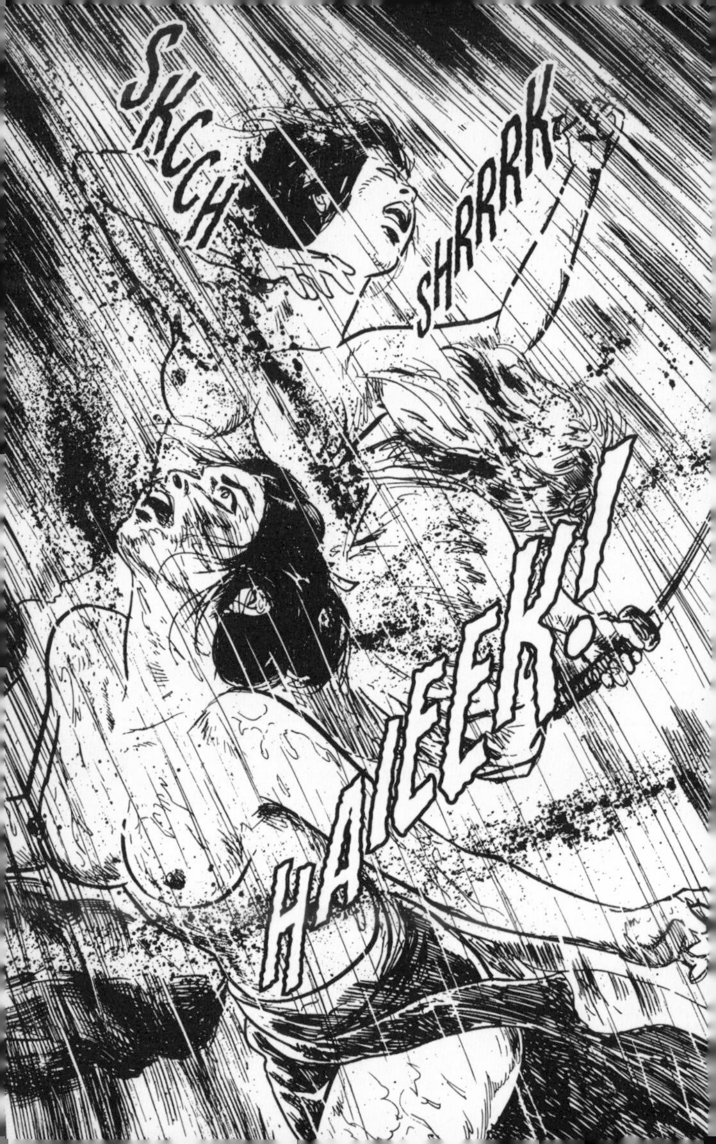
SHRRRK
SKCCH
HAIEEK!

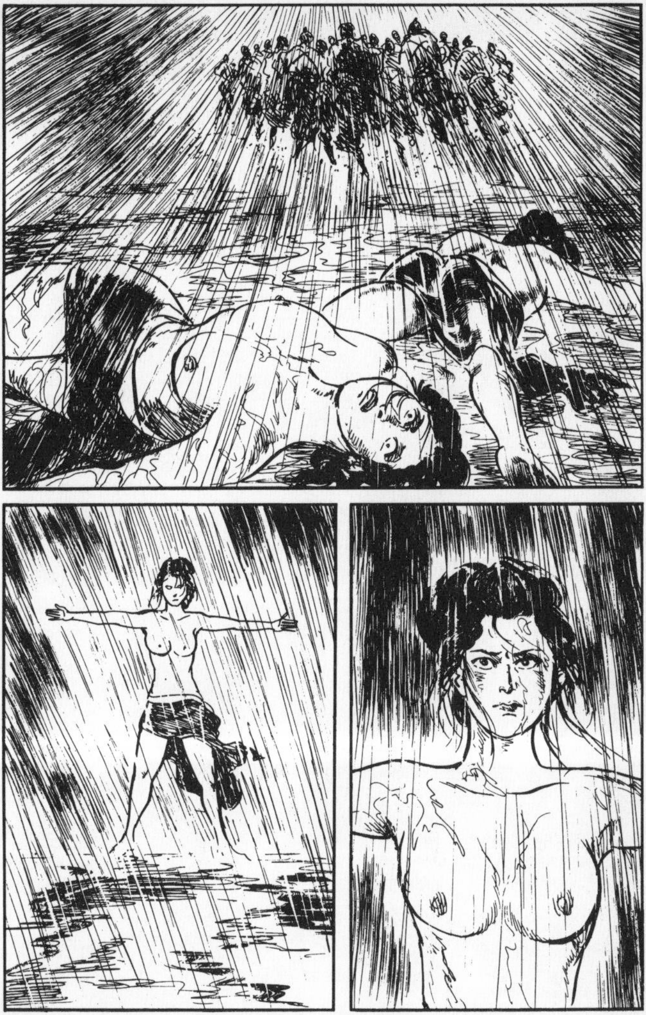

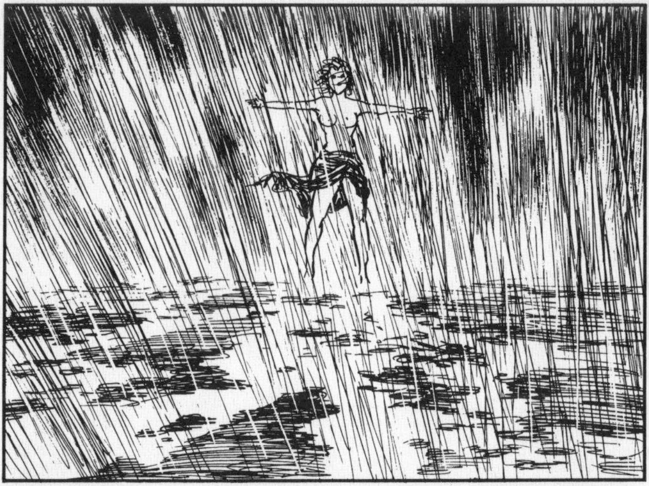
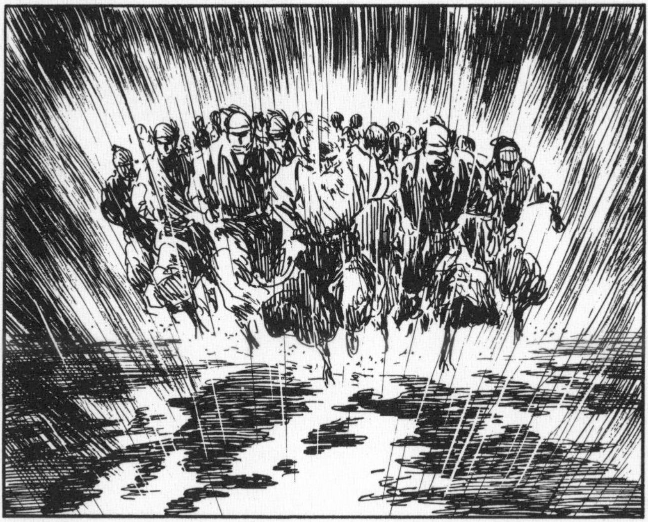

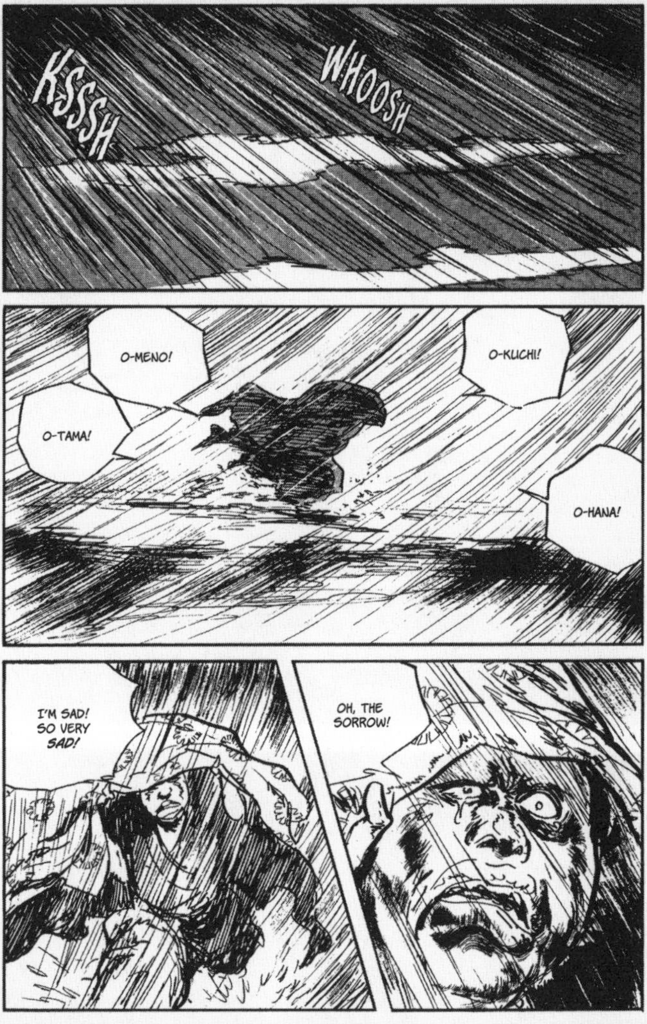
WHOOSH
KSSSH
O-KUCHI!
O-MENO!
O-HANA!
O-TAMA!
OH, THE SORROW!
I'M SAD! SO VERY SAD!

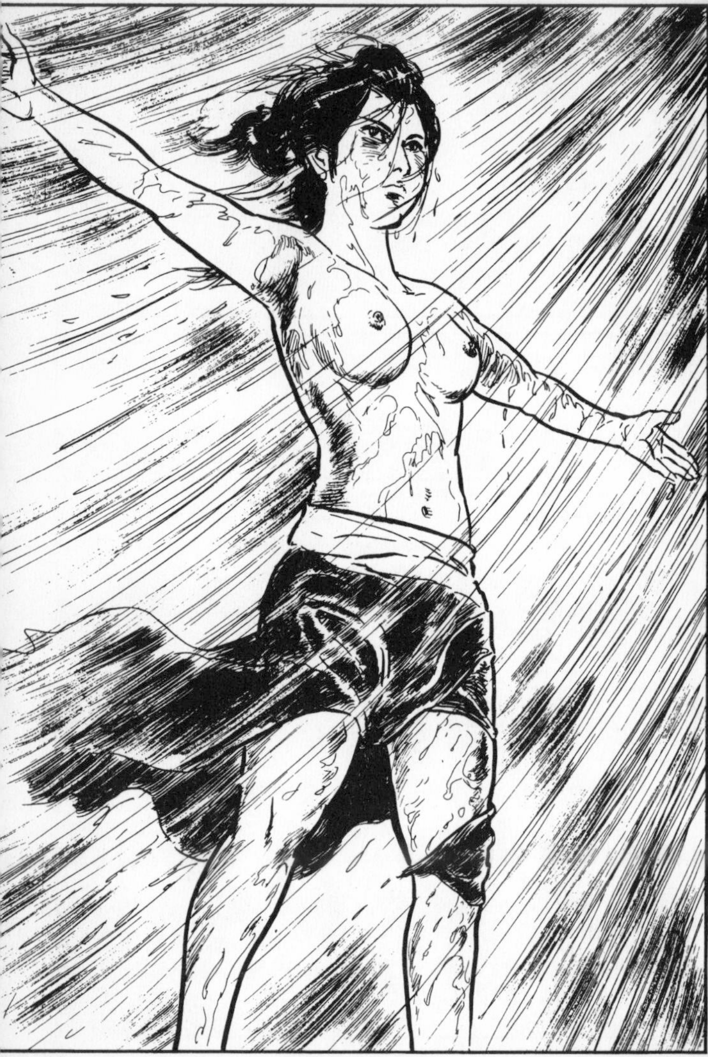

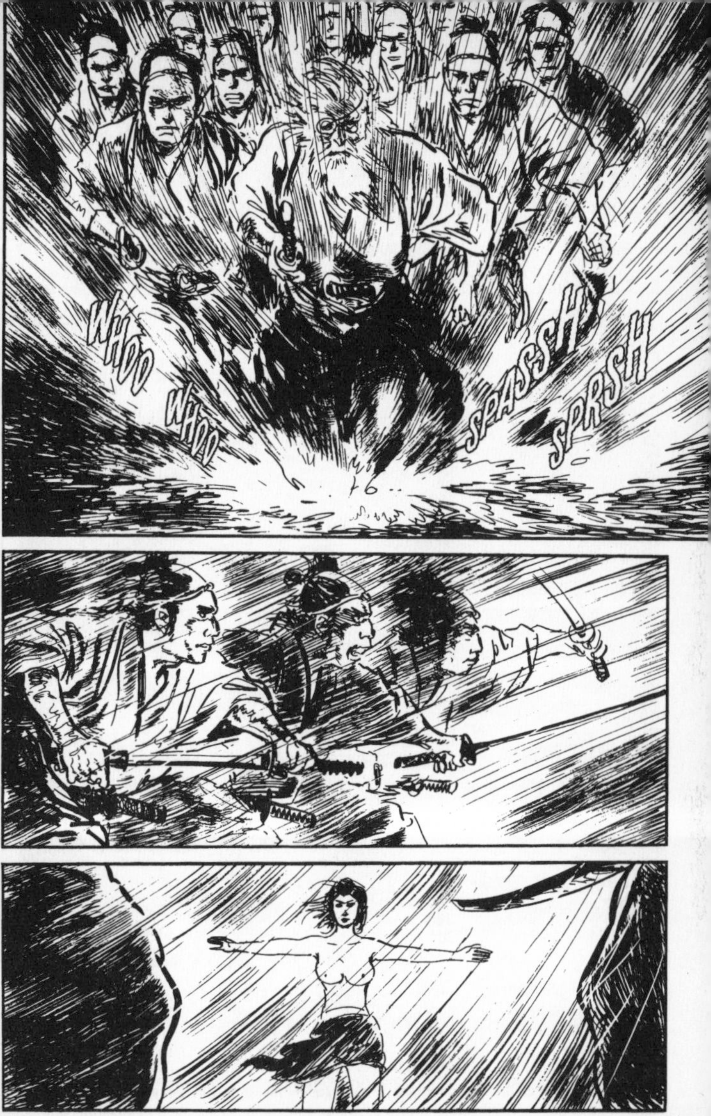
SPASSH
SPRSH
WHOO
WHOO

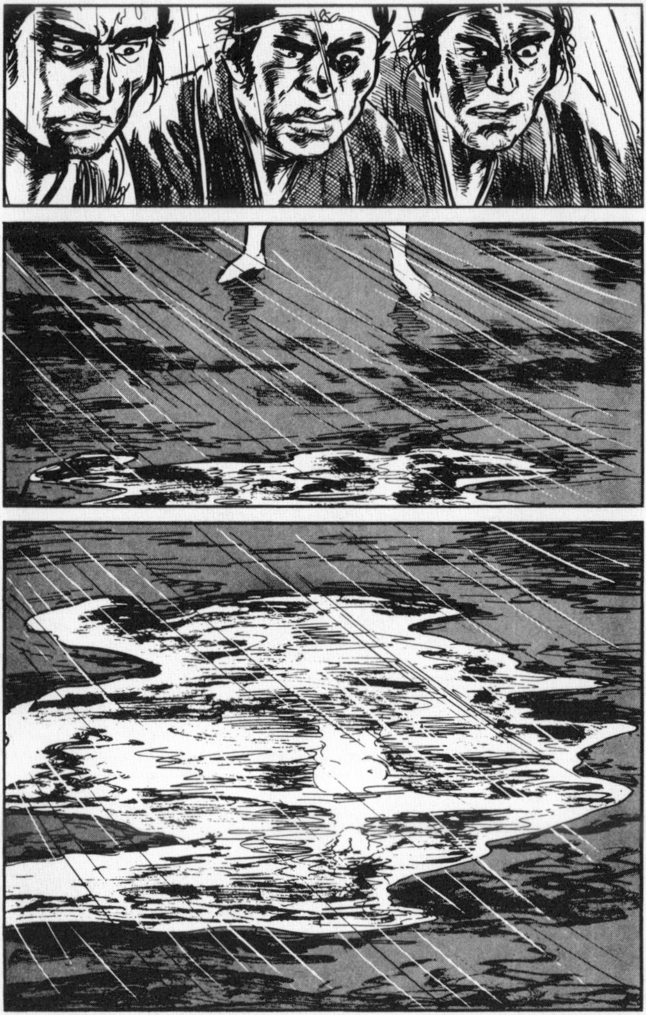

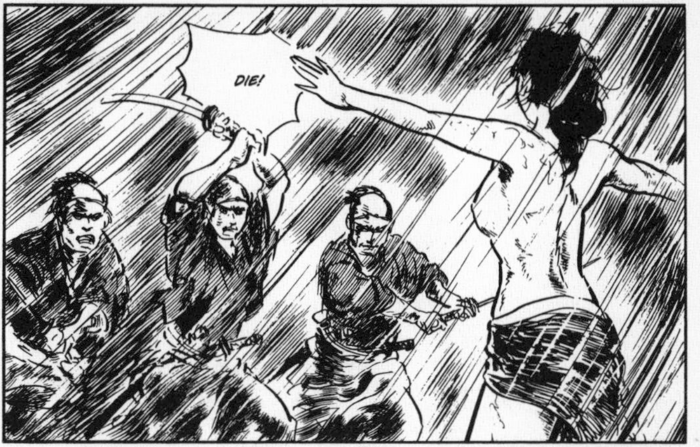
DIE!
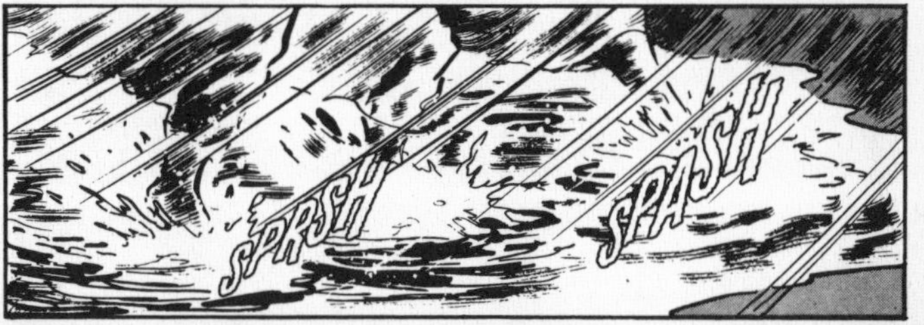
SPASH
SPRSH
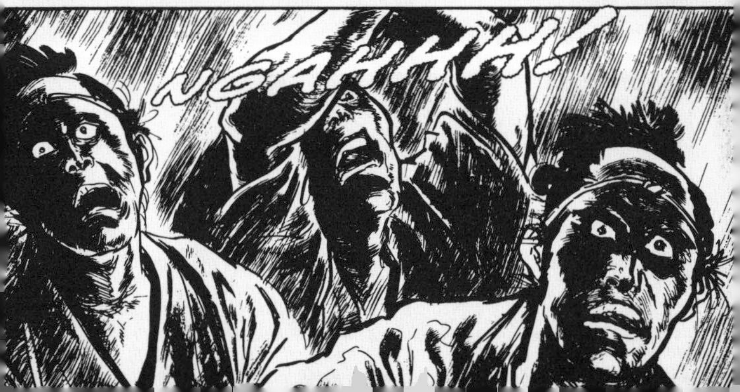
UGAHHH!!

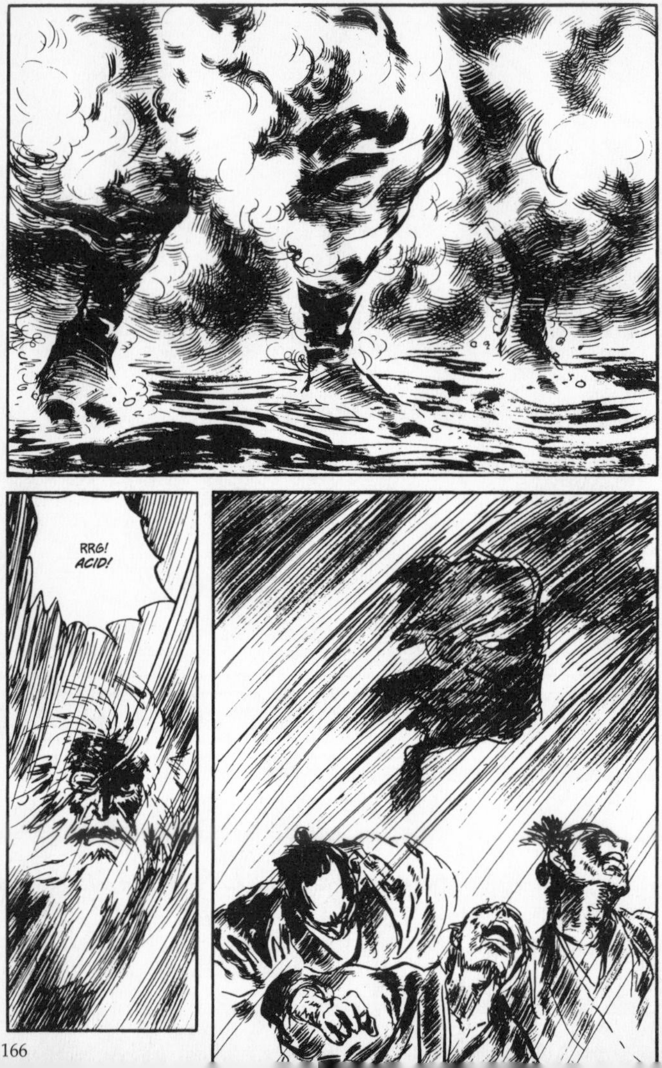
RRG!
ACID!

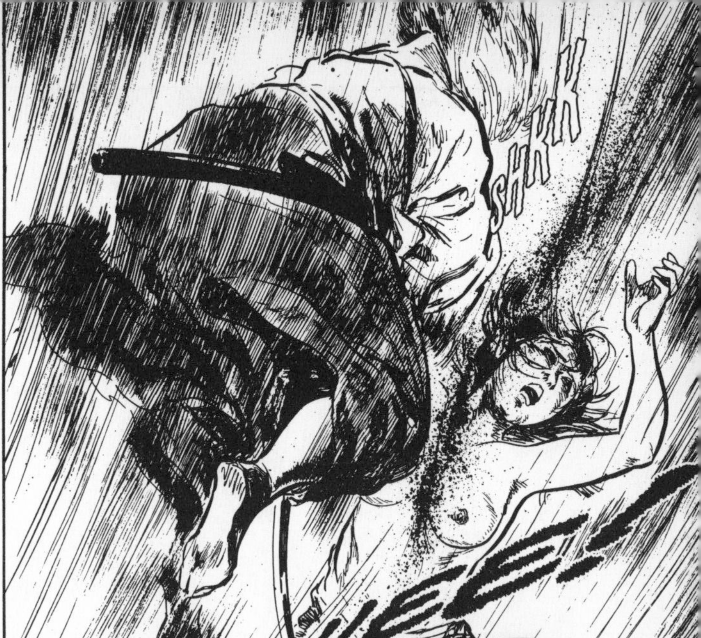
SHKK
HAIIEEE!!

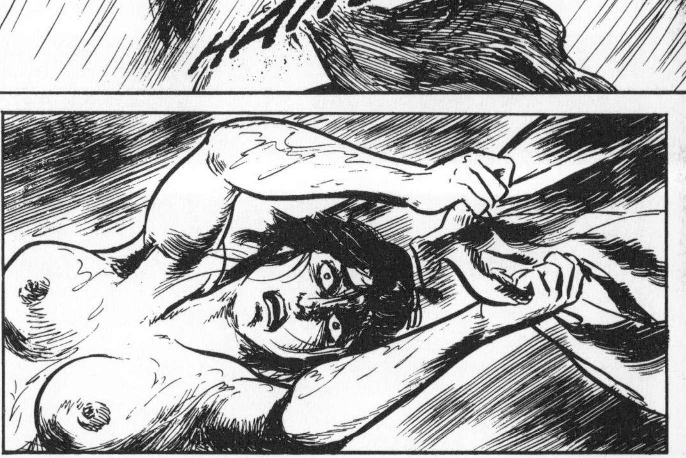

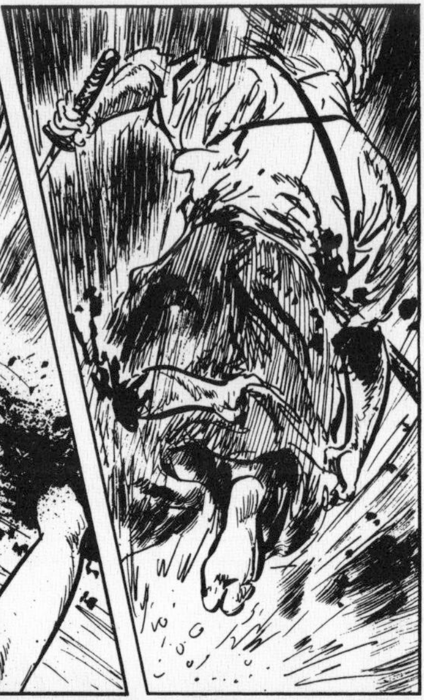
CHOKK
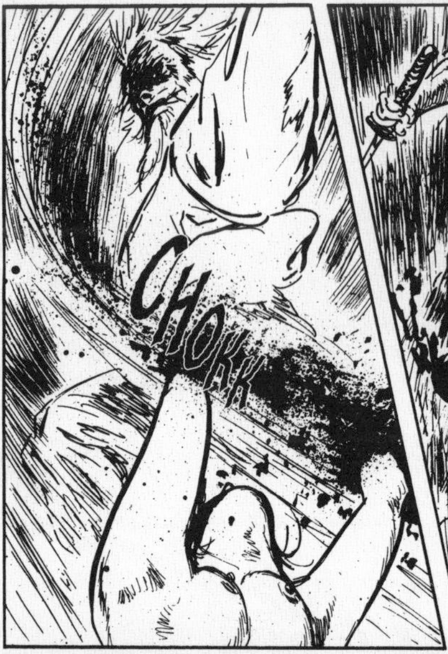
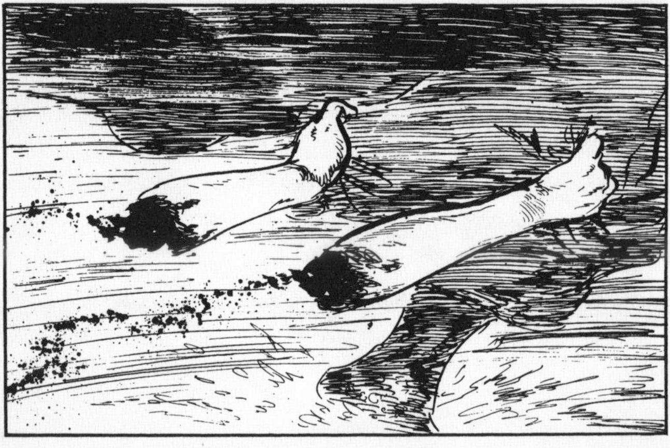

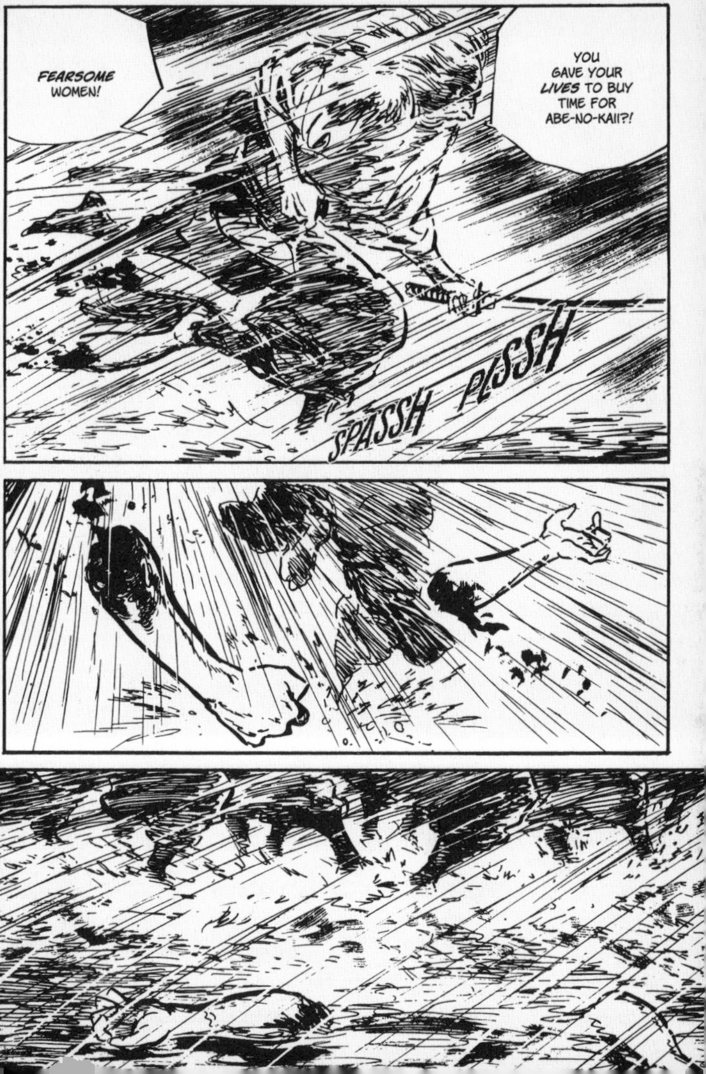
YOU GAVE YOUR *LIVES* TO BUY TIME FOR ABE-NO-KAII?!
FEARSOME WOMEN!
PLSSH
SPASSH

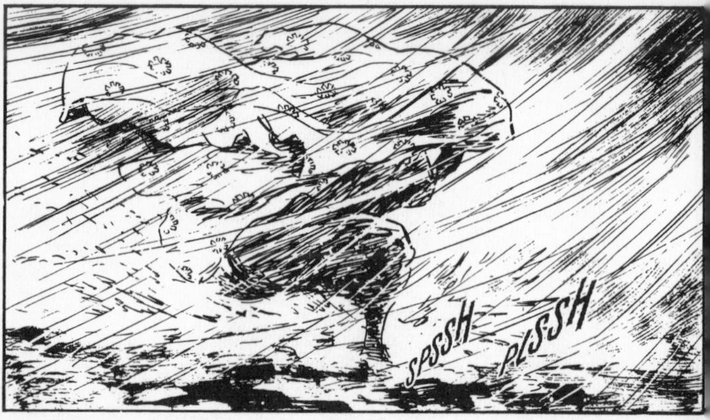
SPSSH
PLSSH

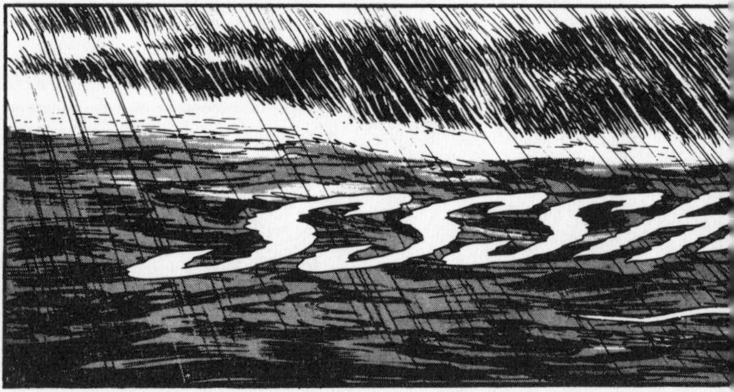
SSSH

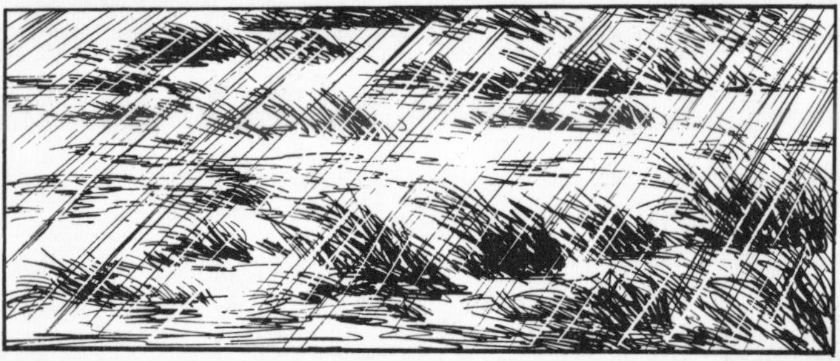

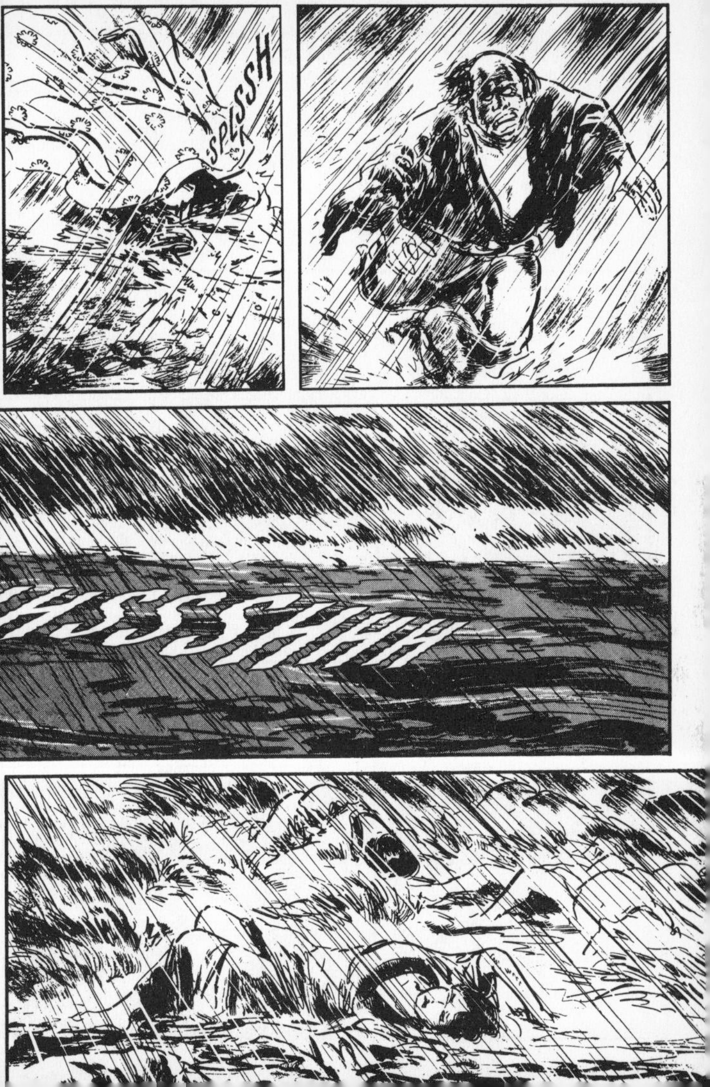
SPLSSSH
HSSHHH

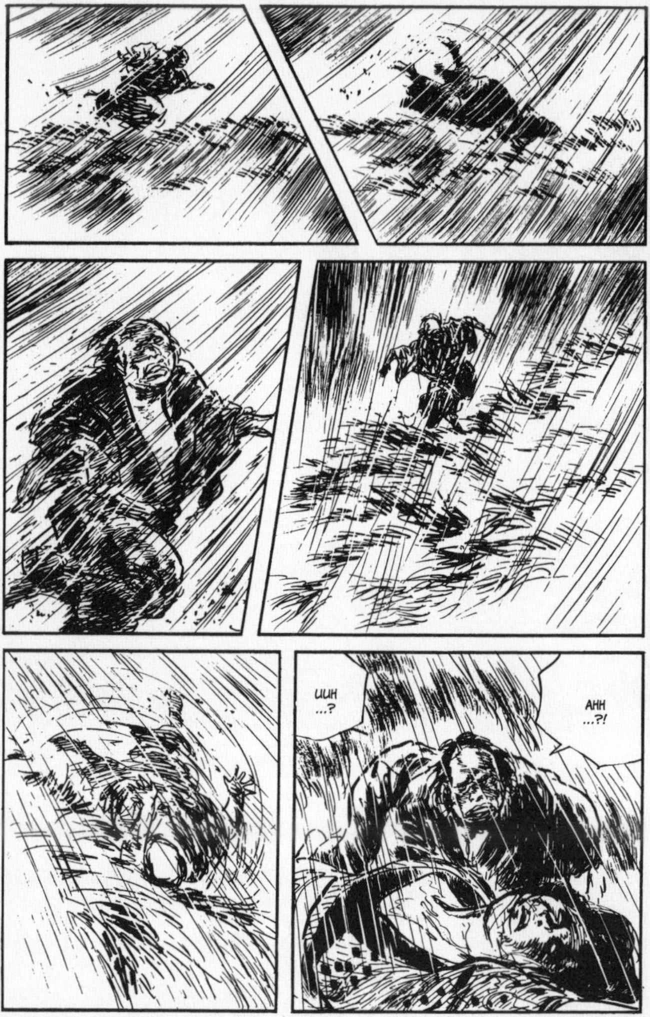
AHH ...?!
UUH ...?

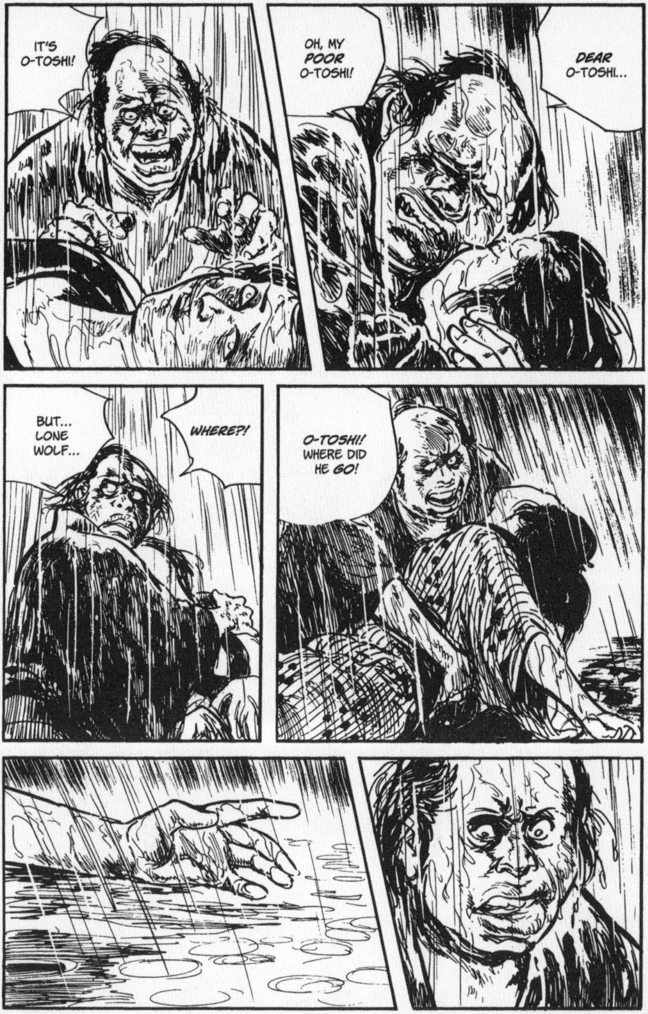
IT'S O-TOSHI!
OH, MY POOR O-TOSHI!
DEAR O-TOSHI...
BUT... LONE WOLF...
WHERE?!
O-TOSHI! WHERE DID HE GO!

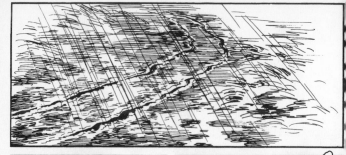

OHH!!
THANK YOU,
O-TOSHI!

YOU
SERVE ME
ALWAYS,
EVEN IN
DEATH!

RMMBBB

BLSSSH

RMMBB

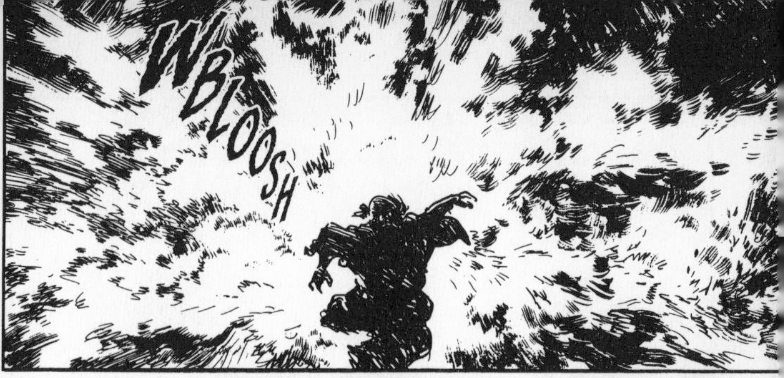
WBLOOSH

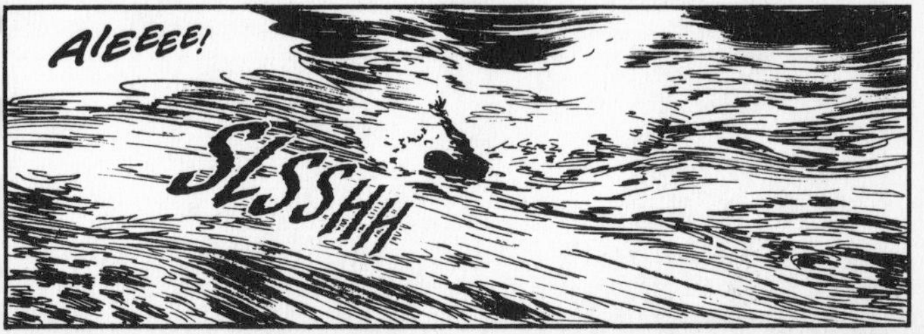
AIEEEE!
SLSSHH

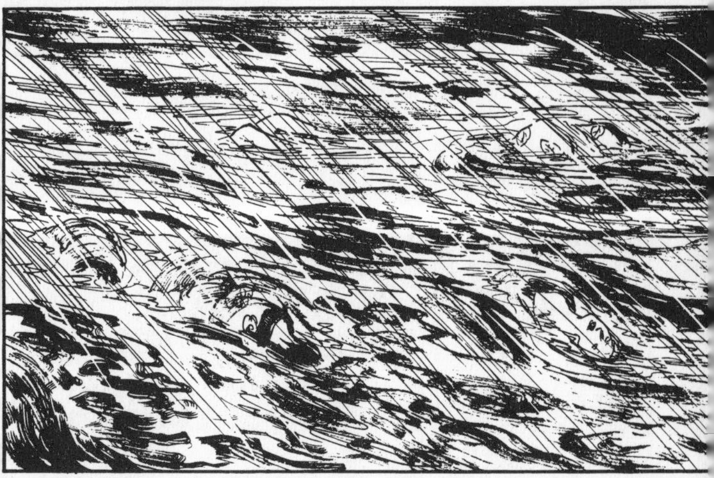

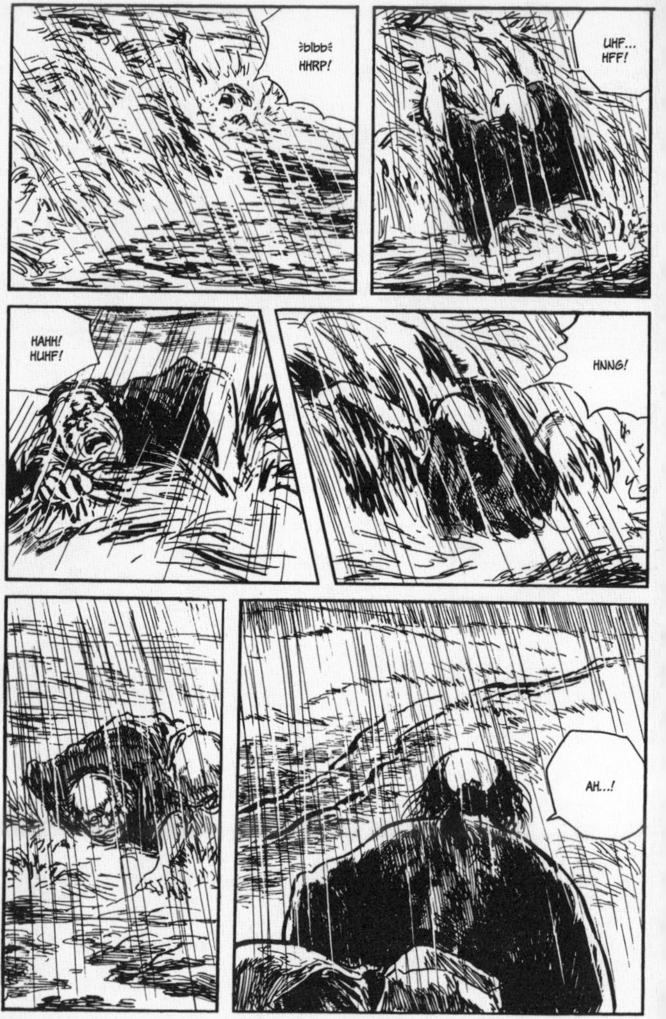
UHF... HFF!
blbb HHRP!
HNNG!
HAHH! HUHF!
AH...!

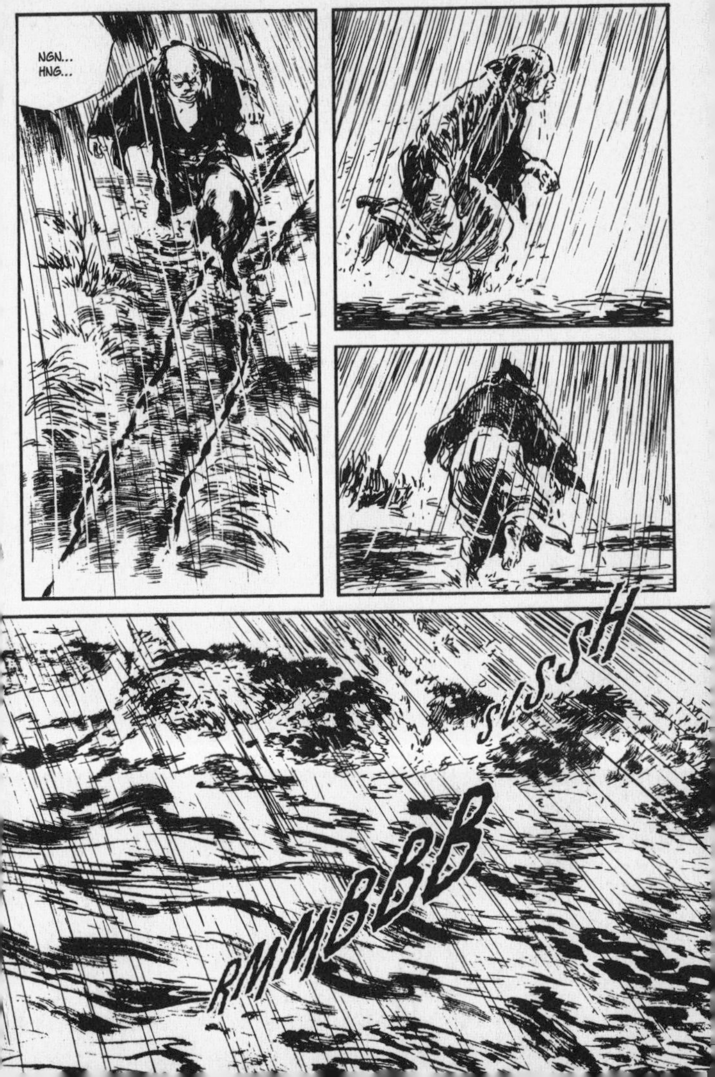
NGN... HNG...
SLSSH
RMMBBB

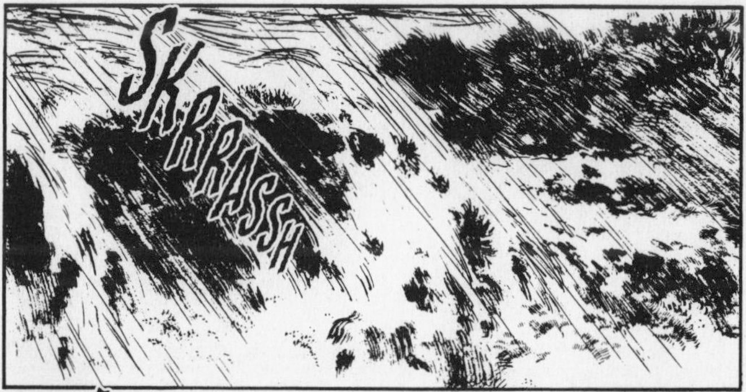
SKRASSH

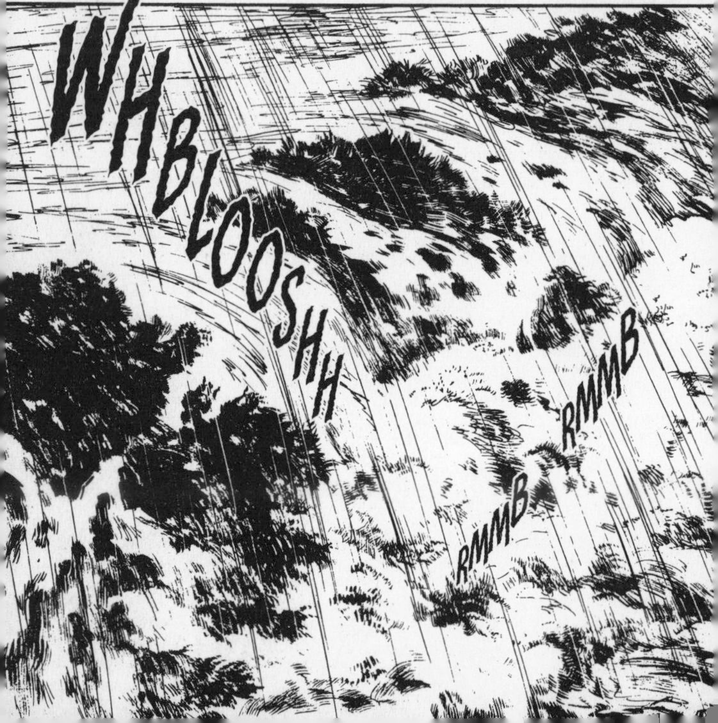
WHBLOOSHH
RMMB
RMMB

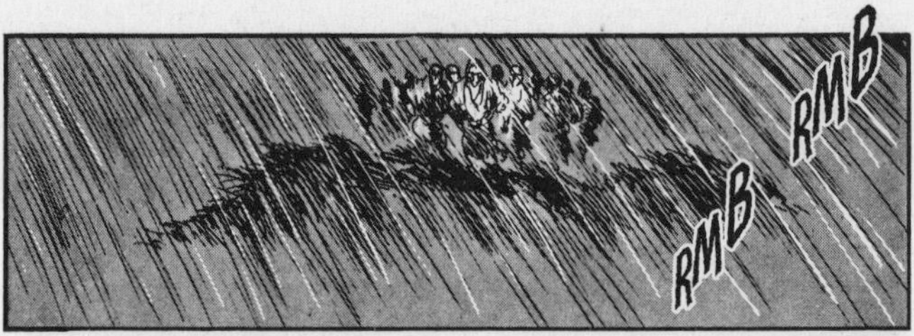
RMB
RMB
RMB
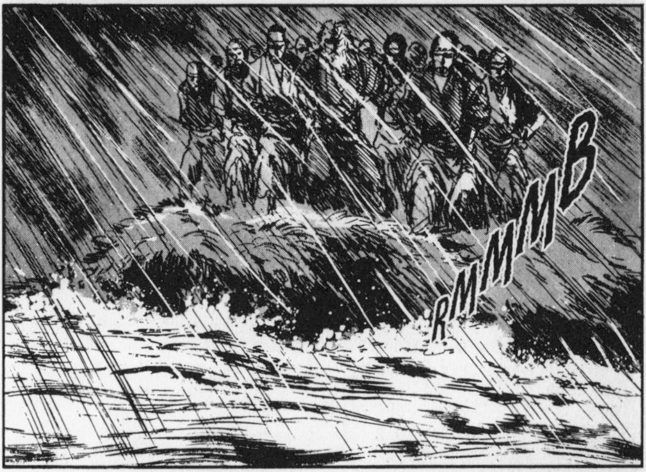
RMMMB
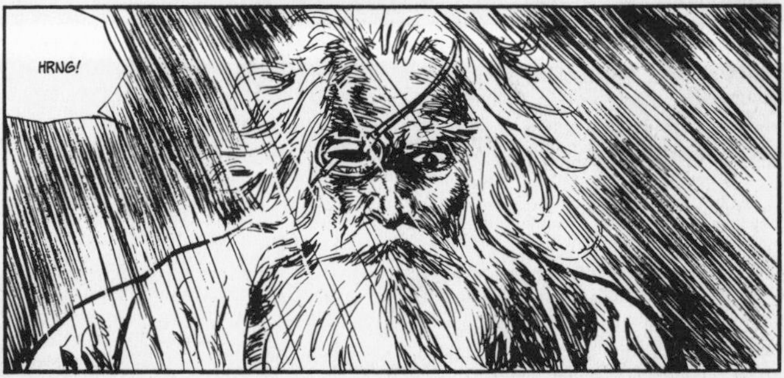
HRNG!

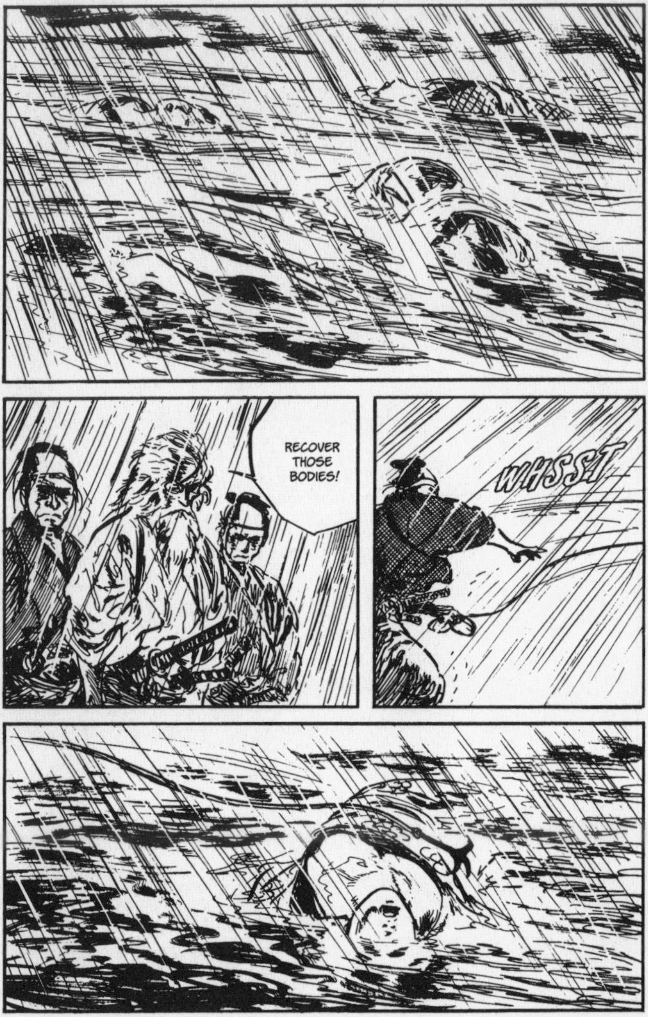
WHSST
RECOVER THOSE BODIES!

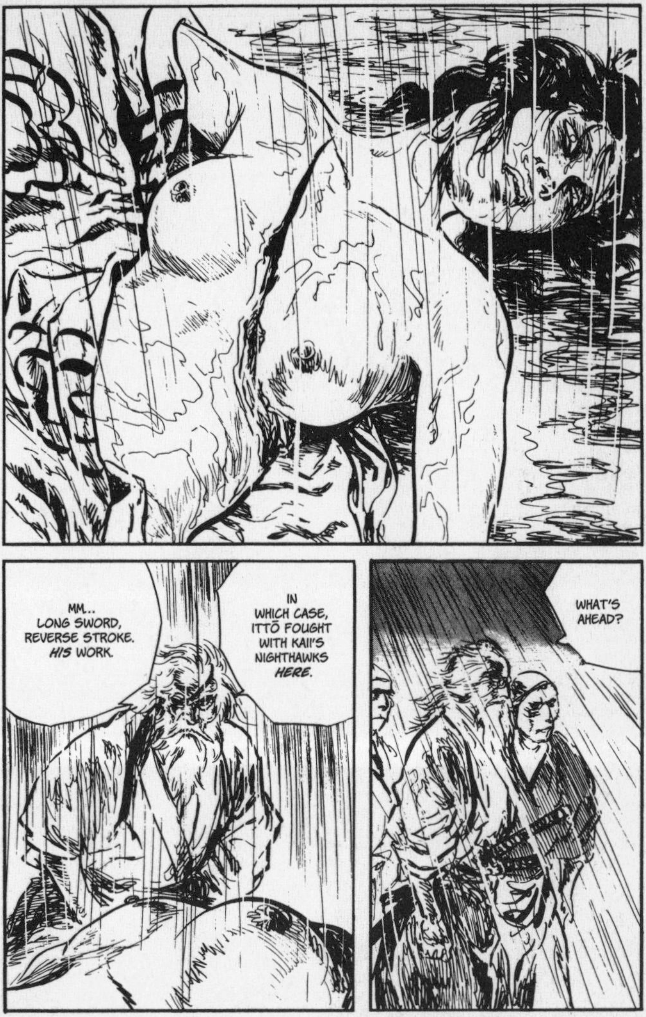
MM.. LONG SWORD, REVERSE STROKE. *HIS* WORK.
IN WHICH CASE, ITTŌ FOUGHT WITH KAII'S NIGHTHAWKS *HERE*.
WHAT'S AHEAD?

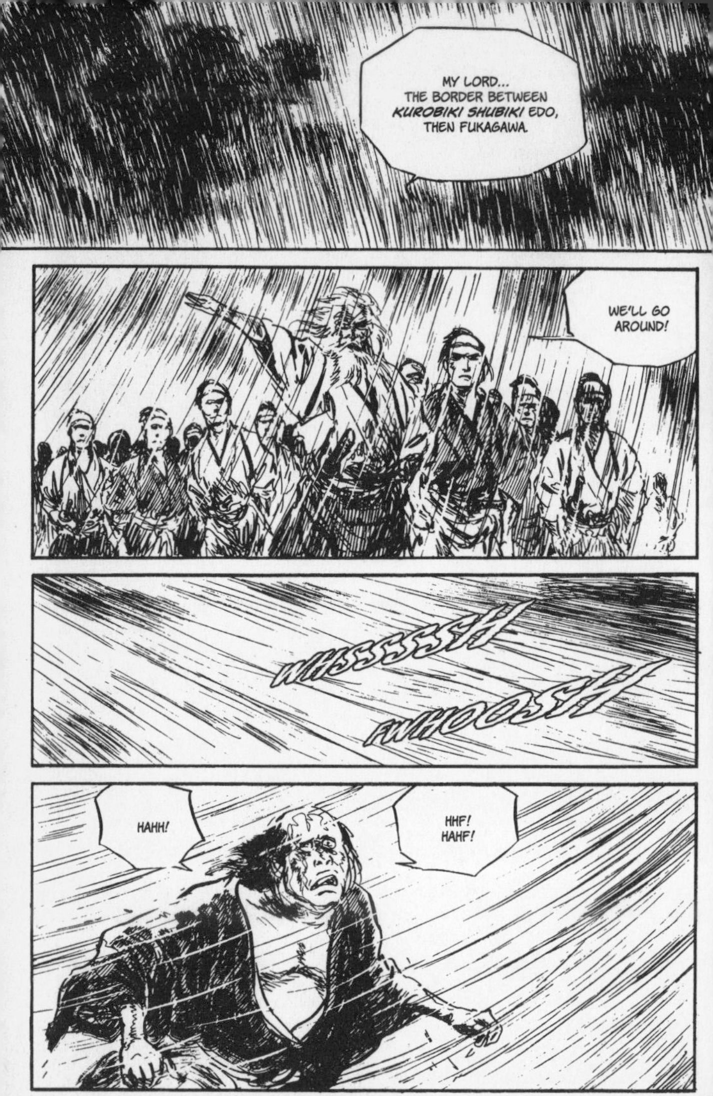
MY LORD... THE BORDER BETWEEN KUROBIKI SHUBIKI EDO, THEN FUKAGAWA.
WE'LL GO AROUND!
WHSSSSSH
FWHOOSH
HHF! HAHF!
HAHH!

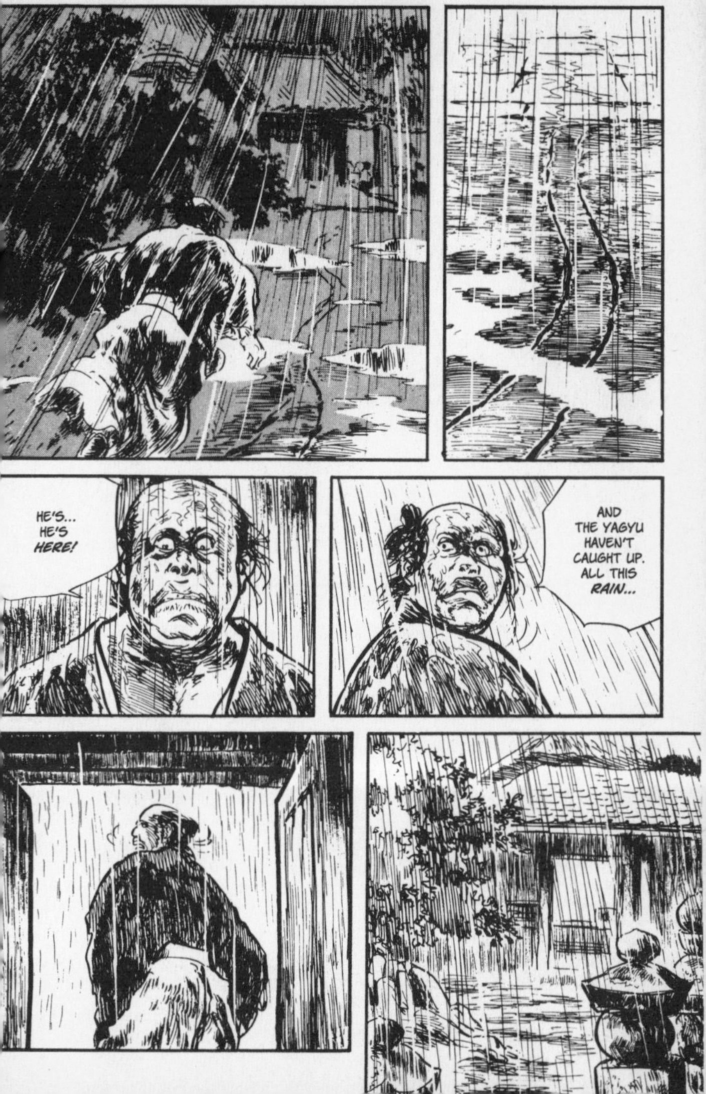
HE'S... HE'S *HERE!*
AND THE YAGYU HAVEN'T CAUGHT UP. ALL THIS *RAIN...*

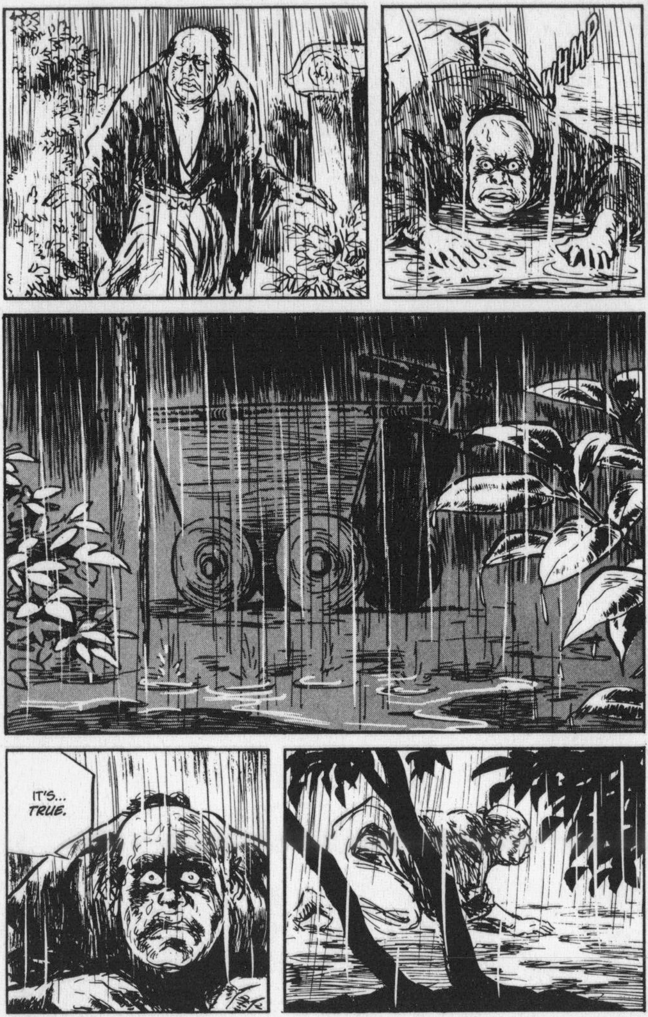
WHMP
IT'S... TRUE.

CHINK
TNK

TNK CHINK

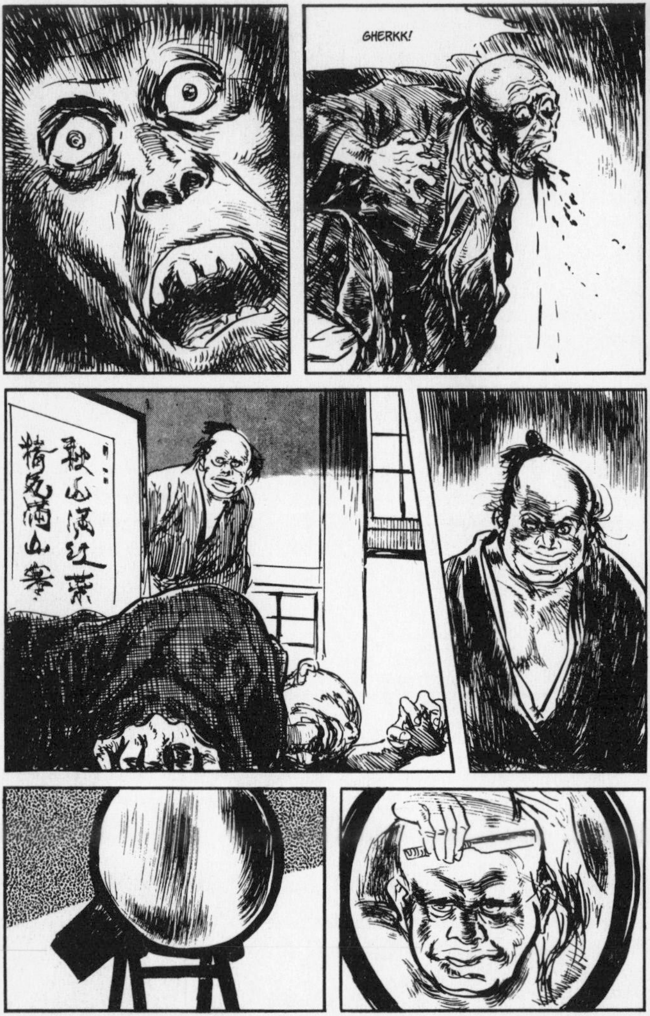
GHERKK!

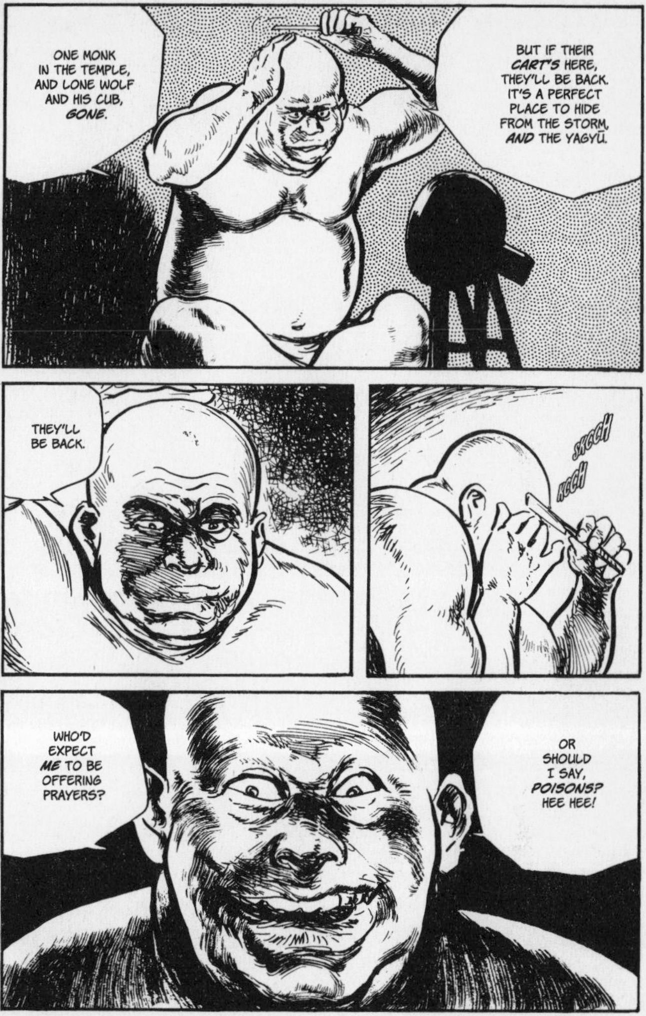
ONE MONK IN THE TEMPLE, AND LONE WOLF AND HIS CUB, *GONE.*
BUT IF THEIR *CART'S* HERE, THEY'LL BE BACK. IT'S A PERFECT PLACE TO HIDE FROM THE STORM, *AND* THE YAGYŪ.
THEY'LL BE BACK.
SKCCH
KCCH
WHO'D EXPECT *ME* TO BE OFFERING PRAYERS?
OR SHOULD I SAY, *POISONS?* HEE HEE!

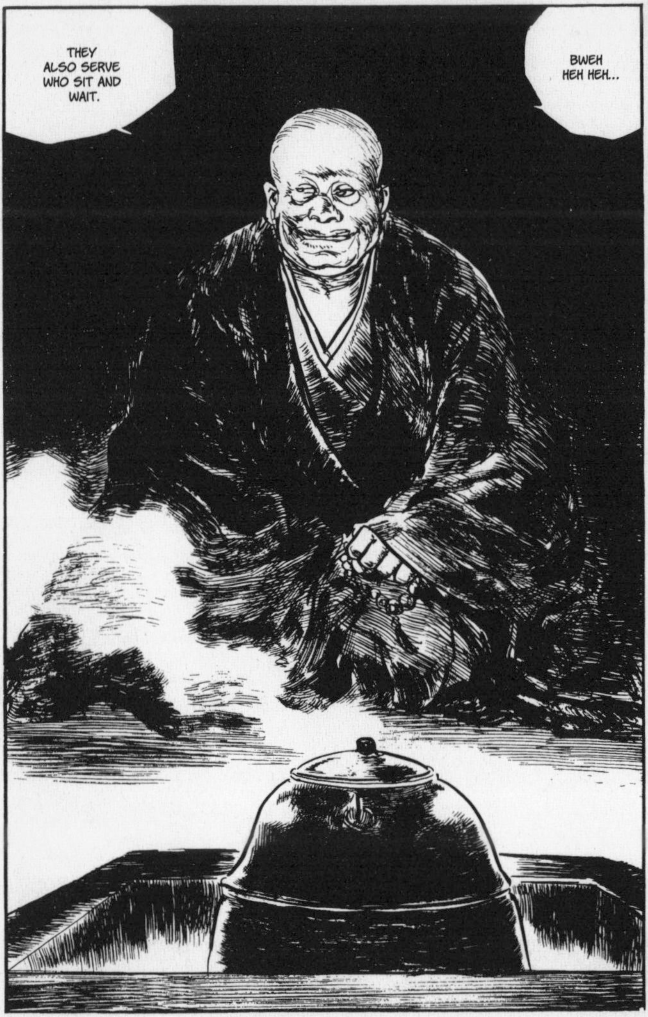
BWEH HEH HEH...
THEY ALSO SERVE WHO SIT AND WAIT.

the hundred
and sixth

Fragrance
of
Death

190

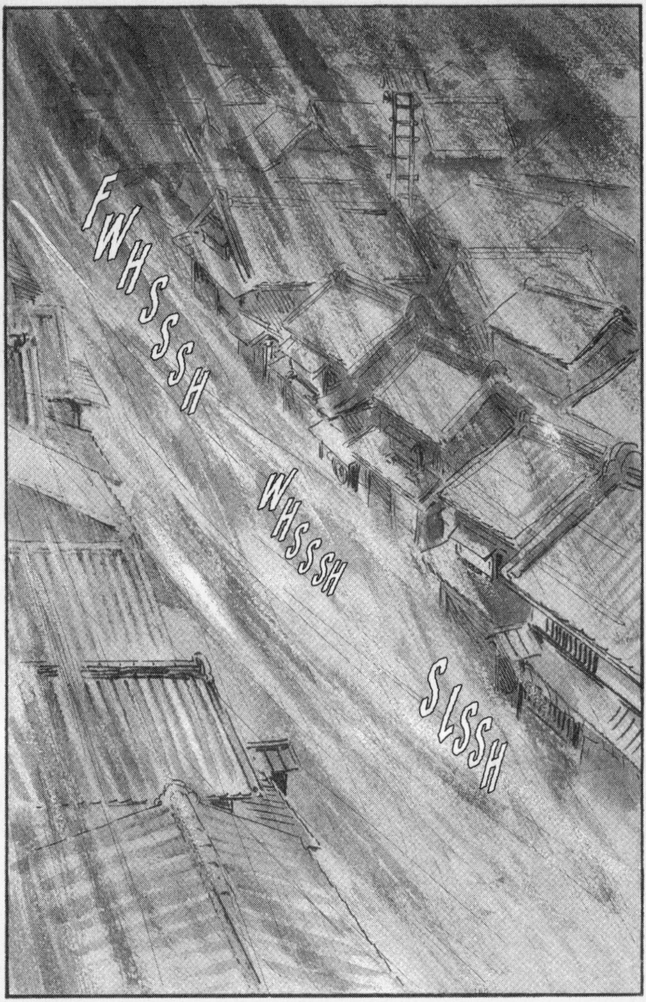
FWHSSSH
WHSSSH
SLSSH

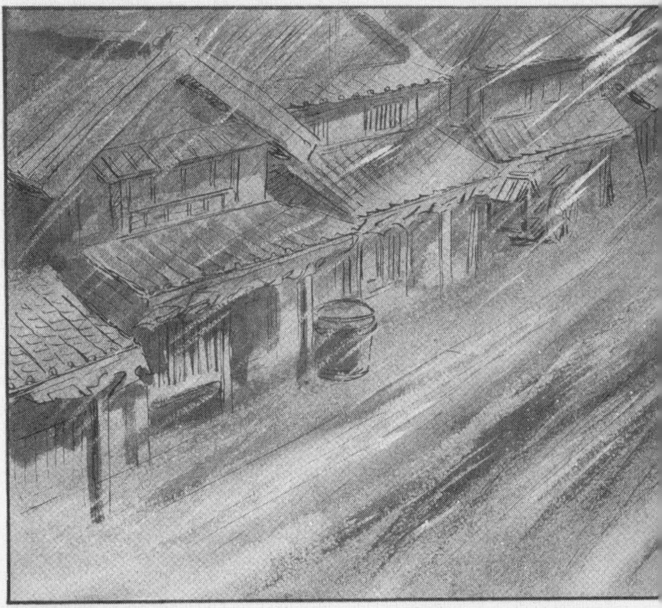

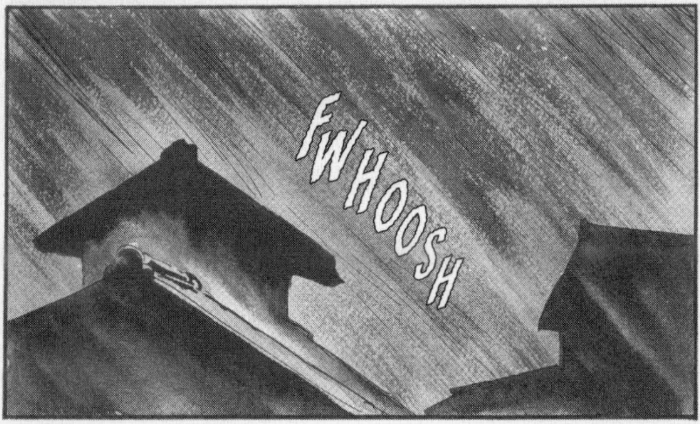
FWHOOSH

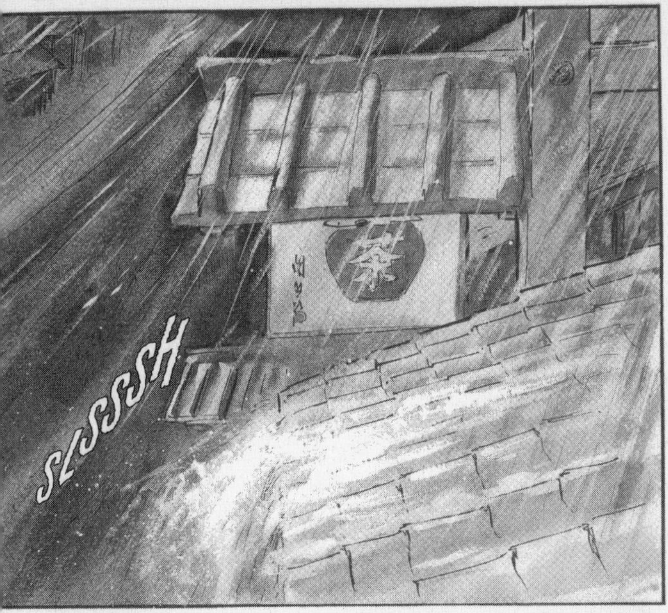
SLSSSSH

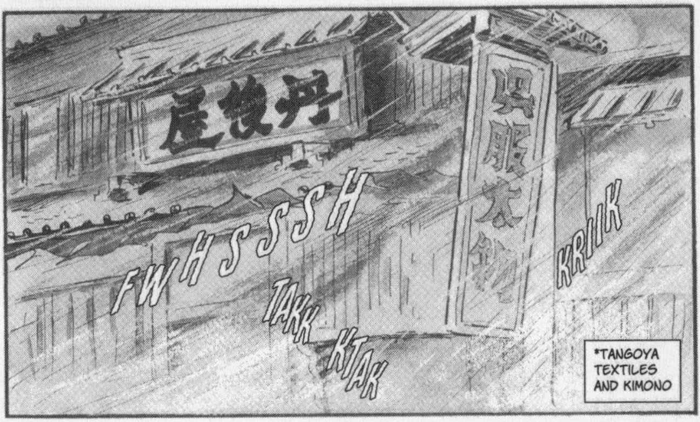
FWHSSSSH
TAKK
KTAK
KRIIK
*TANGOYA TEXTILES AND KIMONO

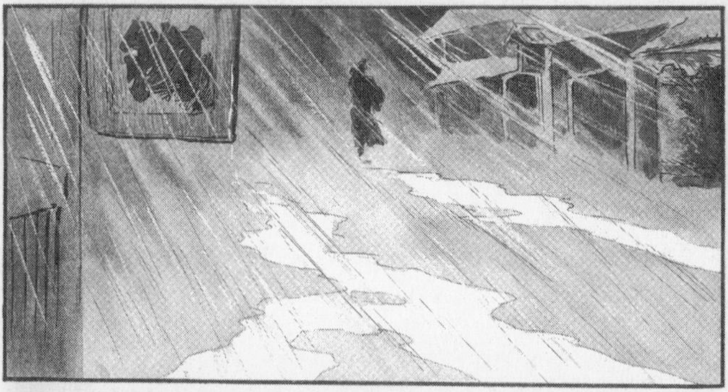
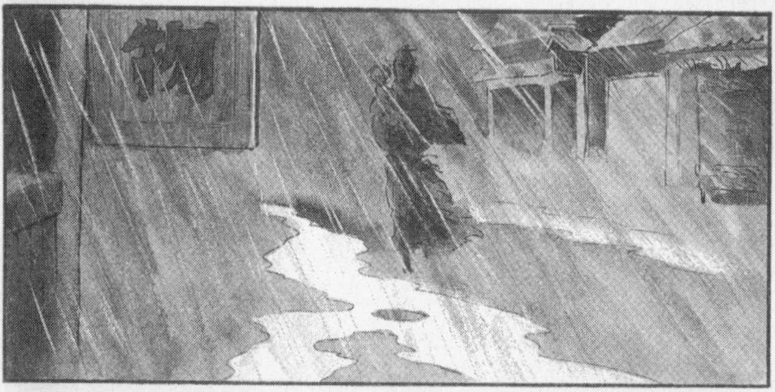
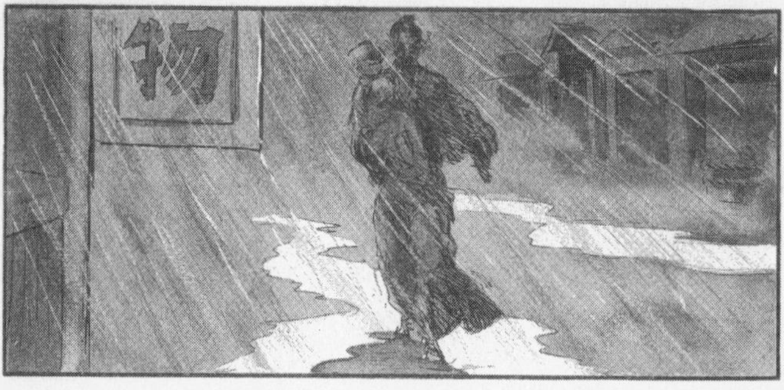

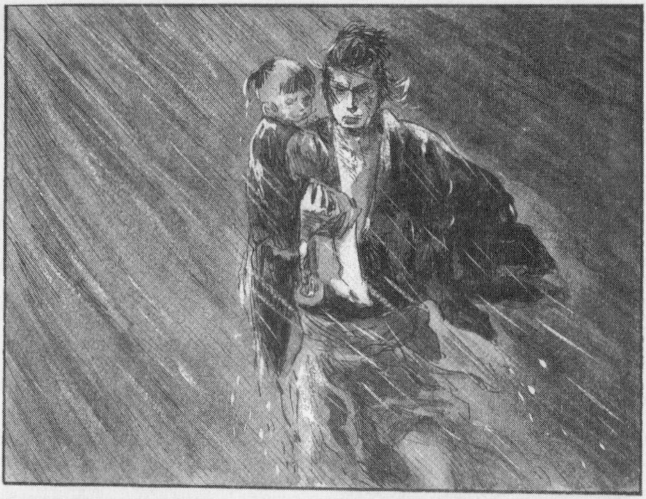
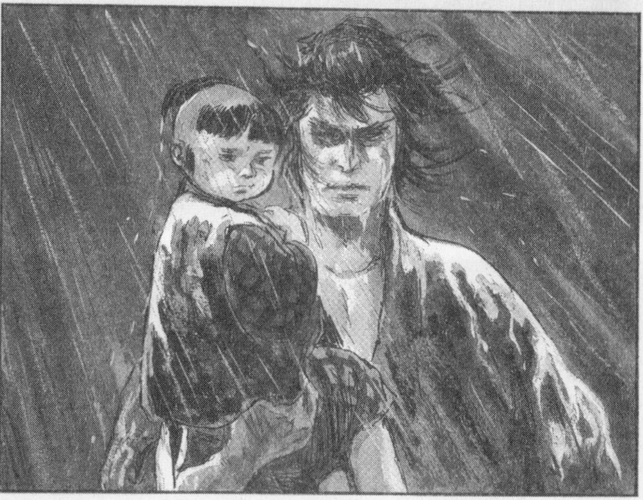

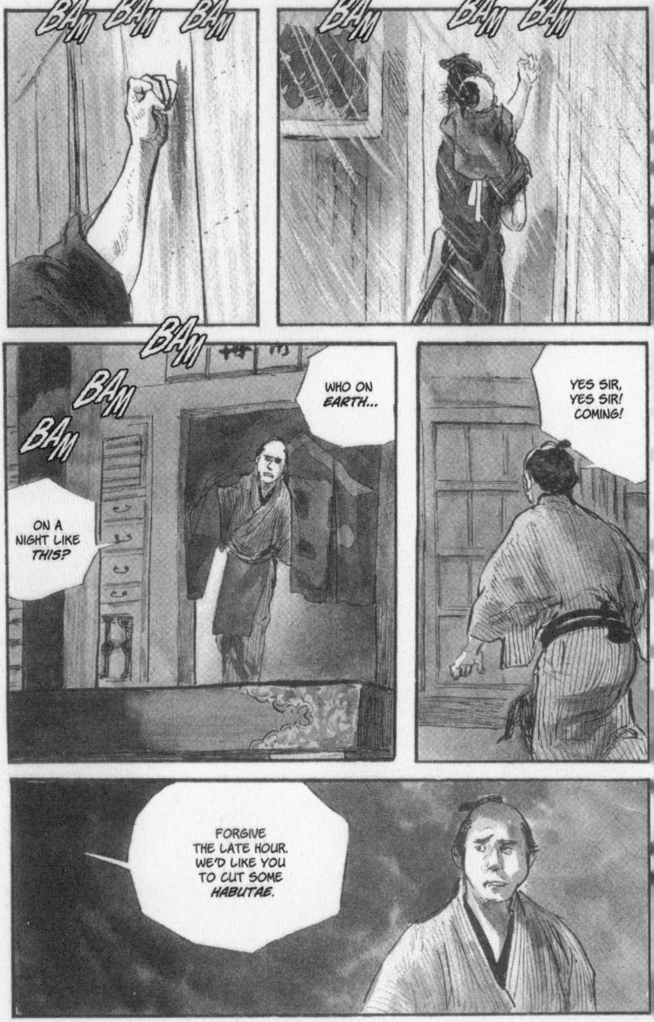
BAM BAM BAM
BAM BAM BAM
YES SIR, YES SIR! COMING!
BAM BAM BAM
WHO ON EARTH...
ON A NIGHT LIKE THIS?
FORGIVE THE LATE HOUR. WE'D LIKE YOU TO CUT SOME HABUTAE.

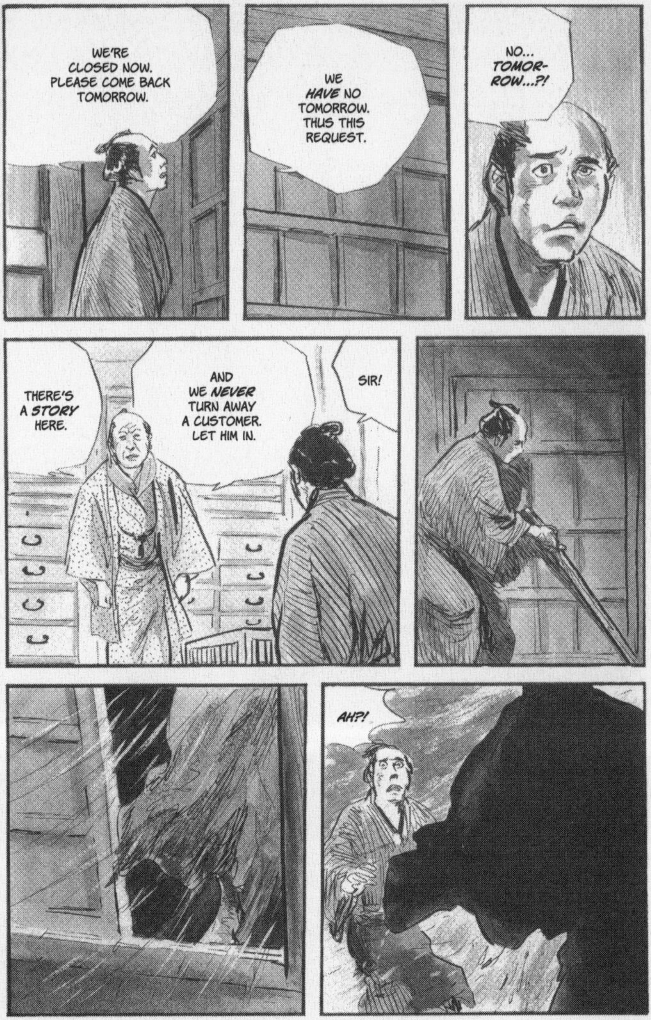
WE'RE CLOSED NOW. PLEASE COME BACK TOMORROW.
WE HAVE NO TOMORROW. THUS THIS REQUEST.
NO... TOMOR-ROW...?!
THERE'S A STORY HERE.
AND WE NEVER TURN AWAY A CUSTOMER. LET HIM IN.
SIR!
AH?!

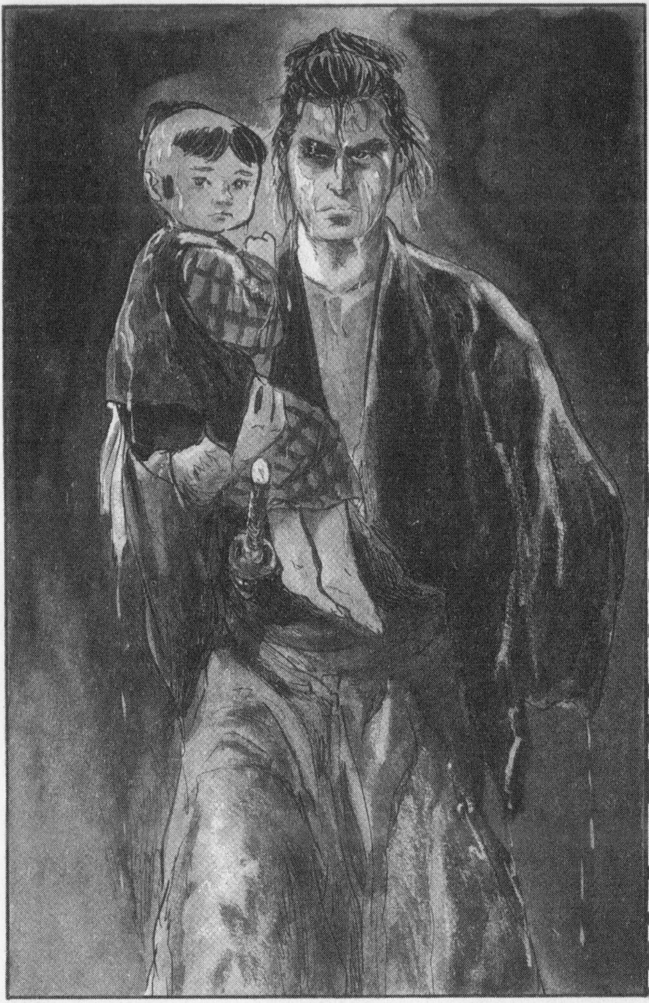

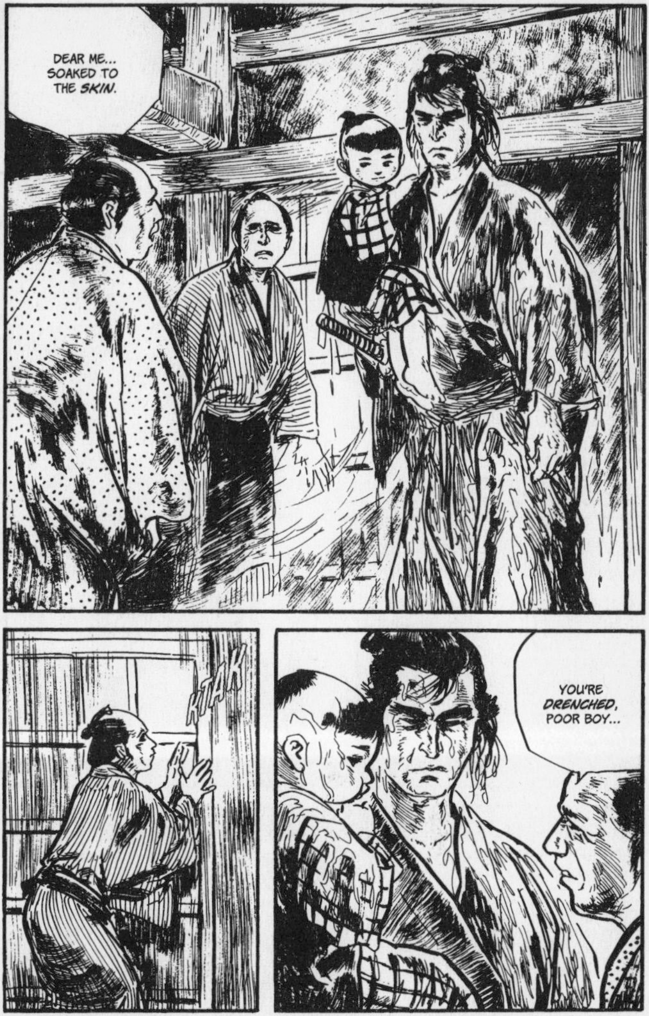
DEAR ME... SOAKED TO THE *SKIN*.
YOU'RE *DRENCHED*, POOR BOY...
KTAK

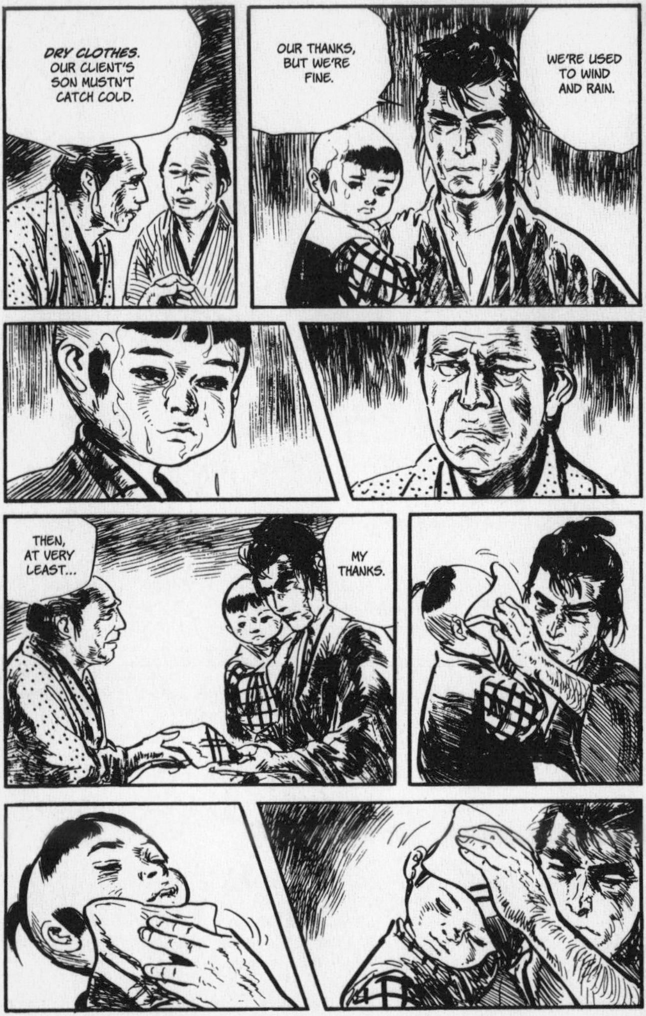
DRY CLOTHES. OUR CLIENT'S SON MUSTN'T CATCH COLD.
OUR THANKS, BUT WE'RE FINE.
WE'RE USED TO WIND AND RAIN.
THEN, AT VERY LEAST...
MY THANKS.

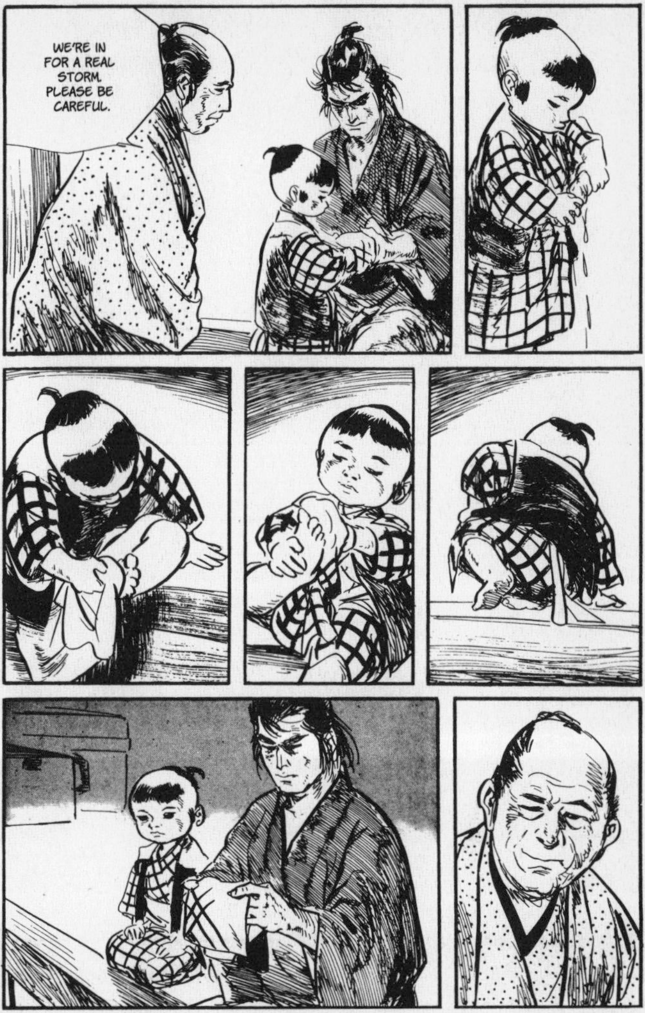
WE'RE IN FOR A REAL STORM. PLEASE BE CAREFUL.

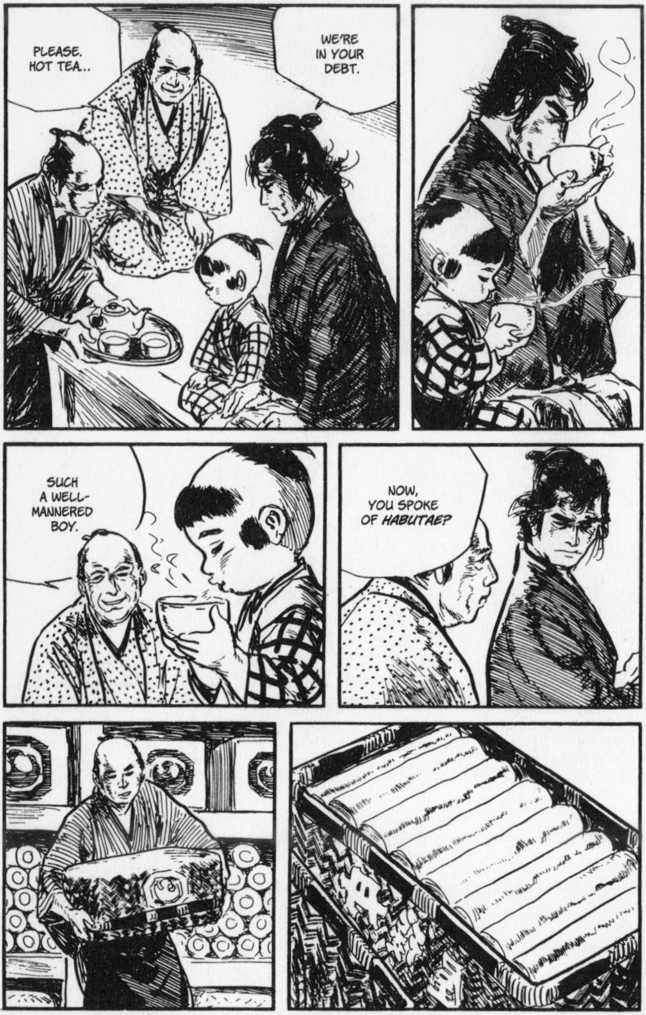
PLEASE. HOT TEA...
WE'RE IN YOUR DEBT.
SUCH A WELL-MANNERED BOY.
NOW, YOU SPOKE OF *HABUTAE?*

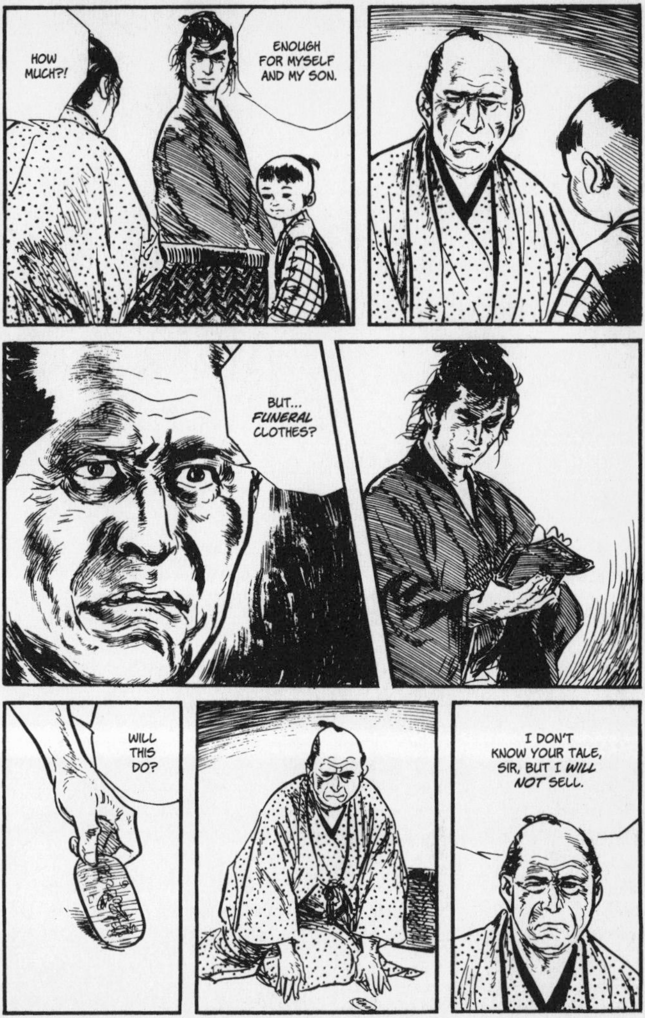
HOW MUCH?!
ENOUGH FOR MYSELF AND MY SON.
BUT... *FUNERAL* CLOTHES?
WILL THIS DO?
I DON'T KNOW YOUR TALE, SIR, BUT I *WILL NOT* SELL.

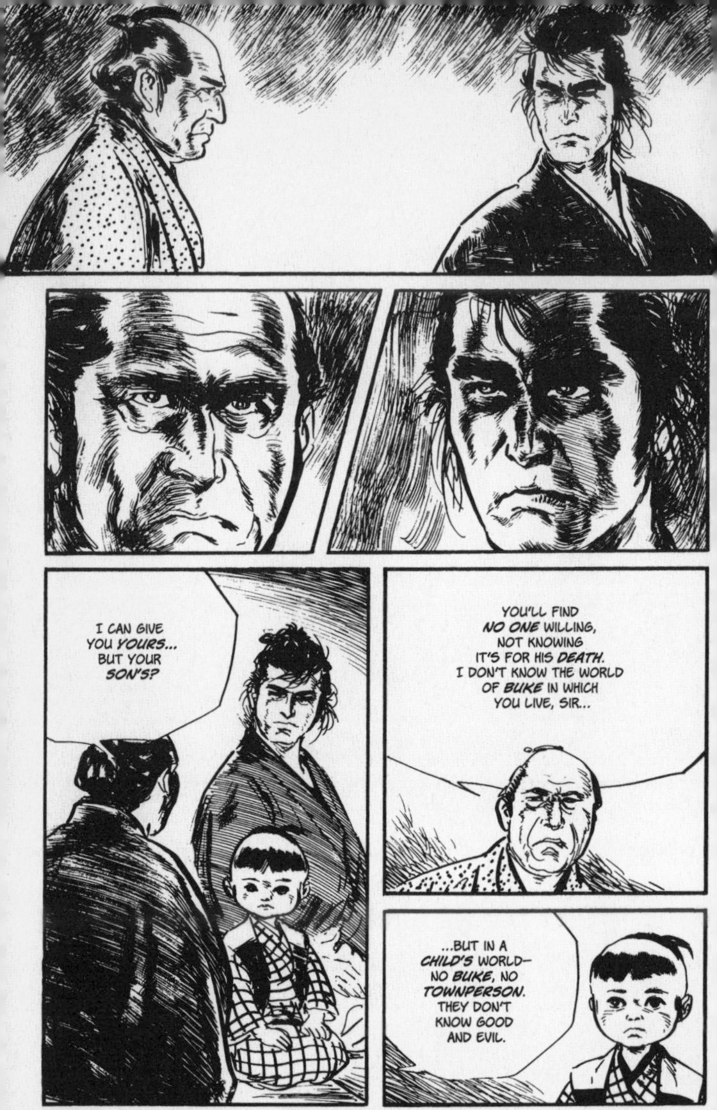
I CAN GIVE YOU YOURS... BUT YOUR SON'S?
YOU'LL FIND NO ONE WILLING, NOT KNOWING IT'S FOR HIS DEATH. I DON'T KNOW THE WORLD OF BUKE IN WHICH YOU LIVE, SIR...
...BUT IN A CHILD'S WORLD– NO BUKE, NO TOWNPERSON. THEY DON'T KNOW GOOD AND EVIL.

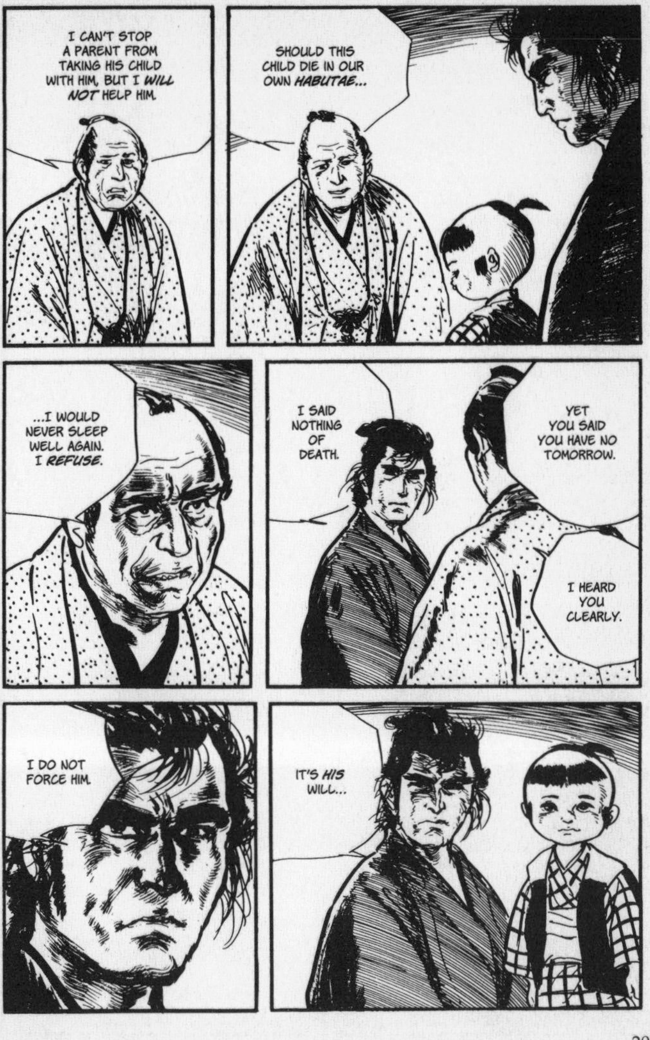
I CAN'T STOP A PARENT FROM TAKING HIS CHILD WITH HIM, BUT I *WILL NOT* HELP HIM.
SHOULD THIS CHILD DIE IN OUR OWN *HABUTAE*...
...I WOULD NEVER SLEEP WELL AGAIN. I *REFUSE*.
I SAID NOTHING OF DEATH.
YET YOU SAID YOU HAVE NO TOMORROW.
I HEARD YOU CLEARLY.
I DO NOT FORCE HIM.
IT'S *HIS* WILL...

GOOD HEAVENS, SIR! YOU SAY...

...THIS CHILD *WANTS* TO WEAR ROBES OF DEATH?

HE CAN'T...

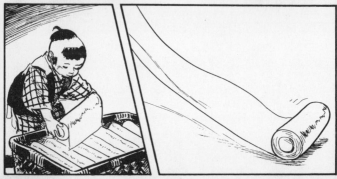

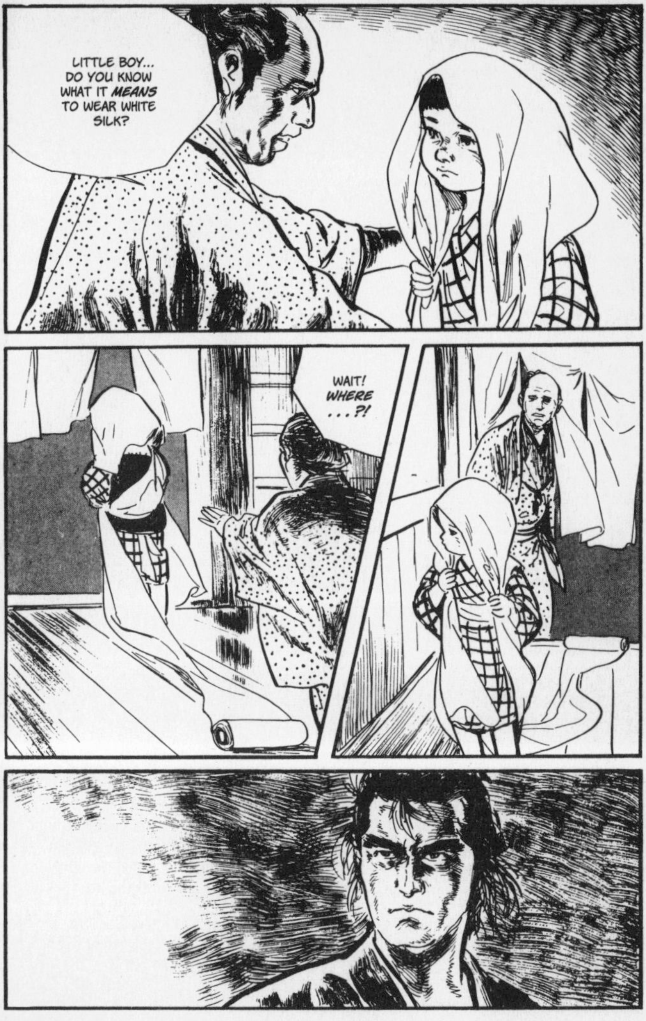
LITTLE BOY... DO YOU KNOW WHAT IT *MEANS* TO WEAR WHITE SILK?
WAIT! *WHERE* ...?!

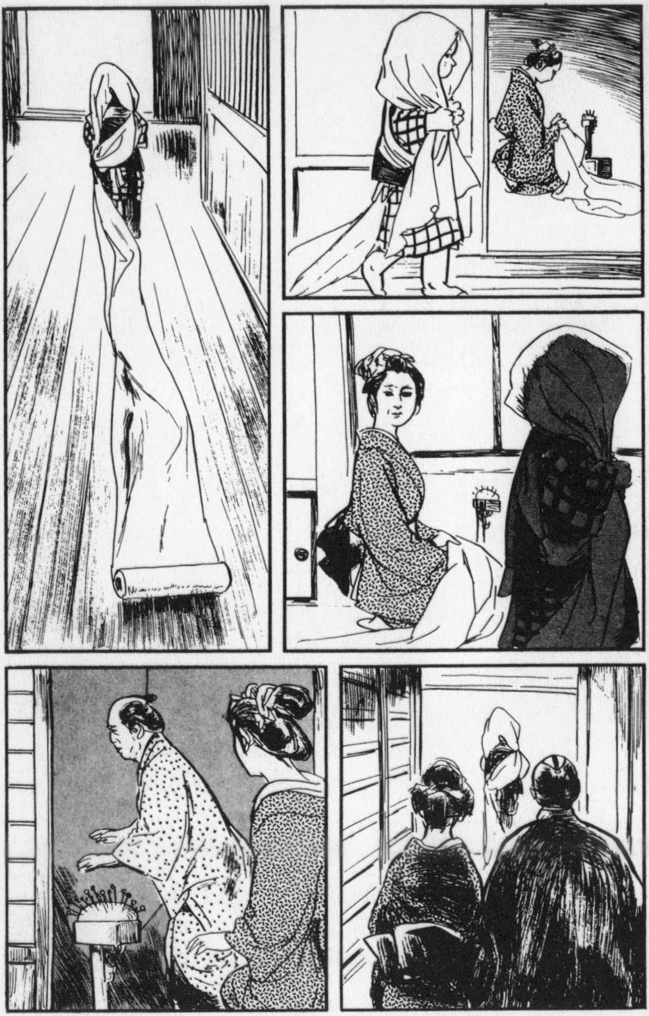

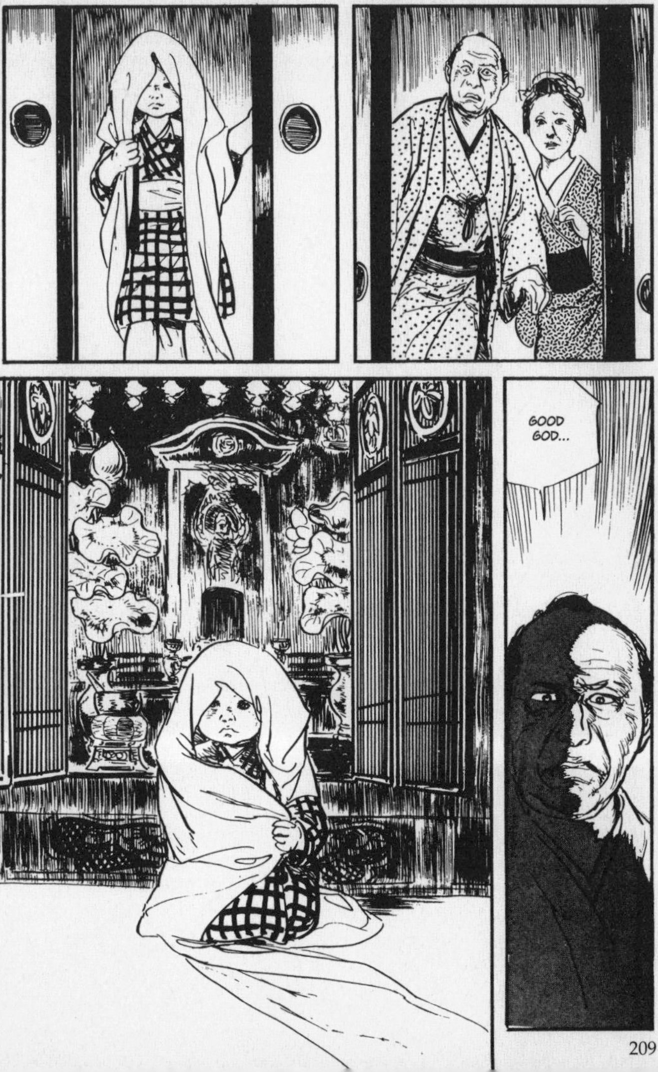
GOOD GOD...

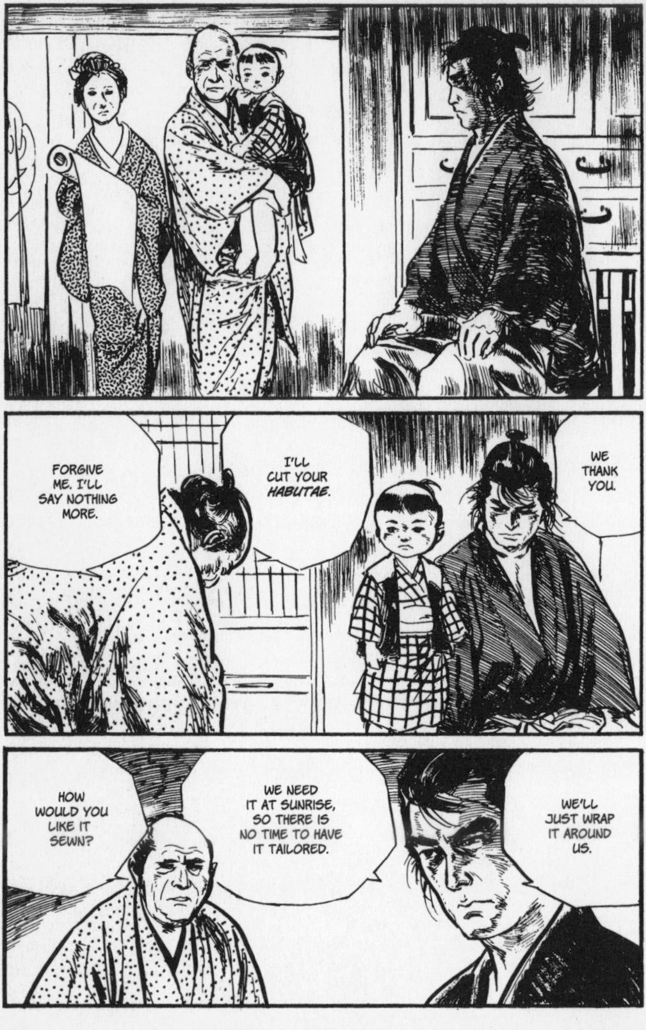
FORGIVE ME. I'LL SAY NOTHING MORE.
I'LL CUT YOUR *HABUTAE*.
WE THANK YOU.
HOW WOULD YOU LIKE IT SEWN?
WE NEED IT AT SUNRISE, SO THERE IS NO TIME TO HAVE IT TAILORED.
WE'LL JUST WRAP IT AROUND US.

BUT IF THEY COULD BE READY BY MORNING...?

YOU WOULD DO THIS?

OF *COURSE!* MY WIFE AND I, *TOGETHER.*

I HELD MANY A NEEDLE WHEN I WAS YOUNG.

WE'D DO ANYTHING FOR THIS YOUNG MAN.

211

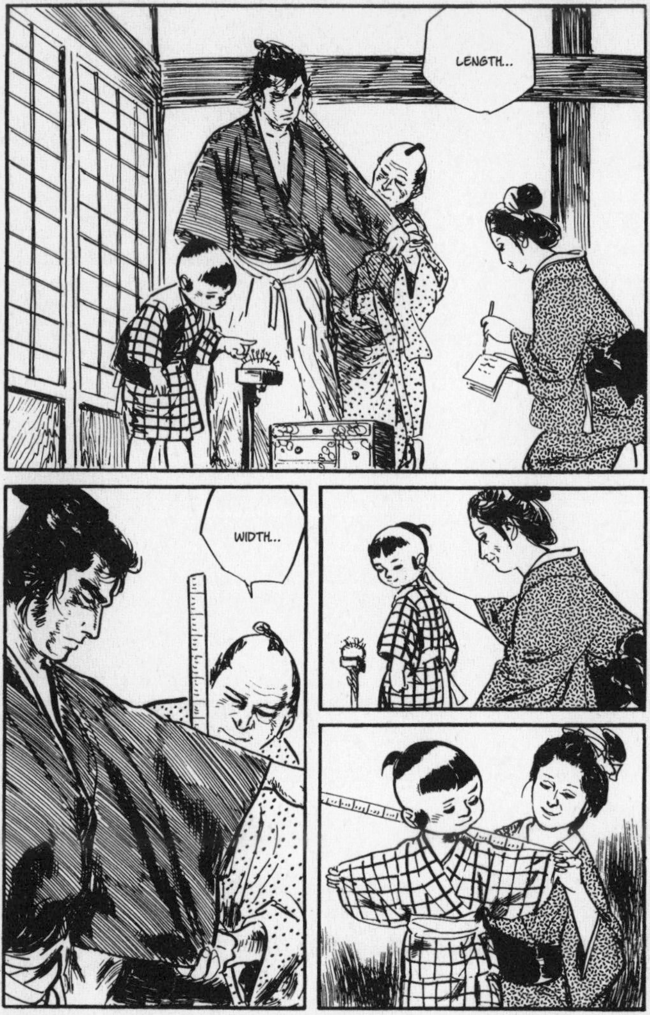
LENGTH...
WIDTH...

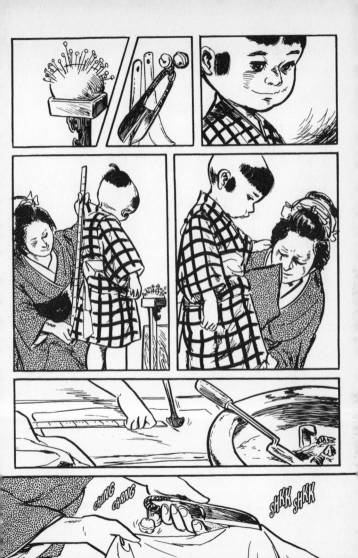

CHING CHING

SHKK SHKK

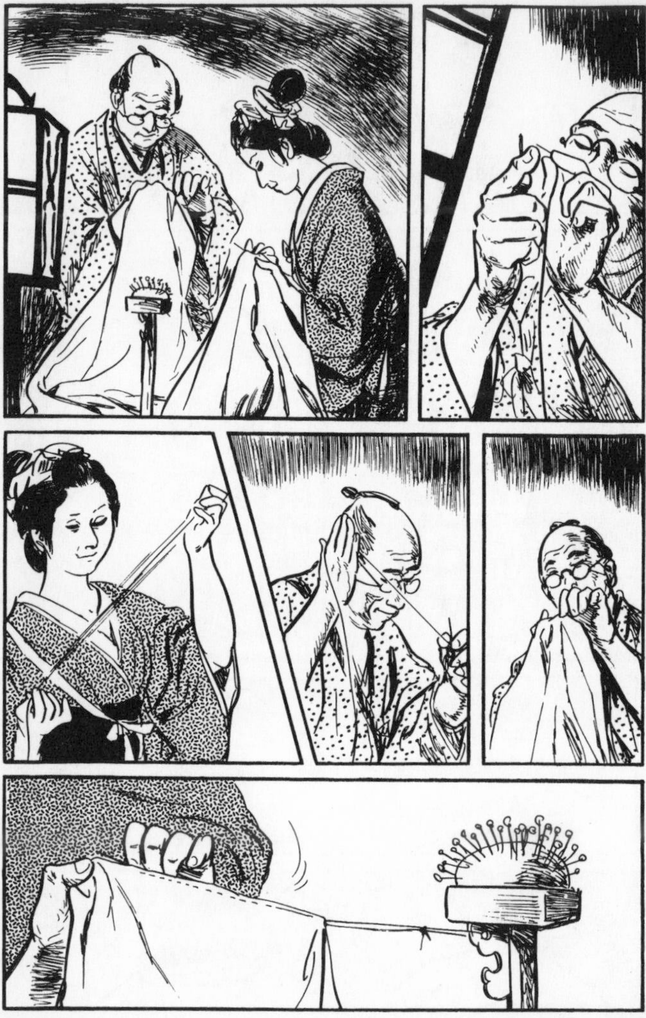

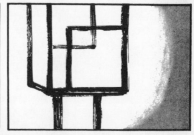

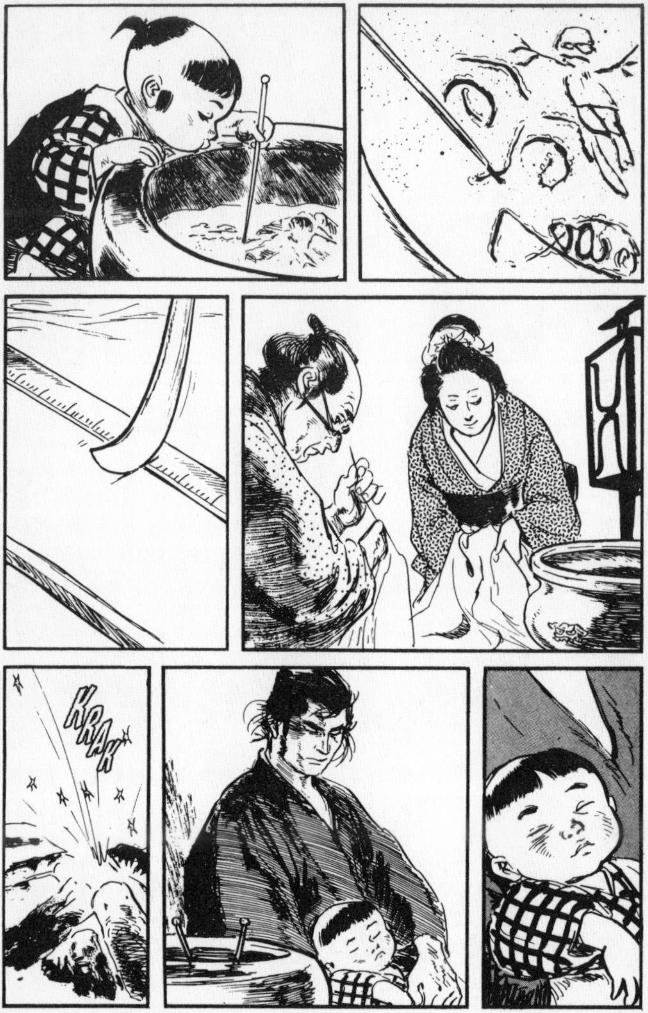
KRAK

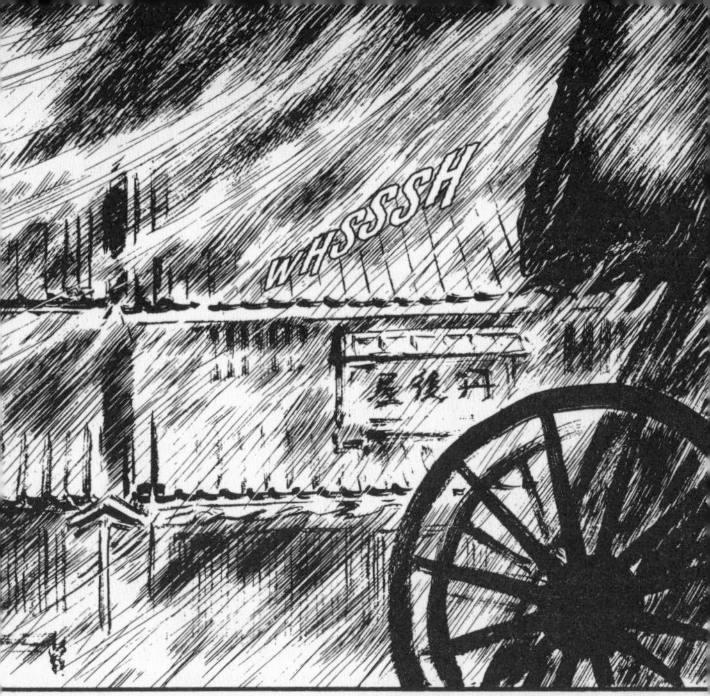
WHSSSSH

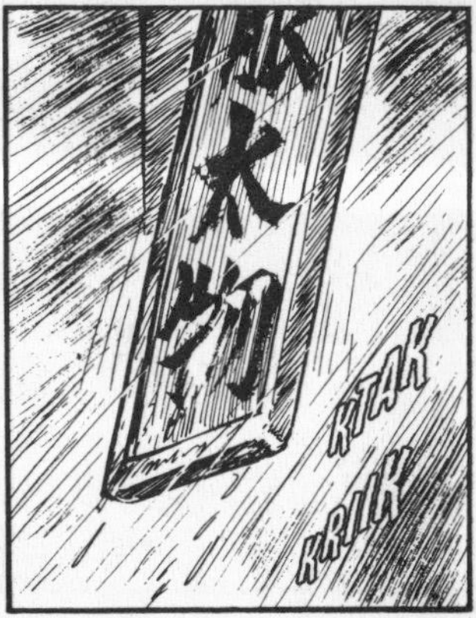
KTAK
KRIIK

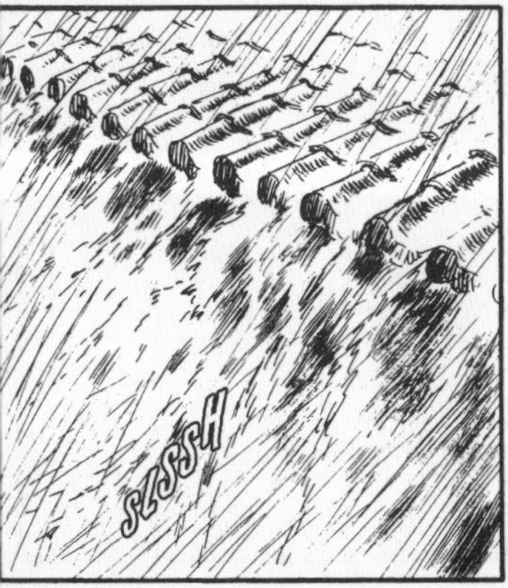
SLSSH

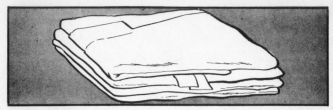

YOUR ROBES ARE READY.

THANK YOU...

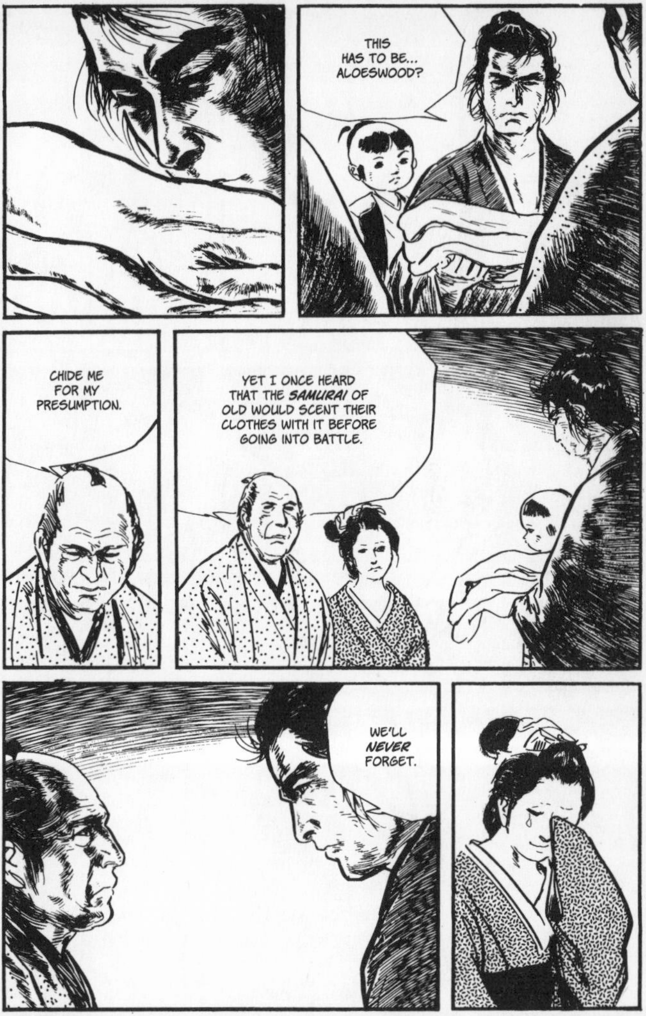
THIS HAS TO BE... ALOESWOOD?
CHIDE ME FOR MY PRESUMPTION.
YET I ONCE HEARD THAT THE *SAMURAI* OF OLD WOULD SCENT THEIR CLOTHES WITH IT BEFORE GOING INTO BATTLE.
WE'LL *NEVER* FORGET.

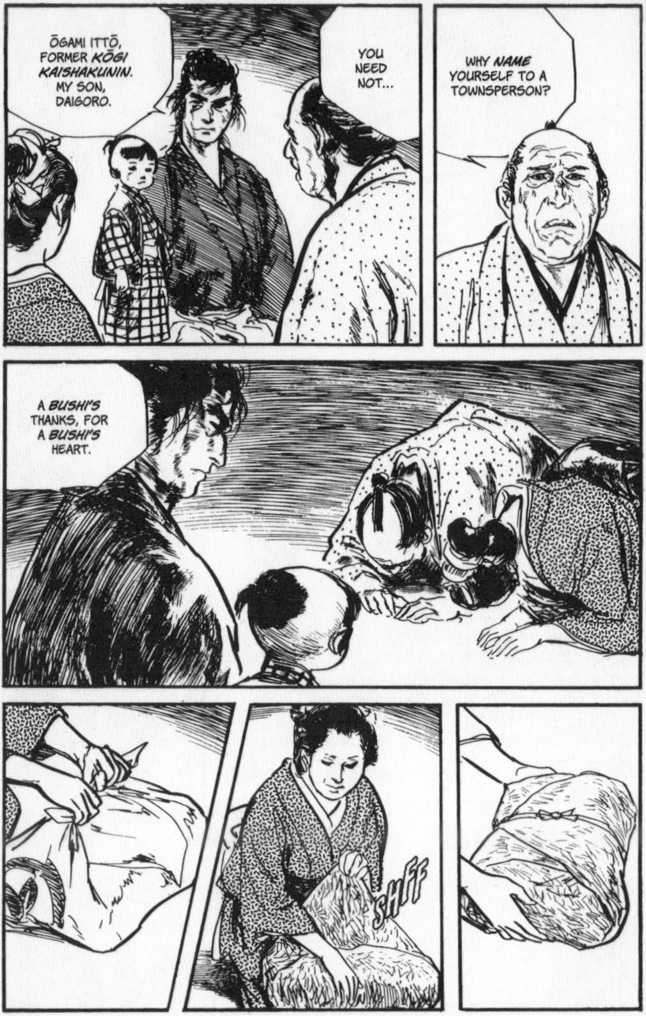
ŌGAMI ITTŌ, FORMER *KŌGI KAISHAKUNIN*. MY SON, DAIGORO.
YOU NEED NOT...
WHY *NAME* YOURSELF TO A TOWNSPERSON?
A *BUSHI'S* THANKS, FOR A *BUSHI'S* HEART.
SHFF

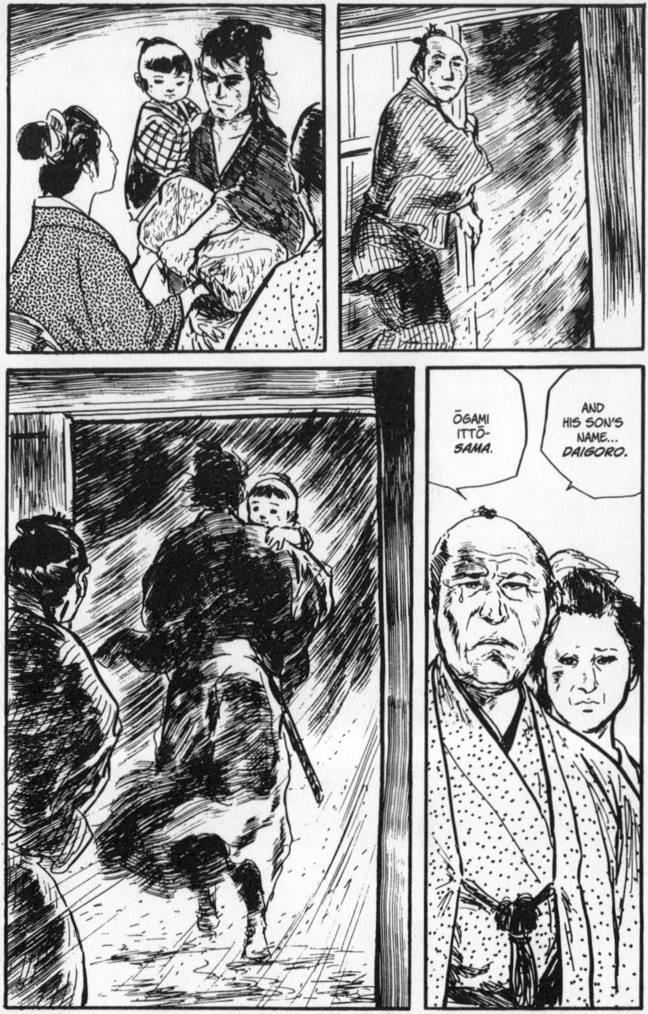
ŌGAMI ITTŌ-SAMA.
AND HIS SON'S NAME... DAIGORO.

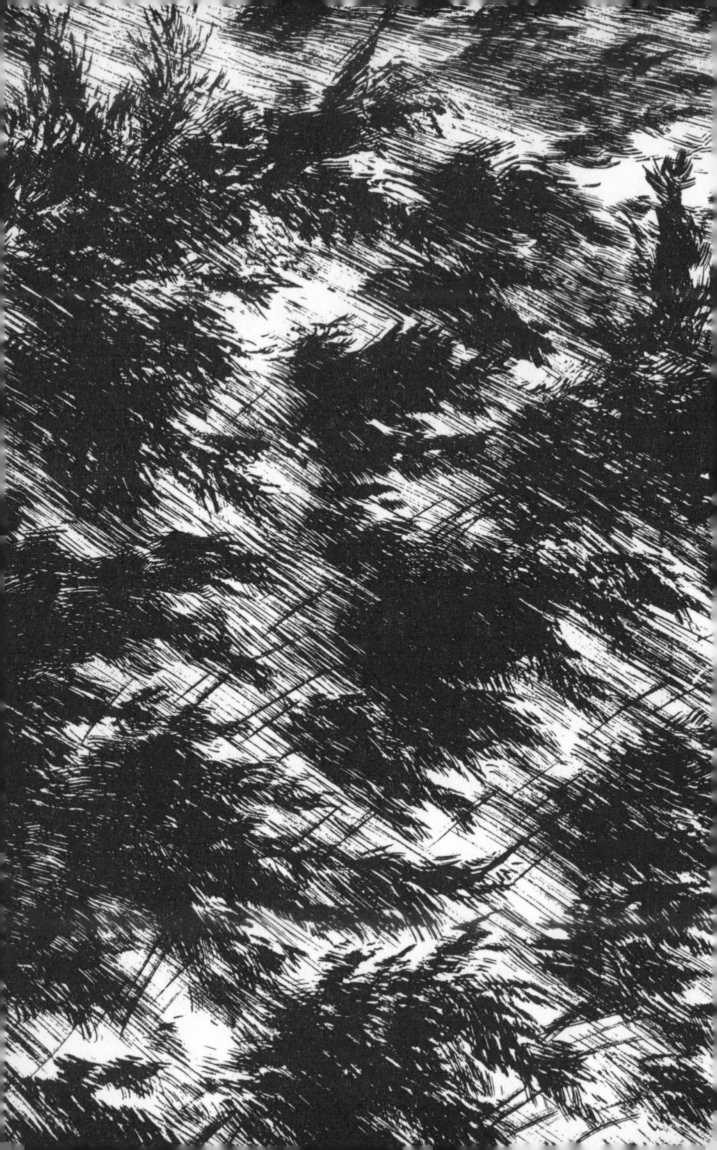

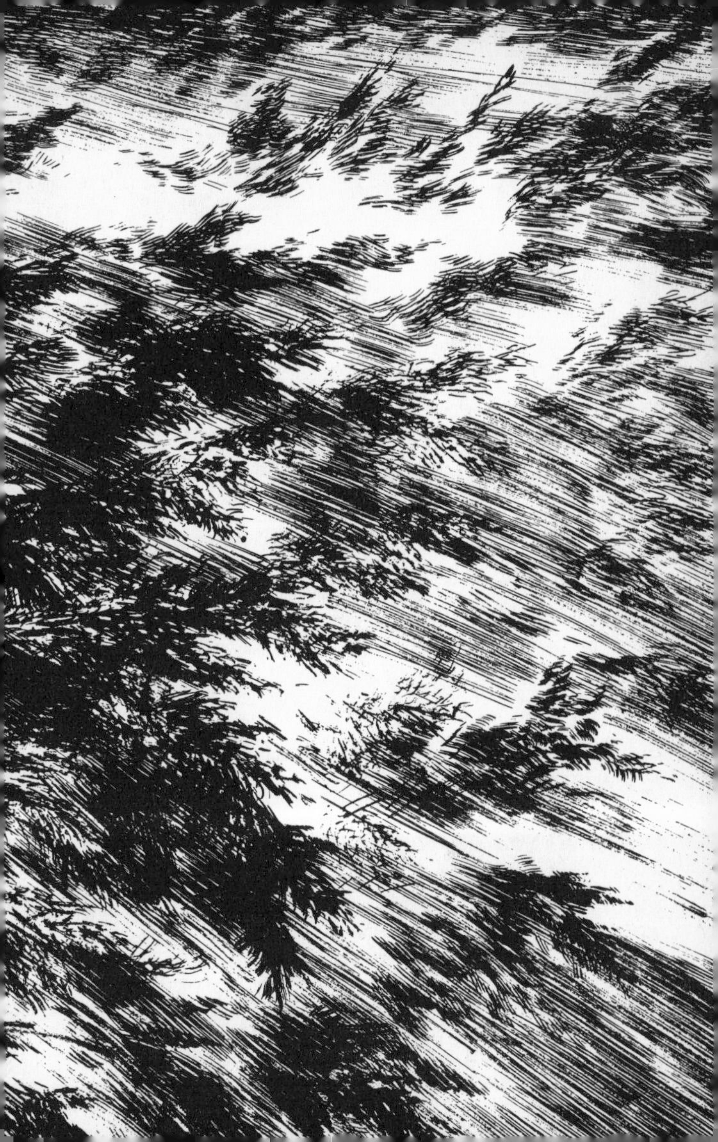

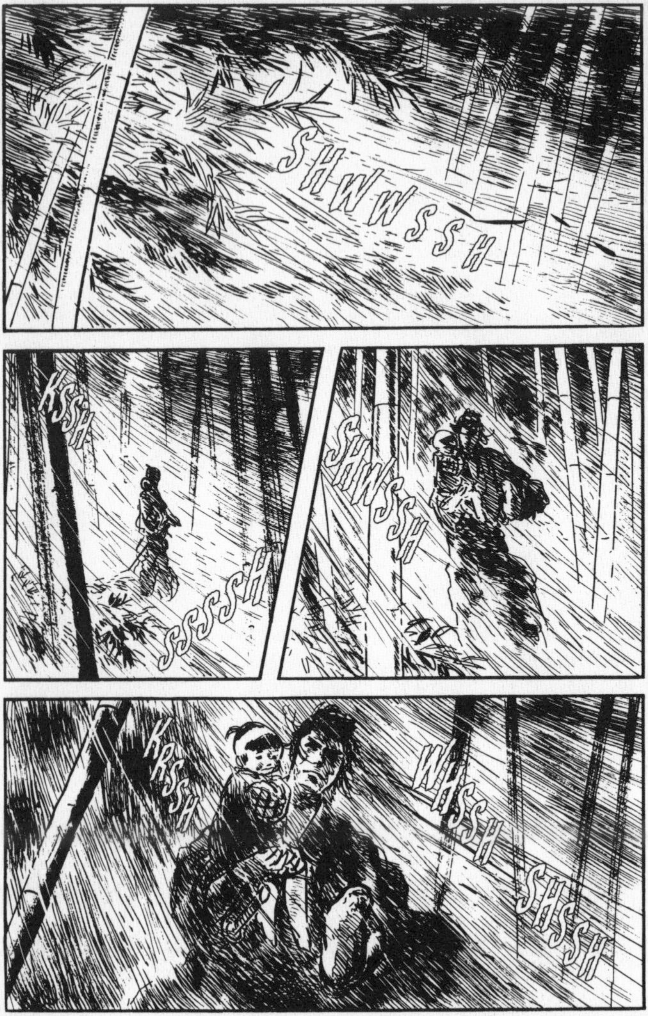
SHWWSSSH
SHWSSH
KSSH
SSSSSH
WHSSH
SHSSH
KRSSH

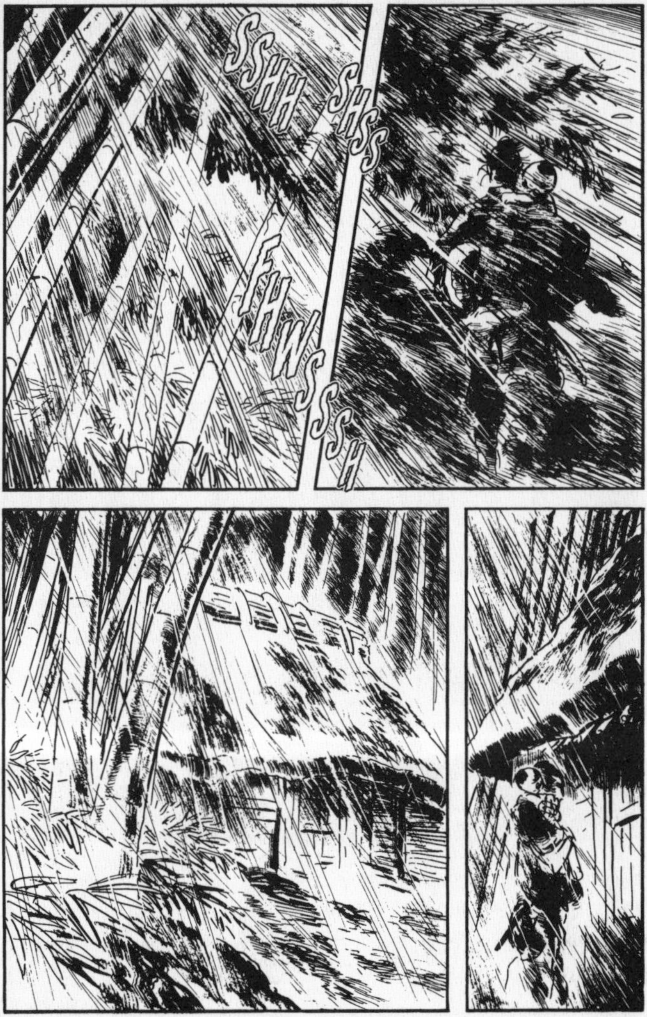
SSHH SHSS
FHWSSSH

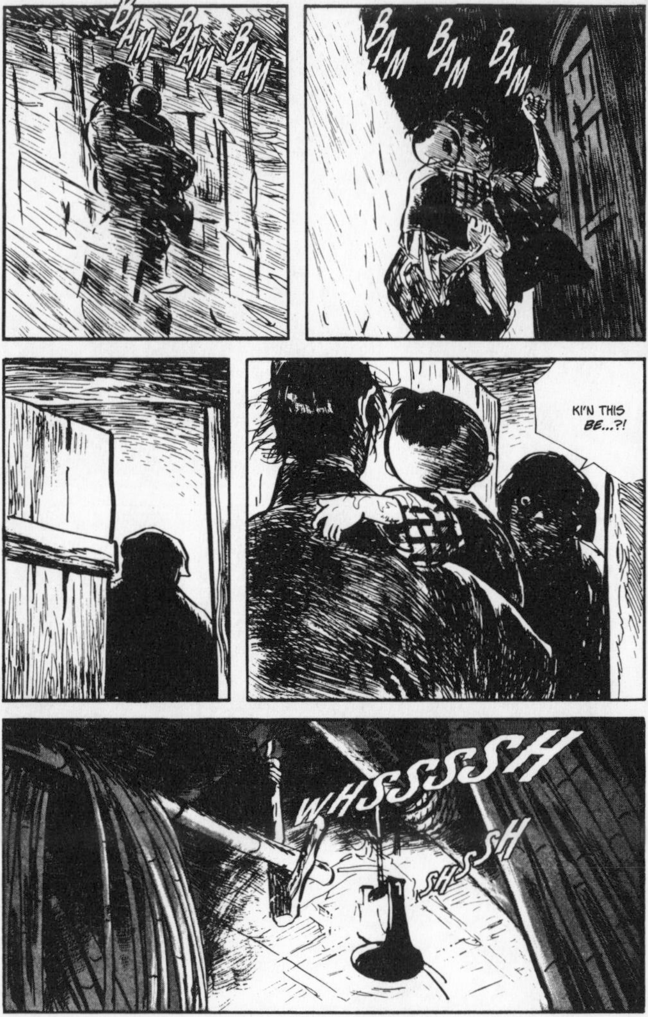
BAM BAM BAM
BAM BAM BAM
KI'N THIS BE...?!
WHSSSSSH
SHSSH

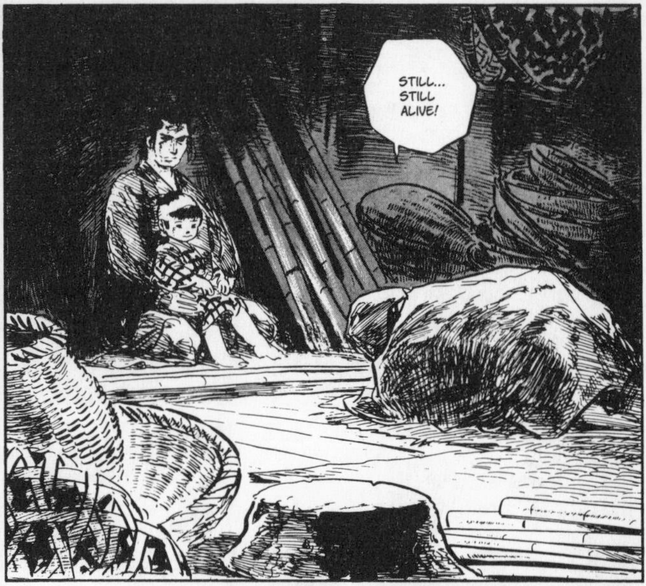
STILL... STILL ALIVE!
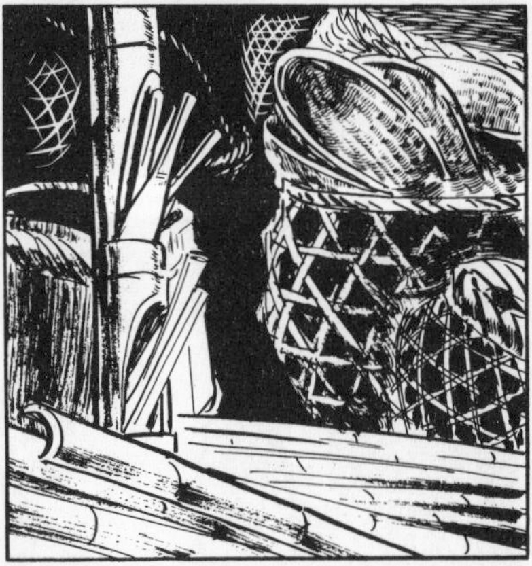
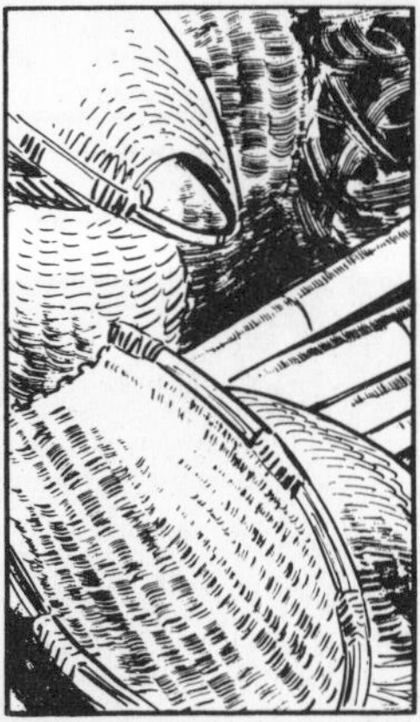

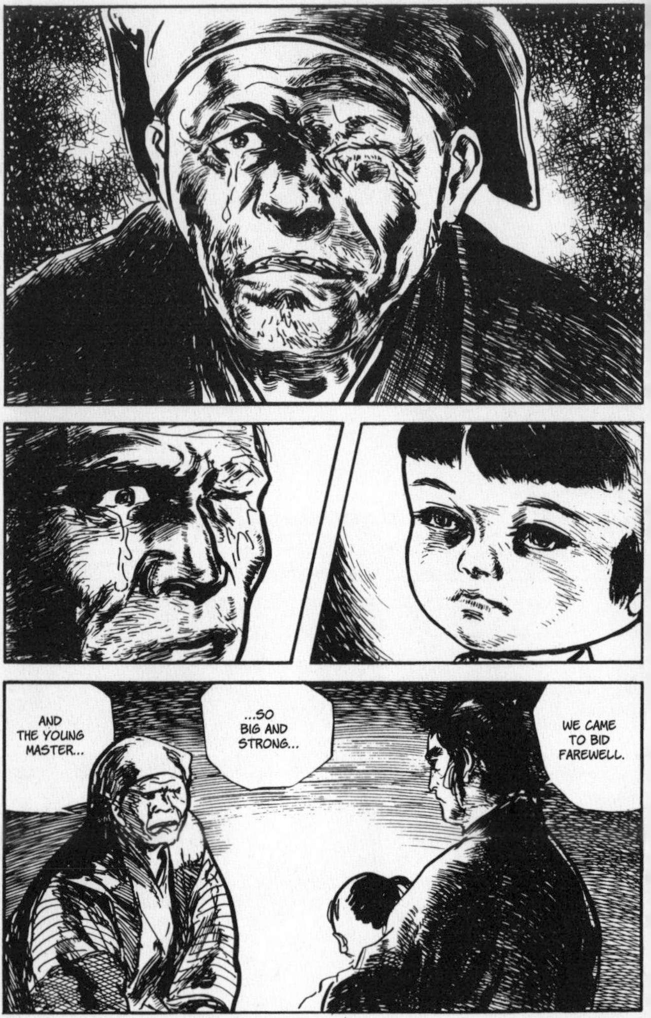
AND THE YOUNG MASTER...
...SO BIG AND STRONG...
WE CAME TO BID FAREWELL.

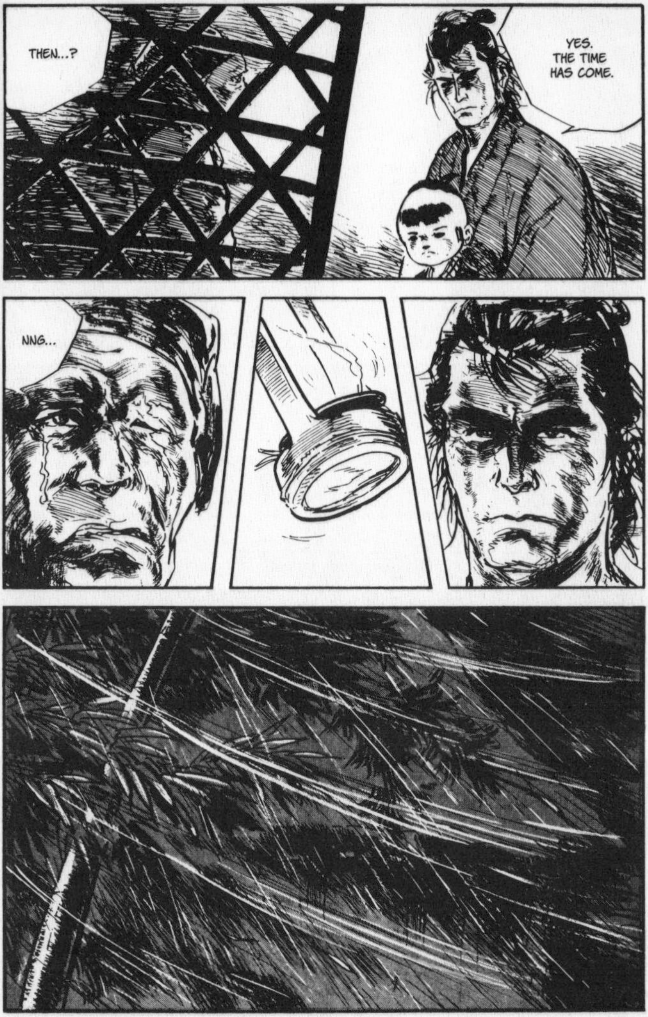
THEN...?
YES. THE TIME HAS COME.
NNG...

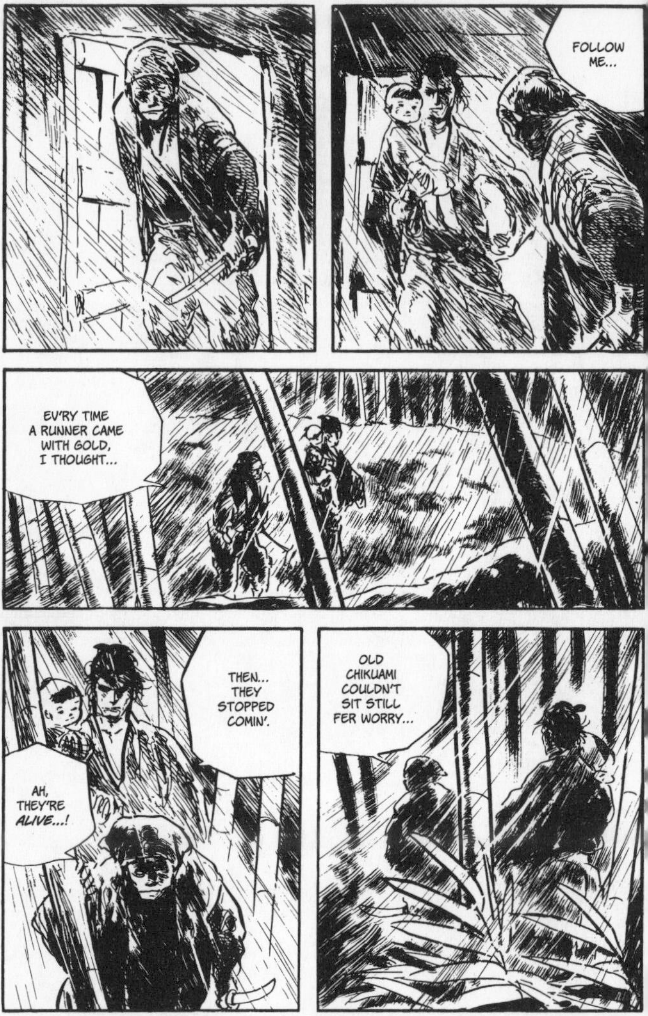
FOLLOW ME...
EV'RY TIME A RUNNER CAME WITH GOLD, I THOUGHT...
AH, THEY'RE *ALIVE*...!
THEN... THEY STOPPED COMIN'.
OLD CHIKUAMI COULDN'T SIT STILL FER WORRY...

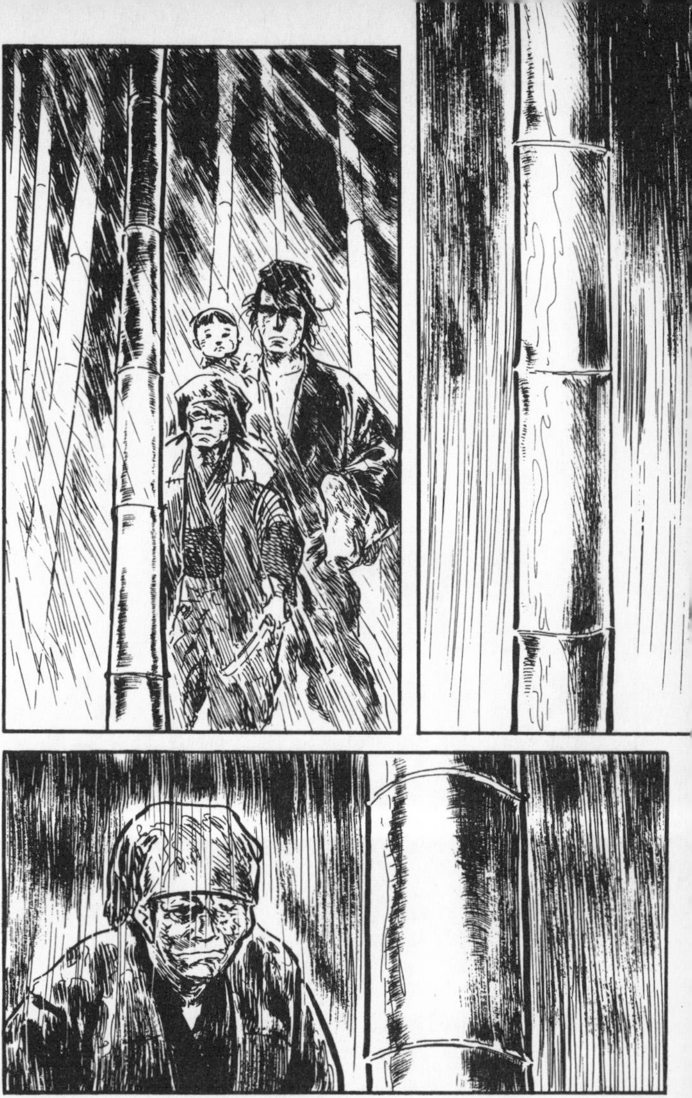

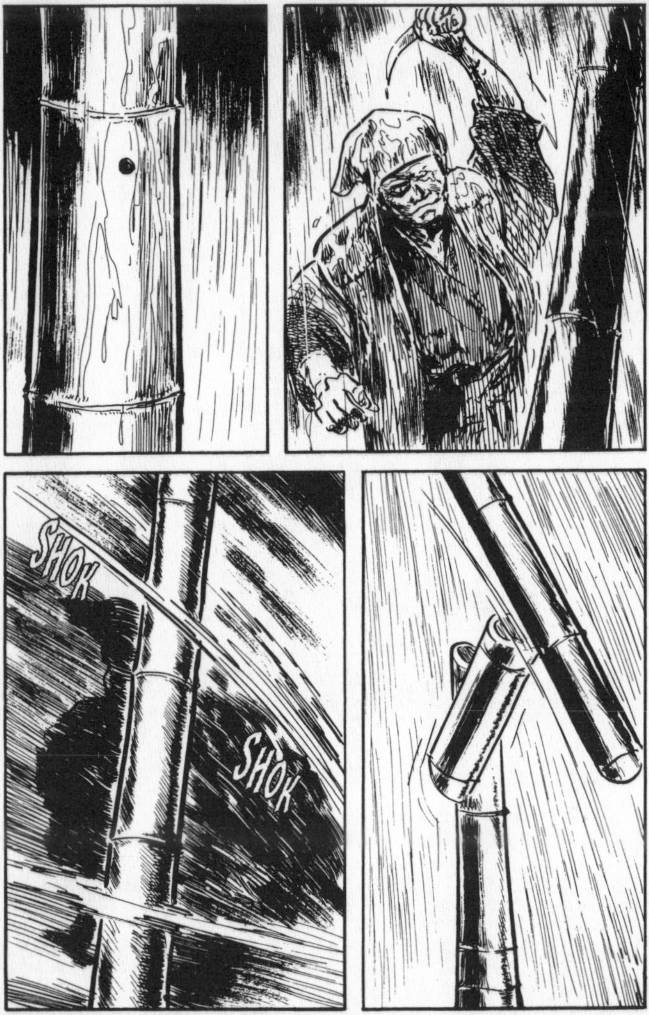
SHOK
SHOK

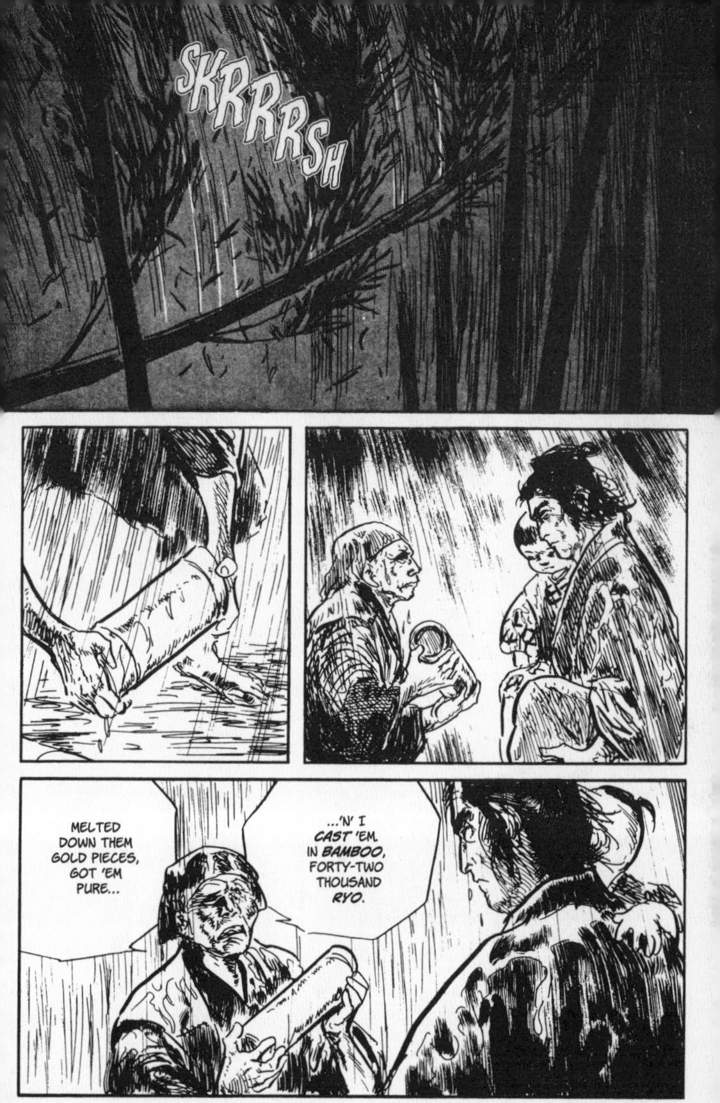
SKRRRSH
MELTED DOWN THEM GOLD PIECES, GOT 'EM PURE...
...'N' I CAST 'EM IN BAMBOO, FORTY-TWO THOUSAND RYO.

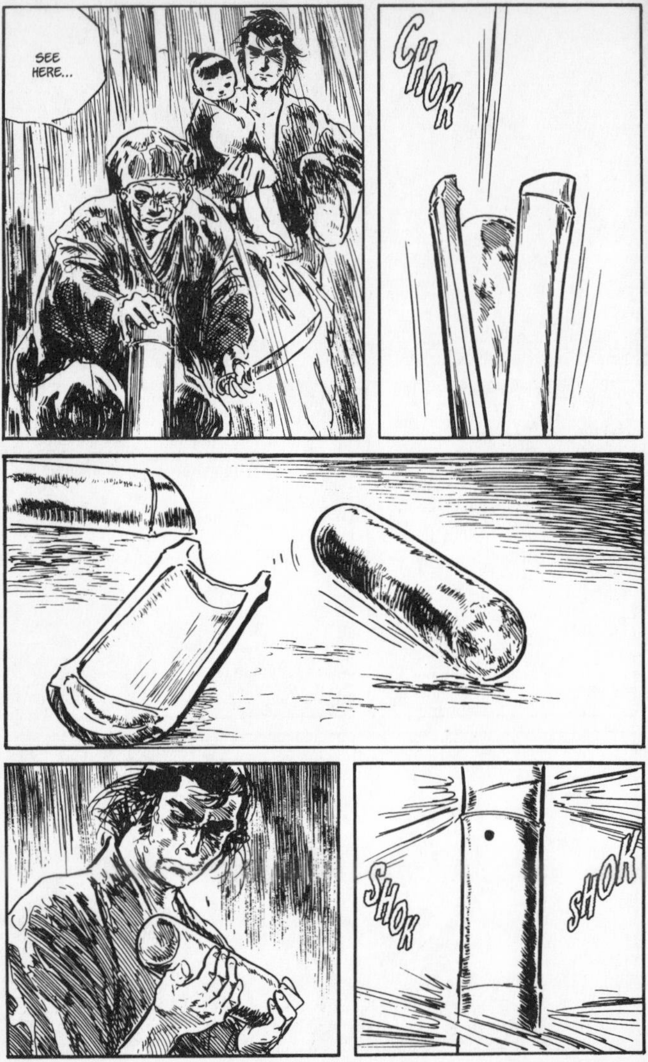
CHOK
SEE HERE...
SHOK
SHOK

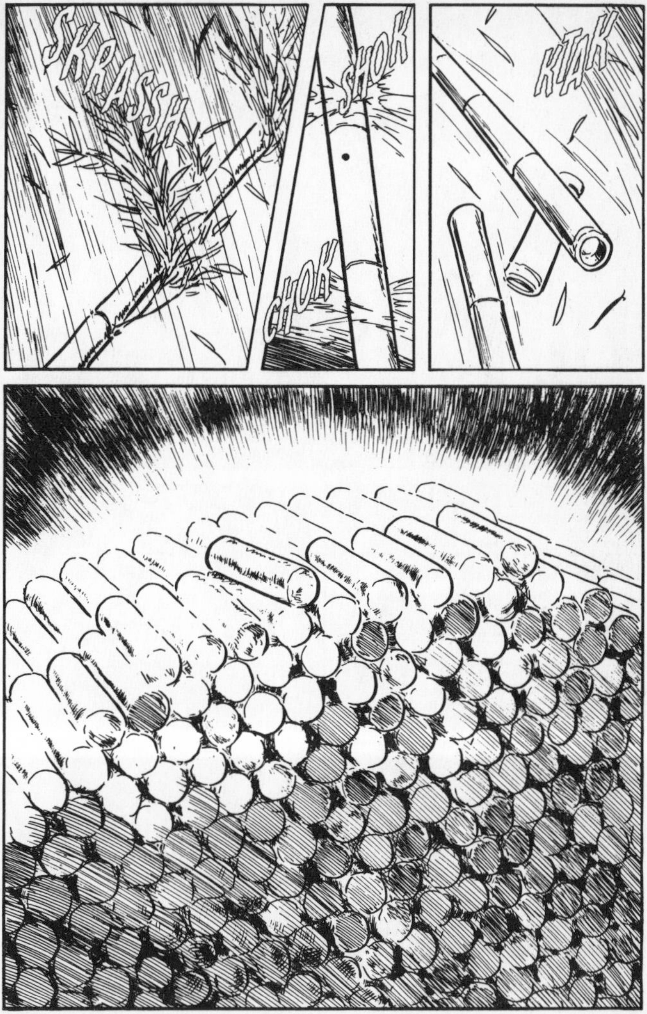
KTAK
SHOK
CHOK
SKRASSH

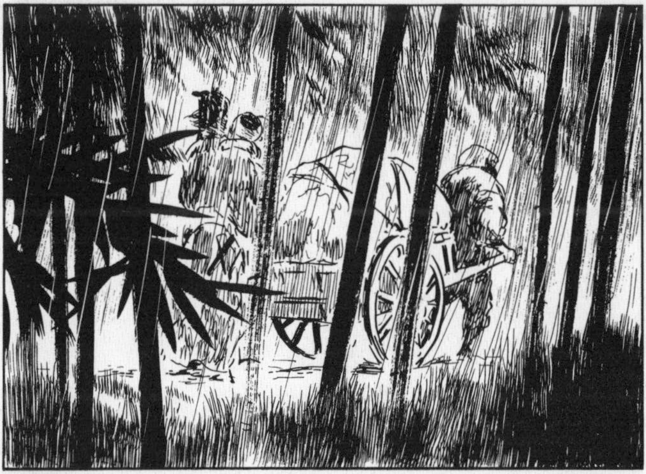
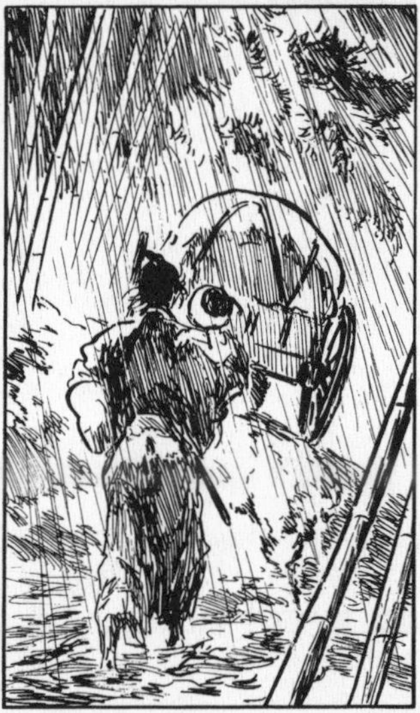
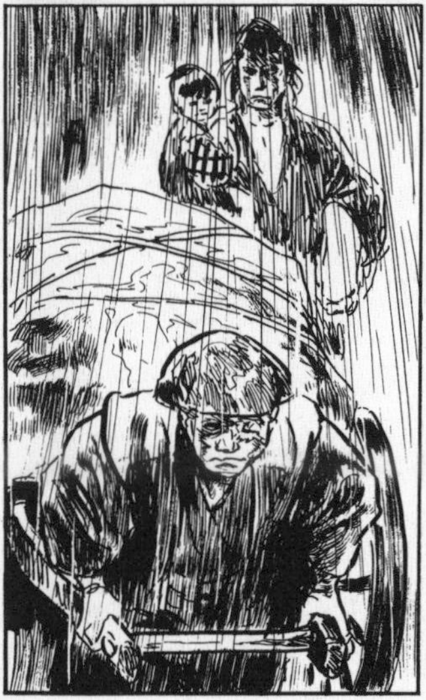

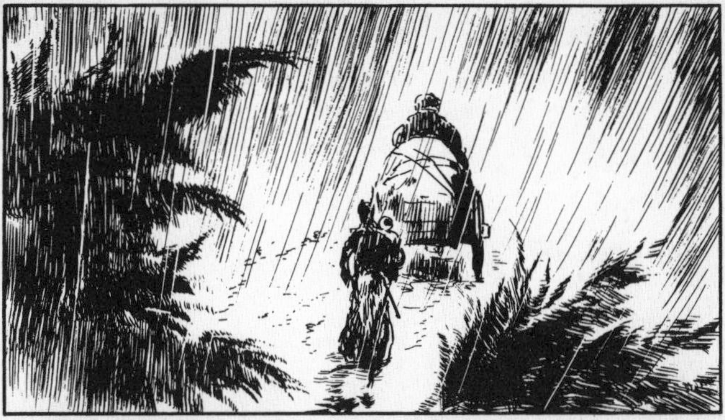
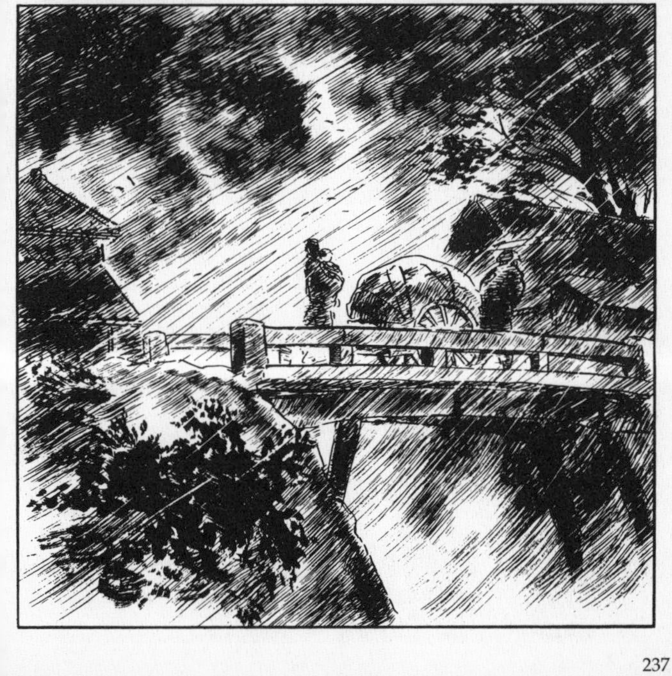

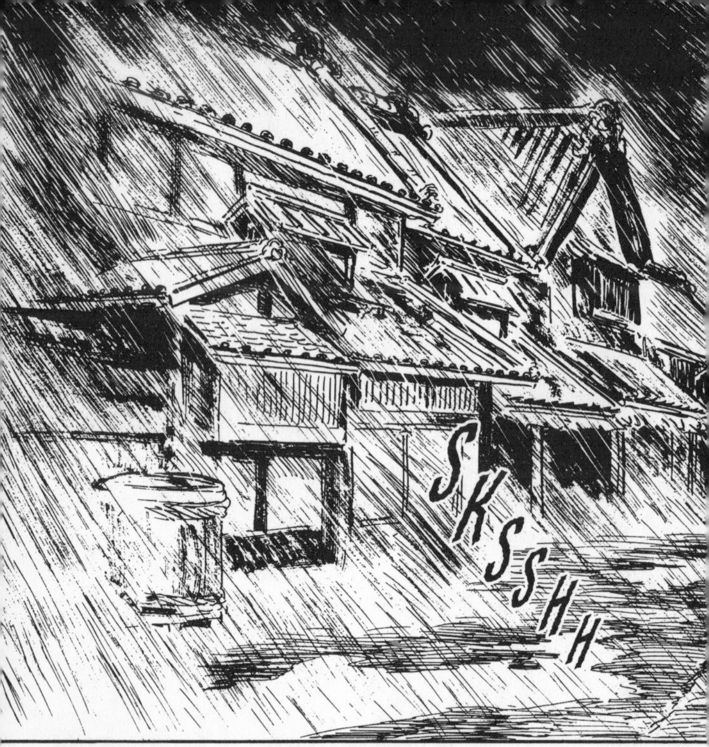
SKSSHH

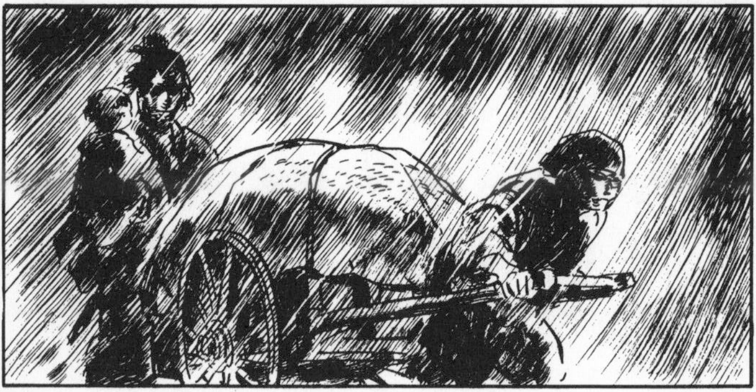

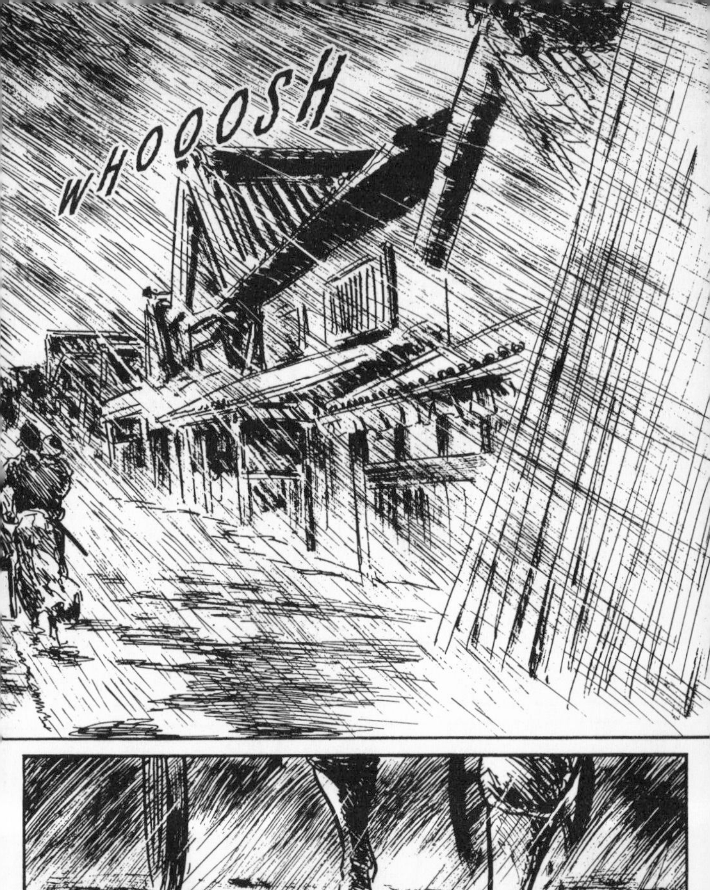
WHOOOSH
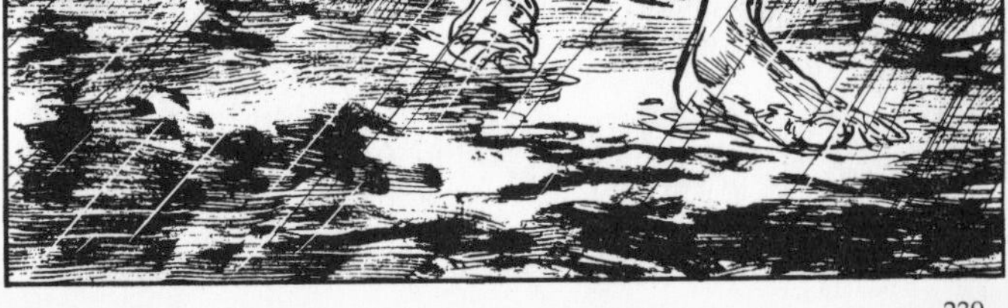

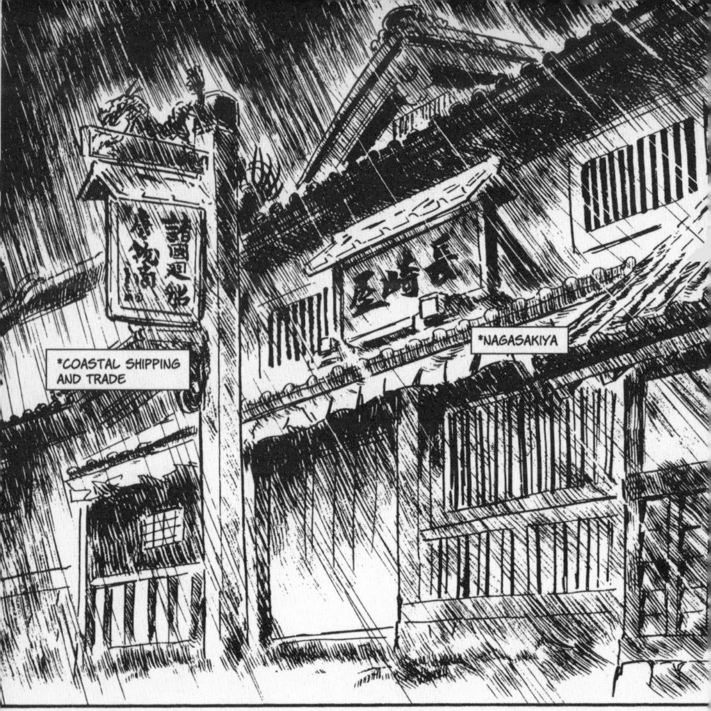
*COASTAL SHIPPING AND TRADE
*NAGASAKIYA

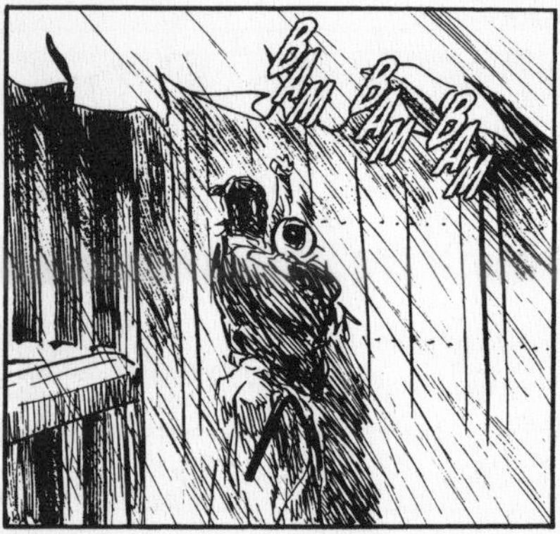
BAM BAM BAM

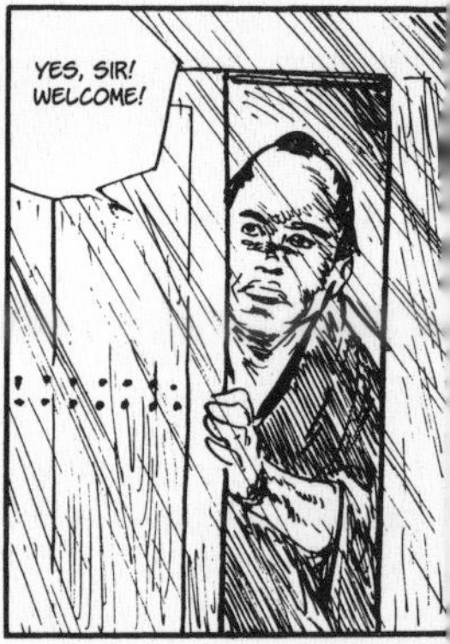
YES, SIR! WELCOME!

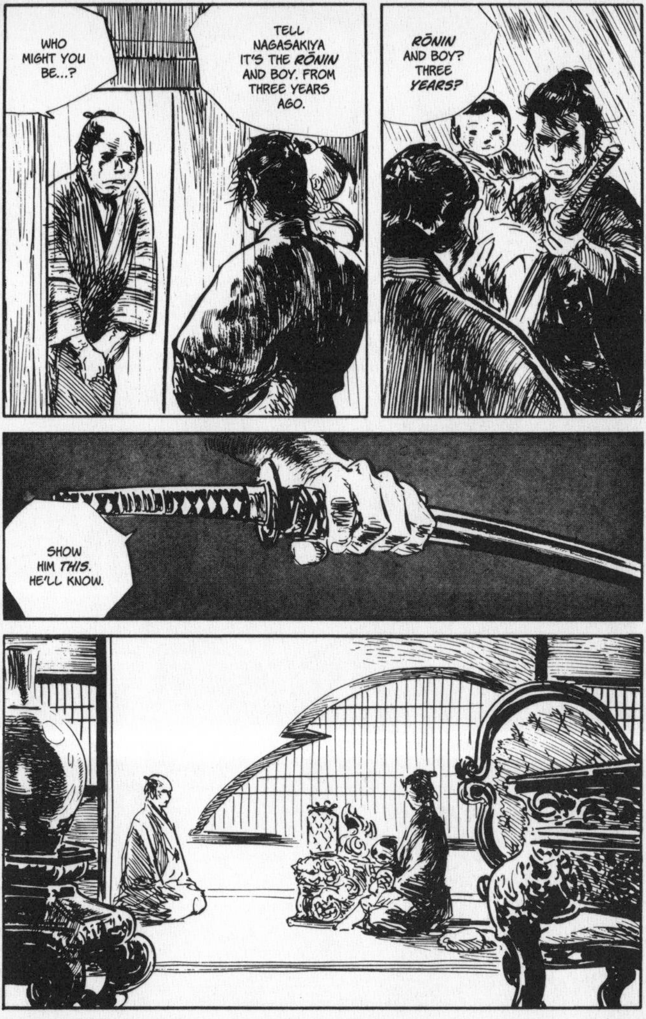
WHO MIGHT YOU BE...?
TELL NAGASAKIYA IT'S THE *RŌNIN* AND BOY. FROM THREE YEARS AGO.
RŌNIN AND BOY? THREE *YEARS?*
SHOW HIM *THIS*. HE'LL KNOW.

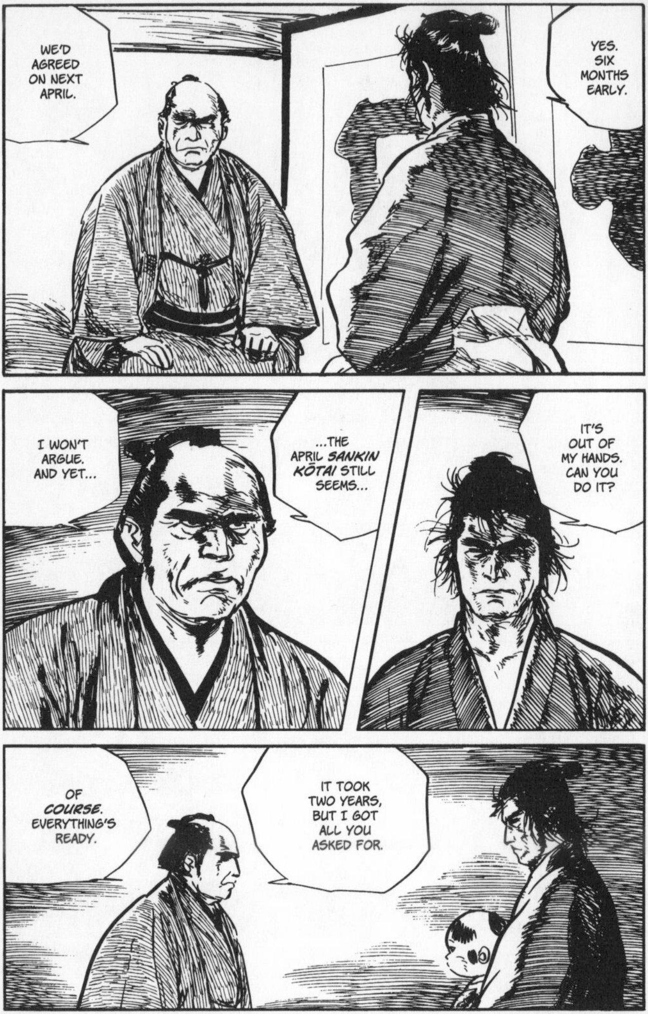
WE'D AGREED ON NEXT APRIL.
YES. SIX MONTHS EARLY.
I WON'T ARGUE. AND YET...
...THE APRIL *SANKIN KŌTAI* STILL SEEMS...
IT'S OUT OF MY HANDS. CAN YOU DO IT?
OF *COURSE*. EVERYTHING'S READY.
IT TOOK TWO YEARS, BUT I GOT ALL YOU ASKED FOR.

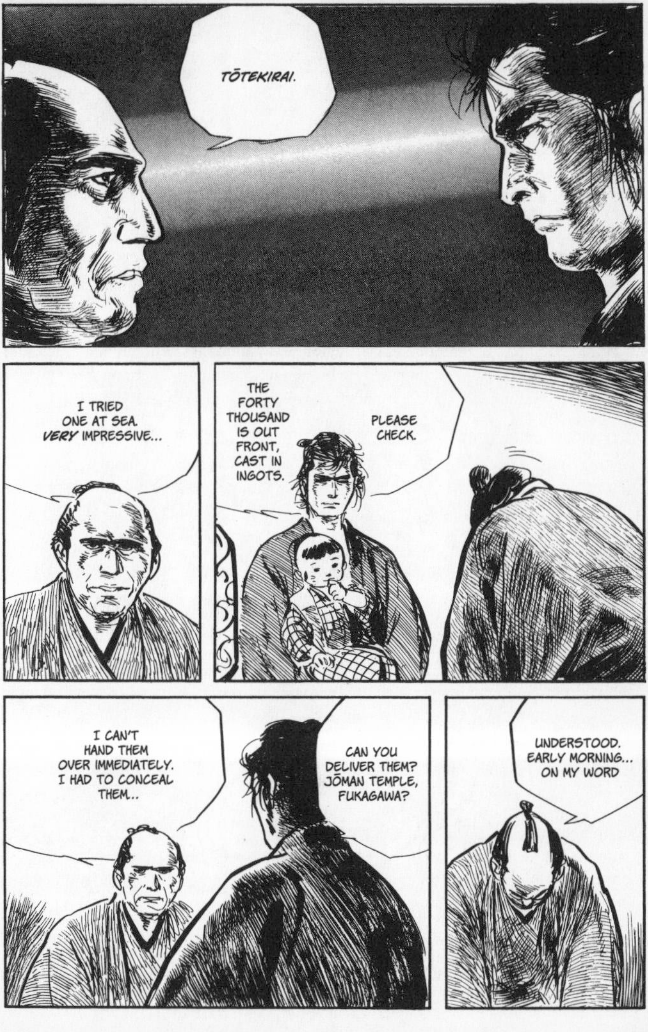
TŌTEKIRAI.
I TRIED ONE AT SEA. *VERY* IMPRESSIVE...
THE FORTY THOUSAND IS OUT FRONT, CAST IN INGOTS.
PLEASE CHECK.
I CAN'T HAND THEM OVER IMMEDIATELY. I HAD TO CONCEAL THEM..
CAN YOU DELIVER THEM? JŌMAN TEMPLE, FUKAGAWA?
UNDERSTOOD. EARLY MORNING... ON MY WORD

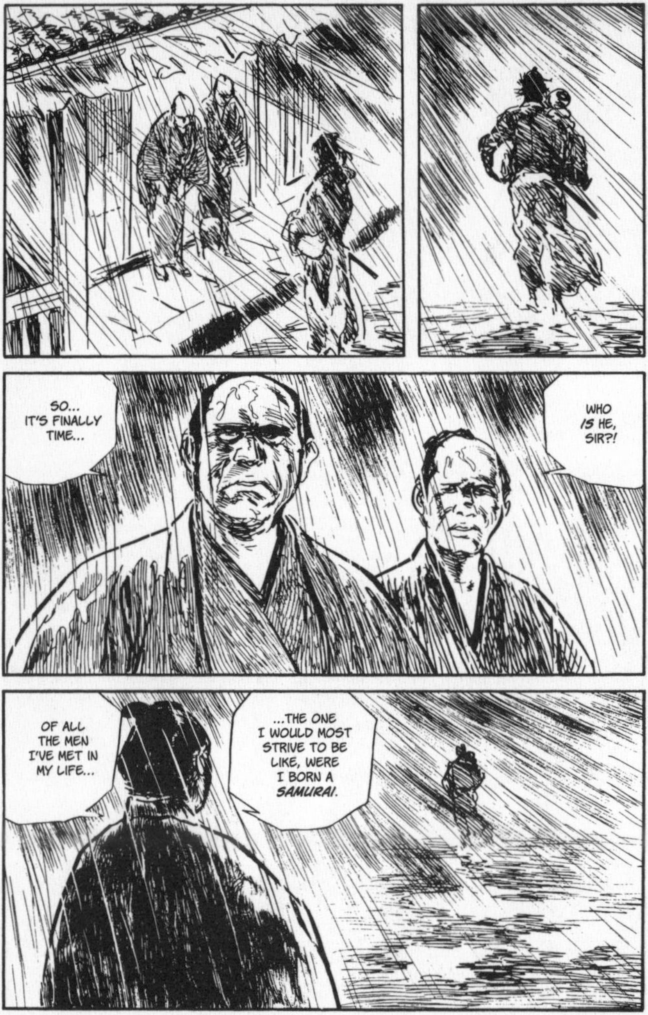
SO... IT'S FINALLY TIME...
WHO *IS* HE, SIR?!
OF ALL THE MEN I'VE MET IN MY LIFE...
...THE ONE I WOULD MOST STRIVE TO BE LIKE, WERE I BORN A *SAMURAI*.

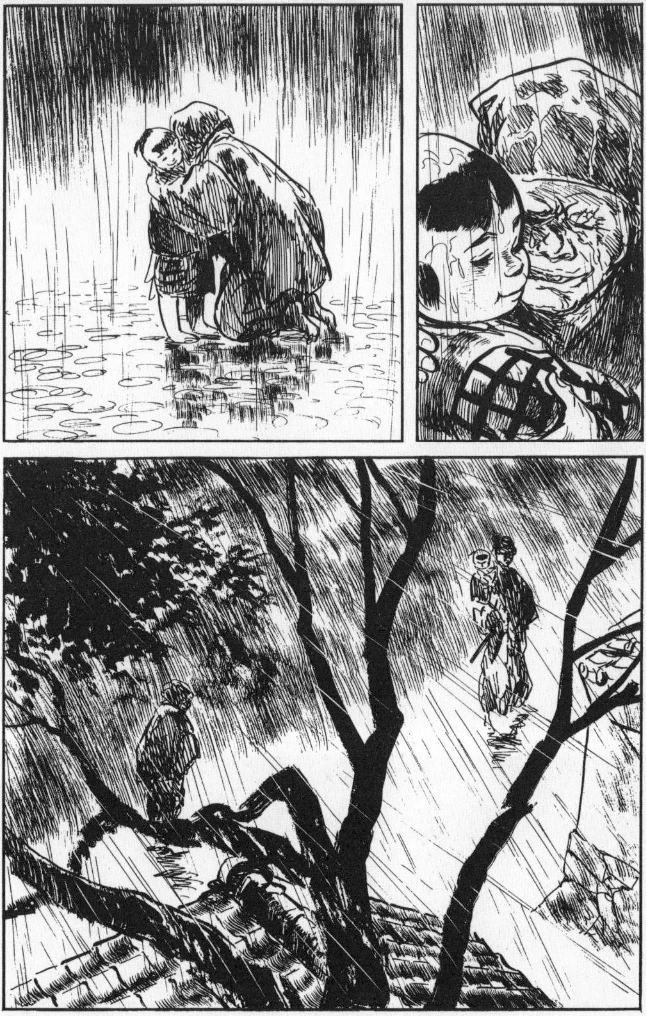

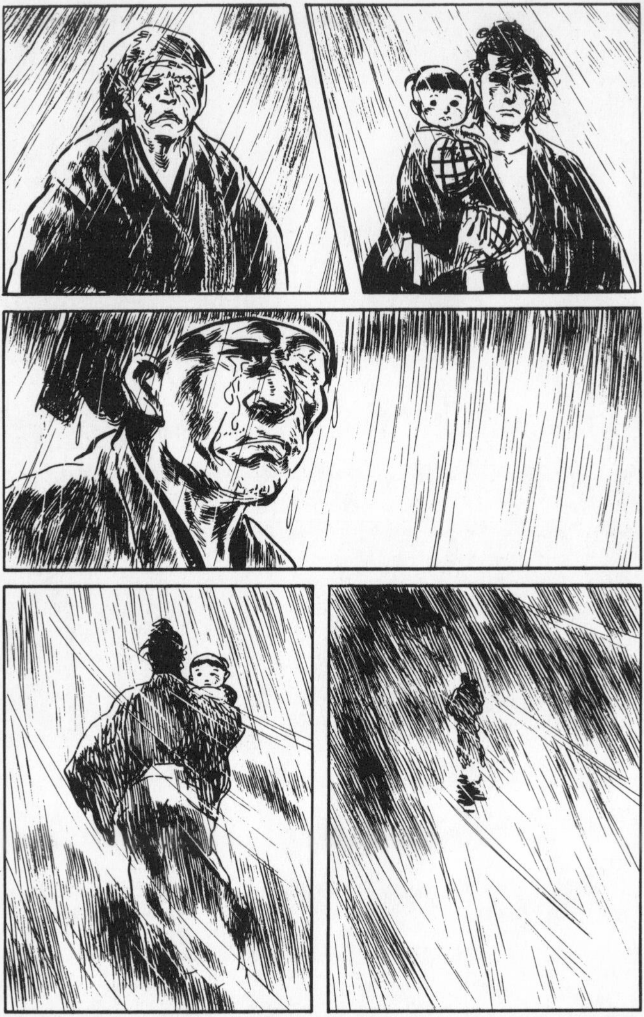

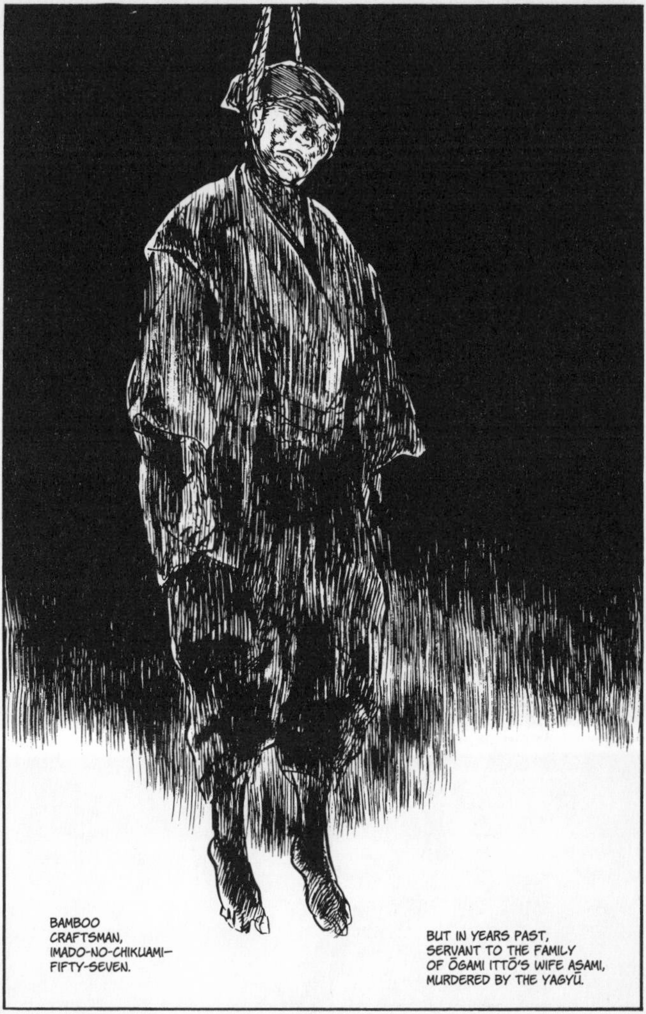
BAMBOO CRAFTSMAN, IMADO-NO-CHIKUAMI— FIFTY-SEVEN.
BUT IN YEARS PAST, SERVANT TO THE FAMILY OF ŌGAMI ITTŌ'S WIFE ASAMI, MURDERED BY THE YAGYŪ.

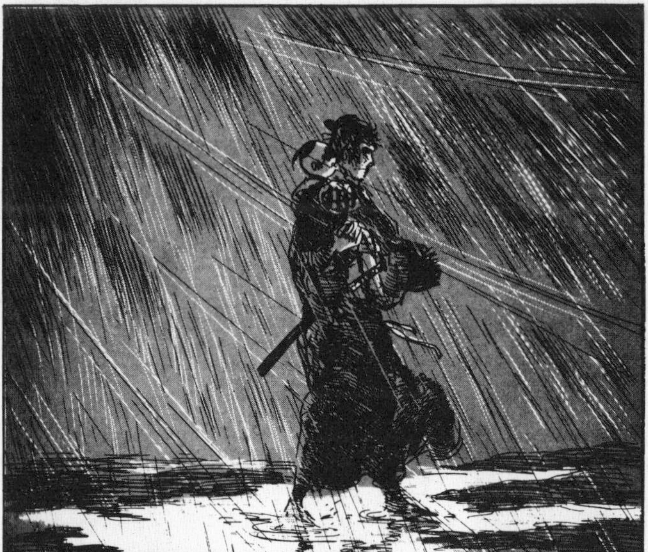

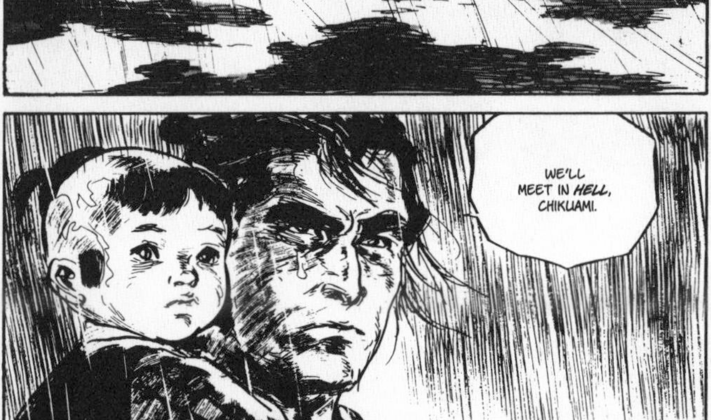
WE'LL MEET IN HELL, CHIKUAMI.

the hundred
and seventh

Kaii's Lullaby

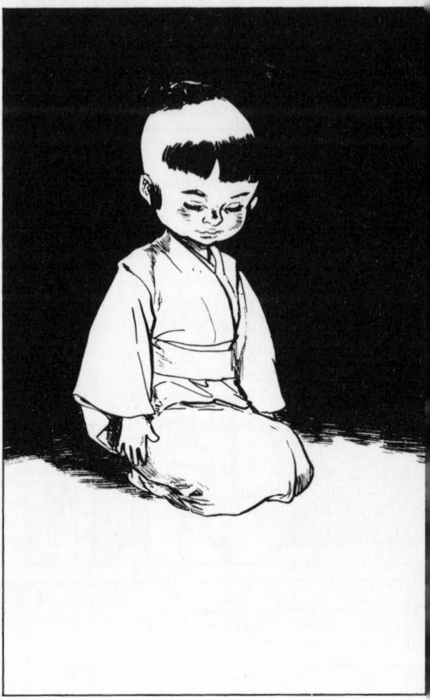

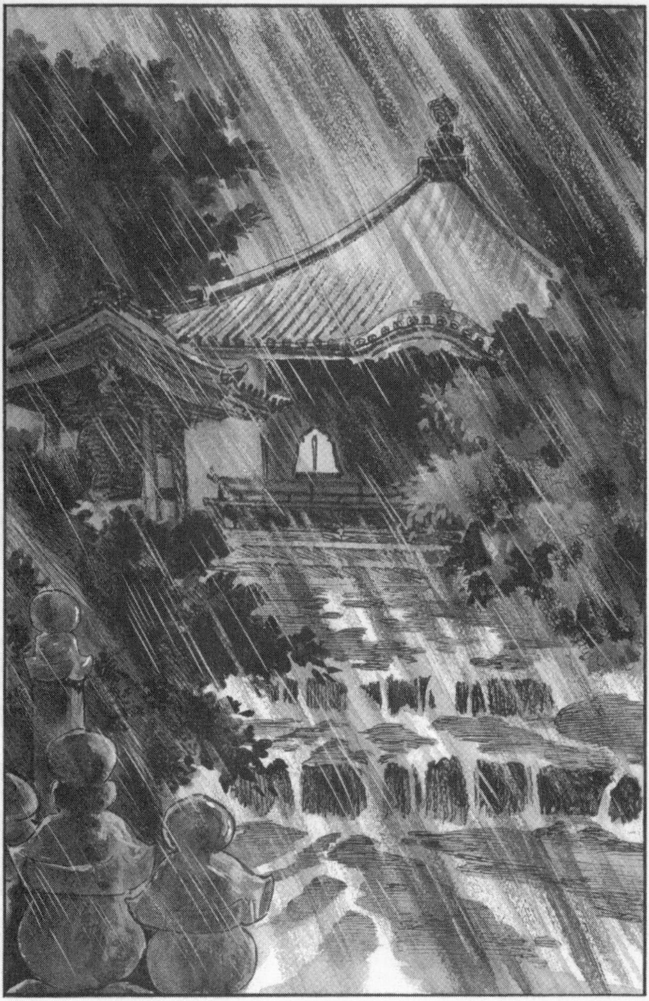

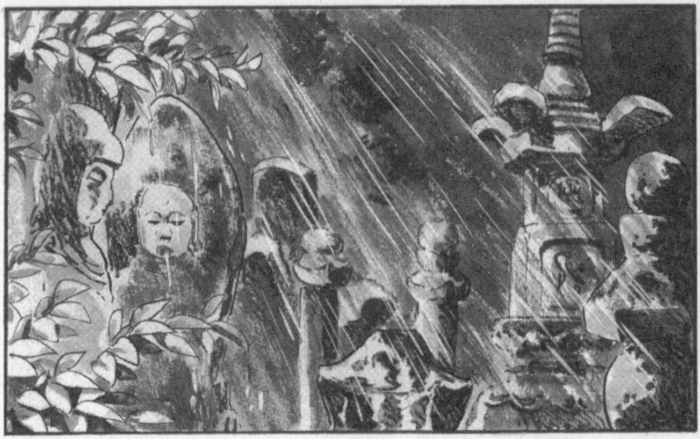
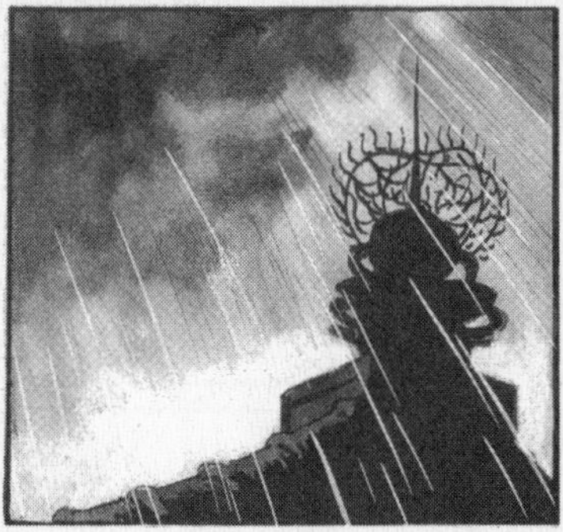
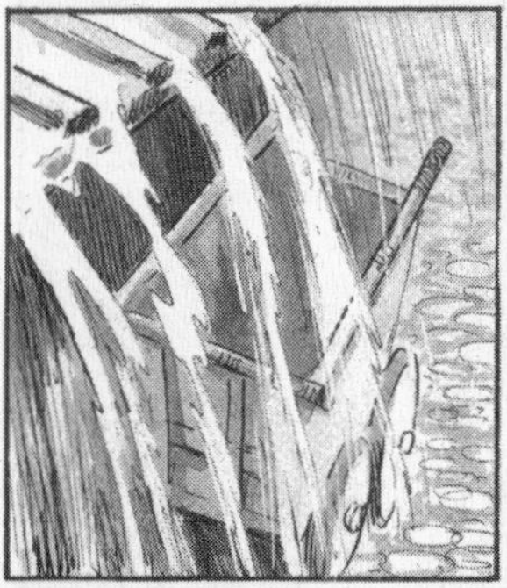
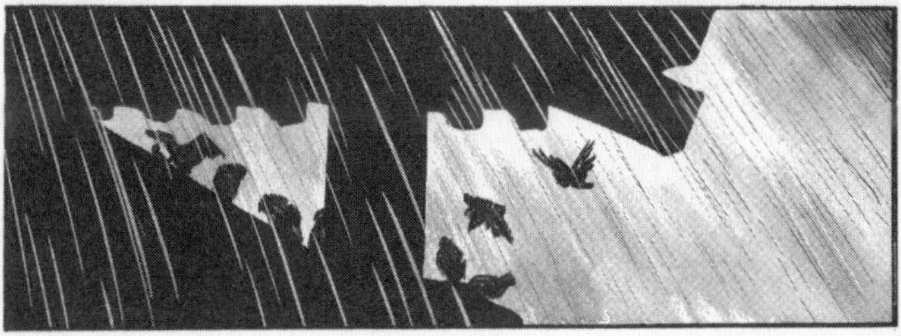

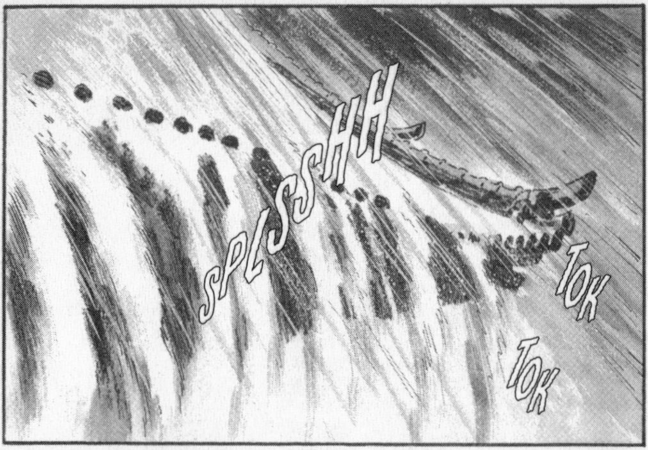
SPLSSHH
TOK
TOK
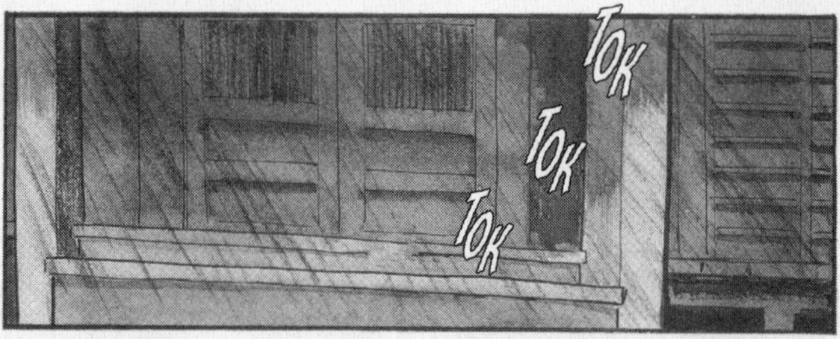
TOK
TOK
TOK
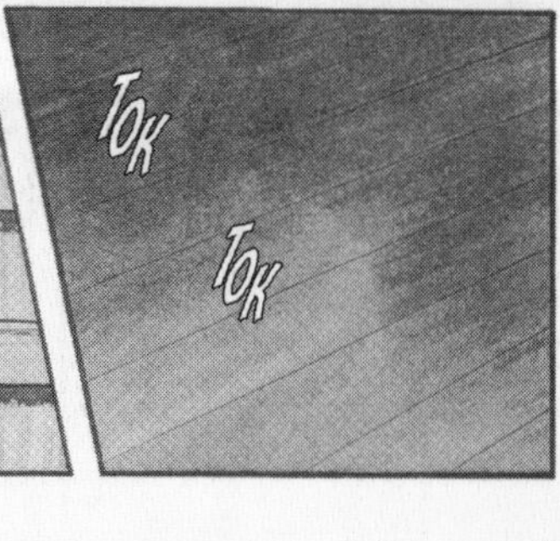
TOK
TOK
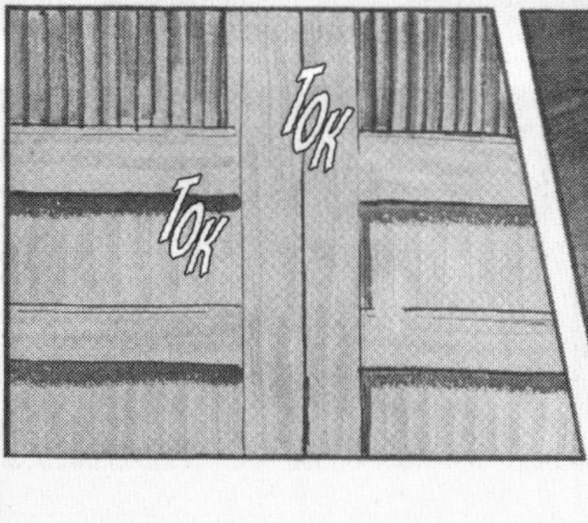
TOK
TOK

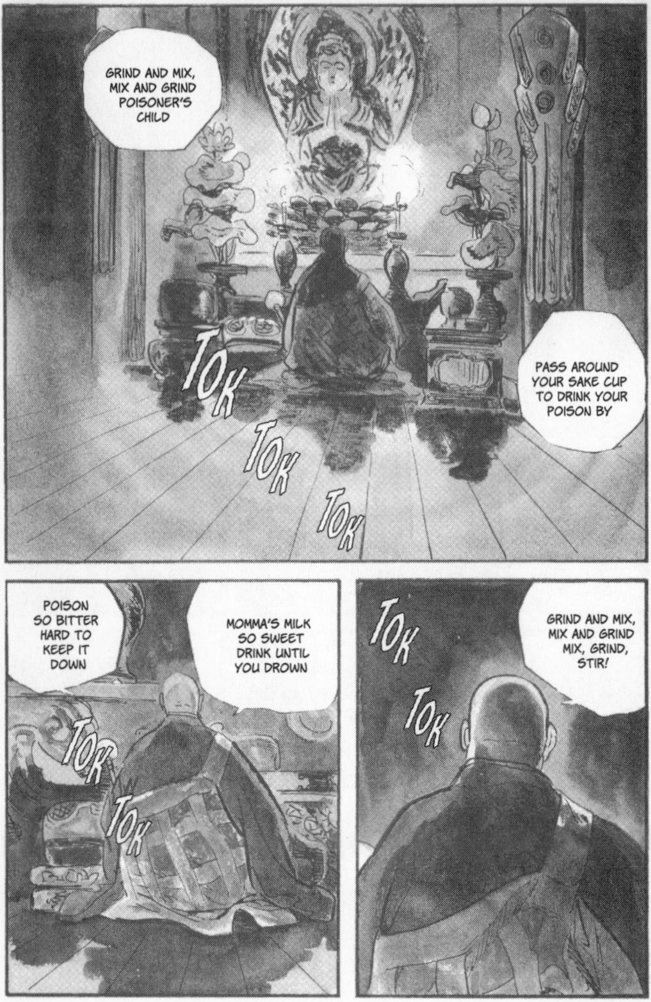
GRIND AND MIX, MIX AND GRIND POISONER'S CHILD
PASS AROUND YOUR SAKE CUP TO DRINK YOUR POISON BY
TOK
TOK
TOK
GRIND AND MIX, MIX AND GRIND MIX, GRIND, STIR!
TOK
TOK
MOMMA'S MILK SO SWEET DRINK UNTIL YOU DROWN
POISON SO BITTER HARD TO KEEP IT DOWN
TOK
TOK

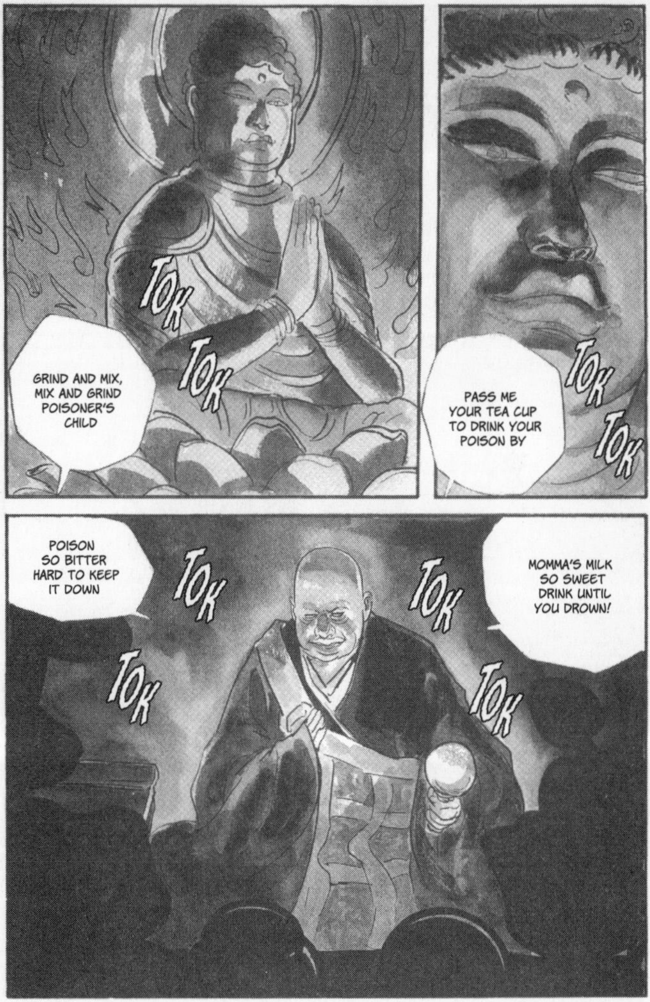
TOK
TOK
GRIND AND MIX, MIX AND GRIND POISONER'S CHILD
PASS ME YOUR TEA CUP TO DRINK YOUR POISON BY
TOK
TOK
POISON SO BITTER HARD TO KEEP IT DOWN
TOK
TOK
TOK
TOK
MOMMA'S MILK SO SWEET DRINK UNTIL YOU DROWN!

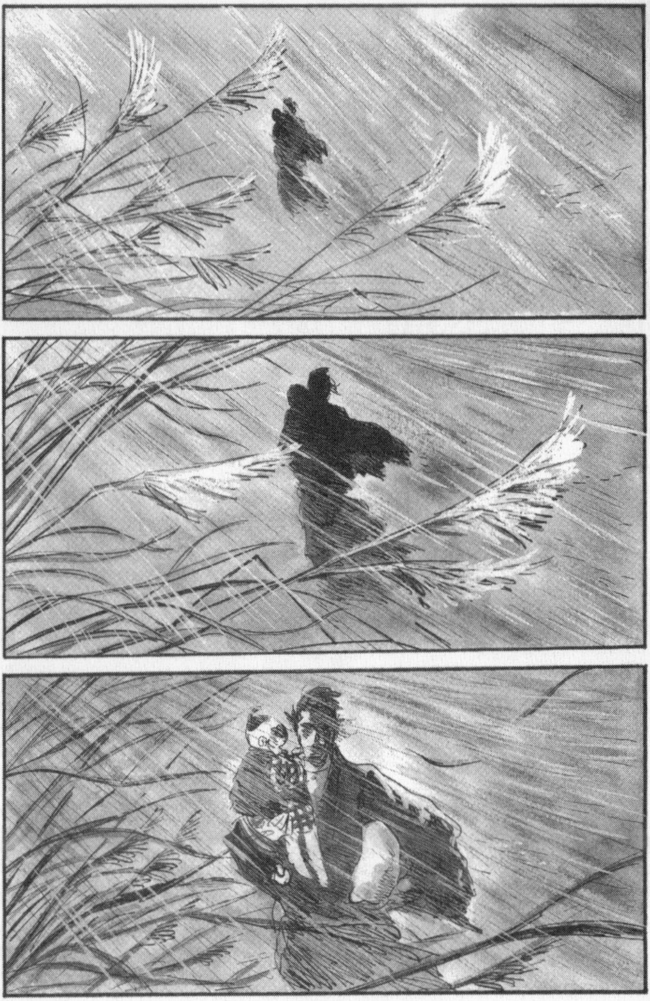

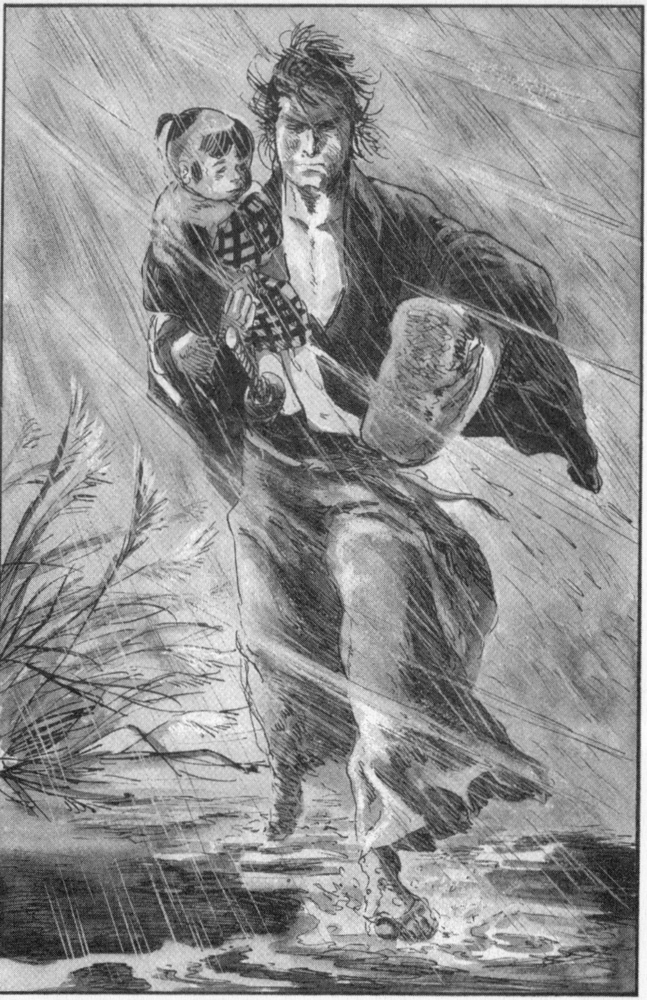

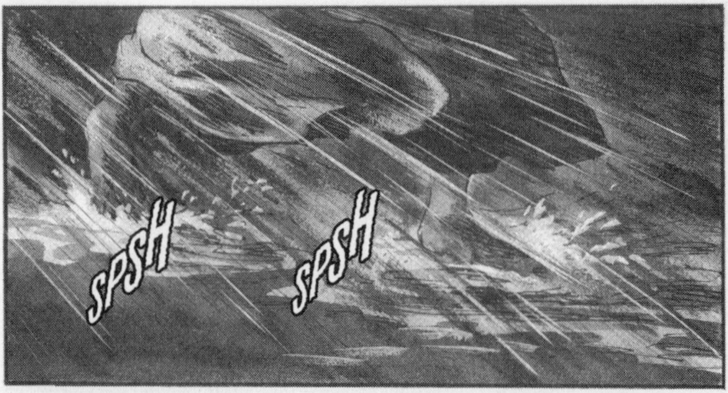
SPSH
SPSH
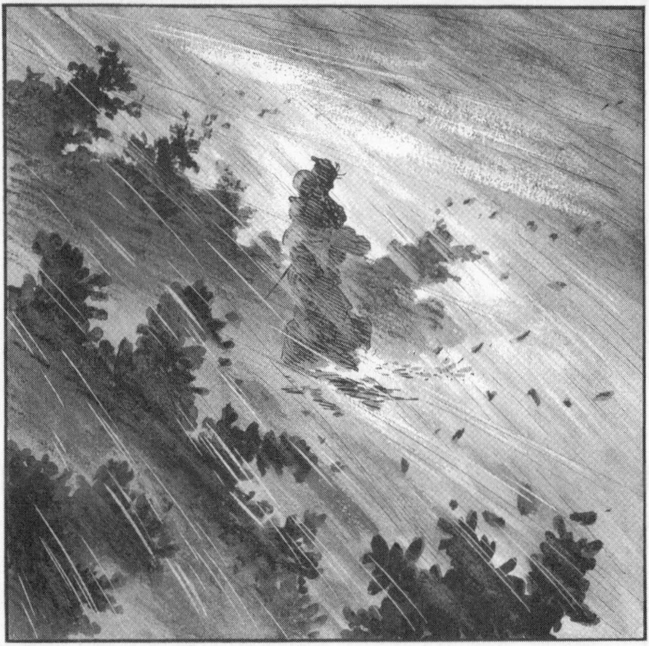

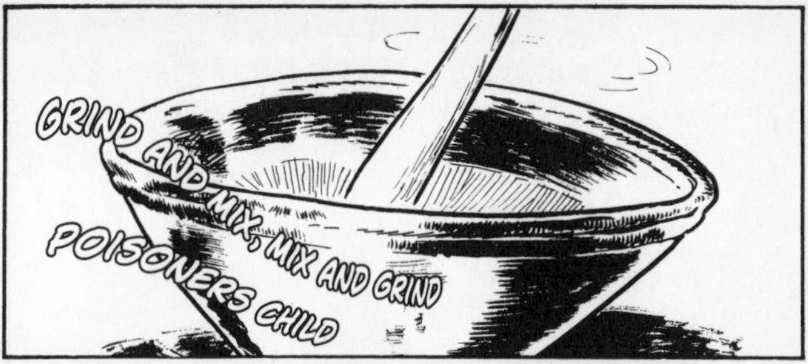
GRIND AND MIX, MIX AND GRIND
POISONERS CHILD
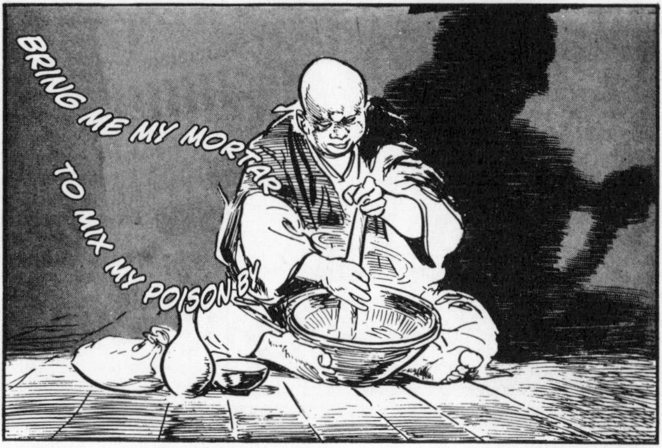
BRING ME MY MORTAR
TO MIX MY POISON BY
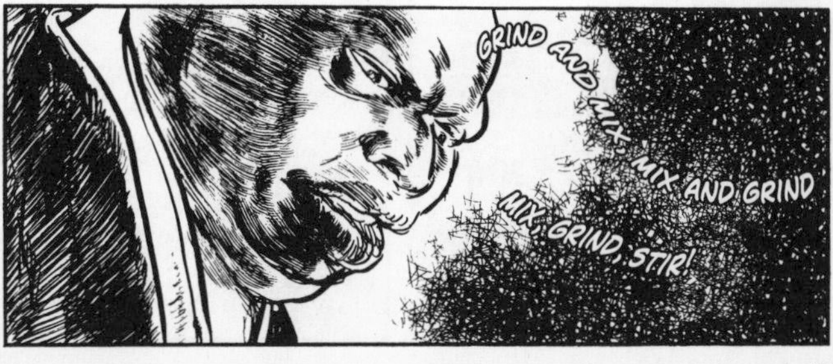
GRIND AND MIX, MIX AND GRIND
MIX, GRIND, STIR!

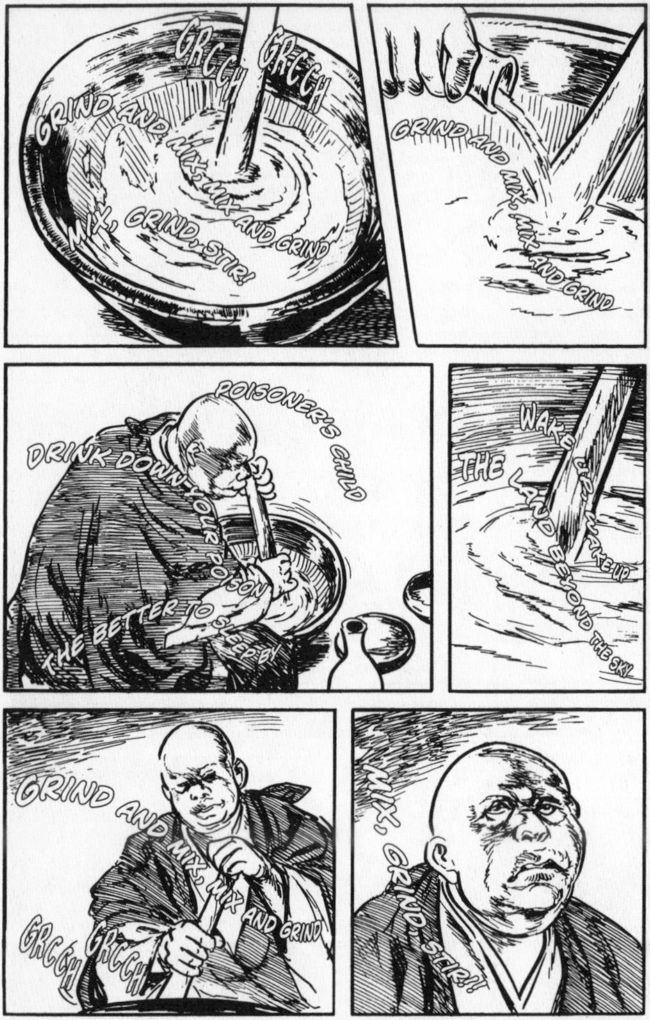
GRCCH GRCCH
GRIND AND MIX, MIX AND GRIND
MIX, GRIND, STIR!
GRIND AND MIX, MIX AND GRIND
POISONER'S CHILD
DRINK DOWN YOUR POISON
THE BETTER TO SLEEP BY
WAKE UP, WAKE UP
THE LAND BEYOND THE SKY
GRIND AND MIX, MIX AND GRIND
GRCCH GRCCH
MIX, GRIND, STIR!!

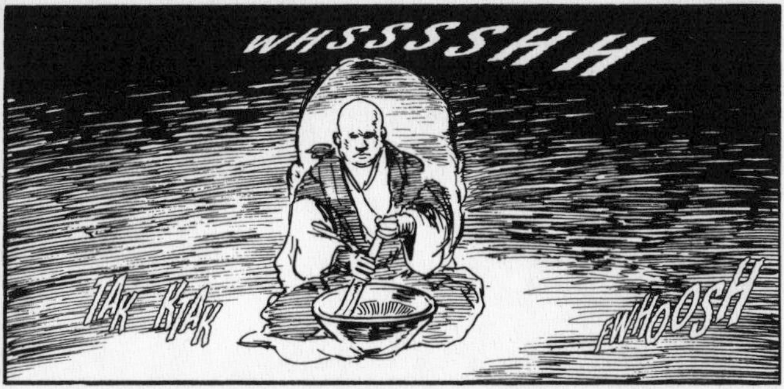
WHSSSSHH
FWHOOSH
TAK KTAK

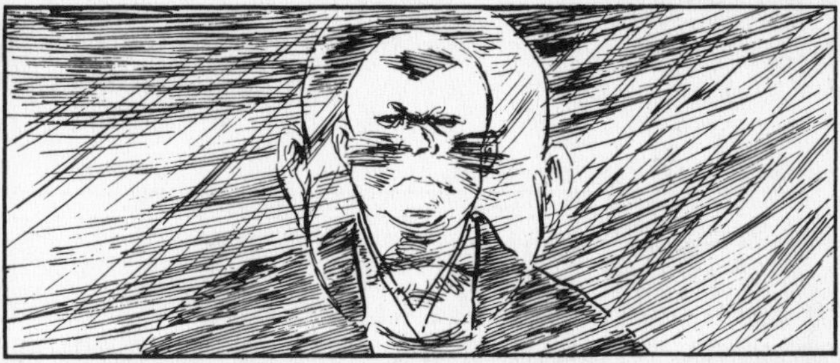

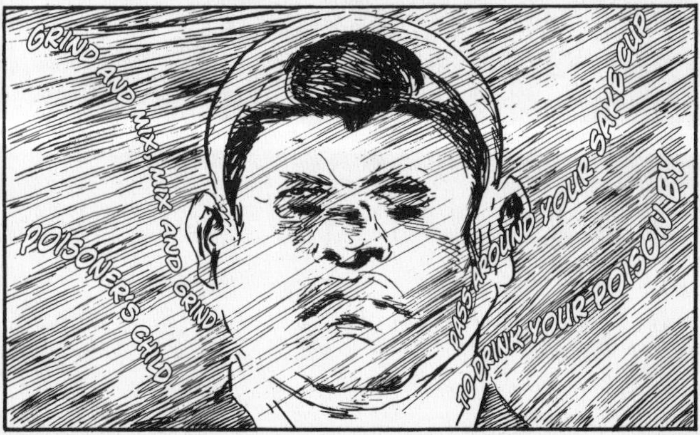
GRIND AND MIX, MIX AND GRIND
POISONER'S CHILD
PASS AROUND YOUR SAKE CUP
TO DRINK YOUR POISON BY

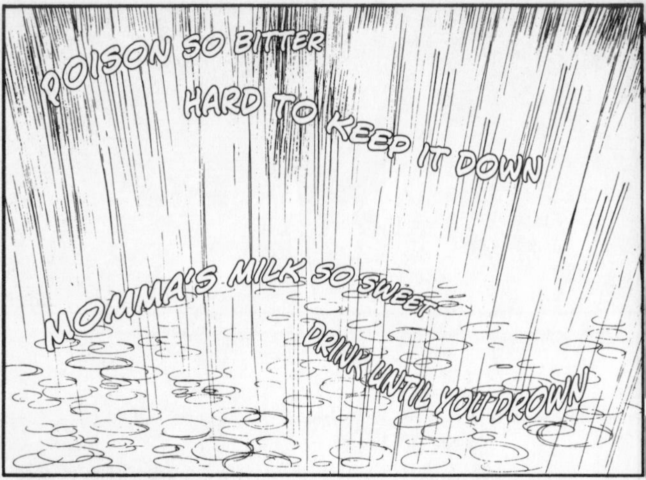
POISON SO BITTER
HARD TO KEEP IT DOWN
MOMMA'S MILK SO SWEET
DRINK UNTIL YOU DROWN
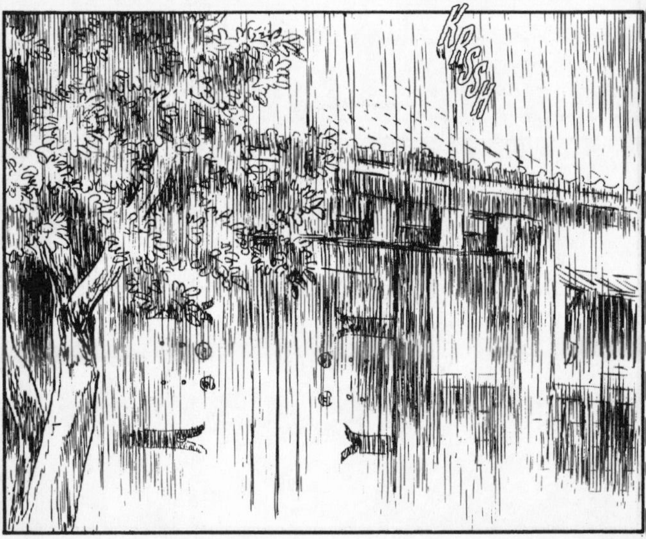
KRSSH

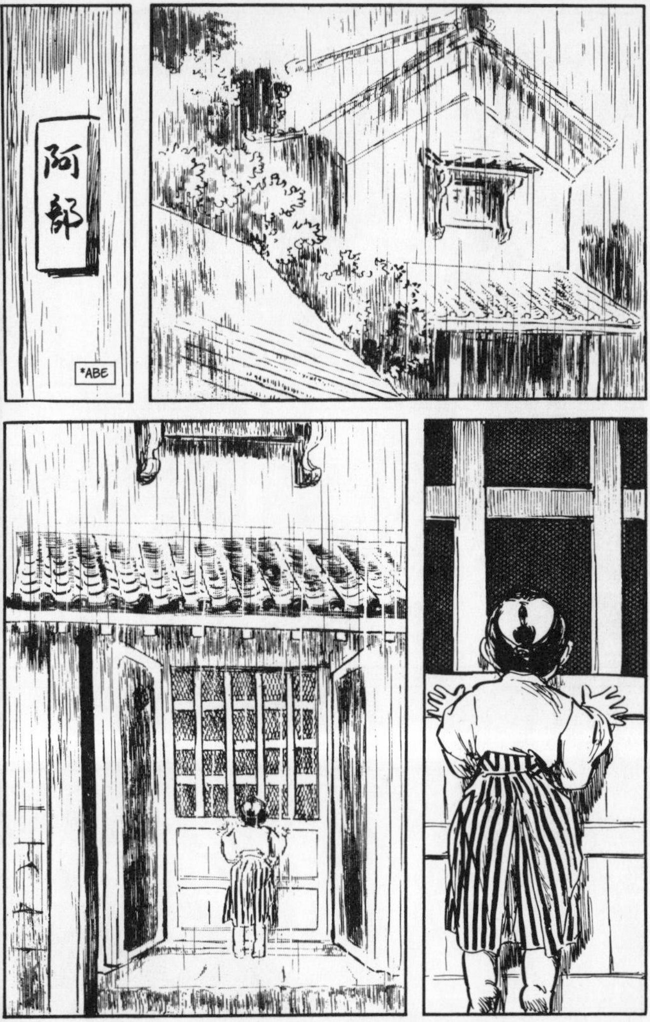
阿部
*ABE

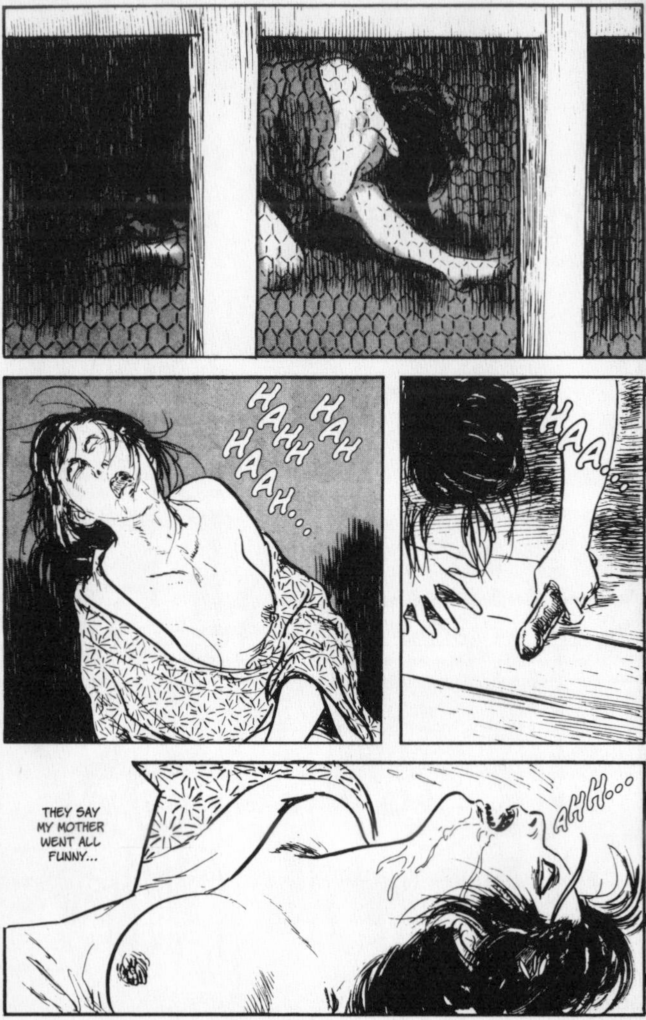
HAA...
HAH
HAHH
HAAAH...
AHH...
THEY SAY MY MOTHER WENT ALL FUNNY...

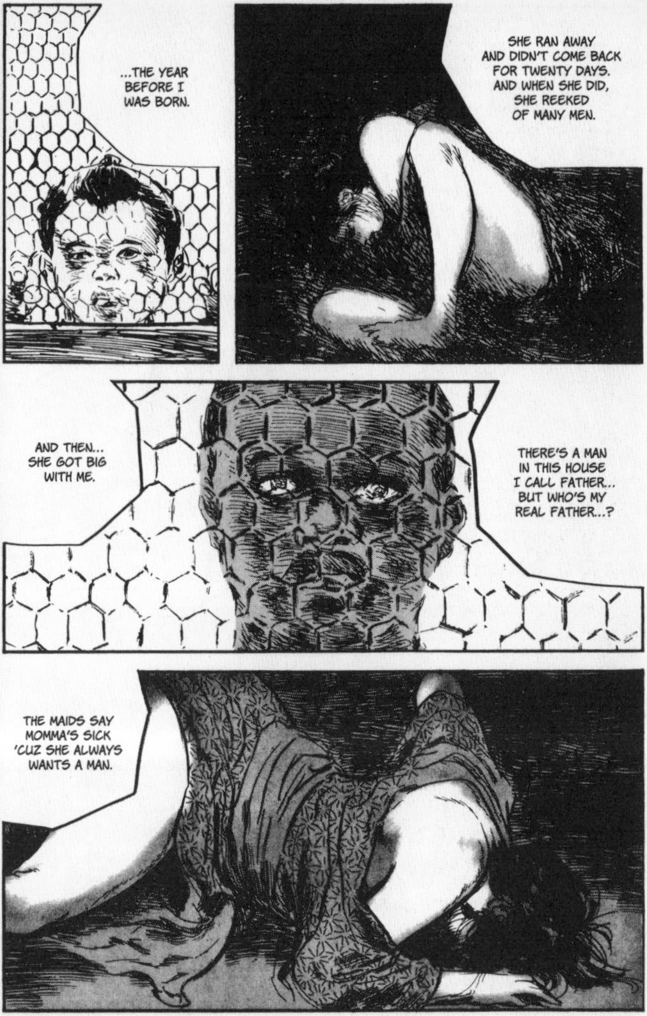
...THE YEAR BEFORE I WAS BORN.
SHE RAN AWAY AND DIDN'T COME BACK FOR TWENTY DAYS. AND WHEN SHE DID, SHE REEKED OF MANY MEN.
AND THEN... SHE GOT BIG WITH ME.
THERE'S A MAN IN THIS HOUSE I CALL FATHER... BUT WHO'S MY REAL FATHER...?
THE MAIDS SAY MOMMA'S SICK 'CUZ SHE ALWAYS WANTS A MAN.

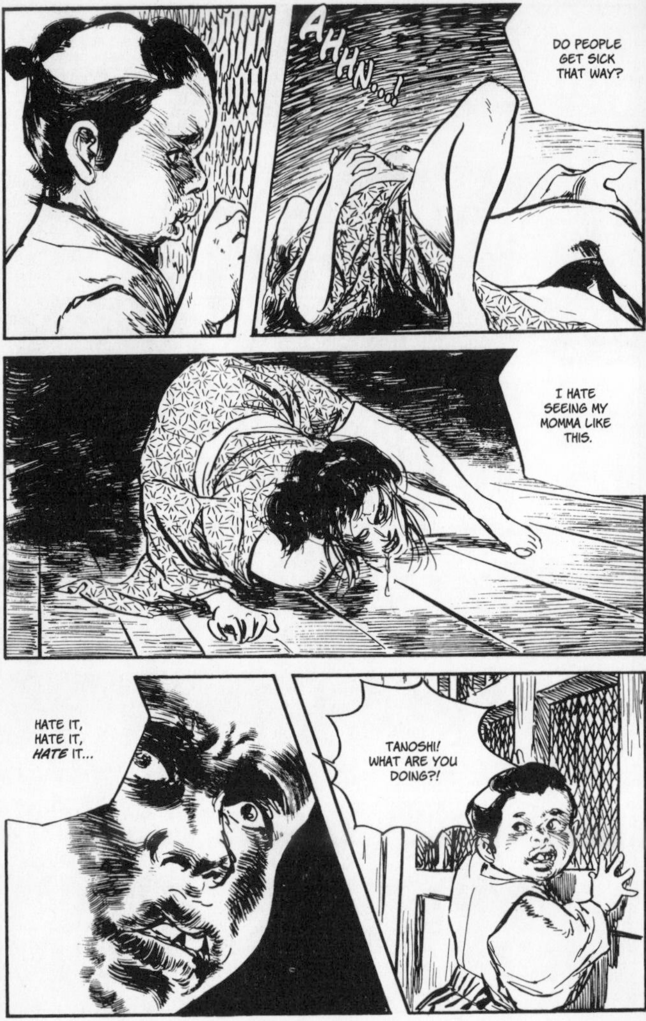
AHHN...!
DO PEOPLE GET SICK THAT WAY?
I HATE SEEING MY MOMMA LIKE THIS.
TANOSHI! WHAT ARE YOU DOING?!
HATE IT, HATE IT, *HATE* IT...

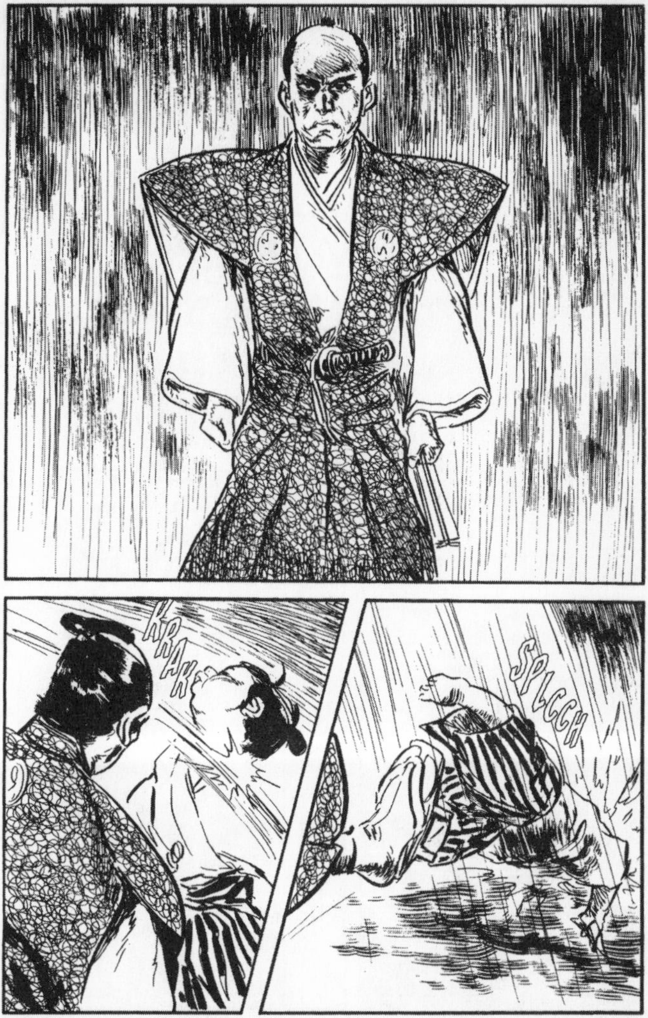
SPLCCH
KRAK

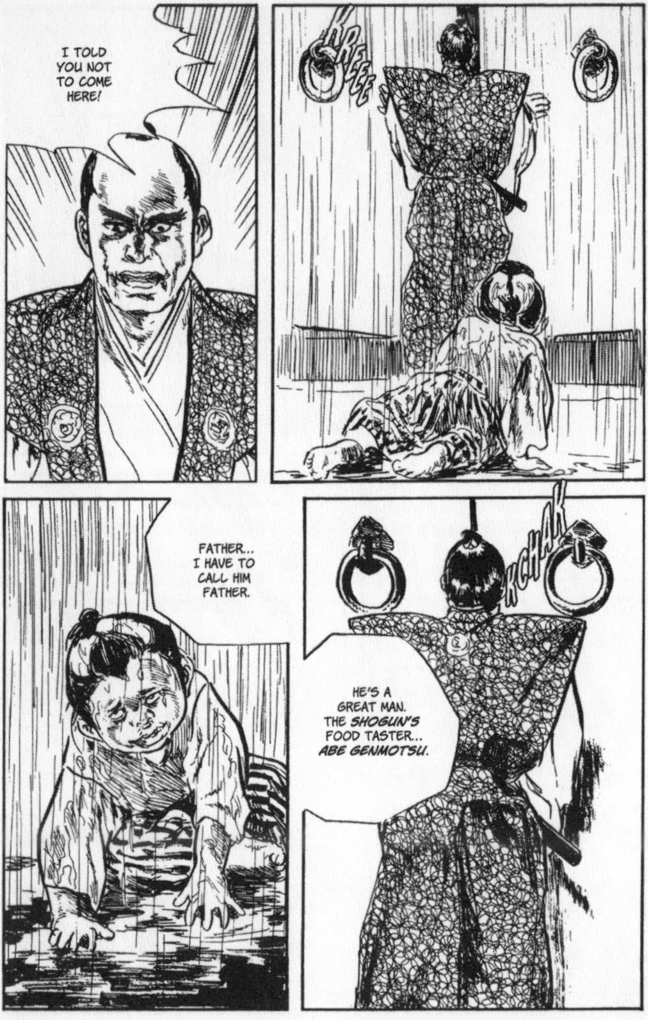
I TOLD YOU NOT TO COME HERE!
KREEE
FATHER... I HAVE TO CALL HIM FATHER.
KCHAK
HE'S A GREAT MAN. THE *SHOGUN'S* FOOD TASTER... ***ABE GENMOTSU.***

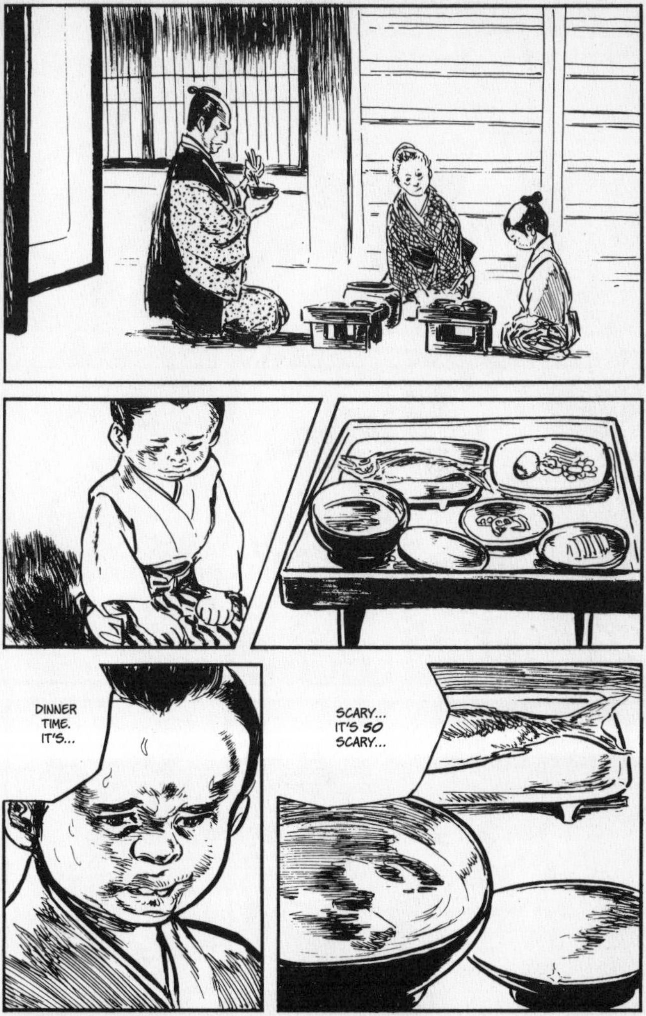
DINNER TIME. IT'S...
SCARY... IT'S SO SCARY...

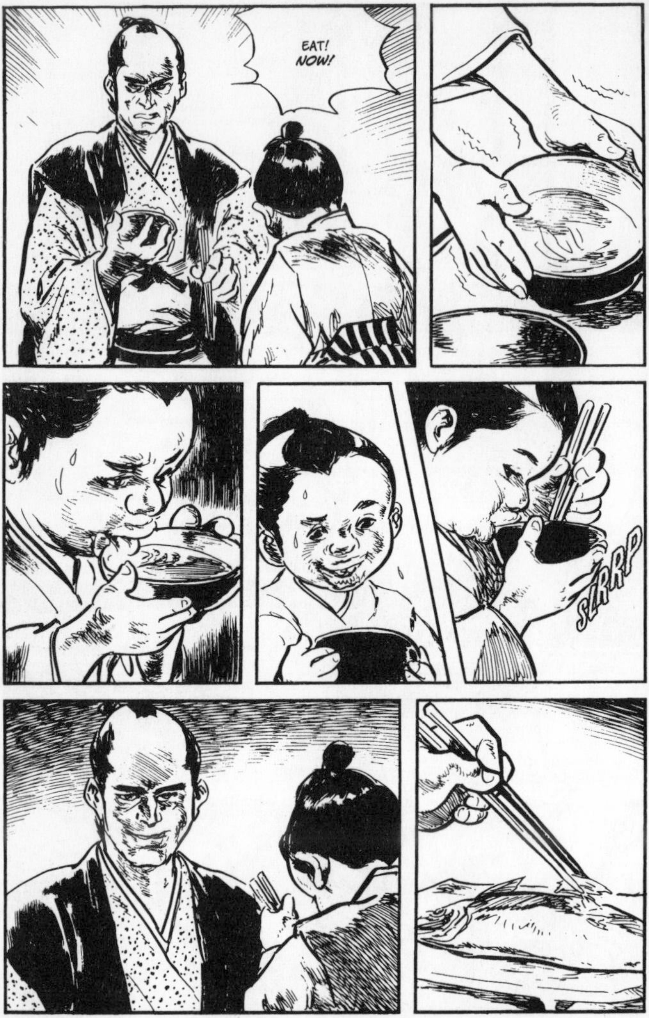
EAT! NOW!
SLRRP

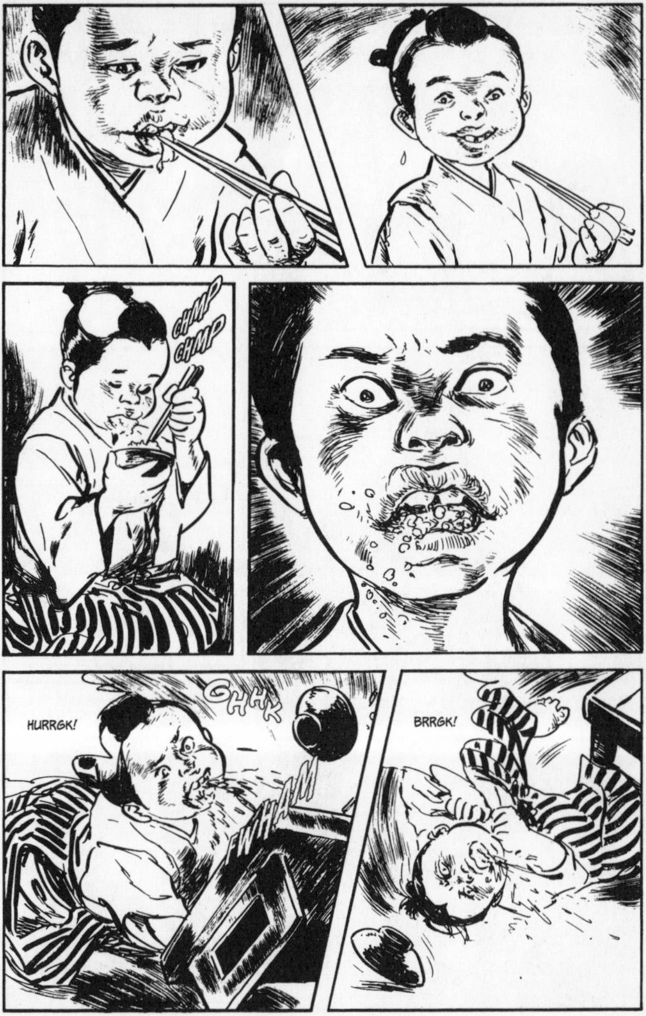
CHMP
CHMP
BRRGK!
HURRGK!
GHHK
FWHAM

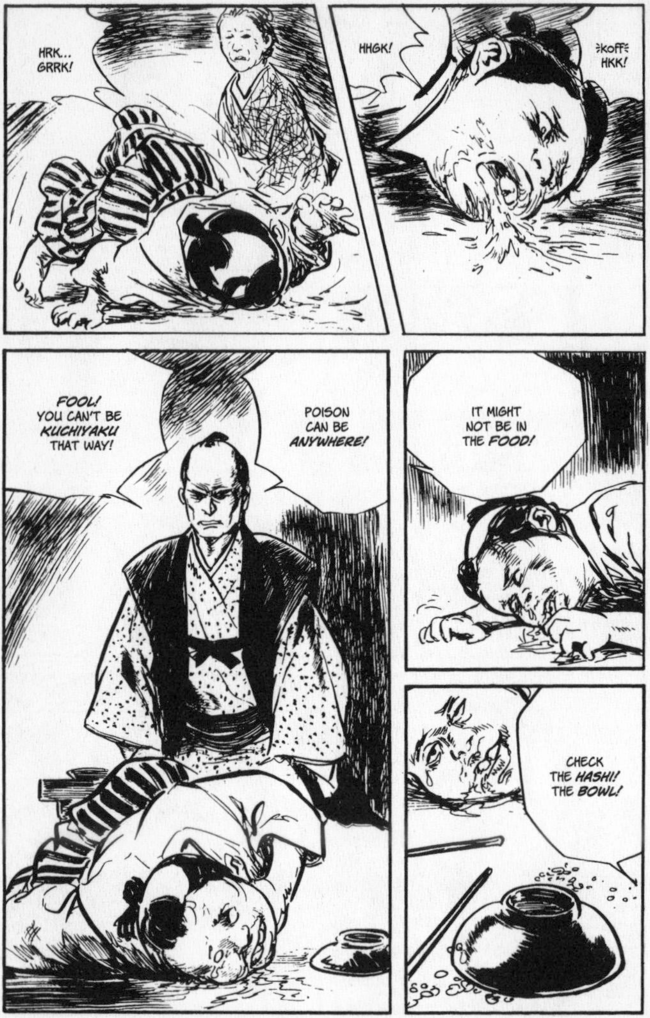
HRK... GRRK!
HHGK!
koff HKK!
FOOL! YOU CAN'T BE KUCHIYAKU THAT WAY!
POISON CAN BE ANYWHERE!
IT MIGHT NOT BE IN THE FOOD!
CHECK THE HASHI! THE BOWL!

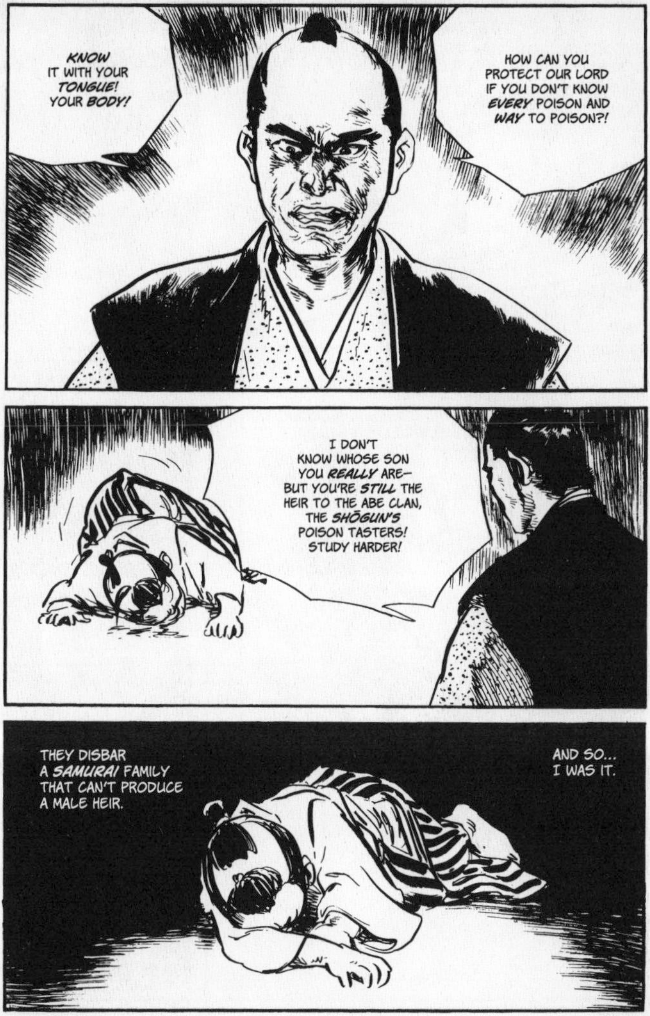

KNOW IT WITH YOUR *TONGUE!* YOUR *BODY!*
HOW CAN YOU PROTECT OUR LORD IF YOU DON'T KNOW *EVERY* POISON AND *WAY* TO POISON?!
I DON'T KNOW WHOSE SON YOU *REALLY* ARE— BUT YOU'RE *STILL* THE HEIR TO THE ABE CLAN, THE *SHŌGUN'S* POISON TASTERS! STUDY HARDER!
THEY DISBAR A *SAMURAI* FAMILY THAT CAN'T PRODUCE A MALE HEIR.
AND SO... I WAS IT.

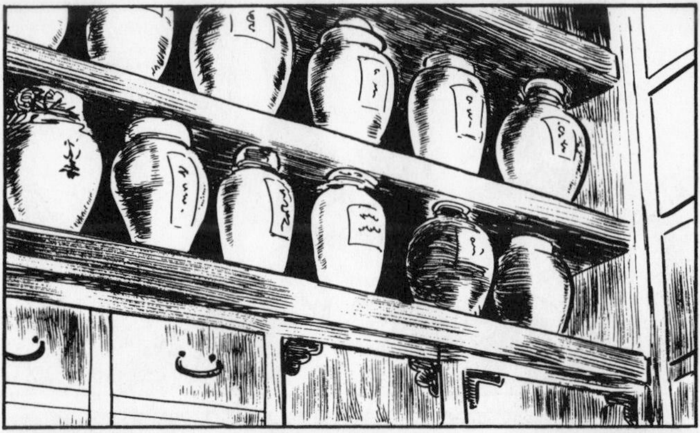

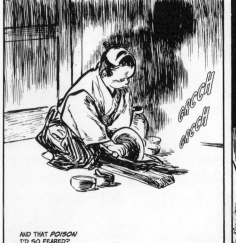

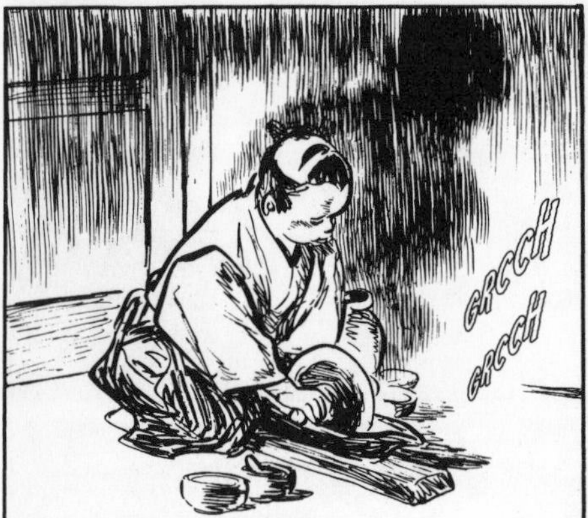
GRCCH
GRCCH
AND THAT *POISON* I'D SO FEARED? AS I GOT TO KNOW IT BETTER, I FOUND...

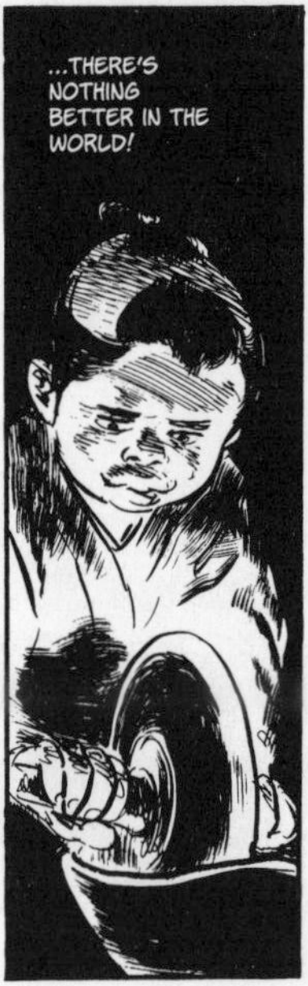
...THERE'S NOTHING BETTER IN THE WORLD!

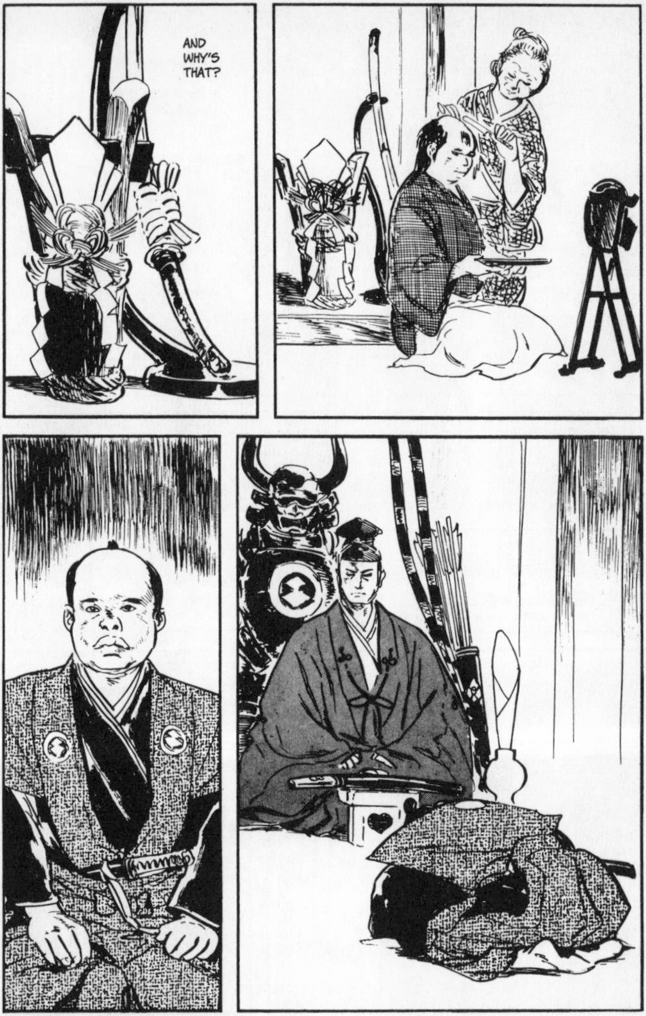
AND WHY'S THAT?

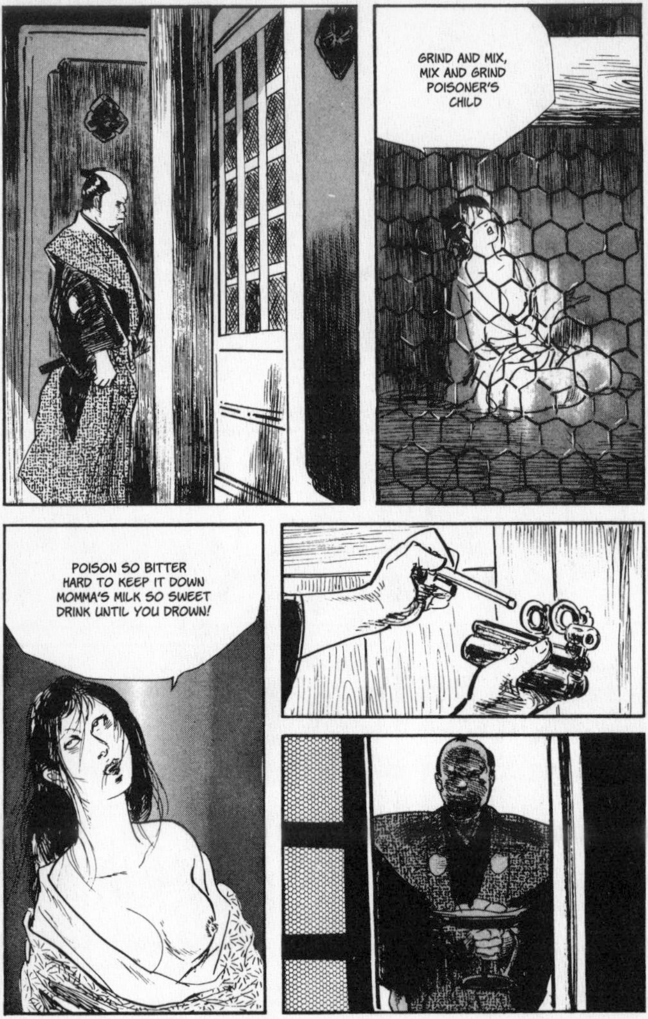
GRIND AND MIX, MIX AND GRIND POISONER'S CHILD
POISON SO BITTER HARD TO KEEP IT DOWN MOMMA'S MILK SO SWEET DRINK UNTIL YOU DROWN!

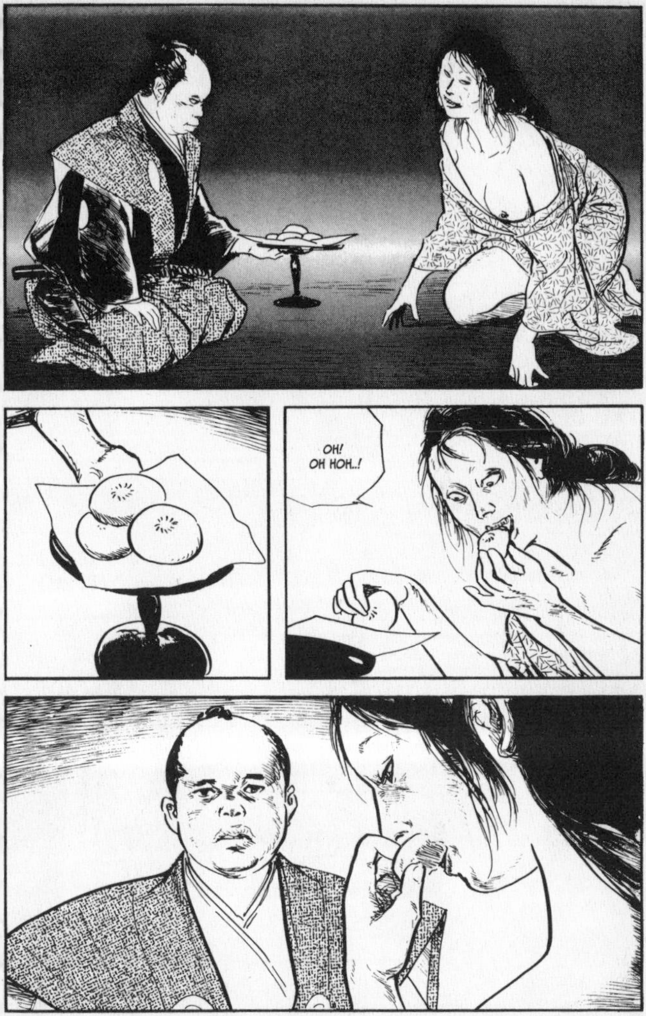
OH!
OH HOH..!

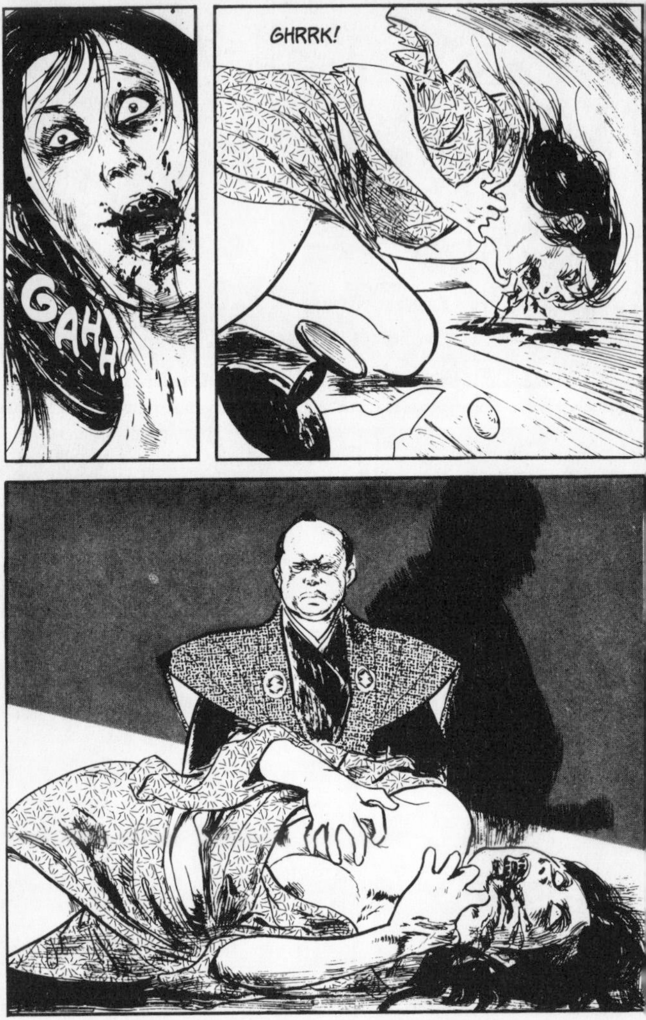
GHRRK!
GAHH!

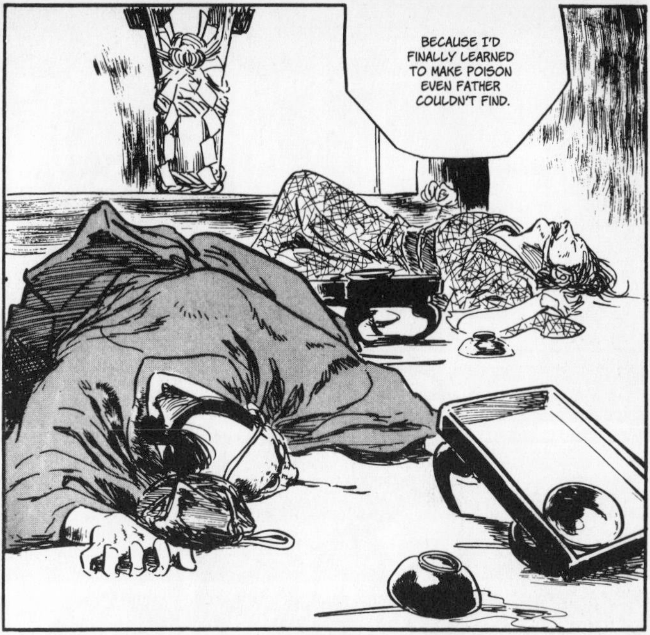
BECAUSE I'D FINALLY LEARNED TO MAKE POISON EVEN FATHER COULDN'T FIND.
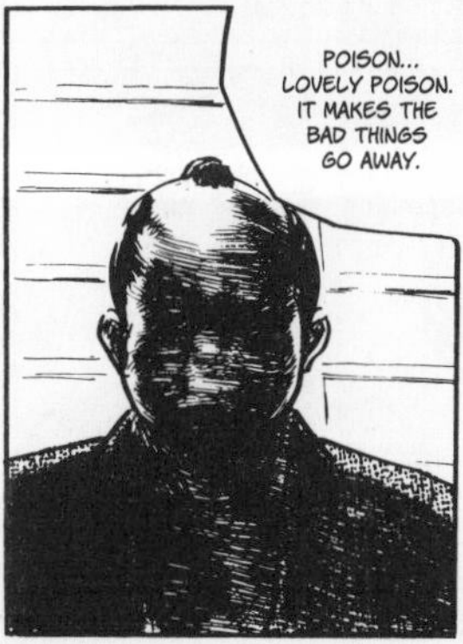
POISON... LOVELY POISON. IT MAKES THE BAD THINGS GO AWAY.
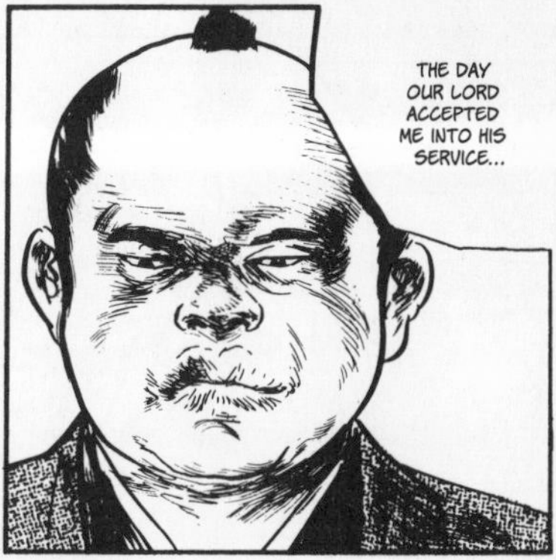
THE DAY OUR LORD ACCEPTED ME INTO HIS SERVICE...

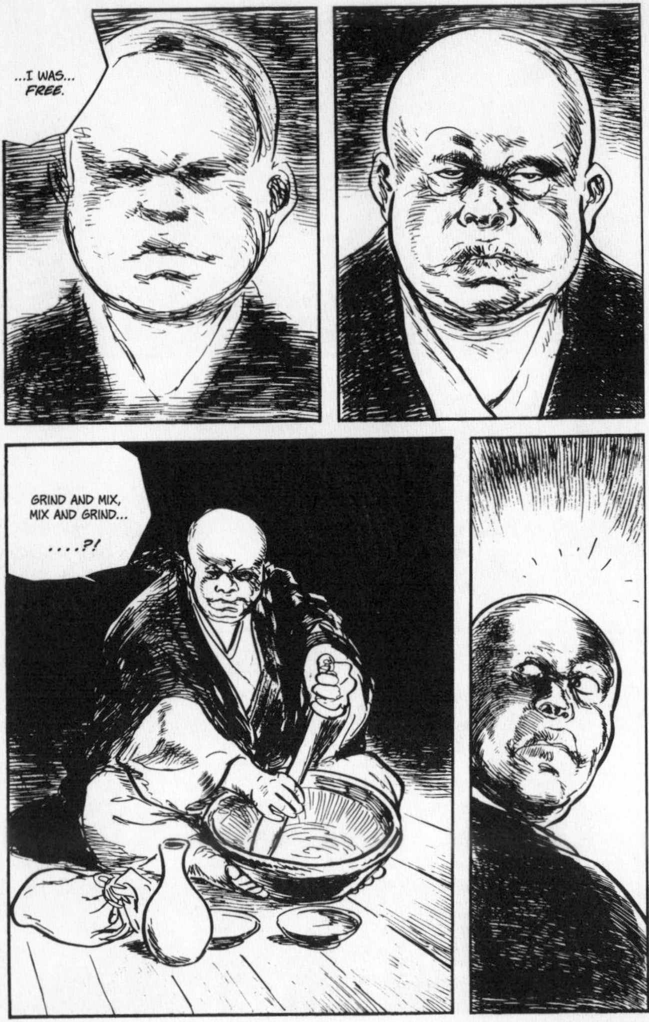
...I WAS... FREE.
GRIND AND MIX, MIX AND GRIND...
....?!

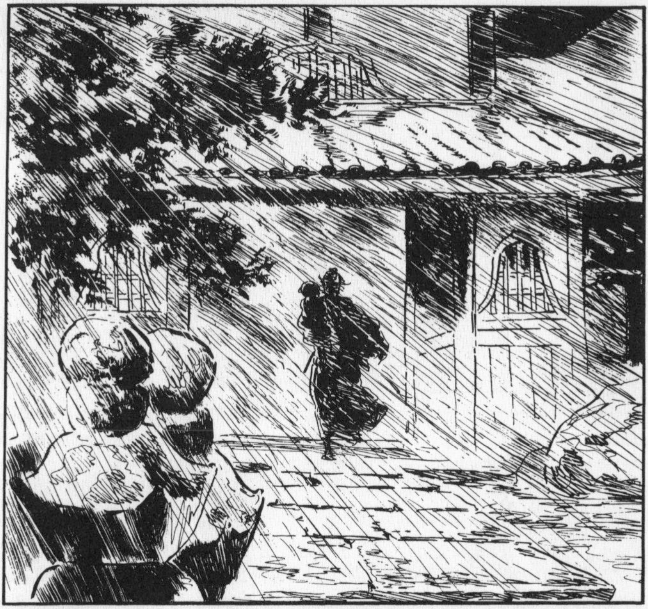
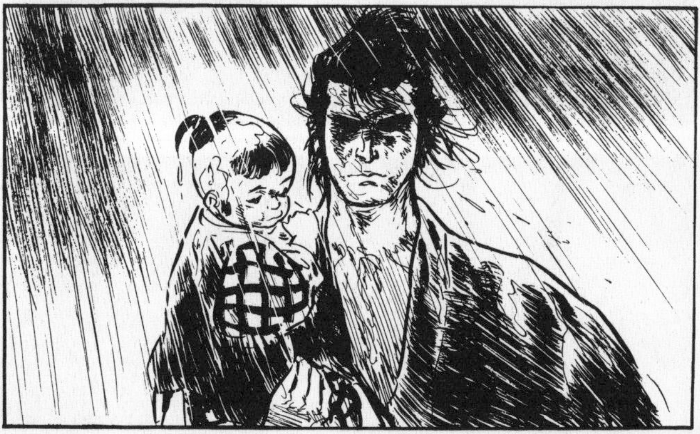

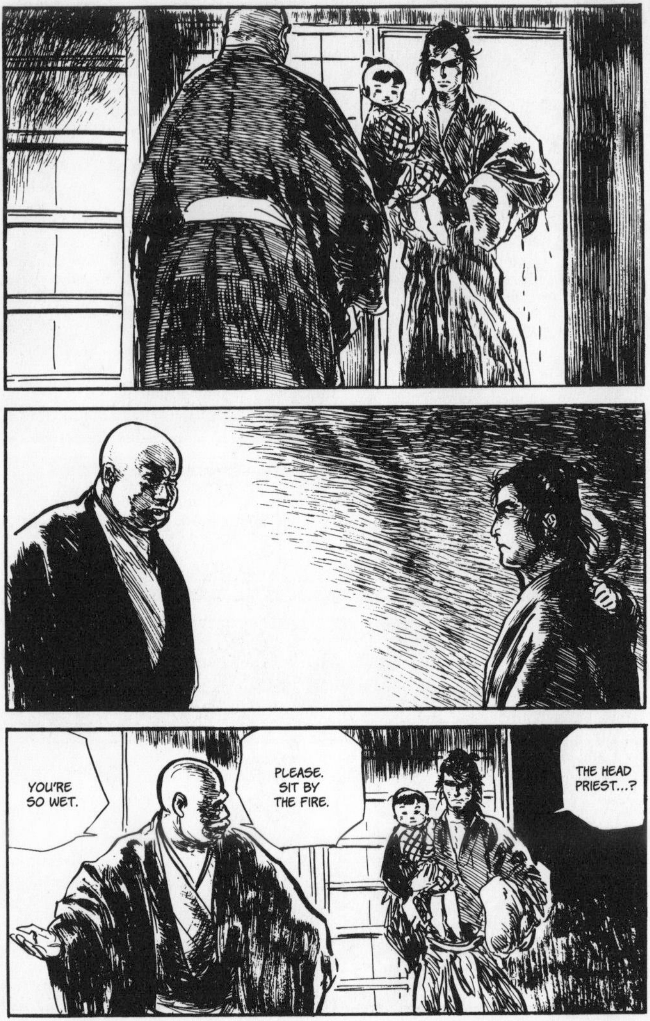
YOU'RE SO WET.
PLEASE. SIT BY THE FIRE.
THE HEAD PRIEST...?

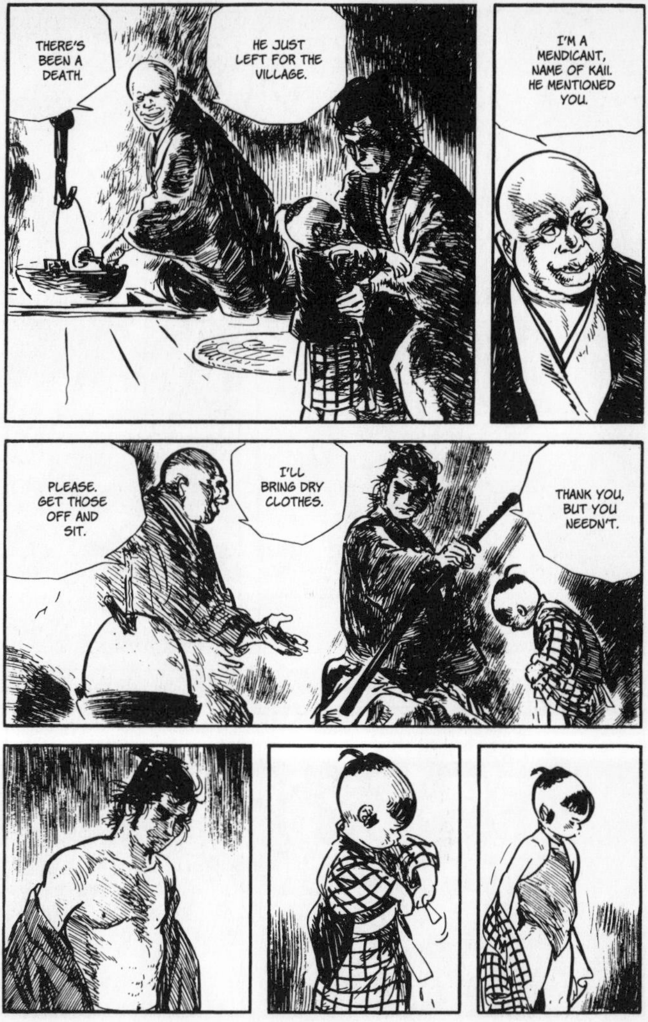
THERE'S BEEN A DEATH.
HE JUST LEFT FOR THE VILLAGE.
I'M A MENDICANT, NAME OF KAII. HE MENTIONED YOU.
PLEASE. GET THOSE OFF AND SIT.
I'LL BRING DRY CLOTHES.
THANK YOU, BUT YOU NEEDN'T.

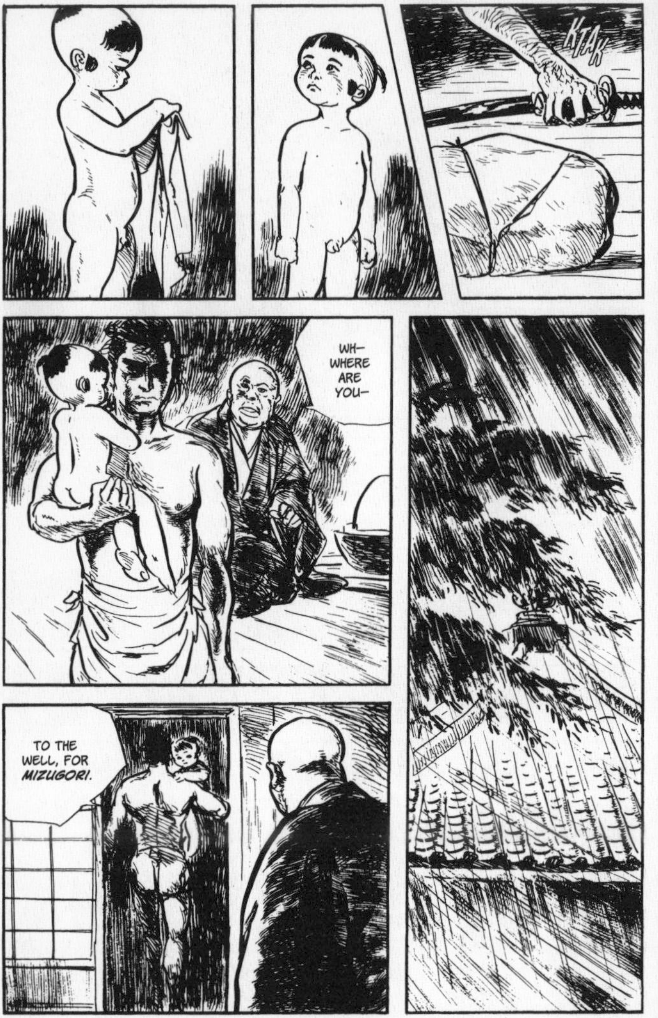
KTAK
WH— WHERE ARE YOU—
TO THE WELL, FOR *MIZUGORI*.

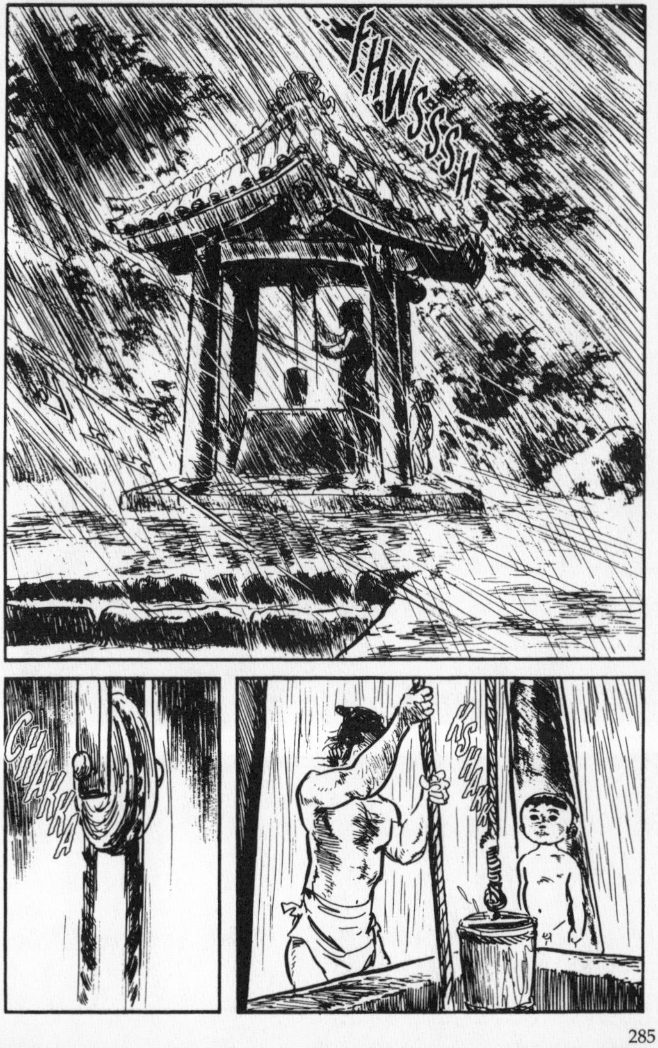
FHWSSSH
KSHAKK
CHAKKA

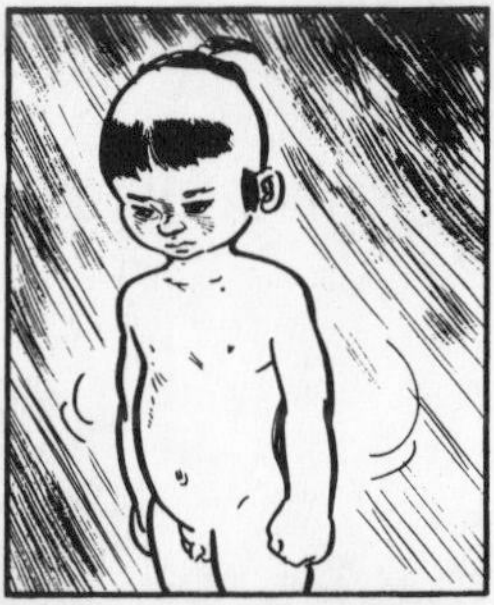

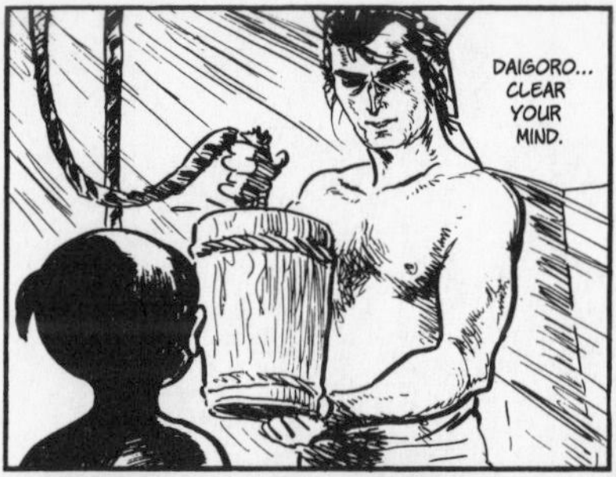
DAIGORO... CLEAR YOUR MIND.

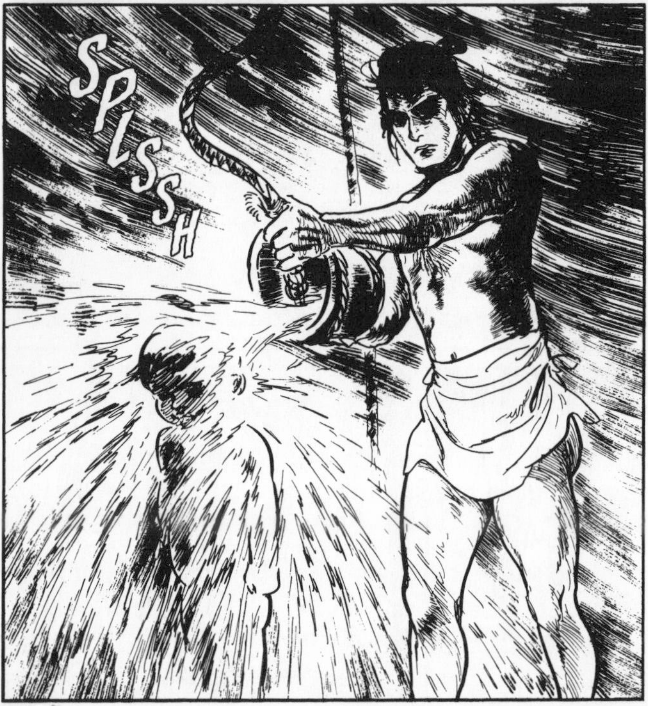
SPLSSH

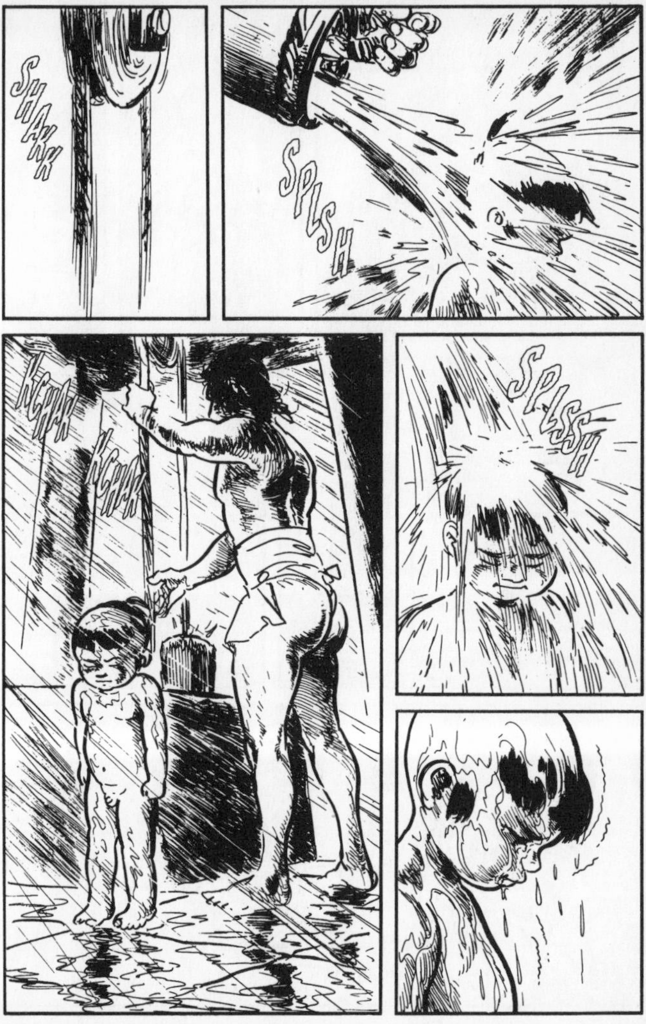
SPLSH
SHAKK
SPLSSH
KCHKK
KCHKK

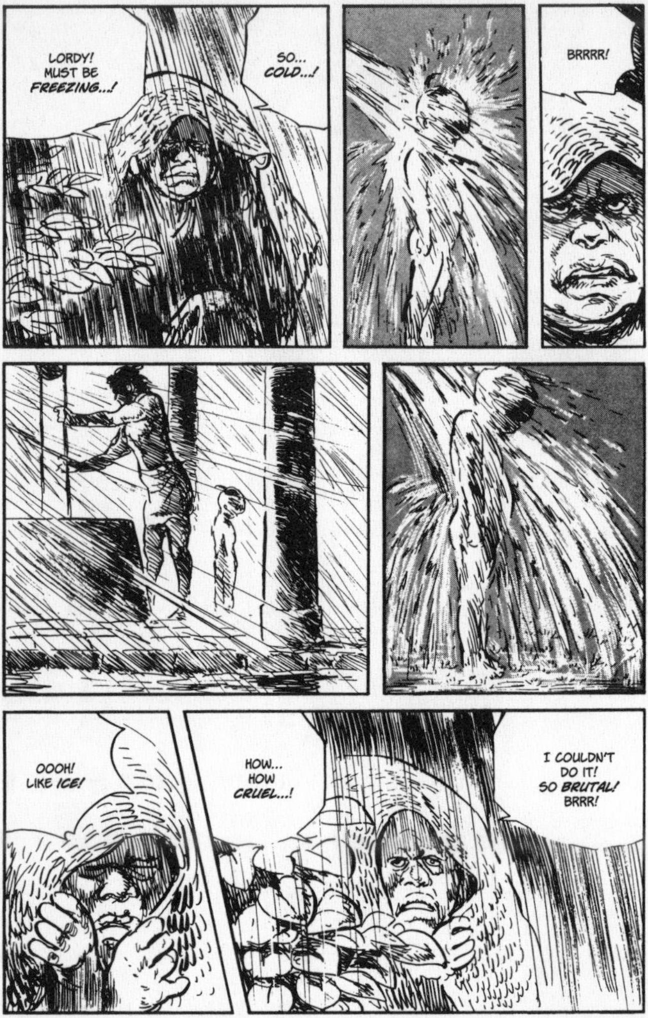
BRRRR!
SO... COLD...!
LORDY! MUST BE FREEZING...!
I COULDN'T DO IT! SO BRUTAL! BRRR!
HOW... HOW CRUEL...!
OOOH! LIKE ICE!

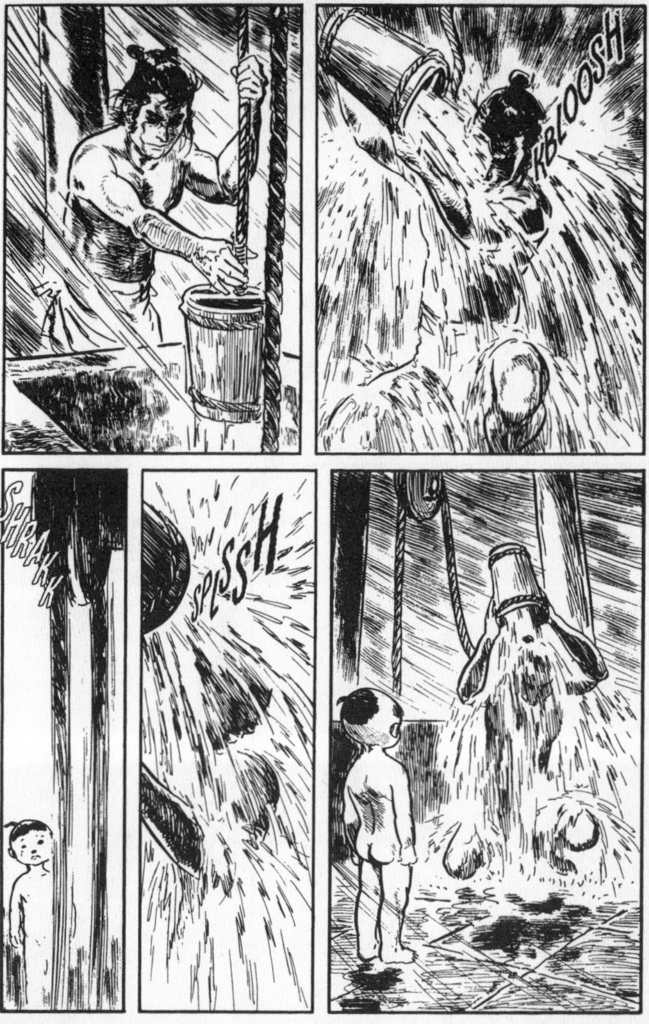
KBLOOSH
SPLSSH
SHRAKK

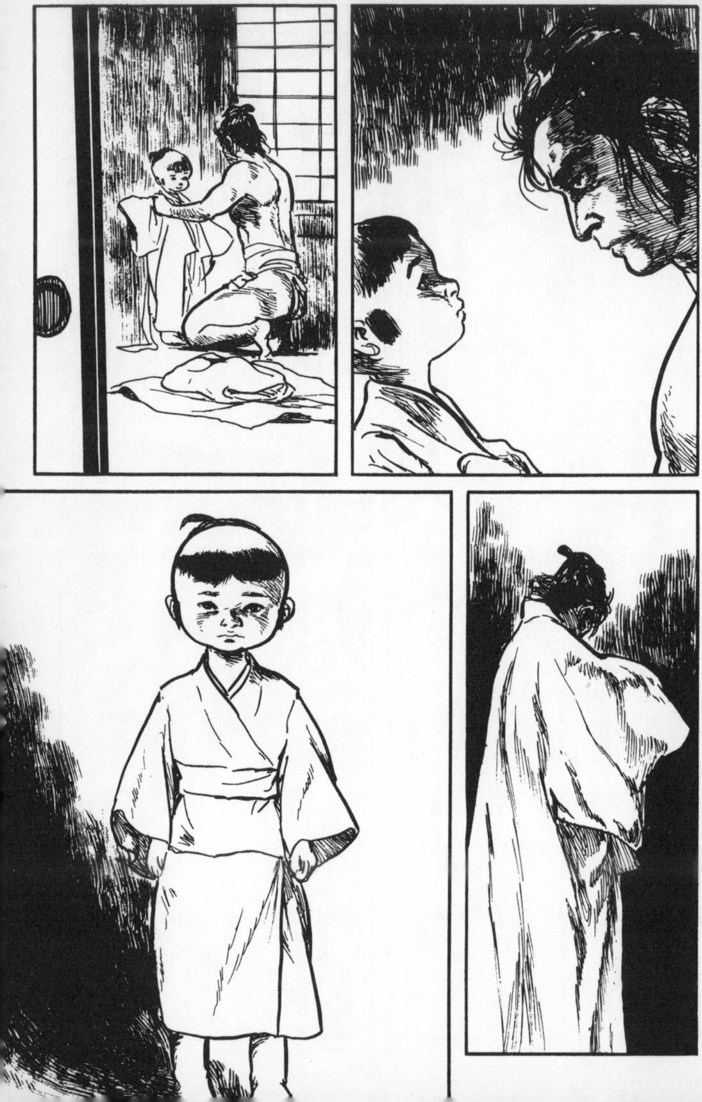

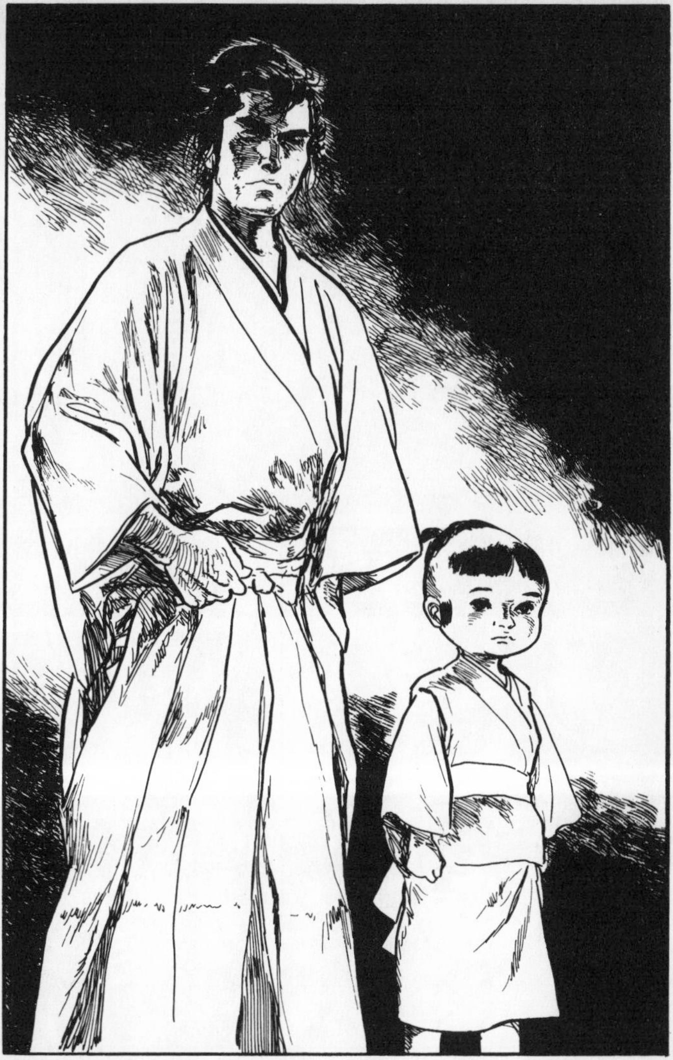

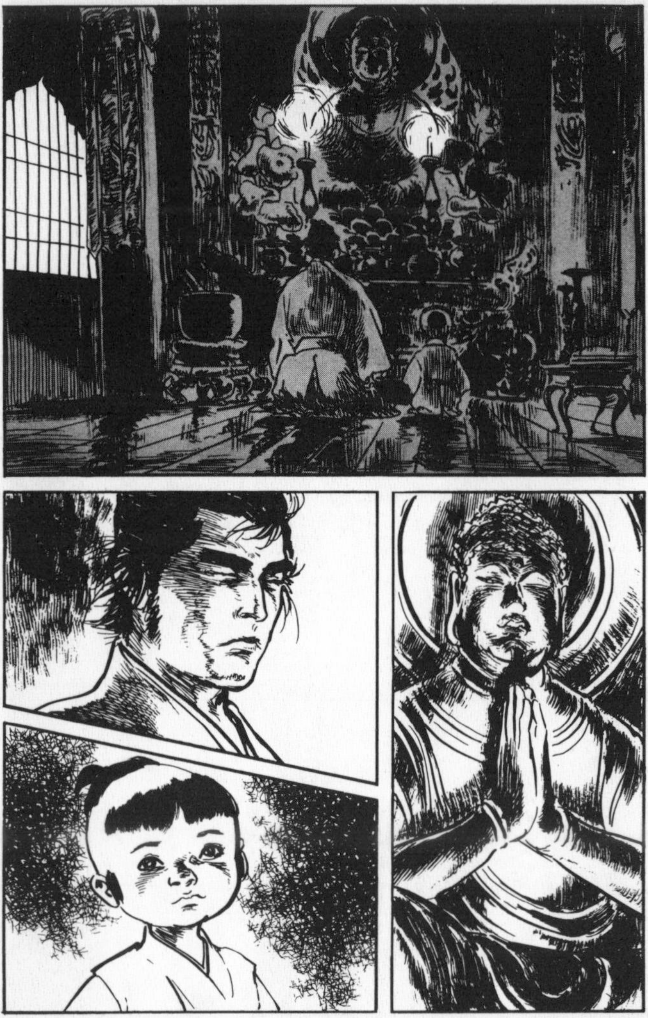

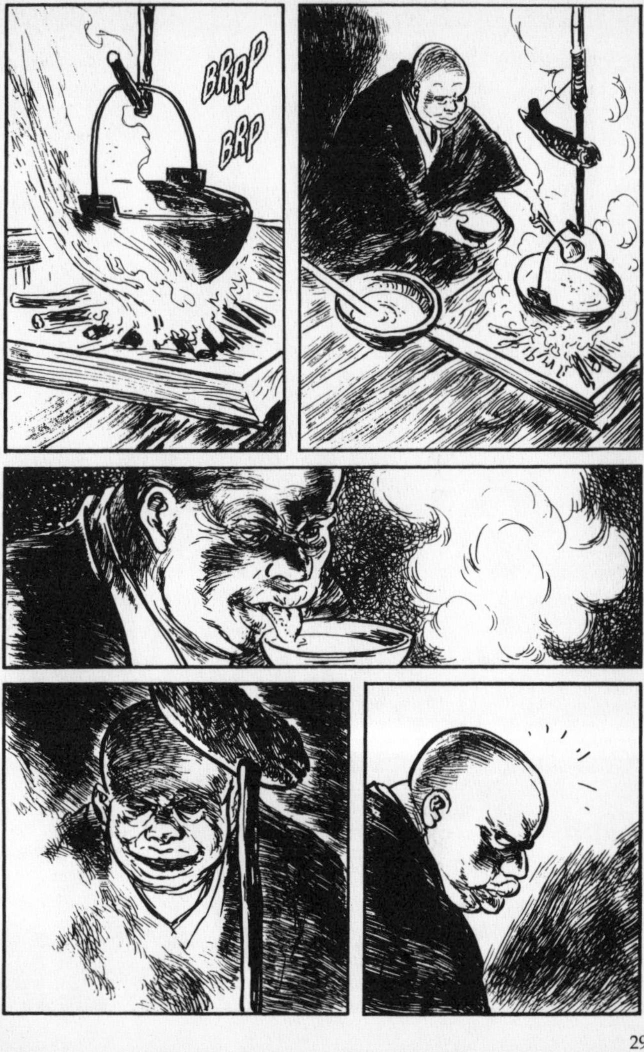
BRRP
BRP

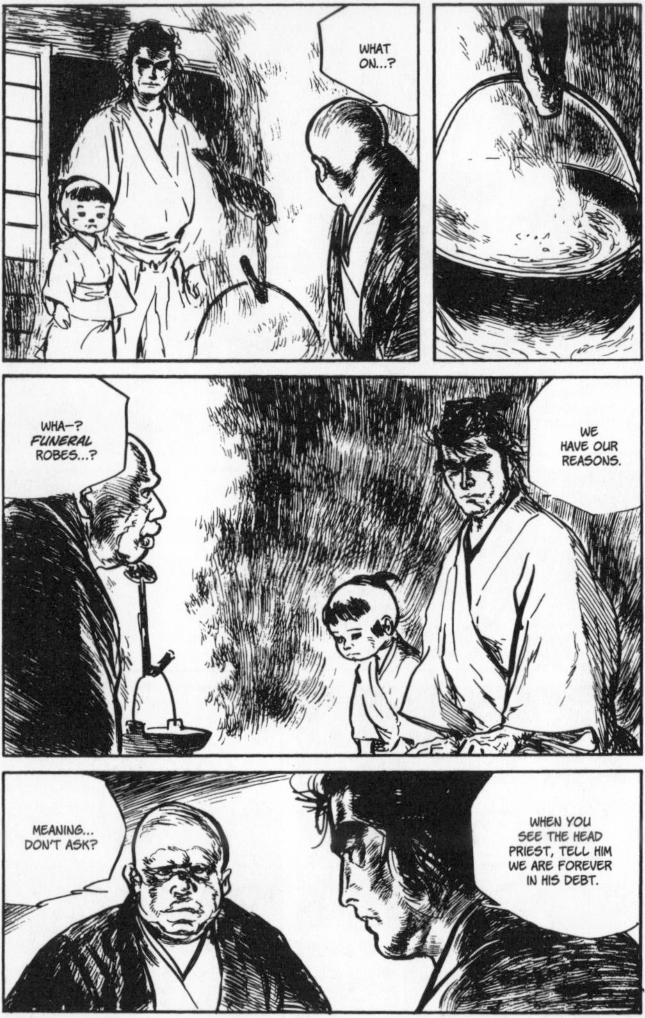
WHAT ON...?
WHA—? *FUNERAL* ROBES...?
WE HAVE OUR REASONS.
MEANING... DON'T ASK?
WHEN YOU SEE THE HEAD PRIEST, TELL HIM WE ARE FOREVER IN HIS DEBT.

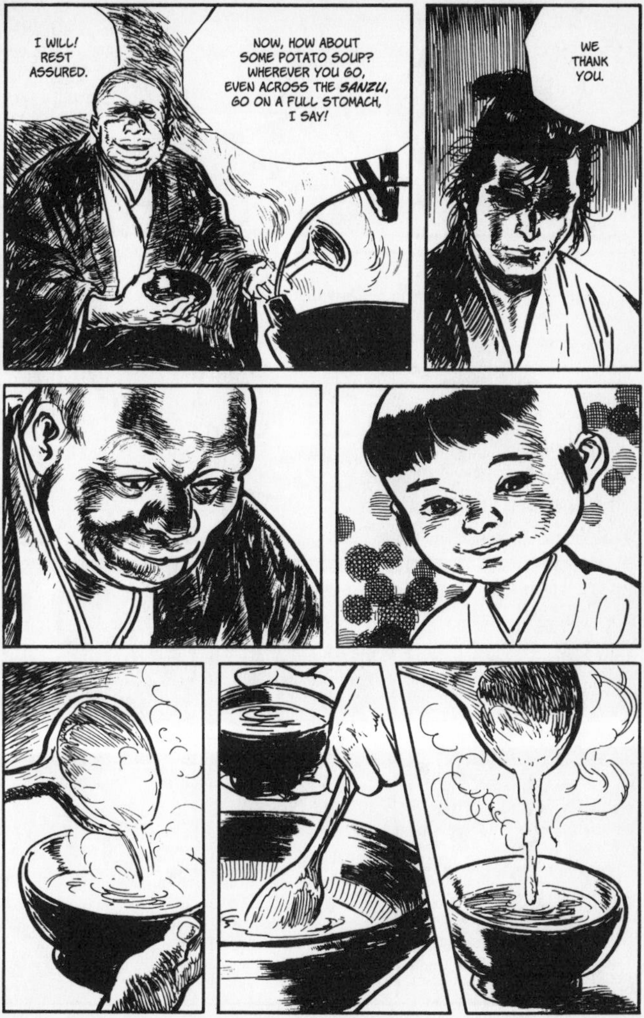
WE THANK YOU.
I WILL! REST ASSURED.
NOW, HOW ABOUT SOME POTATO SOUP? WHEREVER YOU GO, EVEN ACROSS THE SANZU, GO ON A FULL STOMACH, I SAY!

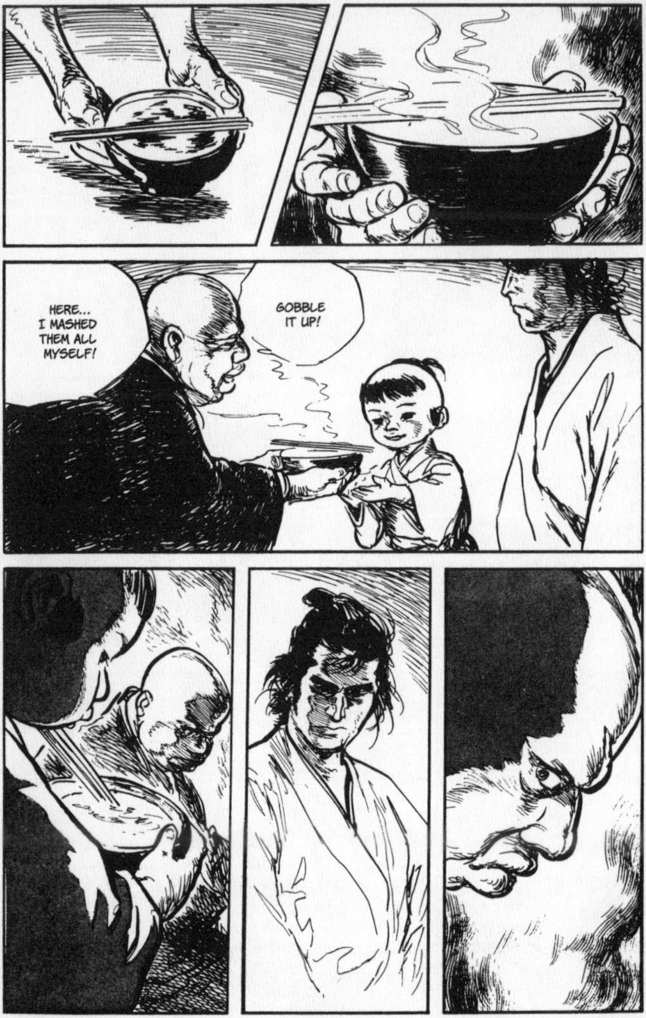
HERE... I MASHED THEM ALL MYSELF!
GOBBLE IT UP!

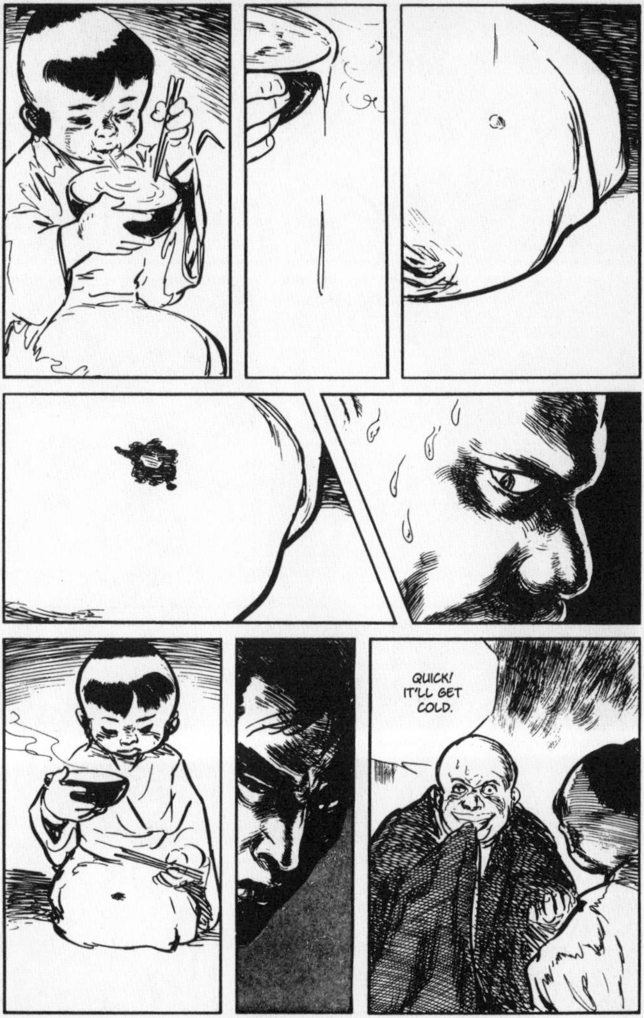
QUICK! IT'LL GET COLD.

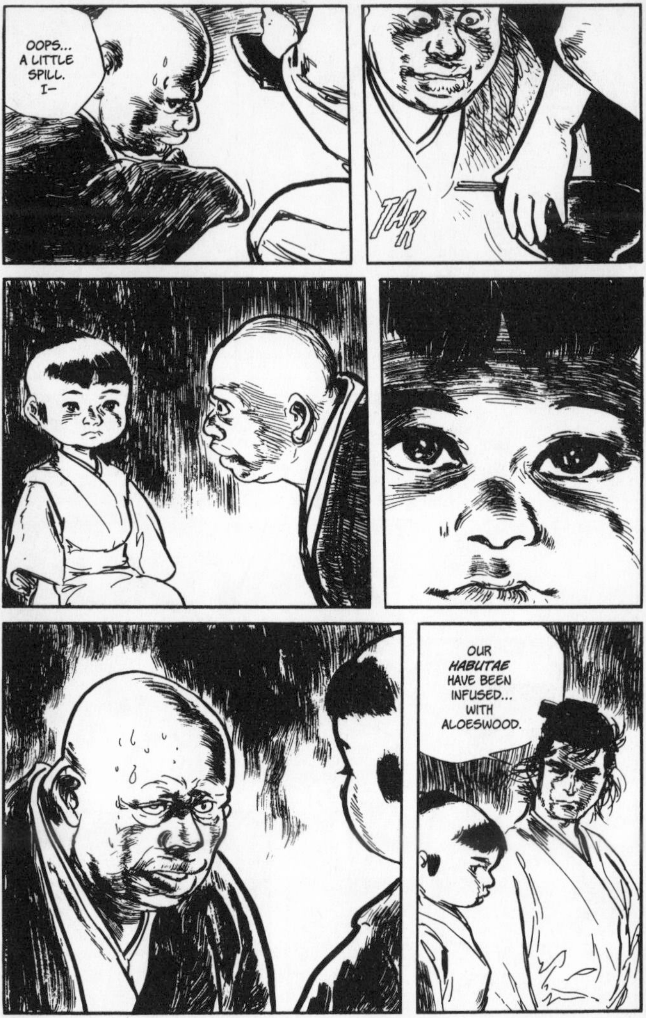
TAK
OOPS... A LITTLE SPILL. I—
OUR HABUTAE HAVE BEEN INFUSED... WITH ALOESWOOD.

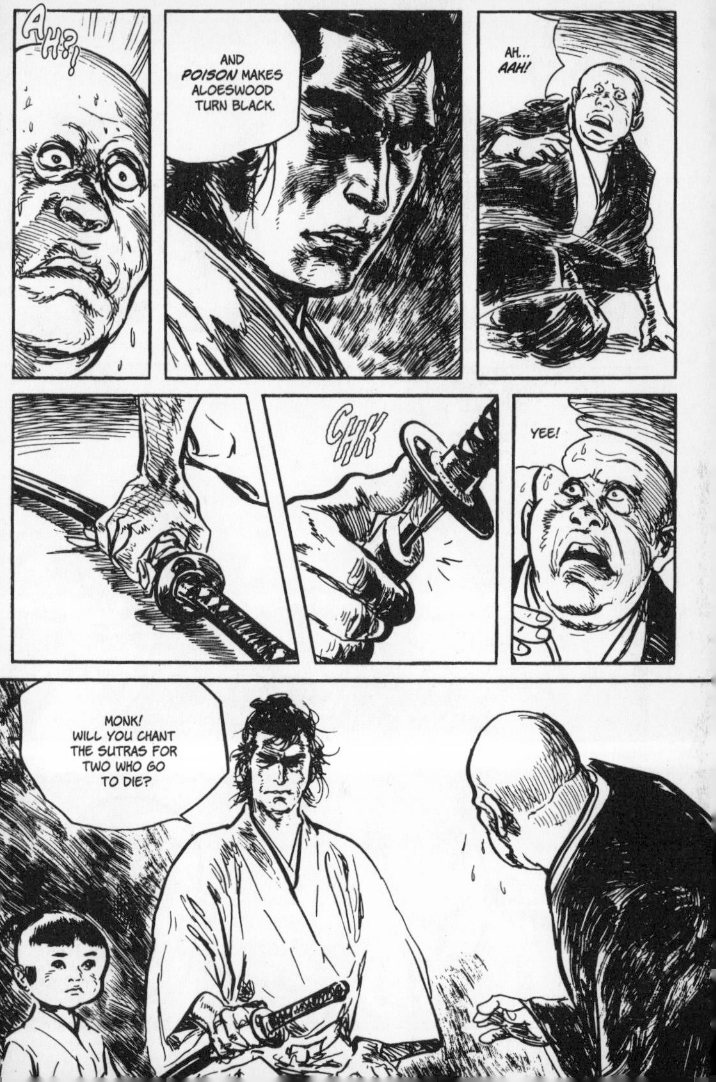
AH?!
AND POISON MAKES ALOESWOOD TURN BLACK.
AH... AAH!
CHK
YEE!
MONK! WILL YOU CHANT THE SUTRAS FOR TWO WHO GO TO DIE?

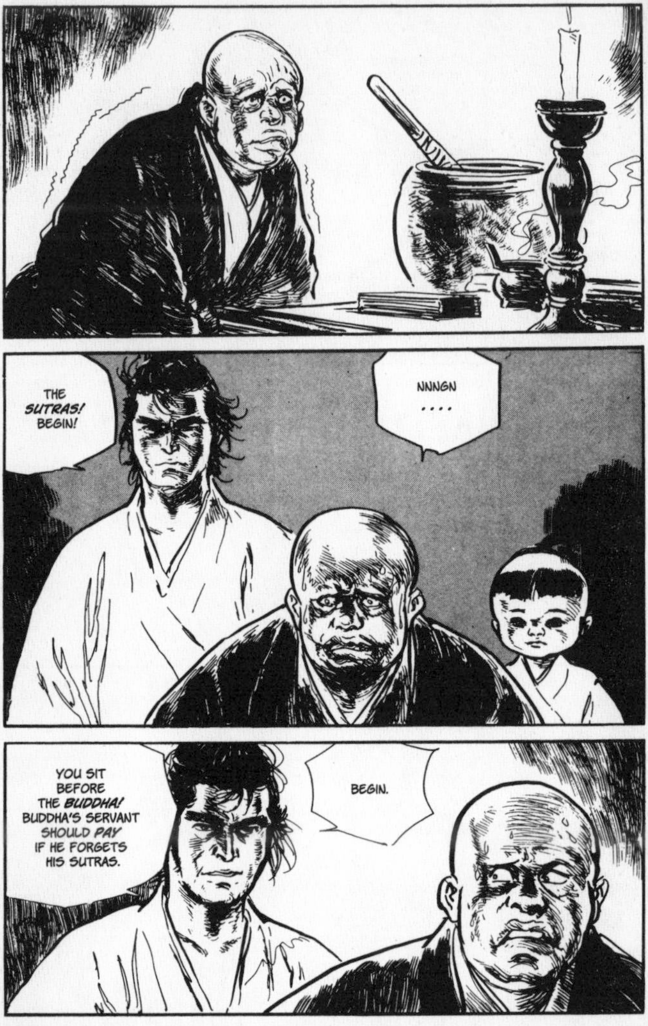
THE *SUTRAS!* BEGIN!
NNNGN ....
YOU SIT BEFORE THE *BUDDHA!* BUDDHA'S SERVANT SHOULD *PAY* IF HE FORGETS HIS SUTRAS.
BEGIN.

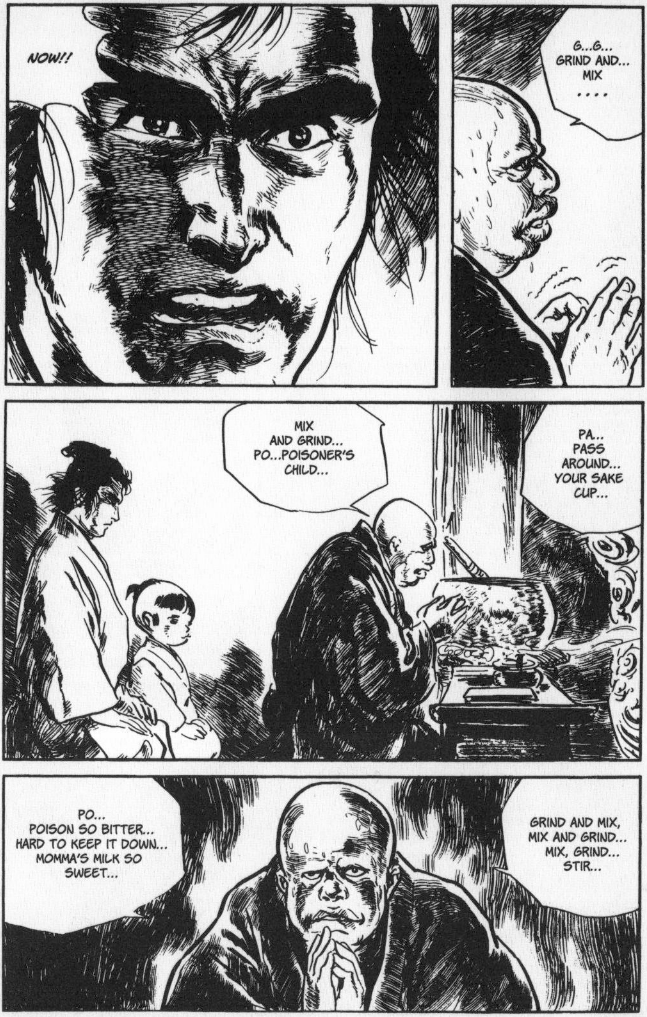
G...G... GRIND AND... MIX ....
NOW!!
PA... PASS AROUND... YOUR SAKE CUP...
MIX AND GRIND... PO...POISONER'S CHILD...
GRIND AND MIX, MIX AND GRIND... MIX, GRIND... STIR...
PO... POISON SO BITTER... HARD TO KEEP IT DOWN... MOMMA'S MILK SO SWEET...

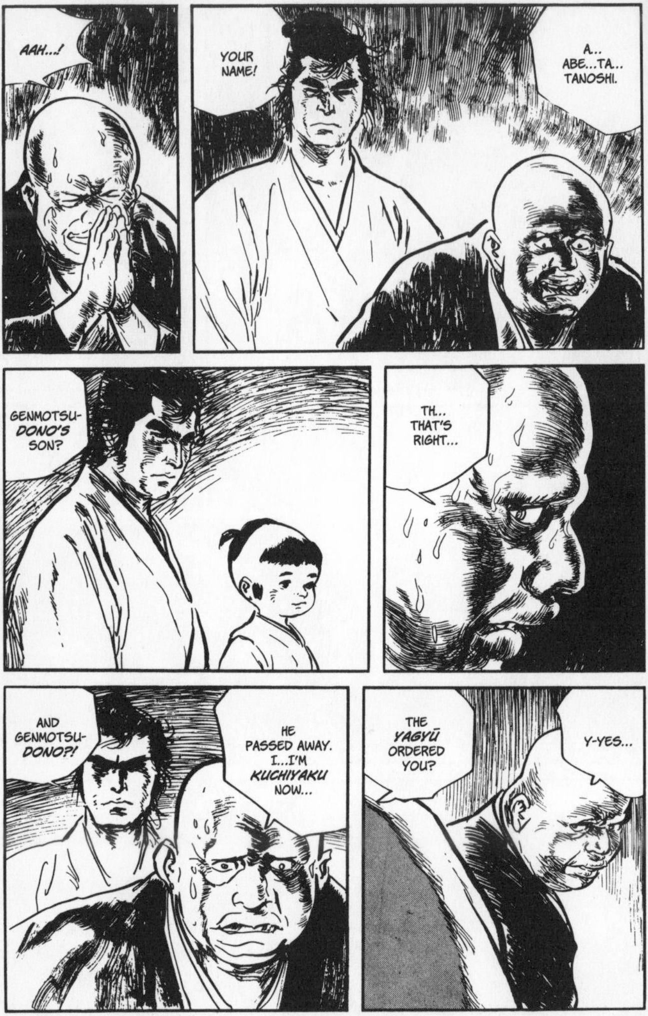
AAH...!
YOUR NAME!
A... ABE...TA... TANOSHI.
GENMOTSU-DONO'S SON?
TH... THAT'S RIGHT...
AND GENMOTSU-DONO?!
HE PASSED AWAY. I...I'M KUCHIYAKU NOW...
THE YAGYŪ ORDERED YOU?
Y-YES...

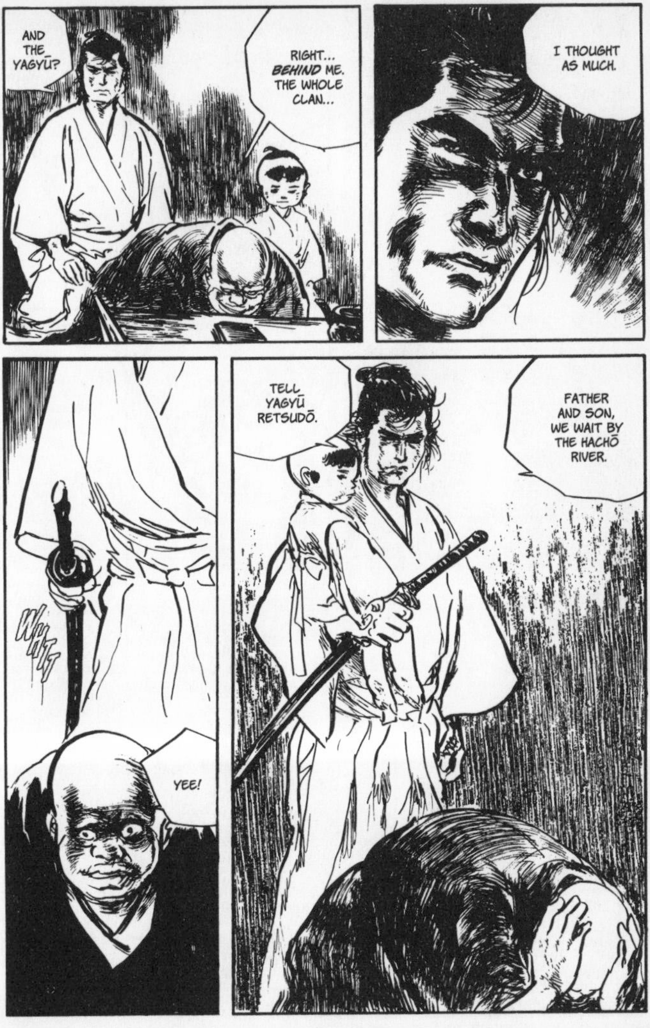
AND THE YAGYŪ?
RIGHT... *BEHIND* ME. THE WHOLE CLAN...
I THOUGHT AS MUCH.
WHTT
YEE!
TELL YAGYŪ RETSUDŌ.
FATHER AND SON, WE WAIT BY THE HACHŌ RIVER.

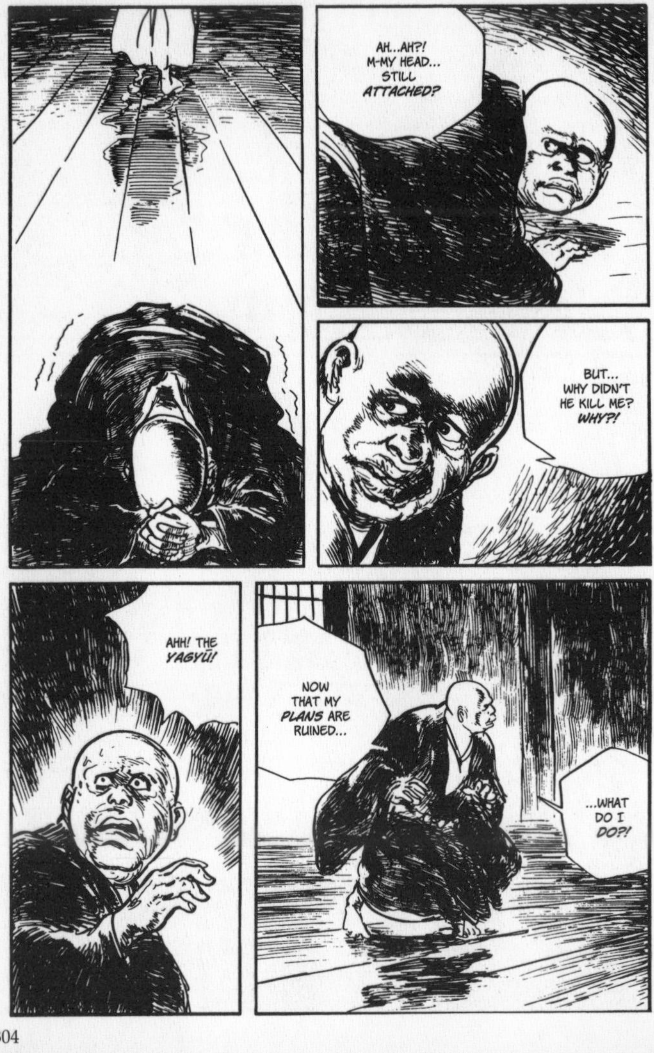
AH...AH?! M-MY HEAD... STILL ATTACHED?
BUT... WHY DIDN'T HE KILL ME? WHY?!
NOW THAT MY PLANS ARE RUINED...
...WHAT DO I DO?!
AHH! THE YAGYŪ!

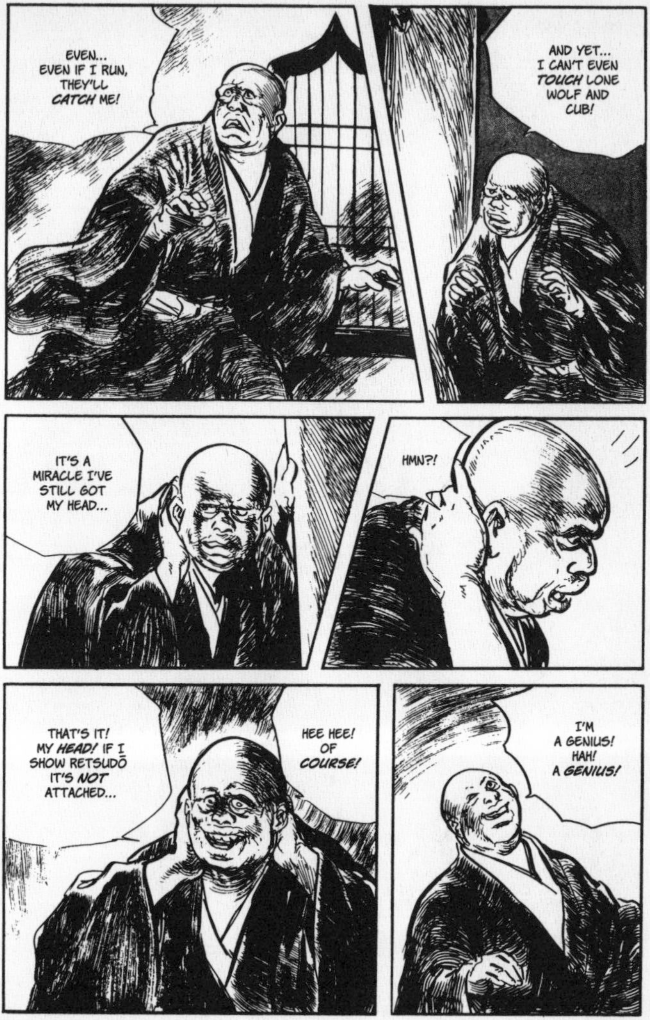
EVEN... EVEN IF I RUN, THEY'LL CATCH ME!
AND YET... I CAN'T EVEN TOUCH LONE WOLF AND CUB!
IT'S A MIRACLE I'VE STILL GOT MY HEAD...
HMN?!
THAT'S IT! MY HEAD! IF I SHOW RETSUDŌ IT'S NOT ATTACHED...
HEE HEE! OF COURSE!
I'M A GENIUS! HAH! A GENIUS!

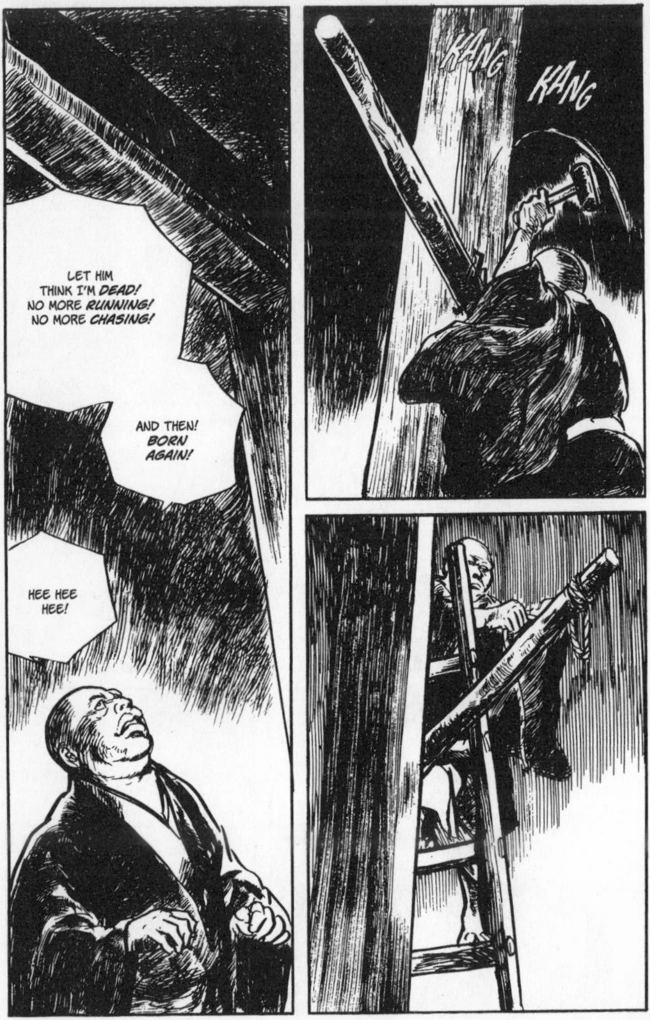
KANG
KANG
LET HIM THINK I'M DEAD! NO MORE RUNNING! NO MORE CHASING!
AND THEN! BORN AGAIN!
HEE HEE HEE!

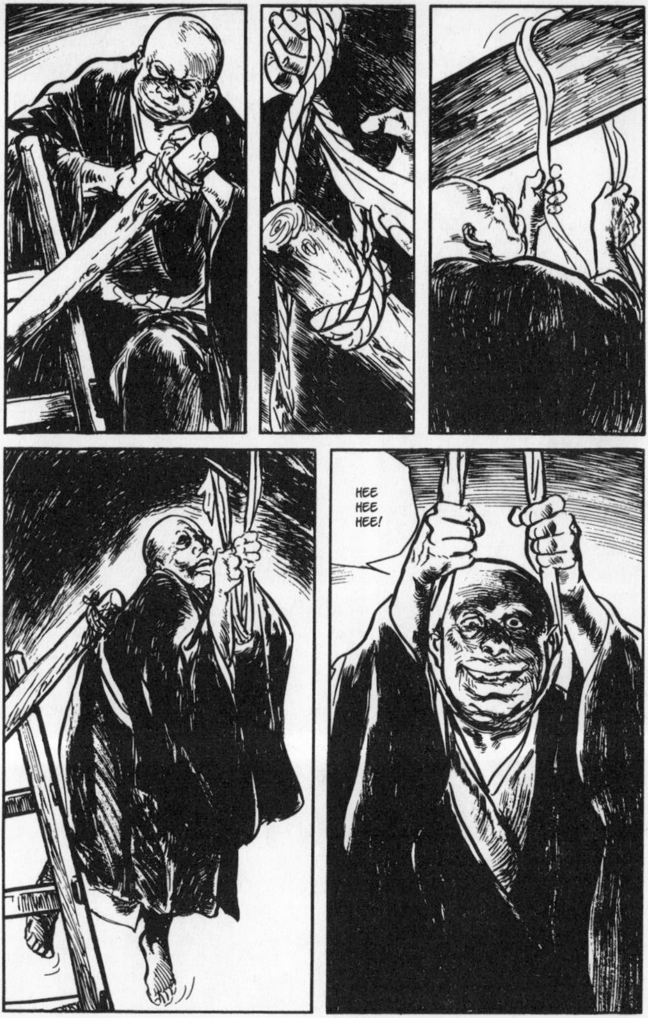
HEE
HEE
HEE!

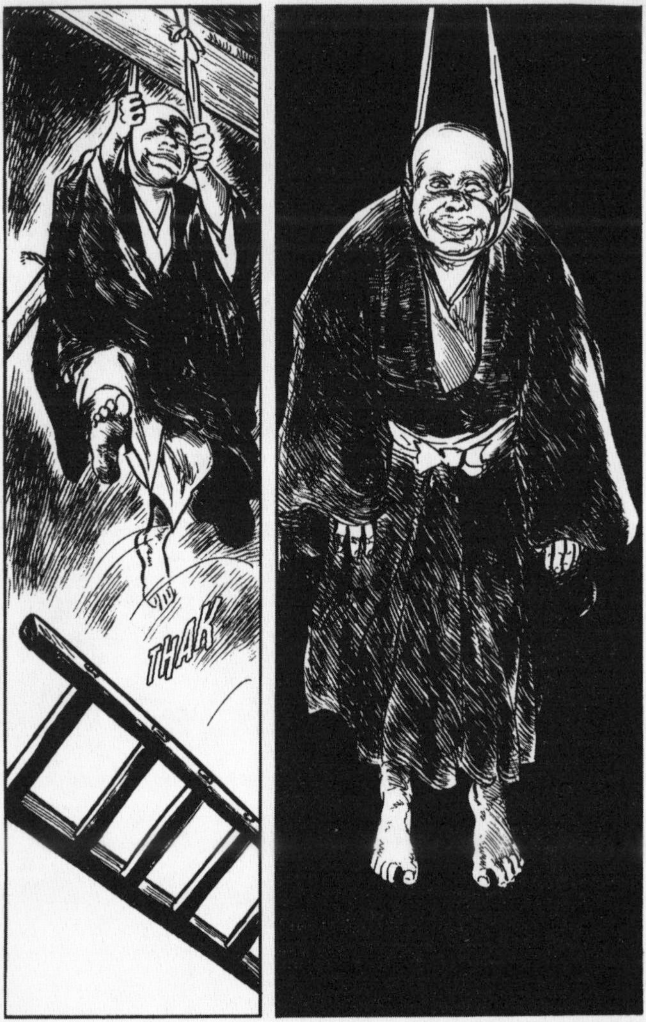
THAK

LONE WOLF AND CUB *VOLUME TWENTY-ONE: THE END*
TO BE CONTINUED

GLOSSARY

afuyō
A type of opiate drug.

buke
Samurai families.

bushi
A samurai. A member of the warrior class.

bushidō
The way of the warrior. Also known as *shidō*.

Edo
Edo was a castle town, that rose up around the moats and ramparts of Edo castle, the stronghold of the Tokugawa clan. The central core of the city, administered by the *machi-bugyō* city commissioner, who reported directly to the shōgun's senior councilors, and was demarcated on official maps by a black line, the *kurobiki*, and was called the *go-funai*.

habutae
Unbleached, white silk.

hashi
Chopsticks

honorifics
Japan is a class and status society, and proper forms of address are

critical. Common markers of respect are the prefixes *o* and *go*, and a wide range of suffixes. Some of the suffixes you will encounter in *Lone Wolf and Cub*:
chan – for children, young women, and close friends
dono – archaic; used for higher-ranked or highly respected figures
san – the most common, used among equals or near-equals
sama – used for superiors
sensei – used for teachers, masters, respected entertainers, and politicians.

ibuki bōfū
Carrot-like root plant with medicinal properties.

ki
Energy. The fundamental mind/body energy of Eastern medicine.

kōgi kaishakunin
The shōgun's own second, who performed executions ordered by the shōgun.

kuchiyaku
Kuchiyaku were the tasters for the shōgun family. They were called kuchiyaku, or "official mouths," because they checked for poison with their own tongues.

machi-bugyō

The Edo city commissioner, combining the post of mayor and chief of police. A post held in monthly rotation by two senior Tokugawa vassals, in charge of administration, maintaining the peace, and enforcing the law in Edo. Their rule extended only to commoners; samurai in Edo were controlled by their own *daimyō* and his officers. The *machi-bugyō* had an administrative staff and a small force of armed policemen at his disposal.

metsuke

Inspector. A post combining the functions of chief of police and chief intelligence officer.

mizugori

To purify yourself with cold water before asking a favor of Buddha or the gods.

mochi

A sticky rice cake, a traditional food to celebrate the new year, made by pounding sweet rice with mallets.

rōnin

A masterless samurai. Literally, "one adrift on the waves." Members of the samurai caste who have lost their masters through the dissolution of *han*, expulsion for misbehavior, or other reasons. Prohibited from working as farmers or merchants under the strict Confucian caste system imposed by the Tokugawa shōgunate, many impoverished *rōnin* became "hired guns" for whom the

code of the samurai was nothing but empty words.

sakayaki

The topknot favored in the Edo period. Still seen on sumo wrestlers today.

sankin kōtai

The Tokugawa required that all *daimyō* spend every other year in Edo, with family members remaining behind when they returned to their *han*. This practice increased Edo's control over the *daimyō*, both political and fiscal, since the cost of maintaining two separate households and traveling to and from the capital placed a huge strain on *han* finances.

sanzu

Three Ways. The river that divides the land of the living from *meido*, the land of the dead.

sumaki

A form of lynching. The victim is beaten, rolled up in a mat, and thrown into a river

tōtekirai

Hand-thrown explosives. A primitive hand grenade.

yakuza

Japan's criminal syndicates. In the Edo period, *yakuza* were a common part of the landscape, running houses of gambling and prostitution. As long as they did not overstep their bounds, they were tolerated by the authorities, a tradition little changed in modern Japan.

子連れ狼

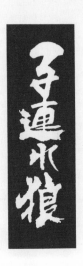

KAZUO KOIKE

Though widely respected as a powerful writer of graphic fiction, Kazuo Koike has spent a lifetime reaching beyond the bounds of the comics medium. Aside from co-creating and writing the successful *Lone Wolf and Cub* and *Crying Freeman* manga, Koike has hosted television programs; founded a golf magazine; produced movies; written popular fiction, poetry, and screenplays; and mentored some of Japan's best manga talent.

Lone Wolf and Cub was first serialized in Japan in 1970 (under the title *Kozure Okami*) in *Manga Action* magazine and continued its hugely popular run for many years, being collected as the stories were published, and reprinted worldwide. Koike collected numerous awards for his work on the series throughout the next decade. Starting in 1972, Koike adapted the popular manga into a series of six films, the *Baby Cart Assassin* saga, garnering widespread commercial success and critical acclaim for his screenwriting.

This wasn't Koike's only foray into film and video. In 1996, *Crying Freeman*, the manga Koike created with artist Ryoichi Ikegami, was produced in Hollywood and released to commercial success in Europe and is currently awaiting release in America.

And to give something back to the medium that gave him so much, Koike started the *Gekiga Sonjuku*, a college course aimed at helping talented writers and artists — such as *Ranma 1/2* creator Rumiko Takahashi — break into the comics field.

The driving focus of Koike's narrative is character development, and his commitment to character is clear: "Comics are carried by characters. If a character is well created, the comic becomes a hit." Kazuo Koike's continued success in comics and literature has proven this philosophy true.

GOSEKI KOJIMA

Goseki Kojima was born on November 3, 1928, the very same day as the godfather of Japanese comics, Osamu Tezuka. While just out of junior high school, the self-taught Kojima began painting advertising posters for movie theaters to pay his bills.

In 1950, Kojima moved to Tokyo, where the postwar devastation had given rise to special manga forms for audiences too poor to buy the new manga magazines. Kojima created art for *kami-shibai*, or "paper-play" narrators, who would use manga story sheets to present narrated street plays. Kojima moved on to creating works for the *kashi-bon* market, bookstores that rented out books, magazines, and manga to mostly low-income readers. He soon became highly popular among *kashi-bon* readers.

In 1967, Kojima broke into the magazine market with his series *Dojinki*. As the manga magazine market grew and diversified, he turned out a steady stream of popular series.

In 1970, in collaboration with Kazuo Koike, Kojima began the work that would seal his reputation, *Kozure*
Okami (*Lone Wolf and Cub*). Before long the story had become a gigantic hit, eventually spinning off a television series, six motion pictures, and even theme song records. Koike and Kojima were soon dubbed the "golden duo" and produced success after success on their way to the pinnacle of the manga world.

When *Manga Japan* magazine was launched in 1994, Kojima was asked to serve as consultant, and he helped train the next generation of manga artists.

In his final years, Kojima turned to creating original graphic novels based on the movies of his favorite director, Akira Kurosawa. Kojima passed away on January 5, 2000 at the age of 71.

THE RONIN REPORT

By David S. Hofhine

An Authentic Example of a Dotanuki School Sword: part two

The tang of this blade is as thick as the blade itself and runs most of the length of the handle to fortify the handle against breakage. This tang is signed on both sides in Japanese kanji, with one side signed Higo Dotanuki Munehiro (fig. 5), indicating that the blade was forged by a smith named Munehiro from the Dotanuki school working in Higo province. The other side is signed *Tenpo ju nen san gatsu nichi* (fig. 6), which is the date that the blade was forged, being "a day in the third month of the 10th year of *Tenpo*," or March 1839. This particular Dotanuki was forged about 180 years after the events depicted in *Lone Wolf and Cub*.

Fig. 5

There is always some question as to whether a signature is false (*gimei*) or true (*shoshin mei*), since faking big-name signatures is an artform almost as old as blade forging itself. A good friend of mine living in Japan is a great authority on Japanese swords and also happens to own another blade made by this exact same smith, which has been authenticated by top experts in Japan. This judgment is made by comparing not only the signatures of the two blades, but also the shape, style, *ji-hada, hamon*, and all other features of the blade collectively.

Fig. 6

A final and sweet bit of history associated with this blade is its original Higo province mountings. This is particularly intriguing because the Dotanuki were based in Higo, and this appears to be the original mounting first crafted for the sword when it was newly forged in 1839. These mountings are largely composed of wood and lacquer and do not normally stand the test of time as well as a steel blade, so having the sword's original mounting is a great boon.

The handle, or *tsuka* (fig. 7), is made of *honoki* wood carefully carved to fit the tang exactly. It is then covered with *samé*, which is the very rough and bony skin of a flat fish, something like a ray, found in the Sea of Japan. The *samé* has been coated in a dark red lacquer to complement the scabbard, and the ends are fitted with metal caps called *fuchi* and *kashira*. The end caps for this handle are made of fine copper covered in *shakudo*, which is a glossy black alloy mixture of copper and gold, and are further engraved with an *oxalis* vine pattern inlaid with silver and gold.

Fig. 7

Typical of Higo mounts, the handle is wrapped with a type of thin, fine leather and is still in very good shape for its age. I have it on good authority that this wrapping is most likely monkey skin! Apparently monkey was a popular handle wrapping material at one time, while today a flat cord of silk is most commonly used.

Under the wrapping are two metal ornaments called *menuki*. These are a traditional part of a Japanese sword handle and help to improve the grip somewhat. The *menuki* are in the pattern of a stylized frog and fish in *shakudo* and gold. Often there is some sort of story or significance to the images and patterns on sword fittings, but what the frog and fish might signify here is beyond my knowledge.

Between the handle and the blade is the guard, or *tsuba* (fig. 8). This divides the blade from the handle, protecting the hands when the blade is in use, and is often covered with elaborate engravings and inlays depicting an infinite variety of themes and motifs. This *tsuba* is in the shape of a particular family crest known as *hiki*, a bar or bars in a circle, most likely indicating the family affiliation of the original owner. This crest was used by the Nitta, Ishiki, Iwamatsu, Sakakibara, Yamane, and Ura families.

This *tsuba* is further engraved with an *oxalis* vine pattern, which appears to have originally been inlaid with gold and matches the pattern of the *fuchi* and *kashira* on the handle. There is also a small dovetailed area at the top of the *tsuba* where a metal inlay seems to have fallen out.

Fig. 8

The scabbard, or *saya* (fig. 9), is carved wood covered in lacquer with carved black horn parts. The lacquer is in a black-and-red swirl pattern, and was done by building up a very thick coating of black lacquer with rippled brush strokes and then covering this with red lacquer. The final surface is then polished down part way through the red lacquer revealing the black in streaks. The final effect is dramatic and very attractive.

This sword is an authentic Dotanuki, but it is a bit different than the one used by Itto Ogami. Its handle and tang are a bit shorter than usual for its blade length, though the handle may have been made shorter at the request of the owner. By this late date, the owner would have likely been more bureaucrat than *bushi* and may not have wanted to bother with carrying around a longer, more cumbersome weapon. This could also have been due to a strong western influence that was creeping into Japan by the mid-nineteenth century. Western swords of the period were generally meant to be wielded in a single hand as opposed to the traditional two-handed *katana* and therefore had much shorter handles.

Fig. 9

There is something a little peculiar about the overall appearance of this blade, however. While it is definitely a Dotanuki blade, it has more in common with the old Hizen school blades than it does with the old Dotanuki school work. The difference between the Hizen and neighboring Higo Dotanuki blades was a major theme of my last article (see *LW&C* vol. 12). The slender shape and exceptionally fine *ji-hada* of this blade are both more characteristic of the refined and elegant Hizen blades, than of the utilitarian choppers the Dotanuki were known to produce during that time period. It seems that 240 years of relative peace finally caught up with the Dotanuki, and they were eventually made to cater more to the aesthetics of the samurai nobleman than the martial penchant of the samurai warriors of old.

At any rate and by any measure, this is a very fine blade with an exceptional mounting, and it has been my great pleasure to share this unique treasure with my fellow *Lone Wolf and Cub* enthusiasts. If you would like more information on Japanese swords or sword polishing in general, please feel free to visit my website at *www.swordpolish.com*.

BIBLIOGRAPHY

Haku, Kozu, and Sato Kan'ichio. *Nihon To Koza*. Trans. Harry Watson. Vol. IV, Shinto 1596-1771. Rio Rancho, NM: AFU Research Enterprises, Inc. 1992.

Hawley, W. M. *Japanese Swordsmiths Revised*. Hollywood, CA: W. M. Hawley, 1981.

Hofhine, David S. *Codex Kensei*. Madison, WI: Kensei LLC, 1992-2001.

Honnami, Koson. *Teiryo Yoji*. Tokyo, Japan: Showa Mizunoe Saru (1932).

Kapp, Leon, and Yoshindo Yoshihara. *The Craft of the Japanese Sword*. Tokyo, Japan: Kodansha International Ltd., 1987.

Nagayama, Kokan. *The Connoisseur's Book of Japanese Swords*. Trans. Kenji Mishina. Tokyo, Japan: Kodansha International Ltd., 1997.

Sato, Kanzan. *The Japanese Sword*. Tokyo, Japan: Kodansha International Ltd., 1983.

Yoshikawa, Kentaro. "The Characteristics of Kyushu Shinto." *Art and the Sword*. Vol. 4. Breckenridge, TX: The Japanese Sword Society of the United States, 1992.

MANGA! MANGA! MANGA! DARK HORSE HAS THE BEST IN MANGA COLLECTIONS!

APPLESEED
Masamune Shirow
BOOK ONE
ISBN: 1-56971-070
BOOK TWO
ISBN: 1-56971-071
BOOK THREE
ISBN: 1-56971-072-4 $14.95
BOOK FOUR
ISBN: 1-56971-074-0 $14.95
DATABOOK
ISBN: 1-56971-103-8 $12.95

BLADE OF THE IMMORTAL
Hiroaki Samura
BLOOD OF A THOUSAND
ISBN: 1-56971-239-5 $14.95
CRY OF THE WORM
ISBN: 1-56971-300-6 $14.95
DREAMSONG
ISBN: 1-56971-357-X $12.95
ON SILENT WINGS
ISBN: 1-56971-412-6 $14.95
ON SILENT WINGS II
ISBN: 1-56971-444-4 $14.95

THE DIRTY PAIR
Adam Warren • Toren Smith
BIOHAZARDS
ISBN: 1-56971-339-1 $12.95
DANGEROUS ACQUAINTANCES
ISBN: 1-56971-227-1 $12.95
A PLAGUE OF ANGELS
ISBN: 1-56971-029-5 $12.95
SIM HELL
ISBN: 1-56971-159-3 $13.95
FATAL BUT NOT SERIOUS
ISBN: 1-56971-172-0 $14.95

DOMINION
Masamune Shirow
DOMINION
ISBN: 1-56971-488-6 $16.95

DOMU: A CHILD'S DREAM
Katsuhiro Otomo
ISBN: 1-56971-140-2 $17.95

GHOST IN THE SHELL
Masamune Shirow
ISBN: 1-56971-081-3 $24.95

GUNSMITH CATS
Kenichi Sonoda
BONNIE AND CLYDE
ISBN: 1-56971-215-8 $13.95
MISFIRE
ISBN: 1-56971-253-0 $14.95

BEAN BANDIT
ISBN: 1-56971-453-3 $16.95

INTRON DEPOT
Masamune Shirow
INTRON DEPOT 1
ISBN: 1-56971-085-6 $39.95
INTRON DEPOT 2: BLADES
ISBN: 1-56971-382-0 $39.95

LONE WOLF AND CUB
New volumes released monthly! Collect the complete 28-volume series!
VOLUME 1–THE ASSASSIN'S ROAD
ISBN: 1-56971-502-5 $9.95
VOLUME 2–THE GATELESS BARRIER
ISBN: 1-56971-503-3 $9.95
VOLUME 3–THE FLUTE OF THE FALLEN TIGER
ISBN: 1-56971-504-1 $9.95
VOLUME 4–THE BELL WARDEN
ISBN: 1-56971-505-X $9.95
VOLUME 5–BLACK WIND
ISBN: 1-5671-506-8 $9.95
VOLUME 6–LANTERNS FOR THE DEAD
ISBN: 1-56971-507-6 $9.95
VOLUME 7– CLOUD DRAGON, WIND TIGER
ISBN: 1-56971-508-4 $9.95
VOLUME 8–THREAD OF TEARS
ISBN: 1-56971-509-2 $9.95
VOLUME 9–ECHO OF THE ASSASSIN
ISBN: 1-56971-510-6 $9.95
VOLUME 10–DRIFTING SHADOWS
ISBN: 1-56971-511-4 $9.95
VOLUME 11–TALISMAN OF HADES
ISBN: 1-56971-512-2 $9.95
VOLUME 12–SHATTERED STONES
ISBN: 1-56971-513-0 $9.95

OH MY GODDESS!
Kosuke Fujishima
1-555-GODDESS
ISBN: 1-56971-207-7 $14.95
LOVE POTION NO. 9
ISBN: 1-56971-252-2 $14.95
SYMPATHY FOR THE DEVIL
ISBN: 1-56971-329-4 $13.95
TERRIBLE MASTER URD
ISBN: 1-56971-369-3 $14.95

…EANCE
…$13.95
…$14.95

STAR WARS MANGA
A NEW HOPE
George Lucas • Hisao Tamaki
VOLUME 1
ISBN: 1-56971-362-6 $9.95
VOLUME 2
ISBN: 1-56971-363-4 $9.95
VOLUME 3
ISBN: 1-56971-364-2 $9.95
VOLUME 4
ISBN: 1-56971-365-0 $9.95
THE EMPIRE STRIKES BACK
George Lucas • Toshiko Kudo
VOLUME 1
ISBN: 1-56971-390-1 $9.95
VOLUME 2
ISBN: 1-56971-391-X $9.95
VOLUME 3
ISBN: 1-56971-392-8 $9.95
VOLUME 4
ISBN: 1-56971-393-6 $9.95
RETURN OF THE JEDI
George Lucas • Shin-ichi Hiromoto
VOLUME 1
ISBN: 1-56971-394-4 $9.95
VOLUME 2
ISBN: 1-56971-395-2 $9.95
VOLUME 3
ISBN: 1-56971-396-0 $9.95
VOLUME 4
ISBN: 1-56971-397-9 $9.95
EPISODE 1—THE PHANTOM MENACE
George Lucas • Kia Asimiya
VOLUME 1
ISBN: 1-56971-483-5 $9.95
VOLUME 2
ISBN: 1-56971-484-3 $9.95

3x3 EYES
Yuzo Takada
HOUSE OF DEMONS
ISBN: 1-56971-059-7 $12.95
CURSE OF THE GESU
ISBN: 1-56971-175-5 $12.95

WHAT'S MICHAEL?
Makoto Kobayashi
OFF THE DEEP END
ISBN: 1-56971-249-2 $5.95
MICHAEL'S MAMBO
ISBN: 1-56971-250-6 $5.95

Available from your local comics shop or bookstore!

To find a comics shop in your area, call 1-888-266-4226 • For more information or to order direct:
•On the web: www.darkhorse.com •E-mail: mailorder@darkhorse.com
•Phone: 1-800-862-0052 or (503) 652-9701 Mon.-Sat. 9 A.M. to 5 P.M. Pacific Time
*Prices and availability subject to change without notice

Dark Horse Comics: **Mike Richardson** *publisher* • **Neil Hankerson** *executive vice president* • **Andy Karabatsos** *vice president of finance* • **Randy Stradley** *vice president of publishing* • **Chris Warner** *senior editor* • **Michael Martens** *vice president of marketing* • **Anita Nelson** *vice president of sales & licensing* • **David Scroggy** *vice president of product development* • **Cindy Marks** *director of production & design* • **Mark Cox** *art director* • **Dale LaFountain** *vice president of information technology* • **Kim Haines** *director of human resources* • **Darlene Vogel** *director of purchasing* • **Ken Lizzi** • *general counsel*